D1248051

YANKEE QUAKER
CONFEDERATE GENERAL

The Curious Career of Bushrod Rust Johnson

YANKEE QUAKER CONFEDERATE GENERAL

The Curious Career of Bushrod Rust Johnson

Charles M. Cummings

Rutherford • Madison • Teaneck
Fairleigh Dickinson University Press

Library of Congress Catalogue Card Number: 76-118805

Associated University Presses, Inc.
Cranbury, New Jersey 08512

ISBN: 0-8386-7706-1
Printed in the United States of America

For Dorothy, Tony, and Geoffrey

CONTENTS

MAPS AND ILLUSTRATIONS

PREFACE

Eighteen West Point graduates of Northern birth and heritage became generals in the Confederate Army. Few attained status among the glittering figures who soar gloriously across Southern hagiography. Encumbered by their antecedents, they never enjoyed the full confidence of their adopted country during the war, nor shared in the acclaim so liberally bestowed afterward. Only New Yorker Samuel Cooper, top ranking as the Confederacy's adjutant general, and Pennsylvanian Josiah Gorgas, the South's chief of ordnance, found relatively unquestioned distinction. At the other extreme, Pennsylvanian John C. Pemberton, lieutenant general at Vicksburg, met bitter vilification then and since. Oblivion has been the portion of the rest.

Three others among the 18 were major generals at the time of Appomattox. Two were 1843 classmates whose loyalty to the South stemmed from ownership of plantations and slaves by marriage: Franklin Gardner of New York, Iowa and Louisiana, who defended and lost Port Hudson, Louisiana in 1863, and Samuel Gibbs French of New Jersey and Mississippi, division commander in the Army of Tennessee. Gardner died in 1873 at the age of 50 and left no personal *apologia;* French spent the remainder of his 92 years of life until 1910 defending his action and in 1901 published his autobiographical *Two Wars* to vindicate his Confederate adherence.

The third was Bushrod Rust Johnson, born in Ohio, classmate in 1840 of William T. Sherman and George Thomas. He was a maverick in vocation and allegiance. His family was Quaker; to them war, arms and slavery were abhorrent. His eldest brother was a vocal and active abolitionist in Ohio and Indiana. He spent seven years in the "Old Army" and was forced to resign after a vague and guileless bribe proposal to a superior during the Mexican War. He operated a military school in Kentucky and Tennessee for thirteen years until he joined the Confederacy. He escaped at Fort Donelson; was wounded at Shiloh. He led the assault on the Union center at Perryville and spearheaded the drive that pierced Rosecrans's lines at Chickamauga. He commanded the sector of the Southern trenches blown up by the Federal mine at Petersburg. A few hours before Appomattox, Johnson, George E. Pickett and Richard Heron Anderson were relieved of their commands and sent home by General Robert E. Lee after they ran away at Sayler's Creek.

Reticent and unassuming, Johnson lacked the personal flair that sets apart some men and their deeds or inspires myths and legends. A tragic flaw in his character deranged the course of his life when he was 30 and haunted him with recurrent disasters until he died. Most of the time he did his best. But it has been his ill-luck that his successes won scant rewards while critics reiterated his failures.

He is worthy of note on several counts. His story points up what can happen to a man who moves entirely counter to his heritage and rearing; what disproportionate consequences can evolve from a character fault; what personality traits can ineluctably dominate a course of action, good or bad, and finally, how, in any life there are, as Santayana found, times when "the spirit blooms timidly and struggles to the light amid the thorns."

ACKNOWLEDGMENTS

Grateful appreciation is expressed to the following for their priceless help in the preparation of this work:

Meredith Johnson, Washington, D.C., fourth-generation nephew of Bushrod Rust Johnson, for family data; Kenneth Owen, Houston, Texas, for special permission to research the papers of Richard Owen, his great-grandfather; Phoebe Andrews, La Jolla, California, for data on Johnson's last years; Mrs. E. Wayne Gibson, Spencer, Indiana, for Spencer family data; Dr. Sidney Forman, former librarian, U.S. Military Academy, West Point, N.Y.; Gertrude Morton Parsley, former reference librarian, Tennessee State Library and Archives; Ruth Long Douthit, former reference librarian, Ohio State Library; Elizabeth Martin, Marian Bates and Conrad Weitzel, Ohio Historical Society Library; Josephine Elliott and Helen Elliott, New Harmony, Indiana; Francis E. Carter, Jr., headmaster, Montgomery Bell Academy, Nashville, Tennessee, for Western Military Institute Register; Anna Loe Russell, reference librarian, George Peabody College for Teachers, Nashville, Tennessee, for Western Military Institute Order Book; Colonel W. M. Slayden II, Nashville, for data on the Johnson portrait painted in 1906; staff members of the Kentucky State Library, Duke University Library, Richmond, Indiana, City Library; Civil War Section of the National Archives; Virginia Historical Society; Chicago Historical Society; personnel of county clerk's offices in Macoupin County, Illinois; Davidson and Wayne Counties, Tennessee; Belmont County, Ohio; Osage County, Kansas; Scott County, Kentucky; Loudoun County, Virginia and Wayne County, Indiana; Robert M. McBride, editor, *Tennessee Historical Quarterly,* for permission to use material from Winter 1968 and Fall 1969 issues; Charles Scribner's Sons for permission to paraphrase passages from Douglas Southall Freeman, *R. E. Lee,* IV, and to my wife, Dr. Dorothy Porter Cummings, for encouragement, loyal support and critical appraisal.

1

A LETTER WRECKS A CAREER

i. "You Can Have From Me a Proffit"

Plague-ridden Vera Cruz sweltered and stank under a steaming sun on the first day of July 1847. Muggy, smothering heat magnified the overwhelming stench of filthy streets and fetid harbor, and any man who was not a native had to make an effort to breathe. To move, even listlessly, was a chore. In the shadows of the low, stone buildings housing stocks of American army rations, a few sentries in dirty blue woolen uniforms slouched and sweated. Indifferently they watched slow-moving Mexican *cargadores* load a few mule-drawn wagons and ox carts in a patio while they cursed the *Yanqui* invaders who would not let work wait until the sun went down.

The warehouses were piled to their tile roofs with barrels of flour, salt beef, hams, sugar and vinegar; with boxes of hardtack biscuit and dripping bacon and with gunny sacks of beans, rice and coffee.[1] These were "subsistence stores" which the commissary officer stocked and for which he was accountable; equipage and gear were stored and issued by the quartermaster. They were here to feed the American occupation garrison in Vera Cruz and the replacements from the United States moving forward to join the army of Winfield Scott, the giant Virginia-born Whig, who dreamed of the White House beyond the glory road he was treading to Mexico City.

Scott, aided by the United States Navy, had taken Vera Cruz in March after his siege guns battered much of it into rubble. Then, before the season of the fevers (the dread *vómito,* called yellow fever or "black vomit" by the Americans, and the malaria), he set out on April 8 with 8500 men for the Mexican capital, 250 miles away. Ten days later at Cerro Gordo he shattered 12,000 men of Dictator Antonio López de Santa Anna. In May he took Puebla, halfway to his goal. Here the enlistments of his one-year volunteers neared an end and he lost nearly one-third of his strength. Now in July he waited in Puebla for dribbles of replacements, who landed in Vera Cruz and tried to survive fevers, sunstroke and guerillas on their way to join him. Such was the unit of recruits drawing their rations at these warehouses in the blazing July sun. At dusk they would leave the walled city and start the long, slow trudge to Puebla.

Their officer was inside signing receipts and manifests at a table cluttered with papers. The forms were handed to him by a tall, brown-haired, big-nosed, square-chinned, 30-year-old lieutenant in his shirt sleeves. His light blue trousers were rumpled and soiled and his dark blue uniform frock coat was draped over a nearby chair. He was recovering from a bout with the *vómito,* his gaunt face was pale and drawn and his body weak and shaking.[2] But he managed to countersign the papers in a full round hand: "B. R. Johnson, 1st Lieut., 3d Infantry, Acting Assistant Commissary of Subsistence." Before this day was done, he would sign one more paper and regret the unfortunate act for the remaining 33 years of his life!

Bushrod Rust Johnson, ninth and last child of an Ohio Hicksite Quaker family whose beliefs he had affronted by entering the U.S. Military Academy at West Point in

1836, had been involved with rations in Vera Cruz since the preceding March. It had been an unending nightmare of pressures and frustrations. He had been bedeviled by demands he could not appease, by inadequate and incompetent assistance, by pilfering Mexican civilian laborers and by insufficient facilities to house and protect the precious stocks upon which so many depended and for which he was personally responsible.

Understandably, his morale was at a low ebb. Since his graduation from West Point in 1840 he had served seven years in the Third Infantry Regiment, first in the dank swamps of Florida against the Seminole Indians, then at Jefferson Barracks near the social diversions of St. Louis, and later in the sandy pine forests of Fort Jesup, Louisiana. The Third had been transferred to Corpus Christi, Texas in the summer of 1845 and had moved with Brigadier General Zachary Taylor to the Rio Grande in March of '46.[3] Lieutenant Johnson had taken part in the battles of Palo Alto and Resaca de la Palma, May 8–9, 1846 and in the bloody fight at Monterrey for five days in September. But his service had been undistinguished. None of the honors garnered by his classmates and juniors came to him. Then in March 1847, the Third took part in the thrilling and relatively safe capture of Vera Cruz. Now it was marching with Scott on the path of adventure, glory and distinction, while he, senior first lieutenant in the regiment, had been left behind to tally barrels, boxes and bags and try to satisfy the demands of everybody.

Johnson had been named to the necessary, but undesirable post by General Scott on March 10. In the army fashion, Johnson probably had been "volunteered" by Captain E. B. Alexander, acting commander of the Third. Johnson did not want the job and he said so. In May he wrote to Washington protesting to Brevet Brigadier General George Gibson who had been the army's Commissary General of Subsistence since 1818.

Johnson felt much like another Ohio-born lieutenant, Ulysses S. Grant, similarly named as a regimental supply officer by Lieutenant Colonel John Garland, commanding the Fourth Infantry. Grant also wrote a letter objecting to removal from "the dangers and honors of service with my company at the front" and asking to be permitted "to resume my place in line."[4] Johnson argued that he was not eligible to be acting assistant commissary of subsistence because he headed the list of lieutenants in the Third[5] and was not a subaltern upon whom such jobs were loaded by custom and regulation. Grant's objections were tactfully denied by Garland; Johnson's were ignored by Gibson.

There often has been an element of ignominy attached to a transfer of a dedicated combat officer from command of troops to mongering supplies. William Tecumseh Sherman, on supply duty, hated the task. "Commissaries are not fighting men," he wrote.[6] Another army commentator saw the commissary as "not necessarily remarkable for dash and valor," but rather "solid, energetic and painstaking."[7] Obviously Johnson had demonstrated no outstanding "dash or valor" in three battles or he would have won a brevet promotion. Whether he was "solid, energetic and painstaking" in the rear echelon of Scott's glory hunters remained to be seen during this period when he controlled thousands of dollars worth of perishable and pilferable commodities upon which the health, efficiency and general well being of the nation's main fighting force depended. He had never before borne such a burden of responsibility, nor ever had worked as hard.

What rankled Johnson most was the different treatment given his classmate, Lieutenant Thomas Jordan, when he was named assistant quartermaster in Vera Cruz on March 3. Jordan had just returned from months of stateside recruiting service, far from the hazards of battle or disease. His task involved equipment, clothing, weapons and other gear on the same scale as Johnson's concern with subsistence. Jordan was promoted to Captain-staff and by regulation was entitled to $10 to $20 a month extra pay.[8] Johnson not only was not promoted, but as an "acting assistant" got no extra money. He might rightly feel he was the victim of discrimination, first in being picked for the job and then in being denied its rewards.

Even the weather had been against him. Three severe "norther" storms had struck in March while Scott was still emplacing his guns around Vera Cruz. Raging winds and heavy seas continued for a week, tossing ships aground on the landing beaches, sandblasting men and equipment, and playing havoc with the tent warehouses on the dunes, stacked with shiploads of food that had accompanied the invasion force. Johnson had to work frantically to save and salvage his stocks.[9]

As soon as the city surrendered on March 29, Johnson searched through its cluttered streets and shattered buildings for safer places to house his rations. He found partly wrecked structures which could be repaired hastily by natives and soldier labor. Into these he brought from the beaches his barrels, boxes and bags. In the midst of his labors came an order from Brigadier General William J. Worth, the temporary American governor, to distribute 10,000 rations of bread, beans and rice to the starving poor.[10] Johnson had the chore of providing these supplies and supervising the dole. When Scott's army moved out, 1000 sick and wounded soldiers were left behind as well as the First Infantry, detailed to garrison the city. These troops also drew their food from Johnson's warehouses. Left in command of Vera Cruz was Colonel Henry Wilson, who as a major in the Third in 1840 had welcomed West Point graduate Johnson to the regiment.[11]

The *vómito* struck, as expected, in May. For years its virulence had given Vera Cruz the ominous title "City of the Dead." Americans were especially susceptible. Johnson contracted a severe case. He had reason to feel that his comrades of the Third had marched off to escape the plague and had abandoned him to its ravages while he was ensnared in a thankless job. For weeks, he said later, he was "wretchedly prostrated in body and mind" as much from the pestilence as from the harsh remedies given to cure it. He was unable to return to his duties until mid-June, and then only for a few minutes daily. Meanwhile, Colonel Wilson provided no replacement, the principal clerk left, and incompetent substitutes got drunk. "Things were in a state of disorder," he wrote.[12]

Physically and psychologically, Johnson touched bottom. He was vulnerable now to the corruption that surrounded the army supply operation. The climate of venality was apparent to all. Lieutenant Richard S. Ewell wrote his brother, Benjamin, on February 12, 1847 that "the government is losing millions by the imbecility and corruption of the Quartermaster Department." He told of old and unsound vessels awaiting discharge at the expense of $8000 daily demurrage, one loaded with only 40 bales of hay which had cost the taxpayers $330 each. One quartermaster, he said, "recently got a service plate worth $2800 from the owners of the ships."[13] Colonel William Bowen Campbell of the First Tennessee Volunteers told his uncle, Governor David Campbell of Virginia, that contractors sold beef to the government at five cents a pound, for which they had paid only a cent. He added:

> I have not space or time to inform you of the great frauds that are perpetrated on the government . . . the great prices paid for old steamboats and other extravagant prices paid, no doubt to favorites or to persons who share with officers the spoils.[14]

Gamblers, speculators and purveyors of all kinds of goods flocked into Vera Cruz as soon as Scott had taken the city. Conniving opportunists fattened on the chaos and confusion born of war, disease, and the collapse of local government. Sutlers' tents crowded the sand dunes before the first American mortars opened fire at Vera Cruz's defenses, and their business boomed even while small boats lightered more stocks from the cargo ships with the invasion fleet. Mexican workers, suddenly made rich beyond all dreams with wages paid to them by the army for their labor, became spendthrift buyers in large numbers. Other natives reaped instant wealth by selling horses, mules and oxen, wagons and carts to the *Yanquis*. Sudden prosperity, inflation and quick profits moved abreast.

As fast as the bombardment debris could be cleaned up, local merchants reopened their stores. They were of all nationalities. Navy doctor Richard McSherry noted the names Jones, Smith and Thompson side by side with Crapaud, Ximénes, García, Rodríguez and Minas painted across the fronts of the shops above which were the owners' apartments.[15] Most of them needed new goods to replace ruined inventories. Other Americans set up places overnight, filling and emptying their shelves with staples from ships in the harbor. A young Tennessee trooper, George Furber, found that within a week or so after the capture of the city, "everything needed could be bought as cheaply as in New Orleans" because such complete "stocks of goods and merchandise were sent in by the vessels."[16]

Some of these enterprising traders, eager to replenish fast-selling articles and to continue to expand their harvest of gains, came to Lieutenant Johnson. They spoke of returns far beyond his $90 monthly pay. He was to act as their agent in procuring and transporting merchandise from New Orleans, disguised as government shipments. Whether they buttressed their persuasive arguments with preliminary retainers is anyone's guess. The unfortunate fact is that he listened to them at a time when illness, low morale, disappointment and resentment had left a tragic flaw in the moral armor inherited from his Quaker background and from the precepts of duty, honor and country he had heard at West Point. He thought over their proposals and did not reject nor spurn them. Instead, he tried to set in motion what had been outlined to him.

On July 1, 1847 he took a sheet of blue paper and penned 160 words that were to finish him forever as an officer in the U.S. Army. This is the letter just as he wrote it before corrections and additions:

Vera Cruz, Mexico
July 1st 1847

Dr Sir–

I venture to inform you of af fact which you may if you think proper turn to your advantage.

If you think proper to ship me 500 Barrils, 2 or 3 hundred boxes of Sale Soap (48 & 24 lbs boxes) and about 100 Boxes of Candles–Sperm–You can have from me a net proffit of between 1200 and 1500 dollars–

Many of U.S. Ships and Steamers run down here lightly loaded and it would be doing no injustice to U.S. to Ship these articles in Small quantities aboard of them.

If my proposition seems improper or impracticable you will please pardon the liberty I have taken in suggesting it to you. In writing this I repose a certain degree of confidence which your descrition will of course not permit to be injurious.

Yours &c
BR Johnson
Lt

To
Maj W Seawell

He reread the letter and made some additions at least twice before sealing it in an envelop which he marked "Private" and addressed to Major Seawell. The first time he interlined the words "of flour" and underlined "flour" after 500 Barrils, wrote a "P" over the "S" in Sale Soap, added a heavy dash after Sperm and cramped the sentence

"Will you let me hear soon from you" in a small space to the left of "Yours &c" after he signed the letter.[17]

Up to this point, the letter might be regarded as a vague, somewhat furtive business proposition, irregular but not wholly dishonest, "doing no injustice" to the army's interests. Virginia-born Major Washington Seawell, 45-year old graduate of West Point in 1825, was the Acting Commissary of Subsistence in New Orleans and thus was the next higher link above Johnson in the subsistence department's chain of operation. He was responsible for filling the ration supply line from the United States to Scott's army in Mexico. If Seawell, using his established connections with New Orleans wholesale grocers and jobbers would obtain the items now in brisk demand in Vera Cruz and ship them to Johnson for disposal to the storekeepers, the two supply officers could share as middlemen in the large profits which were assured. Johnson seemed merely to be sounding out his senior with the inference that if he were agreeable, details of purchase and payment could be worked out later. The "U.S. Ships and Steamers" involved were those leased by the government; their owners and skippers were open to "deals" as both Johnson and Seawell were well aware.

The fatal sentence that was Johnson's undoing was a penciled postscript he added across the bottom of the sheet, shortening the last word to cram it into the lower right hand of the page:

> P.S. You will understand the stores would have to be shipped Commissary propty[18]

This was the clincher giving an otherwise artless proposition the dark hue of conspiracy, dishonesty and betrayal of trust. It was an insinuation that Seawell would have ready knowledge of the role he was to play in the scheme.

Seawell had been in the army for a long time. He had served with the Seventh Infantry on the frontier, then as an Indian agent and later in the Seminole Wars where he earned a major's brevet. He had been on duty in Texas when the Mexican War started and he was assigned the important supply post in New Orleans.[19] As Captain William T. Sherman discovered, five years later, Seawell was not above taking advantage of his post, but he kept within the law and regulations. He made use of the latitude granted him to buy without contract or competitive bids by purchasing most supplies from Perry Seawell & Co., a wholesale grocery firm owned by a relative in New Orleans. He justified this on the grounds that the concern knew better than its competitors how to package the food and prepare it for shipment. After the Mexican War, Major G. T. Waggaman succeeded Seawell. He continued the arrangement and Perry Seawell made Waggaman's brother a partner. A rival grocer in 1852 complained to General David E. Twiggs who ordered an inquiry. Sherman was brought from St. Louis in 1852 to replace Waggaman and abruptly ended the Seawell monopoly.[20]

Major Seawell's reaction to the letter was nothing like Johnson anticipated. The Virginian was affronted at the implied doubt cast upon his honor and integrity by the suggestion that he become a partner in such a subversion of his duties. He acted swiftly to forestall any involvement and to insure that no taint would attach itself to him, especially if he kept silent. At once he copied Johnson's letter and certified on his honor that the copy was true. Then he wrote a description of how it had come to him, written in ink with the postscript in pencil. He mailed the copy and his accompanying note to Washington to Brevet Brigadier General Roger Jones who had been The Adjutant General of the U.S. Army for 30 years. Seawell carefully locked the original letter in his desk.

Less than three weeks after Johnson wrote the "proffit" offer, the copy was being scanned in Washington by General Jones. His righteous indignation surpassed that of

Seawell who had only forwarded the copy without comment other than to tell how it came to him. Turning over the folded two-page document sent to him by Seawell, Jones wrote this indorsement for the eyes of W. L. Marcy, Secretary of War in the cabinet of President James K. Polk:

> The writer [Johnson] stands at the head of the list of 1st Lts in the 3rd Inf and is in charge of the commissariat at Vera Cruz. The station is one of great responsibility involving in a degree the very safety of the Army in the interior—and the officer filling it should therefore possess the highest integrity of character. Upon his honor alone the Gvrt must in a great measure rely for a proper application of the funds and public supplies provided for the use of the troops. That Lieut Johnson has abused the confidence reposed in him his own letter sufficiently shows. Such conduct tends to bring the service into disrepute and cannot be palliated in a disbursing officer whose hands in money matters at least, should be free even from the suspicion of stain.

The Adjutant General recommended that Johnson "be forthwith ordered to New Orleans and a Court of Inquiry there be instituted in his case, the results of which will determine the further measures to be taken."[21]

Secretary Marcy indorsed his approval of Jones's recommendation on the back of the paper and dated it July 20, 1847. The wheels began to turn. Lieutenant Johnson's days in the U.S. Army were numbered. The first and most enduring consequence of the unfortunate malaise in his character was about to engulf him.

ii. *"The President Can Take No Milder Course"*

What he welcomed as good news came to Lieutenant Johnson in Vera Cruz on August 11, 1847. Colonel Wilson, the port commander, informed his Acting Assistant Commissary of Subsistence that he was being transferred to New Orleans at once. Johnson had no idea why he was being shifted. The order, which came from Brevet Brigadier General George M. Brooke (who commanded the Western Division at East Pascagoula, Mississippi) gave no reasons.

Johnson may have thought his unanswered protest in May on his ineligibility for the supply post had finally borne results, or that he was being sent to some other duty after two years in Mexico. Unsuspecting that the order originated with The Adjutant General in Washington, Johnson wrote to that office on August 13 stating his desire to go to New Orleans in compliance with the directive from Brooke. It seems never to have occurred to him to connect this sudden transfer with the letter written to Seawell, who had never acknowledged its receipt.

Cheered to know he was leaving insalubrious Vera Cruz and his vexatious job, Johnson hastened to clear his accounts, shift his responsibilities to a successor and board a steamer for New Orleans about September 1, utterly innocent of the ordeal awaiting him.

Meanwhile Brooke's headquarters set up a court of inquiry. This is not the same as a court-martial, which tries one accused of specific violations or crimes, acquits or finds him guilty and imposes a punishment. The court of inquiry is limited to finding an answer to a question without determining guilt or innocence. In this case the task was to decide if Johnson actually wrote the letter received by Seawell.

General Order No. 28, authorizing the court of inquiry, was written and signed by First Lieutenant Richard B. Garnett, aide-de-camp to General Brooke and acting assistant adjutant general, who had known Johnson for three years at West Point where he graduated in 1841. He was to die in Pickett's charge at Gettysburg. Named as members of the court were Major W. R. Jouett, Third Infantry, who had been in the army since 1818, a year after Johnson's birth; Major A. G. Blanchard, Twelfth Infantry, Massachusetts-born West Point graduate in 1829; and Captain James Monroe, grandson and namesake of President Monroe and for a decade in the Ninth Infantry. Only Blanchard was a West Pointer. Jouett's assignment to the Third Infantry, Johnson's regiment, was on paper only; he had not yet joined it physically.[22] Consequently Johnson probably was unknown to any members of the court.

Major Seawell turned over Johnson's original blue paper letter of July 1 and the court's mission was to ask Johnson, under oath, if he had written it. The stage was thus set for the entrance of the principal actor, who definitely was not playing a hero's role in this tragedy.

Johnson was aghast when he arrived late in September, reported to General Brooke and learned why he had been summoned. His distress and agitation can easily be imagined. Since he was accused of no offence under the military code, he had no defense to prepare nor counsel to consult on trial strategy. With mounting anxiety and apprehension he could only wait to face the inquiry.

His suspense was short. On September 29, 1847 the court was ordered to meet the next day at noon in New Orleans Barracks.[23] Proceedings were brief. Johnson was sworn as the only witness. The original letter of July 1 was shown to him and he was asked by Major Jouett if he had written it.

Johnson hedged at first. He said he did not want to give a "naked answer divested of all its relations." Extenuating circumstances, he pleaded, precluded any simple "Yes" or "No." The court's members discussed his statement and then rejected any explanation as being beyond the scope of the inquiry. The question was repeated:

"Did you write this letter?"

"Depending upon my making an explanation in Washington," Johnson replied, "and for this purpose I will apply for leave to present myself and a full explanation to the authority ordering the court in order that final action can be delayed until I can obtain a hearing upon all the circumstances of the case, I answer in the affirmative."

The court decided this reply was conclusive enough and declared the letter was genuine and written by Johnson. It adjourned *sine die,* after being in session less than half an hour. Jouett signed the proceedings as president and Monroe as recorder. The papers were mailed to Washington.[24]

To Washington, posthaste, also went shaken and fearful Bushrod Johnson, hoping against all odds that he might salvage his career. He arrived as soon as the court's findings reached General Jones on October 11. Jones sent them to Secretary Marcy with this indorsement:

> The genuineness of the letter is established. I recommend action be deferred until Lt. Johnson appears in person.

The next day Johnson delivered a letter to General Jones asking that his request to President Polk for a personal interview be sent to the White House through military channels. The plea said:

> Washington
> October 12 1847
>
> To His Excellency James K. Polk—
>
> I have the honor very respectfully but most urgently to solicit the favor of a few moments interview on matters of the utmost importance to me and essential to the ends of justice in relation to a letter laid before a Court of Inquiry convened at New Orleans barracks on 30th ult.
>
> I am, sir
> Yr exlncy's ob't s'v't
> B. R. Johnson
> 1st Lt. 3d Infantry

General Jones discussed Johnson's request to see the President with the Secretary of War. They agreed that a personal interview with Polk was inappropriate, but concurred that Johnson might write his explanation and submit it to The Adjutant General for consideration by both Marcy and the President. Marcy put this opinion in a note to Jones whose office sent a copy to Johnson on October 14.

Under these conditions, Bushrod Rust Johnson set to work on the greatest literary effort of his life—a desperate attempt to convince the President of the United States that mitigating circumstances existed to explain away the foolishness of his offer of "proffit" to a superior for subverting the responsibilities of their offices. He penned more than 1500 words, many of them misspelled in his haste, in a frantic line of reasoning that ranged from an abject plea for pity to a fantastic statement that somebody owed him an apology for bringing the matter to light. But he seemed unable to convince even himself, and in his conclusion he virtually acknowledged he could not acquit himself and so bowed to the inevitable penalty. The appeal furnishes an amazing measure of the writer.

The letter, covering seven closely written pages, was dated October 15, 1847 and was addressed to General Jones. Johnson began by noting that Jones's office had sent him a copy of Marcy's opinion "indicating the manner in which it is nessary [*sic*] that I should submit what I desired to communicate in person to the President." He continued:

> I therefore hasten to make the following statement which I request may be taken into consideration with the letter addressed by me to Major Washington Seawell and dated Vera Cruz Mex. July 1 1847.
>
> It is true, as I testified to, before the Court of Inquiry at New Orleans Barracks on 30th ult. that I wrote the letter exhibited before it. But to the best of my knowledge I have

never in my life designedly wronged either my country or any individual. On the contrary for 7 years past I have rendered to that country, with the devotion of an honest heart, my most faithful services—and during that period I have never been accused of a fault or received the slightest censure—and every duty entrusted to me has been performed with perfect fidelity—On consideration of these truths in connexion with the fact that it is the aggregate of a man's acts throughout the course of a number of years, and not a single fault totally disconnected with any precedence that indicates the character it will not be unreasonable to inquire whether there are not some extraordinary circumstances under the influence of which this letter to Maj. Seawell was penned. The following facts will I think sufficiently manifest this was the case.

Johnson related that about May 26 he had a sudden, violent attack of yellow fever which "carried me to the brink of the grave." The case was treated with repeated doses of violent remedies until he became "wretchedly prostrated in body and mind." About mid-June, he said, he was able to return to duty for a few minutes daily, but was disabled for six weeks. No proper person was ordered to look after public business, the principal clerk left, substitutes got drunk and "things were in a state of disorder."

"While thus in a weakened condition," he explained, "many importunities came from persons of respectibility and standing in business in reference to transactions of a similar nature to those suggested in my letter to Maj. Seawell." He continued:

I refused to meet these propositions—Though I do not think I ever reflected on them... But after repeated importunities and when worn down to feelings of despair, at the numerous things that constantly demanded my attention without the ability to do justice to any and upon the first impulses of the thought as it occurred to me I turned to an officer of the army and [here Johnson interlined the following phrase] in a careless style that, as it even asks for advice & really expresses the desire to do no injury to the United States, exposed to him without artifice the necked [*sic*] undisguised facts suggested to me by others. Thus I felt I relieved and rid myself of the matter and divested myself of the chance of entertaining for a moment other propositions—I really felt little interest in the matter save that I was troubled with importunities that might be received continually.

And could my condition at that time be now fully realized—My debility from the effects of violent disease and violent remedies—The perplexity and harassing cares of business weighing upon a mind rendered incapable of permanent impressions or connected thought, I cannot but think it would win for me an apology and an acknowledgement that the strongest character might have wavered and sunk or sought the support of others and committed the fault that I have done.

He pointed out that the "style and manner of the letter show it was done hurriedly and impulsively" and an "error in the letter of a most evident character shows that it was not even read over by the writer," a statement contradicted by the corrections and penciled postscript in the original. The whole matter had so far passed from his mind, he wrote, that when word came for him to report to New Orleans he "had no other thought but that the order portended anything but good."

On the sixth day after the date of the letter to Seawell, he said, he sent him another "advising non-compliance with the suggestions in the first." If Seawell ever received such a second letter he did nothing about it, so far as the record shows. By July 10 when the second letter would have reached him, Seawell had already copied the first "proffit" offer and sent the copy to Washington. Beyond Johnson's word, which is suspect since he offered no proof, there is no evidence that, conscience-stricken or with a clearer appreciation of the possible consequences of the offer to Seawell, he ever retracted it.

Johnson stressed that the first letter was written in "a plain undisguised and explicit manner—is signed in full—and exhibits nothing of a determined disposition to do wrong or to tempt others to do so—and no effort is made to shield myself from the ruinous consequences which are always apprehended by the perpetrators of wrong" though it would have been easy to contrive an offer "not to implicate me in the least." He pointed out that he had seen Seawell only two or three times and had spoken no more than "half a dozen sentences" to him and he doubted that "any act so marked with indiscretion" could be committed by "a man of the most ordinary intellect in full possession of his judgement and reason." He went on:

> Indeed the folly exhibited throughout the transaction is a most humiliating evidence of the disqualifying circumstances under which it was perpetrated and has made me shrink from the explanation I now make—it may also be remembered that the amount is not at all sufficient to account for the letter on ordinary principles and motives of action and more particularly so when considered in conexion with the large amount of money and property that my duties required me to handle.

"I shall not attempt to sustain myself on the character of my previous services," Johnson continued, "though they may be found as faithful and bright as some that have been made more glaring and been more fortunate in rewards. If it is deemed worth the enquiry the records of your office will show that in every important position in which my regiment has been placed, from the time I entered it up to the siege of Vera Cruz, I have been with it. And I feel assured that the manner in which I transacted the business entrusted to me in the Commissary department will do me no discredit; though no public records tell of the difficulty and the toil; and of the sacrifice of health and years of existence, which the most favored life may not restore."

He summarized his plea on "the following considerations which I hope will claim special attention.—Firstly; that the letter under consideration was written under disqualifying circumstances.—Secondly; that it was not written deliberately and upon mature reflection or with the usual design and determination with which wrong is ordinarily perpetrated.—Thirdly; that the suggestions contained in the letter are contrary to the whole tenor of my life and character."

Then he added a peroration which virtually admitted the inadequacy of his defense and that the most he could expect was to avoid the disgrace of dismissal. He said:

> ...I am fully sensible of all the consequences that attach themselves to the letter...but I seek no sympathy in the matter and shall at least retain a pride in meeting all the consequences of every act of my life.
>
> The duty I owe to my profession and to my country as well as more private duties prevent me from seeking to abandon a profession in which it has been my pride to serve, at the very moment the country requires new acquisitions to it, and I therefore hope it may not be necessary for me to be cut off from it, but if the foregoing is not deemed sufficient to secure me from further action in the matter I must beg that I be permitted to resign my commission in the army. My previous services and the fact that I have done no injury save to myself will surely entitle me to this privalidge [*sic*].
>
> I have the honor to be, Sir
> Your most obt svt
> B. R. Johnson
> 1st Lt 3d Inf[25]

For six days after he delivered his appeal, Johnson lived in a hell of uncertainty, while General Jones, Secretary Marcy and President Polk reviewed and pondered his statement and considered what action to take. Then Polk reached a decision. It was conveyed to General Jones by Marcy:

War Dept. October 19, 1847

I have laid before the President the letter of Lt. B. R. Johnson to you explaining his letter of 1 of July and was directed to state that the President after due consideration has come to the conclusion that he can take no milder course in the matter than to accept his resignation.

You will communicate this result to Lt. Johnson.

W. L. Marcy, Secty of War.

It took two days to get the word to Johnson. He wrote out the required document:

Washington D.C.
Oct 21/47

To Adj. Gen. R. Jones

I have the honor very respectfully to tender my resignation as 1st Lt. in the Army of the U.S.

B. R. Johnson 1st Lt 3d Inf

Without delay, on the back of this paper, two indorsements were written:

Recommended take effect immediately
L. Thomas, Secy Adj Gen

Accepted.
W. L. Marcy[26]

It was done! Bushrod Rust Johnson was out of the United States Army forever, his world was in ruins and the path of his future was set definitely as a civilian. He could never reenter the army, as did his classmate Sherman, or Henry W. Halleck, or Ulysses S. Grant, or a host of others after their resignations. Any effort by Johnson to return would have opened the files and exposed this questionable chapter in his past. He would always be nagged by the fear that some of the few who knew the story (Seawell, Brooke, Jones, Thomas, Marcy, Polk, or the members of the court, Jouett, Blanchard, Monroe or Garnett) might some day cross his path, drop hints or start gossip. Time and death ultimately removed these hazards, but for nearly a score of years some of them remained to menace his security and his reputation.[27]

He had salvaged one important thing. He had been permitted to quit instead of being cashiered. He could always say, in truth, that he had resigned. No reproach attached to a normal resignation, and as long as the circumstances of his departure from the service remained buried in the files, he was on the same standing as dozens of his classmates and former associates at West Point and in the Army.

Sherman and Grant, in post-Civil War discussions of Johnson with his great-nephew Robert Underwood Johnson, associate editor of *Century* magazine and coeditor of *Battles and Leaders of the Civil War,* never indicated that they knew anything about the 1847 incident and probably were as totally unaware of it as his kinsman. Certainly none of Johnson's colleagues in the educational field before or after the Civil War, in the Confederate Army, or in his postwar business enterprises had any inkling of it.

Those who knew Johnson in later years remarked upon his reticence, his retiring and diffident manner in public, his slow and cautious speech and his carefully considered actions. He was called "modest," "quiet," "studious."[28] If it is true that a man is made by his past, it may be asked if these personality traits were the aftermath of his shattering experience in the summer of 1847, or did they go farther back to his Quaker rearing, his early rural education or the unsophisticated environment of his youth?

Notes

Where two works of a single author are cited, or where two authors of the same name may occur, this device will be used: Freeman, *Lee,* IV, 276 and Freeman, *Lieutenants,* III, 175.

The following abbreviations are used:

B&L for *Battles and Leaders of the Civil War.*

Congress Directory for *Biographical Directory of the American Congress.*

CV for *Confederate Veteran.*

DAB for *Dictionary of American Biography.*

Hamersly for Thomas H. S. Hamersly, *Complete Army and Navy Register of the U.S. 1776–1887.*

OR for *War of the Rebellion, a Compilation of the Official Records of the Union and Confederate Armies.* Since most of the volumes cited are in Series 1, this will not be repeated. Any volume in Series 2 will be so designated. Citations will follow this method: *OR,* XXX, pt. 1, p. 245 meaning Volume 30, part 1, page 245.

SHSP for *Southern Historical Society Papers.*

3d Inf. Ret for Third U.S. Infantry Regiment Returns.

1. George C. Furber, *The Twelve Months Volunteer,* (Cincinnati: U. P. James, 1857), pp. 548 ff.
2. Letter, Oct. 15, 1847, Johnson to Gen. R. Jones, The Adjutant General, U.S. Army. Original in War Dept., AG Files, National Archives. Since Jones's official title was "The Adjutant General" with a capital "T," it will appear in this work in that form.
3. Ethan Allen Hitchcock, *Fifty Years in Camp and Field,* (New York: G. P. Putnam's Sons, 1909), pp. 147 f.
4. Lloyd Lewis, *Captain Sam Grant,* (Boston: Little, Brown & Co., 1950), pp. 168 f. Hereafter: Lewis, *Grant.*
5. Letter, May 10, 1847, Johnson to Gibson in War Dept., AG Files; *Regulations for Subsistence Dept.,* April 11, 1818, Section 6.
6. Letter, Sherman to his wife, Ellen, St. Louis, Aug. 2, 1852 quoted in Lloyd Lewis, *Sherman, Fighting Prophet,* (New York: Harcourt Brace & Co., 1932), p. 87. Hereafter: Lewis, *Sherman.*
7. Henry Coppée, 3d Arty., *Life and Services of Gen. U. S. Grant,* (New York: Richardson & Co., 1868), p. 25.
8. G. W. Cullum, *Biographical Register of the Officers and Graduates of the U.S. Military Academy,* (New York: D. Van Nostrand, 1868), I, p. 619; Thomas H. S. Hamersly, *Complete Army and Navy Register of the U.S. 1776–1887,* (New York: T. H. S. Hamersly Publishing Co., 1888), pp. 333, 340 f.
9. Graphic descriptions of the "northers" and their ruinous results are in *Furber,* pp. 506 f., and *Hitchcock,* p. 246.
10. *Furber,* p. 563.
11. Cadmus M. Wilcox, *History of the Mexican War,* (Washington: Church News Publishing Co., 1892), p. 268.
12. Letter, Oct. 15, 1847, Johnson to Jones, AG Files.
13. Richard S. Ewell, *The Making of a Soldier,* (Richmond: Whittet and Sheperson, 1935), pp. 59 f.
14. William Bowen Campbell, "Mexican War Letters of Col. Wm. Bowen Campbell of Tennessee written to David Campbell of Virginia, 1846–47" in *Tennessee Historical Magazine,* I, pp. 129–67. Campbell was a Union brigadier general in the Civil War.
15. Richard McSherry, *El Puchero,* (Philadelphia: Lippencott, Grambo & Co., 1850), pp. 28 f.
16. *Furber,* pp. 513, 564 *et passim.* "A chaotic state of affairs existed in the wake of the army" wrote Ohio-born Brevet Major Roswell S.

Ripley, later a Confederate brigadier, in his *War With Mexico,* (New York: Harper & Bros., 1849), II, p. 570.

17. Spelling and punctuation are reproduced here as in the original in Record Group No. 153, War Dept., JAG Files, National Archives. Revisions Johnson made while rereading the letter are obvious in the original.
18. *Ibid.*
19. *Cullum,* I, p. 281.
20. W. T. Sherman, *Memoirs,* (New York: Appleton & Co., 1875), I, pp. 90 f.
21. All original papers in this case are in Record Group 153, AG Files and JAG Court of Inquiry No. 476EE, National Archives. These show the sequence of events after Johnson wrote to Seawell.
22. Biographies in Cullum, II, p. 25 and Frances B. Heitman, *Historical Register and Dictionary of the United States Army,* (Washington: Government Printing Office, 1903), 2 vols. I, pp. 304, 548, 644.
23. Orders No. 5, Headquarters, Western Division, E. Pascagoula, Miss., Sept. 29, 1847 in AG Files.
24. JAG Court of Inquiry No 476 EE and AG Files.
25. *Ibid.* Spelling and punctuation as in original.
26. Lorenzo Thomas who indorsed the resignation was The Adjutant General of the Union forces in the Civil War and briefly Secretary of War under President Andrew Johnson. The Third Infantry Returns give October 22 as the date the resignation was accepted.
27. Although he was a Virginian, Seawell remained loyal to the Union in 1861. He was chief mustering officer for Kentucky in 1862–63 and was stationed in San Francisco until retirement in 1866. He died in 1888, surviving Johnson by eight years. *Cullum,* I, p. 281.
28. Statement of Chancellor John Berrien Lindsley to trustees of the University of Nashville in 1870 in University of Nashville *Trustees Minute Books,* I, p. 258.

2
"REMOVE OUT OF THE BLIGHT OF SLAVERY"

i. Diaspora of the Quakers

At least fourscore years or three generations before Bushrod Rust Johnson was born October 7, 1817 on a small farm near Morristown, Union Township, Belmont County, Ohio, his great grandfather, Garrett Johnson, stepped from a ship in New York harbor. He came there from Holland, but he was not a Dutchman. He may have sought refuge in the Netherlands during the troubled times in England when Stuarts and Hanoverians were fighting and when those who picked the wrong side in politics or religion found it safer to flee the country of their birth than face the vengeance of the victors. His distinguished descendant, Robert Underwood Johnson (1853–1937), literary notable and diplomat, said the family tree had roots in Sir Archibald Johnston, Lord Warristoun, a Scottish statesman executed in 1668 after the restoration of Charles II.[1] Sir Archibald's son, James, took refuge in Holland, won and later lost the favor of William of Orange who took the British throne in 1688 from James II, his uncle who was also his father-in-law. James Johnston died in Bath, England in May 1737 at the age of 82.

But no convincing evidence has been found to link these Scottish aristocrats with Yeoman Garrett Johnson, whose name appears sometimes Garet or Garett or Garret. About all that is known of him is that he may have been a Quaker, which might explain his exile in Holland, that he married twice, and that he sired seven sons: Joseph, James, John, Amos, Ira, Charles, and Garrett, and two daughters, Huldah and Joanna, the latter names indicating a Dutch marital connection somewhere on the distaff side.

Among the sons, Joseph Johnson, who may also have been a Quaker, married Hannah Hough and sometime around 1750 moved to Upper Makefield Township, Bucks County, Pennsylvania. They produced six sons: Garrett, John, Charles, Joseph, Noah, and James, and two daughters, Achsah and Hannah. During or shortly after the Revolutionary War the family moved to the Goose Creek Quaker community in Loudoun County, Virginia. Joseph died while some of his children were small and these were parcelled out to relatives to rear.[2]

Such was the fate of Bushrod's father, Noah, born August 10, 1772 in Bucks County, Pennsylvania. He was sent as a lad to live with his older sister, Achsah, who was the wife of Timothy Taylor of Willow Greens at Silcott Spring, Loudoun County. Timothy was Noah's guardian. He acquired some schooling and became a blacksmith, a fairly lucrative occupation in this region of small farmers, most of them either Quakers or Palatinate Germans. What happened to Noah's brothers and sisters is indefinite.

The Society of Friends and the "Dutch" had been thriving in Loudoun County since the 1730s. The Germans came as a result of the colonization policy of Queen Anne, replanting refugees from a homeland devastated in the war bearing her name, 1703–13. In 1730 Alexander Ross and Morgan Bryan of Chester County, Pennsylvania formed a company to bring 70 Quaker families into the Shenandoah region, then a fertile wilderness with few whites. In 1745, Friends from Fairfax County, Virginia who had migrated to the Middle Branch of Goose Creek in Loudoun County got permission to hold meetings, from which ultimately grew the Goose Creek Monthly Meeting located nine miles west of Leesburg, the county seat, and still surviving at modern Lincoln.[3]

Frugal, industrious and better farmers than even the Germans, the Friends flourished. They were clannish and unbending in adherence to their principles. Members were expelled for marrying non-Quakers, for trading in or owning slaves, or for any military service. The devout among them endured fines of tobacco, bedding, livestock and household utensils for refusal to pay "priests' wages" assessed by Virginia as salaries of clergy of the established Episcopal church, for absences at musters of the local militia, or for hiring substitutes.[4]

Names of the children of Garrett and Joseph Johnson are not found in extant records of Quaker meetings in Pennsylvania or Virginia. However, none of them appears in rosters of Revolutionary soldiers raised in their neighborhoods. On the contrary, one Joseph Johnson is listed among "Non Associators" in Upper Makefield Township, Bucks County, on August 9, 1775,[5] stigmatized thereby as a nonparticipant and liable to be fined when the area's manhood rallied as "Associators" in militia units to fight the British. Thus, Quaker or not, he bore testimony to the Quaker creed: "The Society believes war is wholly at variance with the gospel and therefore cannot take part in any warlike measures."

Noah Johnson grew to manhood in this Virginia Quaker community. Placid by religion, the Friends had no overt conflicts with their neighbors who felt otherwise. County records reveal frequent real estate transactions among Quaker Spencers, Hoges, Nichols, Greggs, Bursons, and Janneys with Rusts, Wrights and others who were Presbyterians and Episcopalians. Some of the "bargain and sale" deeds in the Leesburg courthouse are dated in the Quaker manner: "On the ninth day of the fifth month, 1792, etc." Isolated by distance from the aristocratic Tidewater plantocracy, Friends and Germans made common cause against the slaveholding class, but maintained cordial relations with the few in Loudoun who owned Negroes.[6]

The names of Timothy Taylor and his wife, Achsah Johnson, are not found in surviving Quaker records. Nor is Charles Johnson, Noah's brother, who lived nearby. In the area dwelt the numerous Quaker family of Nathan Spencer, Sr., and his wife Hannah Lofborough, who migrated from Abington, Pennsylvania, a suburb of Philadelphia, to Virginia sometime prior to 1761. In 1765 their membership was transferred to Goose Creek meeting. Theirs was a comfortable stone house, about a mile from the meeting house, for Nathan was a man of substance as well as a devout Friend. There were nine Spencer children, eight of whom later were to move to Ohio. The eighth child, fourth daughter, was Rachel, born September 6, 1773. She was an active, practicing Quaker. Her name appears frequently in records of Goose Creek meeting as a witness to marriages of relatives and acquaintances, until finally there is this terse reference to herself and Noah:

> Rachel Johnson (late Spencer) reported married out of unity 28th day 4th month 1794 disowned 26th day 5th month, 1794.[7]

Rachel, in love with the young blacksmith from Pennsylvania, had dared the disapproval of the brethren to become his bride in a non-Quaker ceremony contrary to Friends' rules. Being "disowned" meant she could continue to attend services, but would have no voice or vote in proceedings. If she met certain conditions she could return to the fold, which she did in 1812, by publicly acknowledging her error, condemning her "misconduct," expressing sorrow, and asking forgiveness.

Rachel's marriage involved no break with her family. Actually among younger Friends a spirit of revolt was growing against the sect's strict rules on marriages. Each year, more and more disownments resulted from marriages "out of unity" where one party was non-Quaker, or "contrary to discipline" when both were Friends but preferred to be married by a justice of the peace or minister of another denomination.[8]

Noah and Rachel hastened to join the land-owning class and thereby acquire the local prestige and social status attached to proprietorship. They bought from Timothy and Achsah Taylor for £60 (sixty pounds sterling) "current money of Virginia" a parcel of 30 acres with "houses, buildings, orchards, etc.," on the main road from Snicker's Gap to Israel Janney's mill, about a dozen miles west of Leesbury. The "bargain and sale" deed is dated September 12, 1796, though the property probably had been bought and occupied some time before. Noah's name is spelled "Johnston." His brother Charles signed as a witness. The fact that no mortgage was involved indicates that Noah, at 21, had accumulated enough money at his trade to pay cash in full for the land. The Johnsons sold the place back to the Taylors for $700 in a deed dated December 10, 1810, six years after they migrated to Ohio. In this transaction Noah's name is shown without the "t."[9]

The first children born to Noah and Rachel on December 14, 1794, seven and a half months after their marriage, were twins, a boy and a girl, named Nathan and Hannah after Rachel's parents. As Nathan grew older in Ohio he was to assume leadership of the family. He taught school, learned to be a physician and took an active part in abolition agitation and in the Underground Railroad's aid to fugitive slaves. He practiced in the town of Belmont, Ohio until 1839 and thence for 32 years more until his death in Cambridge City, Wayne County, Indiana. He was to act as a second father to his youngest brother, Bushrod, 21 years younger, and he was always his counselor and help in time of trouble.

Three more children were born before the Johnson family left Loudoun County. They were Lucretia, born about 1796; Joseph, about 1798; and Achsah, namesake of Noah's sister, about 1800.[10] The problem of providing on a small farm for this growing brood, which seemed destined to increase, was apparent. A move westward to cheaper and more productive land was indicated. Equally pressing was the desire of the Friends to escape the encroaching economy of slavery which they regarded with fear and loathing.

Fortuitously, the opening of the new Northwest Territory north of the Ohio River offered a solution to both problems. The first portion of this beckoning Paradise to be surveyed and recorded was the Seven Ranges in eastern Ohio. Under provisions of the Ordinance of 1787 this was to be "forever free of slavery," the land was good and cheaply priced and held a promise of speedy rewards to the hardy and enterprising.

The first Friends moved into eastern Ohio in September 1800 and by December enough had arrived to justify setting up two "preparatory" meetings at Concord in Belmont County and Short Creek in Jefferson. Parts of Belmont County were settled almost exclusively by Quakers. One of the society's historians thus described the diaspora:

> They came chiefly from the southern states . . . stimulated to the movement by a desire to remove out of the blighting influence of slavery against which their religious principles required them to bear constant testimony, and being unwilling that their children should grow up in the midst of its corrupting influences, they left in many instances, good lands in a genial clime to set themselves down to a life of privations and hardship incident to pioneer life in the forest north of the Ohio river.[11]

From as far away as Georgia and North Carolina the Friends came. The entire membership of some meetings moved north in a group. The North Carolina east coast counties of Beaufort, Cartaret, Craven, Hyde, and Jones were almost depopulated of Quakers. The widowed grandmother of Edwin M. Stanton, Lincoln's secretary of war, left Cartaret in January 1800 and arrived nine months later in Bridgeport, Belmont County, her wagon being the first in the group to ford the Ohio. By 1800 there were 800 Quakers in Ohio and by 1826 more than 8000 lived in four eastern Ohio counties alone.[12]

Jacob and Mary Gregg of Goose Creek Meeting in Loudoun bought one of the 640-acre sections in the new Northwest Territory around the turn of the century, although the deed conveying it to them from President Thomas Jefferson was not dated until 1808. They probably paid no more than $2 an acre. The land was in Section 7, Range 5 in Union Township, which was set up in 1804, three years after Belmont County was organized with its county seat, St. Clairsville named for General Arthur St. Clair, first territorial governor of Ohio.

The Greggs roused the interest of the Goose Creek community in favor of a group exodus to Ohio. Noah and Rachel Johnson decided to go. Rachel's brother, Nathan Spencer, Jr., and his wife, Ann Smith Spencer and their children, her brothers John and William; David and Ruth Hoge, Samuel and Mary Hoge and their numerous offspring were among the several score who disposed of their holdings in Loudoun and headed across the mountains to the Seven Ranges in the summer of 1804 or 1805.

The Johnsons bought 120 acres from the Greggs for $600, or $5 an acre. Since Noah sold his 30 acres in Loudoun at the rate of $23 an acre, a comparison of values is available, showing the economics of the migration. The uncleared land was southeast of Morristown, now on U.S. Route 40 west of St. Clairsville and north of the town of

Belmont in Goshen Township.[13] The soil was fairly fertile on gently rolling hills. After the usual three years required to bring it into cultivation, the farm would provide more food than the occupants could eat. Noah's blacksmithing meanwhile brought in additional money. He paid 78 cents taxes on the land in 1810.

The next few years brought three more babies: Aletha during the first year in Ohio; Charles in 1809, who was to die tragically before a dozen years had passed; and Mary, about 1814. Nathan, growing up, acquired enough education in several three-month terms in a log schoolhouse on the Oliver Taylor farm nearby to enable him to get a teaching job in his teens at $10 a month and to tutor his younger brothers and sisters. The Friends had an abiding interest in education and saw to it that provision for schooling went hand in hand with the organizing of their meetings.

The first church of any creed in the area was the Plainfield Friends Meeting house, a building of hewed logs erected in 1806 about five miles from the Johnson farm and a mile south of modern Lloydsville. To this group of Quakers, many of them her neighbors in Virginia, Rachel Spencer Johnson in 1812 made the required penances for marrying "out of unity" 18 years before. She was taken back into membership after Goose Creek Meeting in Virginia gave its consent. The next year, as the Plainfield meeting record puts it: "On the twenty-sixth day of the sixth month," Rachel's daughters, Hannah, nearly 19, and Lucretia, about 17, were received into the Society on their requests,[14] termed "Convincement" by the Friends.

More Johnsons, not joined by blood to Noah, and more Spencers of Rachel's kin continued to come into Belmont County. Her father, Nathan, Sr., died in Loudoun January 30, 1809, leaving £10 (pounds sterling) to Goose Creek Meeting.[15] He had lost his mind and had been a care to his family. Freed by his death, the remaining

Spencer children moved to Ohio. Rachel may have inherited an eighth share of what was left in his estate.

Some of the Johnsons were from Ireland. Others of the name, with and without a "t," were assuming leading roles in the burgeoning community. Robert Johnston bought the first town lots in St. Clairsville in 1803; Sterling Johnson became the first county recorder in 1807 and county commissioner in 1810–11. Most Johnsons and Johnstons had big families; one had sixteen children, another eleven, and counts of six and eight were common.[16] An outsider, or a politician seeking votes, might have thought they were all related and therefore was careful to offend none.

The War of 1812 came and went. The community furnished some soldiers for the army of William Henry Harrison in 1813, but Nathan, 19, was not among them. Quakers had been exempted from military service by the Second Ohio Territorial Legislature in 1801 if they paid $1.25 tax each. None of the Johnsons, Spencers or their Quaker neighbors enlisted.[17] True to their tenets, the Quakers courted community abuse by refusing to join in the parades, bonfires and "illuminations" that celebrated the news of the victory of New Orleans and the later treaty of peace.[18]

The influx of Friends continued. More meetings were set up: at Stillwater in Warren Township in 1808 and Flushing in 1818. By 1828 five monthly meetings were flourishing in Belmont County. The Ohio Yearly Meeting, parent body of 53 monthly meetings in the state, counted 9000 members in 1826. Plainfield, to which the Johnsons belonged, had 170. St. Clairsville, called the "Quaker City," had a newspaper, edited by Howard Jefferson Horton, which dated its issues "Seventh Day, Second Month, Third Day, 1827" for Saturday, February 3, 1827 conforming to the Friends' belief that the names of days and months were heathenish.

Benjamin Lundy, the New Jersey Quaker harness maker and abolition propagandist who lived with his family in St. Clairsville a short distance east of the courthouse, organized the first antislavery group, "The Union Humane Society" there in 1815. Nathan Johnson, now 21, was one of the first members and was proud of the fact all the rest of his life. William Cooper Howells, Quaker father of the author William Dean Howells, was one of the chief spirits in the society.[19] In his saddlery, Lundy made the raftload of horse furniture he floated to St. Louis in 1819 and was unable to sell at a profit because business was deranged by Missouri's uncertain status as a free or slave state. He took the loss and walked back to Ohio in the dead of winter.[20]

Into this quiet, sincere, industrious Quaker environment, Bushrod Rust Johnson was born. He was the ninth and last child of Noah and Rachel, now in their midforties, an age when most pioneer women were past childbearing. A series of tragedies soon darkened their lives, but now the family and friends welcomed the baby who was given two unusual names instead of the traditional Biblical Christian ones.

Why this was done piques curiosity. Robert U. Johnson says the boy was "named for Bushrod Washington of the family of the First President."[21] This is unlikely on two counts: It is improbable that simple Quakers in Ohio or Loudoun County Virginia had any connections with Tidewater Bushrods or Washingtons strong enough to inspire naming a child for George Washington's nephew, Bushrod, justice of the U.S. Supreme Court, 1789–1829; and his statement does not explain the "Rust" as a middle name.

A more plausible reason can be documented. Near the Johnson farm in Loudoun County in 1794 was the home of Captain George Rust who had a son Bushrod, born February 1, 1794, a few weeks before the marriage of Rachel and Noah. The Rust lad was of an age and location to have been a playmate of Nathan, firstborn of Noah and Rachel, who was ten years old when the family left for Ohio. Bushrod Rust became a physician and lived and practiced in the same Virginia neighborhood until 1847.[22] Nostalgic for old scenes and old friends, Noah and Rachel quite naturally could have called their last baby after a former neighbor.

Such a distinctive name set the boy apart from the many Josephs, Charles, Williams, Edwards and Roberts among the Johnsons and Johnstons in Belmont County. It should have marked Bushrod Rust Johnson for a special destiny.

ii. Ambition Rightly Ruled

In the spring after Bushrod Johnson's birth, the Plainfield Meeting community was excited by a prophetic event. The first stage line began operating from Wheeling, in slaveholding Virginia, to Zanesville, 73 miles to the west. The Cumberland Road, under construction since President Jefferson signed the bill in 1806, had crept as far as Wheeling by 1818, bringing the great cities of the East within reach; now the horizon widened toward the boundless West and its promises. Everybody in the countryside gathered at stopping places in St. Clairsville, Morristown and Cambridge to watch Thomas Dryden of Lancaster, owner of the stage, hold the reins of four beautiful bay horses dashing along at twelve miles an hour, the passengers inside and atop yelling and cheering at the applauding spectators. Many a heart was stirred with a desire for a larger part of a future along this road toward the sunset.[23]

Nathan Johnson was such a one. Within a few years the great road would cross Ohio, Indiana and Illinois to the Mississippi River and anyone of vision could see that the primitive villages along the way would turn into cities of business and industry to rival those of the East. A month after Bushrod's birth, Noah sold 40 of his 120 acres to Samuel Hoge, who with his wife Mary and nine children had been among the migrants from Goose Creek to Union Township. The price was $1000, or $25 an acre for land sold for $5 an acre thirteen years before.[24] Here was proof how money was to be made in land.

Nathan, now 24, with money earned as a teacher and probably with some borrowed from his father, traveled west to Centreville, Indiana, eight miles from the Ohio border. Other Virginia Quaker Johnsons had gone to Wayne County even before Indiana became a state in 1816. One of his Spencer cousins, David, came later with eight children.

Deed records of Wayne County, of which Centreville was the seat until 1873 when more populous Richmond succeeded it, disclose an interesting land speculation with a handsome profit for Nathan. On June 6 and 8, 1818 he bought three lots in the town for $631: from William and Nancy Summer, lot 57, and lots 19 and 20 from Arthur and Grace Henry, resident in Cincinnati. Lot 57 was divided into five bits which were sold as follows: on June 27, 1818 to Samuel Louthian, $250; two pieces to S. H. Brannon for $680 on August 7 and 12; one to John Lewis, $105 on August 12 and one to Abel Johnson on August 14 for $100. Lot 19, bought with Lot 20 for $31, he sold on July 30 to James Bailey for $15.[25] In ten weeks he made $620, almost doubling his original investment. Twenty-one years later Nathan would return to eastern Wayne County, which meanwhile became a center of Hicksite Quakers and Underground Railroad operations.

Nathan went back to Belmont County shortly after his real estate enterprise. He married Sarah, one of the eight children of David and Ruth Gregg Hoge, on September 23, 1819. The ceremony was performed by a justice of the peace. Plainfield Quaker Meeting "disunited" her on

March 23, 1820 for marrying "contrary to discipline" which indicated that Nathan was also a Quaker. Otherwise the charge would have been "out of unity" as in the case of Noah and Rachel.[26] The Hoges, (also spelled "Hogue"), had come from Virginia about the same time as the Johnsons, in whose family a legend persists that David Hoge lived at one time on lands owned by George Washington.[27]

Their first child, Nimrod Hoge Johnson, was born September 16, 1820 and therefore was only three years younger than his uncle Bushrod. These two maintained a close association until the Civil War, according to Nimrod's son, the editor Robert U. Johnson.

Sarah Hoge Johnson continued her regular attendance at the meetings of the Friends in Ohio and later in Indiana, her grandson Robert wrote later, and the speech of her sons and daughters and her grandchildren was "thee" and "thy" when addressing her or Nathan. She gave up her strict Quaker dress but retained a liking for dove color and her caps were silk with lace and satin ribbons.[28]

While Nathan's fortunes were rising, tragedy struck his parents. Within a few months between 1818 and 1820, death took Lucretia and Achsah. The causes probably were typhoid fever which struck the area periodically. As the family is listed in the 1820 U.S. Census it may be deduced that the male, 16 to 26, was Joseph, engaged with his father in farming while the two males aged less than 10 were Charles and Bushrod. A female 16 to 26 would have been Aletha and another, more than 26, would have been Nathan's twin, Hannah. A female less than 10 was Mary. There were eight recorded members of the family in the household with two males as farmers and one, Noah, in manufacturing, which meant he was operating his blacksmith's forge alone.

Before May 9, 1822 two more were to die, according to a letter written by Hannah Spencer Burson, Rachel's sister, to a cousin in Philadelphia, Sarah Thomas, giving an account of the fortunes of the Spencer clan. Charles, a promising lad of eleven and a half years, was fatally hurt by a horse's kick, and another of the adult daughters, Hannah, had succumbed to disease. One Joseph Johnston, married to Sarah Stillwell, December 4, 1822 by Sterling Johnson, J.P., may have been the surviving adult child.[29]

Bushrod Johnson's formative years were spent in surroundings dominated by the conviction that Quakerism was the only true faith. Almost from birth he was brought under its training. His mother, who had proved her devotion to the creed by undergoing the reinstatement procedure, his sisters and his brother Nathan's family, conforming to the common practice of their neighbors, "bore testimony" against the fashions of the time in dress and speech. They gathered regularly at Plainfield Meeting House at 11 A.M. on the first and fourth day (Sunday and Wednesday) and ordered their lives in accordance with Friends' precepts. Until he reached his teens, Bushrod may have worn the characteristic "plain dress" of shag-bellied coat and broad rimmed hat common in Belmont County, and spoken the "plain language" without the pronoun "you" at home and among his playmates and classmates. In the meetings he heard exhortations against the evils of holding slaves, of engaging in militia musters, of making or using the peach brandy or whiskey so plentiful in Eastern Ohio, of taking oaths in court or even using such titles as "Mister" or "Mistress" because they bestowed homage due only to God.[30] The Johnsons, grief-stricken by four deaths, may have been more devout than most in a quest for the consolation of religion. Likewise, Bushrod and his sister Mary could have been the objects of more than normal affection and care as the only minor children left at home to Noah and Rachel.

Ambitious Nathan persisted in his efforts to raise his status from the ranks of yeoman artisan and farmer. He took sufficient instruction from a neighboring physician, whose name has been lost, to enable him to pass the scrutiny of the medical board of censors of the 17th Medical District at Canton (modern Bridgeport), Ohio and was licensed by it to practice in 1827.[31] He was elected censor to examine applicants in 1830 by the county medical association, May 25, 1830.[32] In 1828 he was listed among eleven physicians in the county.[33] After he had garnered some income from his patients in the town of Belmont, he went to Philadelphia for several months in the 1834–35 winter to attend lectures of the College of Medicine of the University of Pennsylvania, which advertised its October to March medical courses in contemporary Ohio newspapers. Years later, in 1851, when his second son, Lemuel Riddick Johnson, was graduated by Starling Medical College in Columbus, Ohio, this school awarded Nathan an honorary M.D. degree.[34]

Two events in the mid-1820s had a profound effect upon the whole area, the Quaker element, and on the Johnsons. The National Road reached St. Clairsville in 1825. Ground was broken, appropriately on the Fourth of July, opposite the courthouse, with ringing oratory and fanfare for the next leg of the improved, new road to Zanesville. Survey parties in October were locating the highway 53 miles beyond Zanesville toward Columbus.[35] Ahead of the builders, as contracts were let for grading in one-mile sections, for bridges, culverts and ditches, rolled a wave of optimism. Towns were expanding with stores, manufacturing facilities, schools, churches and newspapers.[36]

The second factor was the Hicksite schism among the Friends which had been simmering for more than a decade and finally erupted beyond return in 1828. The society was rent asunder between the Orthodox and the followers of Elias Hicks, (1748–1830), disputing over the nature of Jesus.[37] The Quaker meetings in Belmont County, as elsewhere, filled their records with entries on members being "disowned" for joining the Hicksites, known variously as "liberal" or "polemical" Quakers. Rachel Spencer Johnson, after seventeen years of affiliation with Plainfield and Stillwater Meetings following her reinstatement, was dropped again. Most of the Hoges and Spencers were also ousted.[38] There were hard feelings and heartaches among the Friends of Belmont County, many of whom had been linked in accord since Goose Creek days. Emotions and tempers were stirred as they can be only by religious differences.

To Noah and Rachel, now in their mid-fifties, all this must have been disturbing. Some of their bright prospects had died with their four children. Aletha, the last adult child left to them, was married to Thomas Leslie, Maryland-born Quaker wagon maker, on March 16, 1826 by Eleazer Evans, a justice of the peace in Goshen Township,[39] and went off to rear a family of five near Bethesda, a few miles away.

Beginning in 1825, Noah disposed of parts of the land left to him after the 1817 sale of 40 acres to Samuel Hoge. Prices had slumped. He got only $1.56 an acre from Ignatious Burns in 1825 and $6.75 each for 80 acres including his home from J. W. Satterthwaite on July 24, 1827. Three years later he bought back two parts for $3.36 and $3.90 an acre and sold them, after three weeks, for $10.50. Pertinent deeds do not disclose what other consideration might have explained this fluctuation in values. He also bought six lots in the town of Belmont between 1823 and 1827 for a total of $236 and sold them in 1833 to Dr. Nathan for $300.[40] By 1833 Noah had liquidated all of his property in Belmont County.

A chance for a new start farther west along the National Road appealed to the Johnsons, psychologically ready to quit the scene of their sorrows and frustrations. In the town of Norwich, Muskingum County, 43 miles to the west, relay stations for the stage lines on the new highway needed artisans like blacksmith Noah. The town, laid out in 1827 by William Harper, a Briton who named it for his birthplace, was midway between Cambridge and Zanesville and between Columbus and Wheeling. It was a good location for hotels and taverns catering to travelers and drovers. As quickly as they could be erected, Norwich boasted a hotel, a boarding house, four stores and a brick house occupied by Harper. The next year, Samuel and James Lorimer began practicing medicine in addition to teaching in the school. A Presbyterian church was started in 1828 and a Methodist soon after, each with its own burial plot. There were few, if any, Quakers and no Friends' meetings within access.[41]

Skills like Noah's were in great demand in places such as Norwich along the National Road. Town lots frequently were offered free to coopers, carpenters, saddlers, wheelwrights and wagon makers as an inducement to settle and ply their crafts.[42] Apparently no such bribe came to Noah, but he doubled his money on town lots, buying two for $500 in 1833 and selling one for the same sum two years later. Noah lived for more than ten years in Norwich, probably working at his trade for one of the numerous competing coach lines passing through the town.[43]

Ten-year old Bushrod and Mary, thirteen, accompanied their parents on the 45-mile removal to Norwich in 1827. They were still at home with them in 1830, census lists reveal. It is probable that both spent some of the three-month school terms each winter living at Nathan's home in Belmont with his children, Nimrod, Ruth, Lemuel, and Elizabeth as companions, though they may also have attended the school taught by the Lorimers in the Presbyterian church in 1829 or an academy which ran a brief course in Norwich.[44]

As he advanced to his middle teens, Bushrod lived permanently in Belmont, less than ten miles from St. Clairsville, where opportunities for an ambitious boy starting out on his own were greater than in Norwich. Records indicate Mary Johnson was married July 4, 1833 to John Winter in St. Clairsville and thus the last of the children of Noah and Rachel left their hearth.[45] The Quaker influence also was fading from their lives.

St. Clairsville was a good location for a young man to start. Edwin M. Stanton began practicing law there in 1835 with Daniel Peck and until 1840 was busy in the courts of Belmont and five adjacent counties. The population was nearing 1500, there were six churches, 20 stores, seven taverns, a bank capitalized at $100,000 and three newspapers, according to W. G. Lyford, the Baltimore directory compiler, who found "the country around is thickly populated and rich."[46] Writer William Dean Howells reminiscently wrote in 1901 of his former residence that the place "was more like an English than an American town . . . an idyll of repose . . . a home of ancient peace."[47]

Bushrod may have been a pupil in a St. Clairsville academy "for young gentlemen" with "pre-college preparatory studies" opened May 1, 1831 by John G. Affleck, later owner-editor of the *National Historian,* weekly newspaper. About 1833 he attended for a short time the preparatory department of Marietta Academy in Marietta, Washington County, 90 miles away, which became a college in 1835. He made a good impression there and displayed a special talent for mathematics,[48] but lack of money cut short his stay. That cogent reason and his Quaker antecedents also may explain why he did not attend Franklin College, the Presbyterian school only 19 miles from St. Clairsville at New Athens.

Probably while he was in Marietta, Bushrod's mother died in Norwich, December 1, 1833. She may have been a victim of the violent cholera epidemic in 1833 when scores perished in towns along the National Road. In June, 153 succumbed in Wheeling and 48 in August in Columbus, while Zanesville and Bridgeport were hard hit. Oddly, St. Clairsville had few victims.[49] Rachel may have been buried in one of Norwich's cemeteries, but time has effaced any memorial.

Noah, now left alone in his sixties, took one Mary Robinson, about half his age, of adjoining Perry Township, Muskingum County, as his wife on March 13, 1835 before Justice of the Peace J. Wylie. Not much is known about her except that she was unable to sign her name, April 27, 1835 on the deed conveying Lot 86 in Norwich from Noah and Mary Johnson to Arthur Taggart. She made her "X" mark instead.[50] They moved back to Belmont County some time before 1840 when the census listed only the two of them residing on rented property in Wayne Township.

When Noah died in 1844, his insolvent estate, inventoried May 31, 1844, listed around $100 in household goods, a set of blacksmith's tools worth $12, eight head of sheep and book accounts amounting to $150 owing to him for work done at his smithy.[51] How and where he died and what happened to Mary Robinson Johnson are not revealed. At that time Bushrod was a lieutenant in Company E, Third U.S. Infantry, stationed at Jefferson Barracks, St. Louis, Missouri and Dr. Nathan had moved to Cambridge City, Indiana not far from Centreville where he had done so well in real estate in 1818. Only the daughter, Aletha Johnson Leslie in Bethesda, a few miles north of Wayne Township, was near at hand.

Nathan's removal to Indiana in February 1839 was the direct result of his persistent, belligerent activity in advancing the cause of abolition and in aiding runaway slaves. Despite Quaker moral opposition to slavery and physical participation in helping black fugitives from across the Ohio river in western Virginia, only a minority of the general community in the 1830s was willing to stand up publicly and be counted on the political "hot potato" issue, which bedevilled office seekers much as Prohibition did a century later. The Belmont County newspapers, *The Chronicle* and *The Gazette,* usually in precarious financial condition, shied away from radicalism likely to lose them subscribers.

Nathan's home in Belmont and later in Indiana, his grandson Robert tells, were stations on the Underground Railroad. Negroes were brought in at night, hidden in the cellar, attic or barn until the following night. Then provided with food, they were taken to the next "station." As lads in Nathan's family, his sons Nimrod and Lemuel, and doubtless Bushrod, took part in these exciting activities.[52]

But such things, perforce, had to be done covertly. Soon Dr. Nathan became more outspoken and publicly zealous. He led a county convention of all antislavery societies on September 9, 1837 and was elected president. The group ratified a constitution and a program of political action in support of candidates favorable to abolition "without regard to mere party names and distinctions." A questionnaire went out to candidates in the state election, due October 10, demanding their stand on abolition in Florida and the District of Columbia, prohibition of the internal slave traffic and banning admittance of any new slave states.

Editors of the Whig *Chronicle* and the Democratic Republican *Gazette* reluctantly printed the society's contributed version of the convention, with explanations indicating Dr. Nathan had put pressure on them.[53] *Chronicle* editor Thomas S. Reid, as a Whig, had worked with Nathan in the 1836 campaign when Dr. Johnson was a vice president of the Whig county organization and helped organize "committees of vigilance" in the townships backing the candidacy of William Henry Harrison. Harrison carried the county, 2666 to 2358 over Martin Van Buren in November 1836.[54]

In forming ranks for the 1837 state races, the Whigs left

off Dr. Nathan's name from committees and "vigilants," perhaps because of his abolitionist activity. Among Whig candidates for the state legislature was Benjamin Wright, a neighbor of Nathan's in Goshen Township, where the Wrights, originally from Ireland, were leading landowners and promoters of the town of Belmont, popularly known as Wrightstown. Because of the Anti-Slavery Society's questionnaire, Wright wrote to both newspapers, calling slavery a "great moral evil," but arguing lengthily for state's rights. To adopt the Abolitionists' view that Congress should deal with slavery, he said, "would be usurpation and usurpation ought to be resisted."[55]

The letter affronted Nathan Johnson. Heedless of his recent allegiance to the Whig party or to the sensibilities and possible reactions of his neighbors, he wrote a long reply signed "An Abolitionist" and sent it to the *Chronicle.* Editor Reid waited to print it until a month after the election in which Wright was defeated. The missive was so long it was published in two issues of the paper. Its theme was an attack on Wright for denying that Congress had the right to abolish slavery in the District of Columbia after Wright had once signed a petition, circulated by Nathan and his son, Nimrod, favoring such a position.[56]

Smarting from his defeat, Wright took considerable umbrage at "being assailed as a private individual" now that the campaign was over. He explained at length in the *Chronicle* about signing the petition "by proxy," made some scathing references to Nathan and asked him for answers to five questions intended to show Nathan's insincerity and inconsistency.[57] The controversy raged for three more months with plenty of turgid dialectic in the contemporary style. The editor of the *Gazette,* John Irons, got into the affray by printing that Nathan had cancelled his subscription when Irons refused to publish his attack on Wright and had been "warning and threatening. We have only contempt for his insolence." Nathan fired back at Irons in the *Chronicle*. By the time the flood of rhetoric subsided in March 1838, columns of type had appeared.[58]

Resentment of Nathan did not die. The Whigs ignored him in the lists of committees named for Washington's Birthday, 1838, but there were numerous Wrights. The county medical society, which annually re-named many of its officers, never picked him again as censor after 1830. The newspapers had enough of abolition and its advocates. The Anti-Slavery Society had to take paid advertising to announce a lecture on May 5 in Belmont and May 25 in St. Clairsville by a Rev. Mr. Howels of Pittsburgh. The notice, over Nathan's name as president, asked "only daylight and fair play." It continued to appear weekly until June 26, a month beyond the date of the second meeting.[59] This was the last time Nathan Johnson's name was printed in the *Chronicle*.

The family was the "target of displeasure," Robert Johnson wrote a century later, and "though they were stoned and egged," they "continued to hold their ground with vigor and even aggressiveness."[60] But the pressures were too strong. Braving the rigors of February weather, Nathan Johnson moved his family across Ohio into friendlier Wayne County, Indiana. There succeeding generations were to find acceptance and honor in medicine, the law, public service and business enterprise for more than 100 years.

Back from Marietta early in 1834, 17-year old Bushrod Johnson took a job teaching in a district school near Barnesville, while his nephew Nimrod, only 15, taught in the "little brick" city school at Church and Chestnut Streets in Barnesville.[61] Some of the latter's pupils were older than himself. Both were paid $10 to $15 monthly.[62] But this activity, as in so many life stories of the times, was only temporary. Both boys were looking ahead. Nimrod hoped to study law and practice at the bar. Bushrod could scarcely do the same in competition with his nephew who was like a foster brother. There was no attraction in going back to his father and young stepmother in Norwich in 1835. To continue to teach school offered little. He had to find a chance for a future somewhere else. Time was pressing. He had reached an age when most young men were getting established.

Occasionally in the newspapers items appeared about the U.S. Military Academy at West Point, New York. The *National Historian* issue of July 20, 1833 told of the graduation of 45 cadets and the entry of a new class of 120. It ended with this comment:

> Those who perfect their course, the severe ordeal of study and conduct are of more than ordinary merit, talent and attainments.

What a challenge for an ambitious boy, anxious to excel! In the summer of 1835 Bushrod made up his mind to attempt it, even though the profession of arms ran counter to everything he had been taught and his Quaker heritage stood for. He had to make the effort for himself; there was no eager parent writing to Washington to promote his chances as in the case of young Ulysses Grant in southern Ohio. The decision and the exertion had to be his alone.

His brother was a success as a physician, a controversial figure in the community, but a man of importance and prestige. His nephews near his own age were destined for the law and medicine. In less than two-score years the Johnsons had risen into the professional class from the ranks of yeoman farmer-blacksmith. Now Bushrod would try to be a soldier.

It was, as his great-nephew put it, "rather a strange career for a Quaker."[63]

Notes

1. Robert Underwood Johnson, *Remembered Yesterdays,* (Boston: Little, Brown & Co., 1923), p. 13.
2. Johnson genealogical data supplied by Meredith Johnson, Washington D.C., eighth in descent from Garrett Johnson.
3. William Wade Hinshaw, *Encyclopedia of American Quaker Genealogy,* (Ann Arbor, Mich. Edwards Bros. Inc., 1950), VI, p. 609.
4. *Ibid.,* VI, pp. 185 f.
5. *Pennsylvania Archives,* Series 2, III, p. 240.
6. Harrison Williams, *Legends of Loudoun,* (Richmond, Va: Garrett and Massie, Inc., 1938), p. 46.
7. *Hinshaw,* VI, pp. 563, 669, 707. Microfilm copies of Goose Creek Meeting records in the Maryland Hall of Records, Annapolis, contain many references to the Spencers, including Rachel.
8. *Hinshaw,* I, pp. ix, x.
9. Loudoun County, Va., *Bargain and Sale Record,* Book X, p. 206; Book 2E, p. 391.
10. Data supplied by Meredith Johnson and Mrs. E. Wayne Gibson, Spencer, Indiana. See also Howard M. Jenkins, *Genealogical Sketch of Descendants of Samuel Spencer of Pennsylvania,* (Philadelphia: Ferris and Leach, 1904), pp. 139 f.
11. Jonathan Schofield writing in J. A. Caldwell, *History of Belmont and Jefferson Counties,* (Wheeling, W. Va.: Historical Publishing Co., 1880), p. 342.
12. H. E. Smith, "The Quakers and their Migration to the Upper Ohio" in *Ohio Archeological and Historical Quarterly,* XXXVII, pp. 35–85.
13. Belmont County, Ohio, *Deed Record,* Vol. D, p. 588.
14. *Hinshaw,* IV, p. 338.
15. *Ibid.,* IV, p. 707.
16. *Caldwell,* pp. 172, 175. *U.S. Census,* Belmont County, Ohio, 1820, 1830, 1840 and 1850.
17. A. T. McKelvey, *Centennial History of Belmont County,* (Chicago: Biographical Publishing Co., 1903), pp. 110 f.
18. William Cooper Howells, *Recollections of Life in Ohio, 1813–1840,* (Cincinnati: The Robert Clarke Co., 1895), p. 33.
19. Andrew W. Young, *History of Wayne County, Indiana,* (Chicago: Robert Clarke Co., 1872), p. 268; *Howells,* p. 33.
20. William B. Hesseltine and David L. Smiley, *The South in American History,* (Englewood Cliffs, N. J.: Prentice-Hall, 1960), pp. 146 f.
21. *Robert Johnson,* p. 12.
22. Ellsworth Marshall Rust, *Rust of Virginia, 1645–1940,* (Washington: privately printed 1940), p. 209.
23. *McKelvey,* p. 70; *Caldwell,* p. 178.
24. Belmont County, Ohio, *Deed Record,* Vol. G, p. 66.
25. Wayne County, Indiana, *Deed Records,* Vol. A, pp. 553, 554; B, pp. 14, 29, 34, 35, 37, 39. Centreville in 1818 is now Centerville.
26. *Hinshaw,* IV, p. 338; Belmont County, Ohio, *Marriage Record,* Book B, p. 24.
27. There is no verification of this in Douglas S. Freeman's detailed biography of Washington.
28. *Robert Johnson,* pp. 11–13.

29. Copy of letter in *Jenkins*, pp. 139 f.
30. *Howells*, pp. 22–27. Howells lived from 1813 to 1816 as a Quaker lad near Mt. Pleasant, Ohio, less than 15 miles from the Plainfield community. He later worked as a printer in St. Clairsville and in Mt. Pleasant.
31. *Young*, p. 268.
32. St. Clairsville *Gazette*, June 5, 1830.
33. *Caldwell*, p. 183.
34. *Catalogue of Officers and Students of Starling Medical College for the Session 1850–51*, (Columbus: Printed by Scott & Bascom, 1851), p. 6.
35. St. Clairsville *Gazette*, October 29, 1825.
36. Thomas Clarke, *Frontier America*, (New York: Scribners, 1959), pp. 313, 344; Philip D. Jordan, *The National Road*, (Indianapolis: Bobbs Merrill, 1948), p. 74.
37. Allan C. Thomas and Richard H. Thomas, *A History of the Friends in America*, (Philadelphia: John C. Winston Co. 1905), 4th ed., p. 125.
38. *Hinshaw*, IV, pp. 410, 413.
39. Belmont County, Ohio, *Marriage Record*, Book 2, p. 30.
40. Belmont County, Ohio, *Deed Record*, Vols. J, p. 30; K, p. 290; L, pp. 42, 251, 371; N, pp. 313, 314, 315; Q, p. 239.
41. J. F. Everhart, *History of Muskingum County, Ohio*, (Columbus, Ohio State Journal 1882), pp. 302, 416 f.
42. *Jordan*, foreword.
43. Muskingum County, Ohio, *Deed Record*, Vols. N, p. 147; P, p. 523.
44. *Everhart*, p. 422. In 1837, W. G. Lyford's *Western Address Directory*, (Baltimore: Printed by Jos. Robinson 1837), listed no schools, six stores, two churches and two taverns in Norwich with 300–400 residents.
45. Belmont County, Ohio, *Marriage Record*, Book 3, p. 214. Winter, British-born and well-to-do, was old enough to be the father of 18-year old Mary Johnson. He died in 1837. A dispute between Mary and Winter's daughter by his previous marriage over his estate dragged through the courts for several years. Meanwhile Mary married John Galbeth and vanishes from the records.
46. *Lyford*, p. 194.
47. Letter regretting inability to attend centennial celebration, quoted in *McKelvey*, p. 92.
48. Letter of D. Hows Allen, professor of mathematics and natural history, Marietta College, November 15, 1836 in West Point appointment document file in National Archives. Marietta's records of preparatory students prior to 1835 are not specific on student names, according to Mrs. T. Gale Sinclair, registrar's office, in letter to author, January 9, 1961.
49. St. Clairsville *Gazette*, July 6, August 24, 1833.
50. Muskingum County, Ohio, *Marriage Record, 1835*; Muskingum County, Ohio, *Deed Record*, Vol. P, p. 523.
51. Belmont County, Ohio *Probate Court Record of Inventory*, Vol. B, p. 387.
52. *Robert Johnson*, 15.
53. *Belmont Chronicle*, September 12, 1837; St. Clairsville *Gazette*, September 16, 1837.
54. *Belmont Chronicle*, August 27, 1836; November 26, 1836.

55. *Ibid.*, September 12, 1837; *Gazette*, September 30, 1837.
56. *Belmont Chronicle*, November 7, 1837.
57. The letter, dated November 28, 1837, was not published until December 18, when it appeared on the front page.
58. See issues of *Belmont Chronicle* and *Gazette*, January to April, 1838.
59. *Belmont Chronicle*, all issues in May and June 1838.
60. *Robert Johnson*, p. 15.
61. Letter, January 1, 1836 from Thomas Shannon, Barnesville, Ohio to Congressman William S. Kennon, Sr., in West Point appointment documents. On Nimrod's teaching job, *Robert Johnson*, 17 and *Caldwell*, p. 319.
62. St. Clairsville newspapers continually carried advertisements for teachers in district schools. Applicants had only to pass a perfunctory examination by the more literate members of school boards.
63. *Robert Johnson*, p. 12.

3

"STRANGE CAREER FOR A QUAKER"

i. A Little Less than Medium

Having decided that he would be the first of his family to become a military man, Bushrod Johnson wrote, in the fall of 1835, to his Congressman, Democrat William S. Kennon, Sr., of St. Clairsville, to whom he was known personally.[1] He asked for information about the Military Academy and was encouraged by Kennon's reply. There was a vacancy in the district's quota of appointments to West Point and the entrance examination was well within the capability of a bright young man with Bushrod's education. From Barnesville, where he still held his teaching job, Johnson asked what he should do next. Kennon replied from Washington that Bushrod should submit two letters of recommendation, one from his brother, Dr. Nathan Johnson, who was a Whig politically but well known to Kennon, and from any other person in whom Kennon "had confidence."[2]

This presented a difficulty. Bushrod already had discussed with Nathan his desire to enter West Point, but the older brother, conditioned by his Quaker pacifistic sentiments, had disapproved. It was apparent to the boy there would be no help from this member of the family whom he regarded almost as a second father. His real father, Noah, was 43 miles away in another county, outside Kennon's constituency, and could not be counted upon. Bushrod would have to turn elsewhere.

He wrote to D. Hows Allen, professor of mathematics and natural history at Marietta College, in whose classes he had sat briefly while attending the preparatory course. Professor Allen responded November 15 in a letter addressed to Kennon. He said:

> Bushrod Rust Johnson was a member of the preparatory department of this institution for several months. I consider him to be a young man of *very good* natural talents and of high promise. He discovered a fondness for mathematical studies and pursued them with success during the short period he was under my instruction.
>
> I have no hesitation in expressing the confident belief that he will be able to pursue with success any course of study to which he may devote himself.

He underscored "very good."

For his second recommendation Bushrod turned to Thomas Shannon, tobacco merchant and leading Democrat in Barnesville. Shannon was an older brother of Wilson Shannon, first native-born governor of Ohio, (1838–40 and 1842–44), and later territorial governor of "Bleeding" Kansas during the struggle between free and slave state forces. With some errors in spelling Thomas Shannon wrote to Kennon that he had "... no hesitation in recommending him [Bushrod] to be a young man of good moral carrector and stedy habits.... What I have stated of Mr. Johnston is from an acquaintance with him since he has resided in the vicinity of this place as a teacher in a district school."

Bushrod sent both recommendations to Kennon in a letter from Barnesville dated December 19, 1835. He explained to the Congressman that after Nathan "manifested some disapprobation" with his design "of entering the Mill [*sic*] Academy" he determined "to trouble him no further with it," hence the letter from Professor Allen which he hoped would be an acceptable substitute. Kennon, of course, knew Shannon, so the boy need have no misgivings there. He continued:

> My age (which you wished to know) is eighteen the seventh of October last.
>
> I have been directed to address a letter to the Secretary of War, but I know of no conexion [*sic*] that he has with the making of appointments, and I am therefore unable to see any necessity for writing to him. If you think there will be any benefit in it, please to inform me. And also if you think the measures I have taken are not sufficient to secure an appointment to the Milt [*sic*] let me know where the defect lies.
>
> Bushrod R. Johnson

The Quaker boy had his heart set on a military education and he was willing to meet any conditions to obtain it. As it turned out he had nothing to fear. Kennon sent the letters from Allen and Shannon to Lewis Cass, Andrew Jackson's Secretary of War, and added a letter of his own. He explained that Shannon was a former member of Congress, though he had actually served only three months of an unexpired term, and he added:

> The friends of Mr. Johnson are members of the Society of Friends and hence the expression of disapprobation of the brother of the applicant. . .
>
> I am *anxious* he would be appointed.

He underlined the word "anxious" to stress that there was something special about getting the young Quaker into the Academy. If President Jackson saw the correspondence he would have recognized Shannon as a member of a family well known to him. Shannon's brother James had been Jackson's *chargé d'affaires* to the Federation of Central American states in 1832 and another brother, David, was "Old Hickory's" private secretary in Florida in 1821.

The appointment was made without delay. Bushrod was notified March 29, 1836 that he would begin his cadetship in the forthcoming summer. There was one final hurdle. Permission of his father as his legal guardian, was required. As soon as he could, Bushrod rode over to Norwich, and wrote a letter for his father to Secretary Cass authorizing Bushrod Rust Johnson "to enter into any agreement for his admission to and connexion for five years with the U.S. Military Academy"; Noah Johnson signed it in a crabbed hand. There was no indication that Noah shared Nathan's Quaker scruples about the military profession.

Then Bushrod, from St. Clairsville, April 16, 1836, wrote to Cass explaining that he had been "absent from my parent" and had not been able "until yesterday to procure his permission."

"I accept the appointment," he wrote and posted the documents to Kennon. The Congressman sent them from the House of Representatives to Cass on April 20 and the formalities were concluded.

The days that followed were too short for all the arrangements Bushrod had to make. He needed money for his fare by stage and steamer to West Point, for new clothing, for luggage and for the deposit of $60 the Academy would require against the chance that he would fail in his studies and have to return to Ohio. Some of this fund he may have saved from his teaching, the balance he probably borrowed from Nathan. There were farewells to be said in Barnesville, Bethesda, Norwich and elsewhere among the numerous kinsmen.

In six other Ohio homes similar thrilling preparations were under way. In May, William Tecumseh Sherman in Lancaster said his goodby to the Thomas Ewing family which had reared him.[3] At the age of sixteen years and five months he was the youngest of the seven Buckeye State cadets entering the class of 1840. One month older was William Spriggs Belt of Chillicothe who would resign in November and return home. Another destined for early severance was George L. Higgins of Norwalk, Huron County, discharged in April 1837. Nearest in age to Bushrod, who at eighteen years, nine months was the oldest, was James Nelson Caldwell, of Franklin in Warren County, one month younger. There were also John McNutt of Cadiz, Harrison County and Job Roberts Hamilton Lancaster of Elizabeth, near Cincinnati, killed by lightning in Florida a year after graduation.[4]

Bushrod probably traveled by stage from St. Clairsville to Baltimore as Sherman did. The trip cost $15 and took 60 hours from Wheeling with meals enroute at 50¢ each.[5] The Quaker farm boy must have been thrilled by his first experiences in the glamorous cities of the East. In Washington to pay his respects to Kennon and receive his best wishes, he saw the Capitol and the White House, and he wandered in awe in Baltimore, Philadelphia and New York. On the steamer going up the Hudson to the Academy he made a few acquaintances among arriving cadets.

As these neophytes disembarked beneath the stone buildings on the heights of an impressive landscape, the glamor and excitement gave way to anxiety and the fear of the waiting examination, the unfamiliar discipline, rigid regimentation, unreasoning authority and restriction. For Sherman, this was eased partially because William Irvin, Lancaster, Ohio neighbor and playmate, was a second year, or sophomore classman who welcomed and guided him.[6] There was none to do this for Bushrod Johnson.

He reported to the Academy adjutant, Lieutenant Charles Ferguson Smith of the Second U.S. Artillery, who in 1838 became the commandant of cadets. Their paths were to cross again on a gloomy February 16, 1862 at a rainsoaked fort called Donelson on the Cumberland River in Tennessee, but that was to be in another age and another world afar. Bushrod passed the mental tests without difficulty, demonstrating his ability to read, write and do simple arithmetic.

On July 1, 1836 the class of 1840 began officially to spend four years at the Academy and four more in the Army. During the summer they lived in tents on the parade ground, called "The Plain," supervised and bullied by the second year classmen. Once they were casually inspected by the superintendent, Major René de Russy, of the Corps of Engineers, known to be somewhat lax in his functioning. In September, when the upperclassmen returned from their summer furloughs, the abasement of the plebes was compounded.

Among the fourth year men, due to graduate in June 1837, were Braxton Bragg of North Carolina; Jubal Anderson Early of Virginia; John Clifford Pemberton of Pennsylvania, fated to defect to the Southland of his wife; John Sedgwick of Connecticut and Joseph Hooker of Massachusetts. The West Point caste system maintained a wide gulf between them and Bushrod. The third year class included the dark-eyed creole, Pierre Gustav Toutant Beauregard of Louisiana, who would insist on Bushrod's elevation to major general in 1864 after two years of pleas and indorsements had failed to move the Confederate War Department; William Joseph Hardee of Georgia, author sometime later of a standard textbook on tactics, who was to be Bushrod's superior in Tennessee in 1862 and '63; Virginian Edward ("Old Allegheny") Johnson with whom Bushrod was sometimes confused in the rebel army; and Ohioan Irvin McDowell from Columbus. Outstanding among the men of 1839 was bug-eyed Henry Wager Halleck, rated as near perfect in brains, conduct and studies.[7]

Bushrod came to know more intimately his own classmates. In addition to the Ohioans, there were Paul Octave Hebert of Louisiana whose brilliance outshone even that of Beauregard; George H. Thomas, the big Virginian against whose lines at Chickamauga a quarter-century hence Bushrod would reach the zenith of his Confederate career; William E. Steele of New York who would marry in Texas and go with the South; Robert P. MacClay of Pennsylvania whose year-old ownership of a Louisiana plantation in 1861 would mean more than loyalty to the Union; and Richard Stoddert Ewell whose funeral in Nashville in 1872 Bushrod would attend. There was also a 21-year-old East Tennesseean, John Porter McCown, who would become a Confederate major general two years ahead of Bushrod.

Of the 100 cadets who moved into their crowded and poorly furnished barracks in August, 1836, only 42 would survive to graduate in June 1840. Fourteen of these would be dead by 1861 and of those remaining eight would join the South, three of them like Johnson, Northern-born. Fifteen of the graduates, five of them Southerners, would fight for the Union.

His first few months as a plebe indicated that Bushrod was a better student than a soldier. He was tardy to class, late to the daily retreat parades, he loitered when he should have been going about his duties with snap and alacrity, and the Officer of the Day on inspection found his room in disorder with his blanket not rolled up with his bedding in the approved manner. All of these minor offenses brought demerits according to an elaborate scale of "criminality" ranging downward from ten demerits for a first grade offense to one demerit for one of the seventh. As cadets advanced in class rank, offenses counted more. A total of 200 demerits in a year brought dismissal.[9]

There were more serious offenses. One or more extra tours of sentry duty were penalties for such things as kicking a horse, tossing bread at mess, possessing liquor, having food in quarters, using tobacco in headquarters, having lights on or visiting after taps. Arrest and confinement to quarters resulted from illicit visits to Benny Havens' Tavern or striking a horse with a saber. Grant, in the class of 1842, made one trip to the forbidden saloon, but escaped detection. Sherman was there several times. If Bushrod ever was, the venture has been veiled in silence.

Church services were compulsory. Cadets marched to chapel by companies and absences meant demerits and arrest. Doctrine and ritual were high-church Episcopalian. Grant resented it, but had to attend for four years. Johnson and Sherman bowed to the inevitable, but the creed to which they were subjected each week until 1840 left both untouched. Sherman had lived from the age of nine in the Roman Catholic atmosphere of the Ewing household and Johnson had never known anything but Quaker simplicity. Both went to chapel at West Point because it was required, neither got any demerits for nonattendance, but once graduated, both forgot it all.

Cadet standings for the first year of Bushrod's class were posted in June 1837. Conduct ratings were based on the 211 men in the entire corps. Merit was based on the 76 members of the class left from the original 100. In the class, Bushrod was No. 23; Sherman, No. 9.[11] Johnson, therefore, stood well in the top third of the class academically, but in conduct he was 87th with 78 demerits while Sherman with 109 stood 124th. These ratings were a factor in Johnson's appointment as cadet corporal during his second year—a distinction not attained by Sherman or Grant. Sherman remained a private throughout; Grant was made sergeant in his third year, but reverted to private because of his low class standing.[12]

The class of 1840 spent the summer of 1837 at the Academy, in tents on "The Plain," imposing their newfound superiority on the arriving plebes of the class of '41. Among these were the Garnett cousins from Virginia,

Richard Brooke and Robert Selden. Richard was to encounter Johnson again in 1847 in the dark hour of the court of inquiry into the Seawell letter. There were Don Carlos Buell from Marietta, Ohio and two Pennsylvanians, John F. Reynolds of Lancaster and Josiah Gorgas of Running Pumps, Dauphin County. Reynolds and Richard Garnett would die at Gettysburg on opposite sides. Gorgas, married to an Alabaman, would be the Confederacy's ordnance expert. From New York was Schuyler Hamilton, grandson of Alexander.[13]

With his corporal's chevrons on his sleeves, Johnson did better in his studies in his second year, but his conduct was worse. Sherman surpassed him in both. Bushrod was 17th, Sherman 5th in merit in the class which now totaled 58. Sherman with 66 demerits stood 78th in the corps, while Bushrod with 87, slumped to 106th.[14] Paradoxically, Johnson got the reward. On June 23, 1838 he was promoted to First Sergeant of one of the four companies into which the corps was divided for drill and parade.[15]

The promotion enabled Bushrod to return to Ohio in the 1838 summer on his first 10-week long furlough with his uniform sleeves emblazoned with the chevron and rocker stripes of his grade. He made an impressive sight on the streets of St. Clairsville as he greeted old friends and his kindred Johnsons and Spencers after an absence of two years. To avoid offending the Quaker sensibilities of Dr. Nathan and his sister Aletha Leslie he probably changed to civilian clothing when he visited their families.

His relatives brought him up to date on the antislavery and abolition agitation in which his eldest brother had been playing a leading role. He may have scanned the newspapers which had printed the vehement and interminable rhetoric between Nathan and Wright in the 1837–38 winter. Certainly he heard all the details of the turmoil which had engulfed his cherished brother. He may have spent part of his vacation helping the aged Noah and his wife move back to Belmont County. But the festering controversy over abolition filled much of the family conversation.[16]

During the same summer, this issue touched the life of "Cump" Sherman in the Ewing family circle. Sherman acquired a contempt for "nigger-stealers," whom he looked upon as cranks and dangerous agitators.[17] One may be sure his attitude was not shared by his classmate Johnson in his more intimate and continuing connection with the principles of abolition, antislavery and aid to runaway slaves as these matters were activated by the Johnsons.

After the hectic summer of 1838, Johnson returned to the Military Academy. There was a new superintendent, Major Richard A. Delafield of the Engineers, as vigilant in tightening up things as DeRussy had been remiss. Back for his third year, Bushrod permitted himself to slump a bit more. Maybe his promotion to First Sergeant gave him an overconfidence or a touch of arrogance that adversely affected his studies or cost him demerits.

The new crop of plebes was unusual. The Ohioans included William Stark Rosecrans of Cincinnati. Johnson met for the first time four men to whom he would be subordinate in the Confederate Army. First was Daniel Harvey Hill of South Carolina, his corps commander briefly in 1863. Next was James Longstreet of Alabama. Temporarily under his wing command at Chickamauga, Bushrod would know his greatest glory, discounted by a miserable and futile campaign later in East Tennessee. Third was Richard Heron Anderson of South Carolina, his chief at Sayler's Creek three days before Lee surrendered, when both of them with George Edwards Pickett galloped away from their fragmenting troops. The fourth was Alexander Peter Stewart of East Tennessee, who would be Johnson's colleague briefly on the faculty of the University of Nashville after both had left the U.S. Army and who also would command Bushrod and his brigade in the Army of Tennessee.

When the lists were posted in June 1839, Johnson had 90 demerits, the most he acquired in four years. Two offenses, of eight black marks each, were for "profane swearing." Others were for inattention and loud talking in drawing class and neglect of duty as orderly sergeant. He stood No. 162 in the corps of 231. Sherman had 57 demerits and was No. 115. But while Sherman was sixth in merit in the class of 46 members, Bushrod had dropped to 26th, into the bottom half. Nevertheless, he was promoted, June 21, 1839 to be captain of one of the four companies.[18]

Johnson probably divided his 10-week furlough in the summer of 1839 among Nathan's family in Indiana whence they had gone in February, Noah and Mary in Wayne Township, and his sister Aletha Leslie who had named her last baby Bushrod for his uncle. Age was imposing its limitations upon Noah. He had no farm to plant; no real estate to trade. A garden plot, a few sheep and some odd jobs of blacksmithing kept him busy for the five years left to him.

Back at the Academy for his fourth and last year, Cadet Captain Johnson scarcely noticed the new influx of 73 hopefuls, the class of 1843. There was another Quaker lad, Samuel Gibbs French of New Jersey, whose later acquisition of a Mississippi plantation by marriage would send him into the ranks of the South and into a lifelong defense of his action. Another destined for a similar future was Roswell Sabin Ripley, born in Ohio but appointed from New York. The Ohioans included Ulysses S. Grant from Clermont County, from whom Johnson was to hide and then walk away at Fort Donelson in February of '62.

Bushrod was able to do only slightly better in his studies than in the previous year. He ranked thirteenth in Infantry among his 42 classmates, but stood thirty-seventh in Ethics; thirty-fifth in Mineralogy and Geology; thirtieth in Artillery and twenty-sixth in Engineering. His demerits were the smallest in his cadetship: fifty-seven for being late, loitering, visiting after hours three times and absence from tattoo. He stood No. 141 in the corps of 223. For the four years his total penalties were 312, compared with 380 for Sherman and only 87 for Thomas.

Thus Bushrod Johnson ended his West Point schooling a little short of medium. He was twenty-third, trailed by nineteen others. Only the Louisianan Paul Octave Hebert had demonstrated enough scholarship to be recommended for the elite Corps of Engineers. Sherman, sixth in the class, could get Artillery as could Thomas, standing twelfth. Dick Ewell, No. 13, picked Dragoons, which besides Infantry was the meager choice for those in the bottom bracket.

Johnson selected Infantry for the practical reason that the officer complement of the Dragoons was full and he would have to wait, as Ewell did, as a brevet second lieutenant until a vacancy developed. In the foot soldiers Johnson was commissioned a full second lieutenant at $778 a year, starting July 1, 1840.

The infantry was not attractive, as Johnson well knew. Its enlisted men were generally hardened veterans of European armies, Germans and Irish predominating, with a leavening of rough, often lawless and unruly, native Americans. These elements generated constant problems of command, dealt with by ironfisted and brutal punishment. As he left West Point forever in June for a three month vacation, Johnson faced a wait of several weeks before he would get orders to join a specific regiment. Once there, in some unattractive outpost, he was doomed to spend his days in plodding routine with promotion coming at snail's pace.

He had little money. Few cadets were able to save anything from the $54.60 credited to them every two months. Most of this went for uniforms and textbooks with a scant margin for petty indulgences. Part of his pay as a second lieutenant was already encumbered for the new infantry uniforms he ordered, according to custom, before he left the Academy.

During the long summer days ahead, among his kinsmen and acquaintances and the scenes of his Quaker upbringing in the midwest, he might well have pondered the results of his four years of preparation for the profession of arms. Physically he had matured; he was taller and heavier, his muscles hardened by exercise and his coordination and responses quickened by drill and discipline.

Mentally he had grown also. He had acquired some technical knowledge and proficency in a specialized vocation. He had learned to accept and exercise responsibility as a cadet officer. His perspectives had been expanded from the narrow limits of Eastern Ohio Quaker provincialism by the aristocratic atmosphere at West Point, its orthodox Episcopalianism and the stress placed on duty, honor and country.[19]

His quiet and retiring personality had been exposed to the enrichment of informal and intimate contacts in barracks, classroom and field with young men from all sections of the country and from a variety of conditions and backgrounds. From these associations he should have developed an appreciation of, if not a tolerance for, points of view divergent from his own on religion, ethics and personal conduct. But in all this, his role was passive. His blank temperament made no lasting impression on his fellows. When his classmates, as old men, reliving the golden hours of their youth, reminisced of their Academy days, he was never mentioned, while "Old Cump" Sherman, "Sam" Grant, "Rosey" Rosecrans, "Dragon" Deshon, "Tom" Thomas and others were recalled with pleasure. In his voluminous letters that have been preserved, Sherman made only one reference to "Bush" Johnson and that was in criticism of his attitude just before the Civil War.[20]

Whatever his cadet associations may have lacked, Second Lieutenant Bushrod Rust Johnson now had an assured social position, a ready acceptance anywhere and a special standing in any community where fate and army orders might locate him.

ii. The South Casts a Magic Spell

In midsummer 1840 Johnson got orders to join the Third U.S. Infantry Regiment at the end of his leave on September 30. The Third could boast of a long and distinguished career. It had served under "Mad Anthony" Wayne against the Indians in the Northwest in 1794. Led by Andrew Jackson it fought the Creeks and then the British at the battle of New Orleans in 1815. In the 1820s it had helped to build Jefferson Barracks, nine miles below St. Louis, one of the loveliest and most desirable posts in the Army. In recent years the Third had been split between Fort Leavenworth, Kansas and the Indian Territory, now Oklahoma.

Since 1835 the Third's commanding officer was Colonel James Many, who had not been near his troops for years. Under an indulgent War Department practice, he was permitted to live in New Orleans on perpetual "sick leave" while drawing full pay, occasionally signing papers and leaving all of his responsibilities to subordinates. He did this until he died in 1852. In 1840 the second in command, Lieutenant Colonel Josiah H. Vose, was on detached service as the Army's general superintendent of recruiting, so the Third in fact was headed by Major Henry Wilson who also commanded the Western Division, one of the geographical military slices into which the nation was divided.[21]

When Johnson's graduation leave of absence expired, he should have reported for duty to Company E of the Third at Fort Jesup, Louisiana.[22] For some reason, he failed to arrive. Through October and November he was listed as "absent without leave." But when he finally reported on December 3 he apparently presented a sufficient explanation, not shown in the record, since he was not compelled to face a court-martial. His two-months' tardiness in reporting for his first duty, which may have raised some eyebrows in the regiment, set a pattern for his ensuing years in the unit. Its records show he managed to get more than the normal leaves of absence and usually was able to have them extended beyond the average length enjoyed by others of his rank.[23]

During the time that Johnson was marked as absent, the Third moved from Fort Jesup, via New Orleans, to Fort Brooke, Tampa Bay, Florida. Consequently he escaped the vexatious tasks involved in the removal, transportation by land and steamboat for 800 miles and resettlement of around 500 men and their equipment. After the Third reached Tampa in November, the disorder was further complicated by breaking up the companies and dispersing them to detached posts through middle and western Florida and along the Georgia border. Their mission was to patrol and scout the swamps and surrounding country in search of marauding Seminoles whose villages, food and canoes they were told to destroy.[24]

In the soldier phrase of the day, Florida was "the infested prison house of the Army." Into this undesirable place elements of the Fourth and Eighth Infantry Regiments also were being poured. In modern Army parlance the duty was "rugged" with a full measure of hardship and privation. Danger was small from hostile Indians, whose ability to resist had waned since the death of Osceola in 1838. But always present were the discomforts of humid weather and devouring insects, the boredom of isolation and the tedium of primitive living conditions and bad food for weeks on end.[25]

In contrast, at the time in December 1840 that Johnson joined Company E at Clay Landing in Western Florida, his classmates Sherman, Thomas and Stewart Van Vliet in the Third Artillery were enjoying the delights of the Florida East Coast with beaches, abundant seafood and frequent reunions.[26]

In February 1841 Johnson was assigned to temporary command of Company H at Fort No. 4, Cedar Keys, Florida, but in April he was shifted to Fort Macomb and Fort Stansbury, both a few miles south of Tallahassee. There, for more than a year, he performed the onerous paper work of acting assistant quartermaster and acting assistant commissary of subsistence; in August, in addition, he became the post commander at Stansbury as well as acting assistant adjutant general of the Western District. This assortment of humdrum jobs was the usual lot of a junior officer, then and since.[27]

At least a desk job was better than trying to survive in the Florida swamps. The first of Johnson's classmates to die was Job Lancaster from Hamilton County, Ohio who had graduated seventh in 1840. He was killed by lightning July 4, 1841 on a scouting foray near Crystal River, north of Tampa. He was 23 years old.

Field command of the Third changed several times. Colonel Vose ended his recruiting stint and took over in November 1841; he was then promoted out to the Fourth. Major Wilson resumed command and then was promoted to the First. Senior Captain John B. Clark ran the regiment until January 1842, when scholarly Lieutenant Colonel Ethan Allen Hitchcock, grandson of the hero of

Ticonderoga, was assigned. Nine months passed before he arrived, due to leaves of absence and time for a roundabout trip from New York.

Hitchcock was a stalwart character little short of fabulous. He traveled with an 800-book library, plus 20 volumes of sheet music. For pastime he played operas on his flute. He was a dedicated soldier with a fighting sense of justice that often got him into hot water with superiors, Congressmen, and President Andrew Jackson.[28] As soon as he arrived at Fort Stansbury he set to work to expand it as headquarters for the Third Infantry. Troops were recalled gradually from their swamp outposts. Parade and exercise grounds were laid out. Hitchcock lyrically recorded in his diary that at Stansbury "the moaning of the wind through the tall pines is like the sounds of a tremendous ocean."[29]

Johnson was fortunate enough to retain his post with the garrison. Charming Tallahassee, its capitol under construction, was a blissful variant to field duty. Its 20-mile railroad, originally mule-powered, to St. Marks on Apalachee Bay, afforded ready transportation from Stansbury and young officers quickly entered into the rounds of social affairs. "The bright button was a passport at all times to the houses of the best" was the way Sherman assessed the Florida social situation.[30]

Two brief incidents interrupted this serenity. Lieutenant Thomas Jordan, who had been Sherman's roommate at West Point, took 20 men and captured Chief Tiger Tail who had reneged on his promise to move to Arkansas. Jordan nabbed the Seminole leader in his swamp hideout without firing a shot and started him and his little band on their way westward. Then in December 1842 Hitchcock sent scouts with amicable messages to Chief Pascoffer, last Seminole holdout of importance. In January, with two companies of troops, Hitchcock floated down the Chattahoochee on a little steamer, sending out friendly Indians to contact Pascoffer who eventually appeared. After parleys, presents and some delays, Hitchcock persuaded him to give up and take his 21 braves to Indian Territory.[31]

Permanent peace was now ensured. The Third had spent two and a half years in Florida at the cost of 3 men killed by Seminoles and 68 dead from disease and accidents. There had been many desertions; in 1841, of 40 runaways, only 10 had been caught. The Third's strength, however, through recruiting, aggregated 690.

Welcome news came in March 1843. Hitchcock was notified to prepare the Third for transfer to Jefferson Barracks. Johnson joined his brother officers in rejoicing that at last they were going to the Army's garden spot. After the customary two years of uninterrupted duty, he had enjoyed a month's leave from January 24 to February 23, 1843 and had been given command of Company E in March. Then he had a bout with "Florida swamp fever," which was the soldier's name for malaria. Treated with massive doses of calomel and quinine, he was unfit for duty for two months. For the second time he missed participation in a move by the regiment.

The troops left Stansbury April 4 and by April 22 were set up in their new home. They went by steamer via New Orleans where yellow fever was epidemic so none tarried. Sharing the 1700-acre Jefferson Barracks reservation, with miles of bridle paths and a 10-acre flower and vegetable garden, were eight companies of the Fourth, their recent comrades in Florida.

Lieutenant Johnson was assigned quarters in one of the whitewashed limestone buildings facing the parade ground on three sides. There was a large hall for fêtes and balls which were frequent and festive in this socially minded post, oriented to the gracious-living first families of St. Louis. On the other hand, St. Louis was an active and bustling river town with saloons, brothels, waterfront dives and gambling houses attractive to certain elements of the garrison with consequent disciplinary problems.

Commander of Jefferson Barracks was the famous Colonel Stephen Watts Kearny, a soldier's soldier, officer of the elite Dragoons and gentleman of urbanity and understanding. He enchanted young Dick Ewell by taking him, a low ranking lieutenant, with him to fashionable parties. Ewell wrote a glowing account of one of these at the home of Colonel John O'Fallon, a kinsman of the Dent family into which Grant later married.[32] Kearny also gladdened the hearts of his officers and men with a liberal policy on passes when work was done. During the fall and winter he brigaded the Third and Fourth into a school for brigade drill and kept them at it until they earned a reputation throughout the service for precision and efficiency.[33] In all of this Johnson had an active role as well as Grant, Longstreet, Georges Sykes and Buell, whom Johnson knew at West Point as underclassmen when he had been Cadet Captain. He was incapacitated by another attack of fever in November.

Hitchcock referred to part of the period as "the doldrums" but contributed some stormy excitement himself. Buell had been tried and acquitted by a court-martial for striking a soldier with his sword. The court decided the blows were no more than necessary for self-defense. The finding went to General-in-Chief Winfield Scott who reviewed the case in Washington and ordered the court to explain why Buell was not found guilty. Hitchcock wrote a letter signed by members of the court protesting Scott's order and declining to obey. The Secretary of War ordered the court to reconvene. Hitchcock wrote another letter for the court charging intimidation and refusing reconsideration. Scott was enraged. Finally President John Tyler ordered the matter ended.[34] Naturally, this joust of a regimental commander with the Army's biggest "brass" was a topic of infinite discussion.

The winter of 1843–44 was filled with parades, reviews, dances and "tea fights," as Ewell called them, wherein "there was no dancing, but flirtation, etc., etc." Hitchcock found them dull, but none of the younger officers did. Grant visited Winter Haven, home of Fred Dent, a West Point friend, and after Fred's sister Julia came home from school, he got excused from retreat parade four times a week to go courting.[35] Longstreet became engaged to Louise, second daughter of Lieutenant Colonel John Garland, acting commander of the Fourth. George Deas, acclaimed the handsomest officer of the Fifth, was to marry her older sister, Bessie. Romance budded and bloomed speedily at army posts. Ewell told his sister that he attended a Christmas ball at Fort Leavenworth where there was "hardly a single girl over 13 in the room, so fast do they get married."[36]

Bushrod Johnson singularly was untouched. His name was never linked as a swain to any local or neighborhood belle and no letter has come to light mentioning him in connection with social affairs. If any final vestige remained in him of aloof Eastern Ohio Quakerism, it should have been tempered now by his association with his pleasure-seeking messmates, by his contacts with polished Colonel Kearny and by the inspiration of his commander, the cultivated Hitchcock, both of whom represented the best in the profession of arms.

Johnson was promoted to First Lieutenant February 1, 1844. He could view the honor with mixed feelings. His monthly income went up to $90, but the higher rank meant transfer from the delights of St. Louis to Fort Leavenworth to join Company I, a unit of the Third which had been sent there when the bulk of the regiment came from Florida. His immediate superior was Captain Clark, erstwhile regimental chief.

Fort Leavenworth had figured in the Third's history for decades. Colonel Henry Leavenworth, back in 1827, had built the outpost with the Third on a range of high bluffs above the muddy Missouri. It was a base for expeditions against the Indians and was a bridgehead for the Santa Fe and Oregon trails toward the West.

Before he could take the steamer from St. Louis to his new assignment, Bushrod was summoned to the deathbed of his father. A special order March 9, 1844, granted him two months leave, later extended to June 30.[37] After looking after the disposal of Noah's meager estate he probably visited around with kinfolk in Ohio and with Dr. Nathan in Indiana.

Johnson's first view of Fort Leavenworth came as he rode from Weston, Missouri, where the steamer from St. Louis landed. It was a far cry from the appointments of Jefferson Barracks. Three two-story brick buildings were officers' quarters. Infantry and dragoons were housed in separate barracks on the east side of the square parade. A row of stables crossed the south end. There were a sutler's store, two warehouses, a small hospital and a "bedlam" for mental cases.[38] Facilities were even bleaker at Council Bluffs Sub-agency where Johnson spent August on detached service.

Nearest civilian activities were at Weston, 15 miles upriver, with a few hundred inhabitants, and at Independence, 35 miles southeast, where floods in the 1844 spring wrecked most of the wharfage. The disaster insured the prosperity of rival Westport, a few miles up the Missouri, destined to become Kansas City. The town of Leavenworth, south of the post, was not founded until a decade later.

Meanwhile, unexpectedly in April 1844, most of the Third and Fourth were ordered from Jefferson Barracks to Fort Jesup, Louisiana, ostensibly "to prevent filibustering into Texas," which had been an independent republic since 1836. Hitchcock skeptically thought the troops were "to carry the flag intoTexas upon annexation," an objective he privately opposed.[39] Lieutenant Ewell, briefly post commander at Jefferson Barracks after all the foot soldiers left, found it "most disagreeable" with no garrison and "only a few grass widows from the Fourth."[40]

Johnson missed for the third time a mass migration of the Third. The regiment went by steamer down the Mississippi and up the Red River to "Nackitosh" as Hitchcock spelled Natchitoches, thence footslogging through the woods with supply wagons for 25 miles southwest to Jesup. Colonel David Emanuel Twiggs and the Second Dragoons, now dismounted, were there already, occupying the barrack buildings. They made room for the Third which named its area Camp Wilkins. The Fourth had to move 20 miles northeast and set up a place of their own, called in grim jest, Camp Salubrity. In a letter to Mrs. George Bailey, back home in Bethel, Ohio, Lieutenant Grant of the Fourth described the primitive living conditions there, with swamps "full of Aligators" and woods crawling with "Red bugs and ticks," but free of mosquitos because of its elevation. Only one death from fever hit the Fourth during the first six months.[41]

In June, Brevet Brigadier General Zachary Taylor took command of the two infantry regiments and the horseless dragoons making up the "Army of Observation." Hitchcock found that Taylor had secret instructions to be ready to move at short notice to any point designated by the newly appointed *chargé* in Mexico, Andrew Jackson Donelson. He had the Third build huts for winter housing anyhow. When news came to Camp Wilkins on November 28 that James Knox Polk had been elected president over Henry Clay, Hitchcock prophesied in his diary: "I look on this as a step toward the annexation of Texas first and then, in due time, the separation of the Union."[42] His first forecast came to pass when President Tyler, three days before bowing out to Polk, signed the bill to annex Texas passed near the close of the short session of Congress of 1844–45.

In April 1845, after another thirty-day leave in March, Lieutenant Johnson came to Camp Wilkins with Companies I and K after nearly a year at Fort Leavenworth. The concentration of the Third was complete. After his "exile" in Kansas, Bushrod now could renew his contacts with friends he had not seen since Jefferson Barracks. At Camp Salubrity were others in the Fourth. They introduced him to the diversions they were enjoying: visiting among the citizens of Natchitoches and Grand Ecore, four miles north, attending parties given by wealthy planters along the Red River bottom lands, betting on and often taking part in horse races, and gambling interminably at cards. In camp, "gander pulling," which Hitchcock called barbarous, helped pass the time.[43]

As in Florida and St. Louis, these Northern-born boys from small towns and farms moved in the best social circles. George McCall, speaking of such officers, put it this way:

> Here he encountered and mingled with a people strangely differing in manners and habits from those of his native state, but who, nevertheless, possessed traits of amiability and gentleness in the women and love of pleasure in the men, which rendered them uncommonly unobtrusive but sometimes fiery and vehement when they thought their rights were invaded.[44]

This experience in gracious living was pleasant, but it also was subtile. The South was weaving an enchantment around these young Northerners and some of them would never break the spell. Even Bushrod must have compared Natchitoches with St. Clairsville, Ohio or Cambridge City, Indiana and felt a glowing euphoria in his present situation, brief though it was to be.

Two months after arriving at Camp Wilkins, Lieutenant Johnson and Company I were aboard the steamboat *Monmouth* on the way from New Orleans to Corpus Christi, Texas when the rest of Taylor's forces moved. The "Army of Observation" had become the "Army of Occupation."[45]

Bushrod Johnson now had nearly nine years as a cadet and as an officer in this "strange career for a Quaker." Most of it had been a dull round of routine unimaginative duties. Material advancement had been small. But all this might be changed in the impending war with Mexico. At the least there was a promise of adventure in a faraway country amid a strange people in an exotic setting. More important to an ambitious professional soldier, meeting the test of battle could bring honor and promotion, or point the way to subsequent success.

As he steamed southward in the Gulf of Mexico, Lieutenant Johnson could fill his cup of hope.

Notes

1. Born in 1793 in Uniontown, Pa., source of many of the Quakers in his constituency, Kennon served as a Democrat in the 21st and 22d Congresses (1829–1833) and the 24th (1835–1837), later as a common pleas judge and on the Ohio Supreme Court. He died in 1881. *Biographical Directory of the U.S. Congress, 1774–1961,* (Washington: Government Printing Office 1961), p. 1404.
2. Originals of all correspondence quoted here are in U.S. Military Academy Appointments File in National Archives.
3. Lewis, *Sherman,* p. 48.
4. Records in U.S. Military Academy Archives, West Point N. Y., called WP Archives hereafter. McNutt was the only Ohioan to remain continuously in the Army spending most of his career as an ordnance officer. *Cullum,* I, p. 597.
5. Lyford found the westward fare was $2 higher: $17 from Baltimore to Wheeling. Schedules were haphazard, but coaches ran night and day.
6. Descriptions of daily routine in Lewis, *Sherman,* pp. 52 f.; Lewis, *Grant,* pp. 60 f.; Glenn Tucker, *Hancock The Superb,* (Indianapolis: Bobbs Merrill, 1960), pp. 31 f.; U. S. Grant, *Personal Memoirs,* with notes and

introduction by E. B. Long in one volume, (New York: World Publishing Co., 1932), pp. 14 f. Grant, *Memoirs* hereafter.

7. Biographies of Union generals in *Cullum*, I, pp. 533, 536, 559 and 573; Confederate generals in Ezra J. Warner, *Generals in Gray*, (Baton Rouge: Louisiana State University Press 1959), pp. 22, 30, 79, 84, 124 and 158.
8. *Cullum*, I, p. 690 *et passim* and *Warner*, pp. 131, 199, 289. Steele was a Confederate brigadier general; MacClay was assigned to duty as a brigadier but not named to that rank by President Davis.
9. Explanation of Conduct Roll in WP Archives.
10. Lewis, *Grant*, p. 75; Lewis, *Sherman*, p. 63.
11. *Official Register of Officers and Cadets, 1836–1850* and Roll of the Cadets in *ibid.*, 1837–1840 in WP Archives. *WP Register* hereafter.
12. Grant *Memoirs*, pp. 15 ff.; Lewis, *Sherman*, p. 64.
13. *Cullum*, II, pp. 20, 22, 26; *Warner*, pp. 99, 100, 112.
14. *WP Register*, 1837.
15. *Post Order Book, No. 1 Headquarters U.S. Military Academy*, February 19, 1838 to June 3, 1842 in WP Archives.
16. *Robert Johnson*, pp. 15 f.
17. Lewis, *Sherman*, p. 61.
18. Post Orders No. 39, p. 129 in *Post Order Book No. 1*, USMA in WP Archives. Conduct and merit ratings in *WP Registers* for 1836–50 and 1837–40.
19. *WP Registers*, 1836–50; 1837–40.
20. Letter, Sherman to Sewell L. Fremont, April 12, 1865 in *The War of the Rebellion: A Compilation of the Official Records of the Union and Confederate Armies*, (Washington: U.S. War Dept., 1880–1901), XLVII, pt. 3, p. 271. Fremont, born in Vermont, 1841 graduate of West Point, resigned in 1854 and served as a Confederate colonel.
21. Lt. J. H. McRea "The Third Regiment of Infantry" reproduced in T. F. Rodenbaugh and W. L. Haskin, *The Army of the United States*, (New York: Maynard, Merrill & Co., 1896), pp. 432 f. *McRea* hereafter. Vose later was promoted to command the Fourth, joined by Grant in 1843. Vose, like Many, remained away on "sick leave" until the Mexican War was imminent and fell dead as he directed his first drill at New Orleans Barracks.
22. Named for Brig. Gen. Thomas L. Jesup, quartermaster general of the Army since 1818. Now spelled Jessup, it is 20 miles south of Natchitoches, La., not far from the Texas border.
23. *Third Infantry Regiment Returns*, 1840 in Record Group 94, War Dept., AG Office Files, National Archives. Called *3d. Inf. Ret.*, hereafter.
24. *McRea*, p. 434. The Third had approximately 21 officers and 446 soldiers, including sergeants, corporals, musicians, clerks and artificers. A company numbered 35 men.
25. Maj. Gen. George Archibald McCall, *Letters from the Frontier*, (New York: Lippincott 1868), pp. 380 f. In the Great Cypress Swamp, McCall slept in mud for five months, waded constantly in knee-deep water and barely survived on starvation rations. Similar experiences are detailed in Erasmus D. Keyes, *Fifty Years' Observation of Men and Events*, (New York: Chas. Scribner's Sons 1884), pp. 163 f.
26. Lewis, *Sherman*, p. 67.
27. *Cullum*, I, p. 597.

28. Lt. Col. William G. Bell, "A Test of the Academy's Independence" in *Military Review,* XLIV (April 1964), p. 57 f.
29. Ethan Allen Hitchcock, *Fifty Years in Camp and Field* (New York, G. P. Putnam's Sons 1909), p. 167.
30. Letter, Sherman to Ellen Ewing in Lewis, *Sherman,* p. 69.
31. *McRea,* p. 435; *Hitchcock,* p. 174. Hitchcock calls him Pascofa.
32. *Ewell,* p. 54. He told his sister Rebecca of the delicious food, champagne and variety of wines.
33. *McRea,* p. 435.
34. Details in *Hitchcock,* pp. 182 f.
35. Lewis, *Grant,* pp. 102 f.; Grant, *Memoirs,* p. 19.
36. Ewell, pp. 40 f., 44, 48, 52 f., 54.
37. *3d. Inf. Ret.,* March, May 1844.
38. Lt. Col. Edward W. McGregor, "The Leavenworth Story" in *Military Review,* XXXVI, (May 1956), pp. 62 f.
39. *Hitchcock,* p. 184.
40. Letter, Ewell to his brother Benjamin, Aug. 1, 1844 in *Ewell,* p. 51.
41. Lewis, *Grant,* p. 115; Grant, *Memoirs,* p. 22.
42. *Hitchcock,* p. 187.
43. Details in Grant, *Memoirs,* pp. 118 f.; *Hitchcock,* p. 189. In "gander pulling" a rider passed a tethered bird at a gallop, leaned from his saddle and tried to grab the fowl by the neck.
44. *McCall,* p. iv.
45. *3d. Inf. Ret.,* June–July 1845.

4
FOUR BATTLES WITHOUT A BREVET

i. Bright Prospects for Advancement

The sea was rough and the steamer *Alabama* pitched and rolled at anchor in Aransas Bay, north of Corpus Christi, Texas, on July 25, 1845. Most of the crowded soldiers aboard were sick, many with diarrhea. Lieutenant Colonel Ethan Allen Hitchcock had a touch of it, but he managed to stay on his feet. He dispatched a lieutenant ashore to plant a small American flag and he duly took credit in his diary for this symbolic act in a venture he privately opposed. Then he ordered three companies ashore in rowboats without their mess chests. A few days later in calmer weather, the rest of the troops disembarked and gear and equipment were landed. Hitchcock personally led Companies G and K into Corpus Christi on August 1.

Lieutenant Bushrod Johnson and Company I, having left New Orleans eight days after their comrades, arrived the next week aboard the *Monmouth.* Others dribbled in. Then the diarrhea became epidemic and Hitchcock was prostrated for two days.[1]

Corpus Christi was a hamlet of less than a hundred inhabitants on the west coast of a bay formed by the entrance of the Nueces River into tidewater. A small American trading post sold tobacco and cloth to Mexican smugglers, evading their government's monopoly. As soon as the troops moved in, every hut became a saloon or a brothel to exploit the soldiers who drew only $7 monthly pay at irregular intervals. Gone were any social contacts for the officers unless they could wangle an official trip to San Antonio or Austin, both more than a hundred miles away, as a paymaster's escort or on a supply mission. Grant took such a trip in December.[2]

The camp stretched for two miles along the bay shore on soil formed of powdered shells. Abundant fresh water was only slightly brackish. Living was good because nature provided many tasty additions to the army fare. Storms stranded scores of green sea turtles; oysters could be raked from the river mouth by the bushel. Deer, duck, wild turkey and jacksnipe abounded on the prairies and were bagged by the dozens.[3] Trouble was plentiful, too. After the Second Dragoons arrived August 28, there was a rash of "disgraceful brawls, quarrels and drunken frolics," Hitchcock recorded. "The Dragoons made themselves a public scandal. One officer resigned to avoid a court martial . . . and two other officers were tried for fighting over a whore."[4]

During September other units arrived until Taylor could muster nearly 4000 men from the Third, Fourth, Seventh and Eighth Infantry Regiments, four light artillery batteries, (then called companies), a regiment of heavy artillery serving as infantry and seven companies of the mischief-making Second Dragoons.[5] One of the artillery units was Company E of the Third Artillery, commanded by Captain Braxton Bragg, West Point '37, and Lieutenant George H. Thomas, classmate of Bushrod Johnson. In another company was Lieutenant Daniel Harvey Hill of the class of '42.

When not occupied in trying to make soldiers out of the recalcitrant immigrant recruits, officers bought and broke Mexican mules to draw supply wagons and to carry packs. They also added to their strings of personal mounts from the wild horses caught and sold for $10 apiece by the Mexicans. By regulation, officers could feed their own mounts at government expense.

Company I, Third Infantry, had become so settled in camp routine by October 1 that Johnson managed to get another 60-day leave. He traveled north to Cambridge City, Indiana to visit his brother's family and had a recurrence of swamp fever. Dr. Nathan's certificate of ill health gained Bushrod an extension of his leave of absence until February 1846. After an absence of five months, Johnson returned to resume command of Company I on February 28, 1846.[6]

Hitchcock rejoiced in November when 761 of his books and 20 volumes of his music arrived in good order from Camp Wilkins. He estimated Corpus Christi now housed "2,000 adventurers and speculators; no ladies and few women."[7] Because "Old Zach" Taylor was lax on sanitation, there was much disease and some deaths during the winter.

In March 1846 Taylor's army left Corpus Christi and moved south 150 miles to the Rio Grande River through territory in dispute between Mexico and Texas. Hitchcock, ailing and unfit for duty, was scandalized. "The United States are aggressors," he wrote. "We have outraged the Mexican government and people by arrogance and presumption that deserve to be punished." Grant shared this opinion, calling the movement a provocation designed to force Mexico to start hostilities in an "unholy war of conquest by the United States." George Deas thought the United States and not Mexico was to blame for starting a war by "going there with the Army, driving poor people away from their farms and seizing their customs house at Point Isabel" at the mouth of the Rio

Grande.[8] On the contrary, other inarticulate junior officers were generally thrilled. Cadets in the class of 1846 at West Point, including Cadmus M. Wilcox and Thomas Jonathan Jackson, were so excited they volunteered for immediate service without waiting three months more to graduate. Academy authorities scotched the idea.[9]

Taylor formed his troops into three brigades for the 150-mile hike to a point on the river opposite Matamoros. With Twiggs, the Dragoons, and Major Samuel Ringgold's artillery as an advance party, Taylor left March 8 for Point Isabel, debarkation port for supply ships and reinforcements coming from New Orleans. The first and second brigades followed. March 11 the Third Infantry, led by Captain Lewis N. Morris while Hitchcock was ailing, with the Fourth Infantry and Captain Bragg's artillery making up the Third Brigade, followed 66-year old Colonel William Whistler, brigade commander who also led the Fourth. Bushrod Johnson, leading Company I, rode with the rear guard and Grant went with the 307 wagons, including 80 ox carts, in the supply train.[10]

Hitchcock went along in a bed installed in a wagon. He grew no better after the army reached its target and in April he was granted leave to go North and recover. He did not return until November, thereby missing Taylor's battles in May, June and September.

Heat and thirst plagued the marchers through the uninhabited area where prairie fires had left the ground covered with black ashes. Thousands of wild mustangs galloped within sight of the troops, churning up suffocating clouds of dark dust. Water holes, often brackish, were miles apart. Ten miles from Matamoros the army halted until Taylor and the Dragoons returned March 28 from Point Isabel with a train of supplies. The next day a camp was set up opposite Matamoros and all hands began to build a fort strong enough to be held by a few troops while the balance, with every available vehicle, went back to Point Isabel to unload more supplies from vessels riding at anchor off Brazos Santiago.

Native women bathing naked across the river within sight of the toilers at the fort brought an immediate discipline and morale problem. Mexican offers of 320 acres of land to turncoats were noised about. Catholic church bells, processions and ceremonials in Matamoros stirred the European immigrant recruits. Within a week, 30 deserters fled across the river, 14 of them in one night. Negro "body servants" of officers, including one of Bragg's, followed. Sentries were ordered to shoot fugitives, white or black. A few were killed, some were wounded, but most got away, including some of Johnson's Company I.[11]

Mexican bullets made permanent the absence of some. Major Trueman Cross, assistant quartermaster general, failed to return from a ride on the night of April 10. An officer and a soldier, hunting for him, were ambushed and killed April 14.[12] On April 25, Taylor sent Captains Seth Thornton and W. J. Hardee with 63 dragoons to see if Mexican General Mariano Arista had sent 2500 horsemen over the river above the American fort. Thornton's men let themselves be trapped in a *rancho* corral, and 16 were killed and the rest captured. They were treated kindly and later exchanged.[13]

When Taylor's little fort was finished late in April, Major Jacob Brown, veteran of the War of 1812, took command with 500 men of the Seventh Infantry as a garrison, backed by the guns of Company E, Third Artillery, with Lieutenant Thomas. Taylor gave them most of his remaining food, retaining only enough for the time it would take for 2000 men and 250 wagons to get to Point Isabel to pick up the rations, ammunition, gear and forage on the supply ships.

Johnson, still commanding Company I of the Third, left with his men at 3 P.M. May 1, marched until 3 A.M., halted for a nap and went on again, reaching Point Isabel at noon, May 2.[14] Two days later, Philip Narbourne Barbour from Company A, by virtue of promotion to captain, took command of Company I. He was a Kentuckian, West Point graduate in '34, and had a brevet captaincy from the Florida war in 1843, the same year he married. He wrote often to his wife and kept a detailed, graphic chronicle of his duty in Mexico in a journal intended for her.[15]

At Point Isabel, Johnson got a first hand acquaintance with the back-breaking method of unloading supplies from ships, a task which was to concern and harass him a year later in Vera Cruz. Vessels from New Orleans were compelled to anchor in deep water off Brazos Santiago and unload cargo into light draft steamers which carried it four miles across the shallows to Point Isabel. Then it was transferred again into smaller craft to cross the sand bars at the mouth of the Rio Grande. The little boats took the supplies to an improvised dock 350 yards up the river where they were unloaded and stacked. In a high wind and heavy seas, havoc and disaster were the rule at the transfer points.[16] Once ashore, the cargo was loaded again by soldiers or hired Mexican laborers into four-wheeled wagons drawn by six mules and capable of carrying a ton.

While slow-moving Mexicans and reluctant soldiers filled his wagons under a blazing sun, Taylor on May 3 heard a rumble as of thunder borne on the west wind. He rightly guessed that the shooting war had begun in earnest and that Brown's garrison was under attack. For four more days the booming guns were heard while the loading was finished and the defensive works protecting the supply depot at Point Isabel were strengthened. Taylor began his return to Brown's fort on May 7 with the supply train, knowing that in the interim Arista had moved his force across the river to the Texas side and was massing them athwart the road back. The first pitched battle of the Mexican War was in the offing.

Lieutenant Johnson, Ulysses Grant and other younger officers looked forward to the morrow with some apprehension. This was to be virtually their first practical application of what they had been taught in classroom and drill ground. Each weighed his own ability to meet the test. Grant was sorry he was in the Army. He wondered how Taylor felt under the burden of his responsibilities. He was not afraid until a soldier next to him was killed, but when it was all over, he slept soundly.[17]

Taylor's 2200 troops marched seven miles along the path from Point Isabel before bivouacking for the night of May 7–8. Next morning, after a hasty breakfast, they fell into step again. Because of the heat, many wore Mexican straw hats instead of their short-brimmed uniform caps which gave no protection from the sun. Many doffed their woolen jackets and tossed knapsacks into the wagons atop the piles of rations, gear and ammunition.[18]

Soon they reached a spacious plain, actually an ancient river bed, on the left (east) side of the road. It was covered with shoulder-high needle-pointed grass and bordered by tall trees. This was Palo Alto. Then they saw the glistening bayonets and the long lances of 6000 Mexicans.

This enemy was not a ragtag rabble of barefooted peons. The Mexican troops were fully uniformed in blue or green tunics trimmed in red, with white pants. They were shod in sandals which were more suited to the sandy terrain than the heavy shoes worn by the *Yanquis*. Headgear was the leather "tar bucket" shako of the French army, some with red pompoms. This infantry was armed with a British Tower musket; the cavalry carried a British carbine as well as the formidable 10-foot long, razor-sharp lance. Most of the troops had been battle-tried in the perennial Mexican civil wars of the decade or in the Texas fight for independence. Each regiment had its own band, besides trumpeters and buglers.[19]

Taylor formed his line of battle carefully. On his right he put the Fifth Infantry, then Ringgold's four guns, next the Third under Captain Morris, two 18-pounders just unloaded from the ships, then the Fourth Infantry. The Third and Fourth made up the Third Brigade under Garland. With two squadrons of Dragoons, this was Taylor's right wing, led by Twiggs. The left wing, under Lieutenant Colonel William G. Belknap, included the Eighth Infantry and the heavy artillerymen fighting as infantry. Safely behind this line along the road was the supply train close to a stream available to its thirsty animals.[20]

Bushrod Johnson, supplanted in command of Company I by Barbour, got into the fight very early with the rest of the Third. Eight squadrons of Mexican lancers came pounding through the chaparral on the American right rear. The Fifth formed the hollow square prescribed in the books for countering such a gambit and its concentrated musketry stopped the charge cold. Reinforced with two guns, the Mexicans returned. Ringgold's battery countered. The Third was ordered out of the line to pass to the rear of the Fifth and further discourage the hostile horsemen. The Mexican lancers withdrew behind Arista's lines, reformed and supported his infantry in a strong attack on the American left. Largely through the skills of the American artillery this was broken up. Thereafter the Mexicans made only several feeble attempts to advance before falling back at dusk. Taylor moved forward into the position Arista had occupied at the start of the battle. He counted 9 killed and 47 wounded. None of his precious 40 yoke of oxen had been hit.[21]

Bushrod Johnson and his brother lieutenants could view the results of their first battle as disappointing. Mostly they had been compelled to endure artillery fire from a distance and to shoot at elusive cavalrymen with only fleeting chances to prove their mettle in a standup fight. But they had the exhilaration of knowing they had met and withstood an enemy almost three times their size.

Before the next dawn the Mexicans began to retire down the road to Matamoros, and by 10 A.M. they reached a Y-shaped ravine, oblique to the road, 6 to 8 feet deep and from 40 to 60 yards wide. The two extremities were pools of water. Woods and thickets encumbered the approaches. This was Resaca de la Palma and it was a good defensive position. Taylor approached the Mexicans, spread at right angles to the road, with the Third and Fifth abreast, followed by the Fourth, the Dragoons and the Eighth in the rear. He left the wagons back at Palo Alto.

As skirmishers in advance, Captain George McCall led 150 men of the Fourth. They were soon targets of heavy infantry and artillery fire. The Third, with Johnson, swung wide to the right around both McCall and a pond in the ravine and hit the Mexican left flank, while the Fourth and Fifth moved up against the enemy center. Dense undergrowth impeded Arista's cavalry and the American infantry pressed forward, pouring a murderous fire into the Mexican front and flanks. They fell back, then fled in panic, abandoning baggage, wagons and headquarters in a frantic scramble to get to the river, across it and back to the safety of Matamoros. Many were drowned. Taylor lost 39 killed and 82 wounded. In the two battles, the Third lost 2 killed and 7 wounded.[22]

Johnson's part in the two fights had been without distinction. Captain Barbour's detailed account of the events in his journal mentioned four other officers, but was silent on Bushrod, his chief lieutenant. Barbour was awarded a brevet as major for his conspicuous gallantry, as also was Captain Lewis N. Morris, the regimental commander.

Taylor's troops spent the night of May 9 at their former camp near their fort, which had been under constant artillery fire since May 3. George Thomas had traded shell for shell from his guns with the Mexicans across the river. Major Brown had been mortally wounded on the sixth and died on the ninth. The fort was named in his memory, perpetuated in the modern city of Brownsville.

The Third got a new commander when Major William W. Lear returned to duty from a long sick leave and took over from Captain Morris. Because of the scarcity of officers present, Companies A, B, E and G were temporarily broken up and their personnel was absorbed by other companies. Eight officers as well as sergeants and musicians of the disbanded units were sent North as recruiters. Among them were four lieutenants who had been with the Third only a short time: Barnard Bee, James N. Ward and John C. McFerrin of the class of '45 and Henry B. Schroeder of '44. Three of Johnson's '40 classmates, William B. Johns, Thomas Jordan, and Oliver B. Shepherd, also got this welcome release from danger and discomfort and were the objects of envy. Currently enjoying the same pleasant duty back in Ohio were Sherman, who was hunting foot soldiers in Zanesville and frequently galloping down to Lancaster to court Ellen Ewing, and Dick Ewell, seeking cavalry recruits in Columbus.[23]

Bushrod Johnson was not so lucky. He was now one of a dozen officers left of a normal complement of 21 in the Third, whose strength had fallen to around 250 men.

After Taylor moved his army on May 18 across the Rio Grande to a camp outside Matamoros, abandoned by Arista, his soldiers settled down to enjoy its delights for two months. There were dance halls, brothels and gambling dens aplenty. The *cantinas* and their potent beverages were the downfall of two young officers of the Eighth, one the brother of Lieutenant George Deas and the other, Jordan Bibb of the class of '44. Bibb vanished on an overnight drunk. Lear sent Johnson to hunt for him. Johnson caught up with Bibb at noon, roistering in the plaza and brought him back to face charges. Barbour loaned Bibb the money to travel home after he resigned.

Barbour and Johnson found saner pleasures in strolling through Matamoros. They got permission from a Mexican gentleman to visit his garden, lush with flowers and loaded lemon and orange trees. They also went swimming together in the river. Barbour was proud of his variegated mess, listing two menus served to visitors including mutton chops, eggs, hash, beans, tomatoes, onions, squash, "excellent baker's bread and butter," coffee and a bottle of claret. Taylor tried to enforce a rigid policy of paying for everything, to protect the native shops and market places from thefts or pillage by his soldiers and generally to treat the Mexicans with "humanity and consideration."[24]

Johnson had a bout with illness in June. Barbour had to take over some of his duties, but he managed to get twenty days' leave to go to Galveston to visit his wife. He did not return until July 5. Meanwhile Lieutenant W. H. F. Brooks commanded Company I. As soon as Barbour returned, Johnson got thirty days leave to go to New Orleans, then reported himself sick at Pass Christian, Mississippi on August 8 and did not rejoin the company until September 12 after it had moved to Camargo, 125 miles up the Rio Grande on the way to Monterrey. In nine months of 1846 Johnson had been off duty by illness or leaves of absence for a total of six and a half months, vastly more than normal during a war.

Taylor's army, meanwhile, was being strengthened by the arrival of the first regiments of 12-month volunteers, pursuant to an act of Congress signed by Polk in May. The first came from Tennessee in June, followed by regiments, or smaller units, from Ohio, Kentucky, Mississippi, Alabama, Indiana and Missouri. Colonel Jefferson Davis of the First Mississippi, former son-in-law of Taylor, insisted that his troops be armed with rifles instead of the usual smoothbore muskets, hence the unit added "Rifles" to its title. The Second Mississippi was led by Charles Clark, Ohio-born Mississippi planter and politico, later a Confederate general. The Third Ohio Volunteer Regiment included Company D, recruited in Belmont County by Captain John Patterson of St. Clairsville. If the memories of some of its men went back a decade they might have recalled young Bushrod Johnson who had gone off to West Point in 1836. Their paths were not to cross, however, for Company D spent its year on garrison duty at Fort Brown and reached there after Johnson rejoined the Third in Camargo.[25]

In the Second Ohio, Lieutenant Grant found an old friend: Thomas L. Hamer, the Congressman who had named him to the Military Academy in 1839. Hamer was a major, soon would be a brigadier general, leading the First and Second Ohio in the battle of Monterrey.[26]

Taylor now had 6000 men, half of them volunteers. Except for the troops guarding depots at Point Isabel and Matamoros, most were concentrated at Camargo by September 1, 1846. The volunteers were grouped into two divisions headed by Major General William O. Butler, one of Andrew Jackson's officers in 1812, and by Major General Robert Patterson, Irish-born wealthy Pennsylvania Democrat. The regulars also were in two divisions led by Twiggs and William J. Worth, who was touchy about his brevet brigadier rank. The Third, with Johnson and the Fourth, with Grant, were brigaded under Garland in Twigg's division. Taylor bolstered his volunteer generals with West Pointers as adjutants: McCall to Patterson, Lorenzo Thomas to Butler and Joseph Hooker to Hamer.[27]

Taylor left Patterson at Camargo with Kentucky, Illinois and Indiana troops and moved sixty miles southwest to Cerralvo with the two divisions of regulars plus Butler's division which grouped the brigades of Hamer and another of Mississippians led by John Anthony Quitman, New York-born cotton planter who had so much money he personally paid the expenses of his headquarters officers. On September 14, the day after Bushrod Johnson returned from a 64-day absence, the army, now at 6500, moved out of Cerralvo to Monterrey, a city of 15,000, the capital of the state of Nuevo León. Twiggs was in the van with the Third and Fourth. Johnson was still second in command of Company I, led by Barbour.

General Pedro Ampudía, who had replaced Arista, posted 10,000 infantry and cavalry behind strong defenses in Monterrey. A citadel dubbed the "Black Fort" by the Americans dominated the north and northwest roads; on the west was the fortified Bishop's Palace on an elevation whence its guns commanded part of the road from Saltillo. On the East, along the bank of the Caterina River were three detached defensive works: The Tannery (*La Tenería*), the Devil's Corner (*Rincón del Diablo*) and Fort Liberty (*La Libertad*). In the city's central plaza cannon were mounted behind barricades and sighted to sweep the streets in all directions. On the roof-tops of many houses, riflemen crouched behind sandbags. Across the river to the Southwest was a strong point called The Soldier (*El Soldado*).[28]

Three miles north of Monterrey in the grove of San Domingo, labeled Walnut Springs by the Americans because of its trees and plentiful mountain spring water, Taylor's army assembled on September 19. Old Zach ordered Worth's troops to march out of range of the Black Fort around to the West and South to the Saltillo road and then make the main attack from the West, while cutting the Mexican supply and communications line with Saltillo. At the same time Twiggs and Butler would hit the north and east sides of the city.

Worth started around the west side of the city in early forenoon of September 20. In the evening of the same day, Barbour wrote his last entry in his journal. He had seen in a newspaper on September 1 that he had been brevetted major and on September 17 he got the official word. Unaware this was his last night on earth, Barbour recorded his pride as a light rain fell on his tent. His widow in Galveston read the journal a fortnight later.

At dawn September 21, the main force north of town heard the booming of guns and knew that the battle, the first one for the volunteers, had begun. The Third with its 262 officers and men and the Fourth, reduced to six companies, with a Maryland volunteer company and Bragg's battery, all under Garland, edged out between the Black Fort on the right and the Tannery on the left toward the white stone and stucco houses on the northeast edge of Monterrey. They were caught in a three-way fire from the forts on each flank and from the rooftops in front. Barbour was mortally wounded.[29] The drive, which Grant called "ill-conceived or badly executed," bogged down.

Taylor dispatched Butler toward the Tannery and the town to support Garland, then hurried Quitman's force against the Tannery, after Butler with the First Ohio pushed into the streets to the right of Garland. Charging on the run, these recently civilian volunteers carried the fort and grabbed a foothold in the nearby dwellings. Across town, Worth's regulars took *El Soldado* and were poised to assault the Bishop's Palace the next day.[30]

A night rain drenched the bodies of the dead and the moaning wounded as Taylor counted his losses, a total of 394 casualties. The weakened Third and Fourth had been still further reduced, but a bloodier day was ahead for both. Not the next day; that was spent burying the fallen, resting and gathering strength for the impending showdown. Only Worth's force was active. In a fierce charge, it took the Bishop's Palace.

At daylight, September 23, both pincers of Taylor's army began tightening. Worth's Texans in Monterrey's west end dug holes from house to house to foil rooftop snipers. His regulars pushed toward the plaza where Ampudía, abandoning the Black Fort, the Devil's Corner and The Liberty, had massed his defenders. The Third and Fourth advanced doggedly along the streets from the East, easy targets for the riflemen on the roofs and the guns behind the barricades.

Bushrod Johnson, leading Company I, was not far when the regimental commander, Major Lear, was hit. Trying to pull him to safety, Captain Morris (who had won a brevet majority for gallantry at Palo Alto and Resaca) and Second Lieutenant Robert Hazlett suffered fatal wounds. The regimental adjutant, Lieutenant Douglas S. Irwin, and Captain George P. Field were killed. Captain Henry Bainbridge, who took command after Lear's wound, also was injured. Lear lingered until October 31 and died.[31]

Five officers dead, one dying, sixteen soldiers killed; Bainbridge and twenty-nine wounded out of twelve officers and five companies present for duty. This was a ghastly tribute to the valor of the Third and the unstinting bravery of its leadership. No other unit in the red carnage of Monterrey could equal such a record!

Meanwhile the volunteers were moving down the eastern edge of the city, passing the Devil's Corner and The Liberty, inching their way toward the central plaza. Worth's wall punchers, taking fewer losses, continued to burrow from house to house. Ampudía's broken thousands, penned and cramped in the center of the city, knew it was all over. September 24 at dawn he proposed to surrender on terms permitting him to take his survivors, their weapons and six guns, and march seventy miles southward during an armistice of six weeks. Taylor accepted. His men needed rest and reinforcements. He had lost 488 killed and wounded in three days, but many felt he had virtually ended the war.[32]

Honors were showered on the Third. But in the rewards for valor and gallantry passed out to the surviving officers, Bushrod Johnson was not included. Two first lieutenants, Brooke and Buell, both junior to him, and his classmate Thomas won the right to sign themselves "Brevet Captain." To four captains of the Third went the brevet rank of major: Daniel T. Chandler, Lewis S. Craig, Joseph H. Eaton and William S. Henry. Johnson had led Company I for part of the battle after Barbour's death. The exclusion of his name from the list must have stirred comment and speculation among his brother officers to whom rank and status were a way of life.[33]

His long absences from duty may have been a factor in prejudicing those who made the recommendations, or his performances under fire may not have impressed his superiors. Even if his own character was free from envy or rankling resentment, he must have been keenly disappointed.

Bushrod Johnson, three times in combat, had not won prestige and standing among the honored elite. One more Mexican War battle was ahead of him, but in it he was to be denied a warrior's part. The opportunity to add lustre to his career passed when firing ceased on the bloody streets of Monterrey.

ii. Sidetrack off the Glory Road

There was a quietness for weeks after Monterrey. Taylor's army treated its wounds, welcomed replacements and shifted men and officers to fill vacancies made by enemy bullets. Into the battered Third from the Seventh came three members of the West Point class of '45, all eager to build their reputations: Henry B. Clitz, William Rhea, and William H. Wood. Captain Bainbridge recovered sufficiently to retain field command of the regiment. Its official chief, Colonel Many, still enjoyed his "sick leave" in New Orleans.

In November, Bushrod Johnson was shifted from Company I to command Company C. Assigned to assist him was Barnard E. Bee, class of '45, made a full Second Lieutenant in September after a year of serving with brevet rank.[34] But Bee was still in the North on recruiting duty and would not return until early 1847. Fifteen years distant for him was Bull Run and his death and the distinction of indelibly labeling Thomas J. Jackson as "Stonewall."

One-third of the army was disabled with "chills and fever" attributed to overindulgence in the fruits abounding in the area, such as the oranges and pomegranates Lieutenant George G. Meade described to his family.[35] Nobody blamed the utter lack of either sanitation or precautions in food preparation or the malaria-carrying mosquitos. Fortunately, deaths were few.

A new phase of the war was shaping up in Washington. The Democratic administration of Polk looked with a jaundiced eye on the acclaim showered on Taylor, a potential Whig candidate for president in 1848. At the same time another Whig presidential hopeful, general-in-chief Winfield Scott, was urging his politically hostile superiors to let him win the war by taking Vera Cruz and striking Mexico City. Gradually the Democrats became aware of the chance to neutralize Taylor by letting Scott go ahead and perhaps destroy himself at the same time.[36] So Scott was put in chief command in Mexico and promised the help of the U.S. Navy in the first amphibious operation in American military annals against Vera Cruz.

Scott started for the mouth of the Rio Grande in December. At the same time Taylor sent Twiggs with the First, Second, Third and Seventh Regiments, and Patterson and the volunteers, afoot to Victoria, 155 miles southeast of Monterrey. Trooper Furber was amazed, as the hungry and dirty men trudged along the dusty road, at the huge amount of discarded and abandoned rations and equipment. The ground was littered with broken saddles, old harness, clothing of every kind, bars of soap and bags of beans, rice, flour, bread and pork. All of it was thrown away because instead of two wagons, only one had to carry everything for two companies.[37]

Delays and countermarches prolonged the ordeal until late in January. The low morale of the plodding volunteers was not raised by the exhibition of General Gideon J. Pillow, erstwhile law partner of President Polk, eating and drinking a plentiful Christmas dinner in sight of his weary and famished men. Pillow was to figure in several episodes in the later life of Bushrod Johnson, who was footslogging along with Company C of the Third.

Scott lost no time in taking charge. More than 4700 men were taken from Taylor and sent toward Vera Cruz, some through Tampico; they included Johnson and the Third, Patterson, Twiggs and Quitman. Worth with Grant and the Fourth went north to Point Isabel to embark. Others came from New Orleans. Taylor was left with about 5000 men, mostly volunteers, but with them he won the battle of Buena Vista in February and that virtually ended the war in Northern Mexico.

Time was breathing on Scott's stalwart neck. He had to reduce Vera Cruz and start for the interior before spring brought malaria and yellow fever to the coast. But agonizing delays came in January and February with scant transport to convey forces from New Orleans, Brazos Santiago at the mouth of the Rio Grande, and from Lobos Island, the rendezvous and debarkation point below Tampico.

Johnson's Company C hoofed into Victoria on January 4. Two days later because of the return of Captain James M. Smith from stateside recruiting duty, Johnson was shifted from command and returned to Company I. With this unit and the rest of the Third, he endured a nine-day forced march from Victoria to Camp Watson, near Tampico, going 174 miles between January 14 and 23. Then, after a month's idle waiting, the Third embarked on February 27 from Lobos Island for a week of misery and tedium aboard the steamer *Barling* before sighting their goal, Antón Lizardo, 16 miles south of Vera Cruz. They were luckier than Grant and the Fourth who came from the Rio Grande and were on shipboard in frightful heat for more than a month.[39]

Covered by the fires of five gunboats and two steamers blasting away at the sand hills above and below the landing place, Collado Beach, the troops began climbing down into surfboats manned by sailors on the afternoon of March 9. Worth's 4500 regulars, including Grant and the Fourth, Fifth, Sixth, and Eighth Regiments were in the first wave to hit the beach at sundown. Charging and slipping through the sand toward the dunes where any defensive force could be expected, the Americans were amazed to find they were unopposed. Worth moved inland. Then Patterson's volunteers were rowed ashore and finally Twigg's regulars, including the Third and Johnson. Nobody fired a shot at them. By 10 P.M. the entire force of 13,000 Americans was safely on the beach without loss or accident. All through the night and for days to come, except when frustrated by storms, the rowboats would continue to ply from the ships to the sands bringing in siege guns, mortars, shells, animals, harness, wagon parts, equipage of all kinds and tons upon tons of food.[40]

Johnson was to be concerned with these rations from now on. March 10 he was designated by order of General Scott as acting assistant commissary of subsistence for the army. This meant, as far as the assault of Vera Cruz was concerned, that his fighting days were ended. Henceforth he was to be involved in a nightmare of receiving, unloading, storing, protecting, issuing and replenishing the substantials which 13,000 men, their appetites whetted by sea air and outdoor activity, would devour three times a day. It was a tremendous financial responsibility and an overwhelming physical chore.

A week previously, on March 3, Thomas Jordan, Bushrod's 1840 classmate, who had just returned to the front after months of pleasant, stateside recruiting service, was named assistant quartermaster and promoted to Captain-staff.[41] Johnson must have expected a similar promotion and the extra pay of $10 to $20 monthly for such duty as provided for by regulation. He got neither and continued to be designated "acting assistant," though his tasks were as numerous and onerous as Jordan's.

Johnson's commissary supply dump was set up a few hundred yards from the water's edge, not far from the landing beach and adjacent to Scott's headquarters. A short distance up the beach toward the city Jordan had his depot. Mounting stacks of barrels, boxes, casks and loose equipment were piled helter-skelter in the deep sand. More came with each rowboat from the ships at anchor off shore. Eager for fast profits, sutlers crowded their tents side by side along the beach and navy carpenters worked hastily to build floors, sides and counters for these private enterprises, neglecting the pressing military business at hand. Boxes of goods and fancy groceries filled the tents and a brisk trade began almost as soon as the first troops came ashore.

The roar of the sea was drowned out, Trooper Furber noted, by the hammering, cursing, commanding and shouting, mingled with the "jabbering" of Mexican civilians hired at once as laborers. Horses and mules, restive after long confinement aboard ship, reared and jerked wagons through the drifting, cloying sand amid the crowds of soldiers, laborers and seamen moving painfully slow in the dunes behind and around Vera Cruz, out of range of the Mexican guns.[42] Worth went into position on the American right, Patterson in the center to be followed by Twiggs on the left.

A violent "norther" storm, first of several to spread chaos and destruction along the beach, struck on the night of Wednesday, March 10. Rain and wind and the raging seas continued for three days, halting further unloading of wagons or pack animals. Johnson's rations had to be carried on the backs of men from his disorganized stocks to the ravenous men trying to dig trenches and gun emplacements in the sand along the investing line. Pennsylvania Volunteer J. Jacob Oswandel, who had acquired a remarkable aptitude for stealing hams on the transport *Statesman* on the way down, had to go two days without a good meal, and then only salt pork, hard crackers and coffee were brought to the diggers in the sands.[43]

As soon as the blow diminished, Johnson resumed the frenzy of unloading, piling up, sorting and distributing. He was forced to compete for human burden-bearers with the ordnance people who had to land, carry and store copper boxes of powder, 10-inch shells, mortars big enough for a man to stand up in, 8-inch howitzers and 24-pounders and huge Paixhan guns weighing two-thirds of a ton apiece. These were ferried through waves still running high and dragged across deep, soft sand into hastily built magazines and dumps. Colonel Hitchcock, who had rejoined the war as Scott's inspector general, meticulously kept track of the guns brought ashore, the number of Mexican shells fired at the Americans, and incidents like the one on Saturday, March 20, when an excited sentry mistook Captain Robert E. Lee and Lieutenant P. G. T. Beauregard for Mexicans and fired at them with a pistol, the bullet passing between Lee's left arm and his body, singeing his coat.[44]

Another "norther," this one more violent, struck on the same Saturday night. On that day, Mexican guns lobbed 400 shells and round shot into working parties within 600 yards of the city walls, according to Hitchcock's tally. The wind-blown sand was worse than enemy gunfire, blinding and choking humans and animals. The gale drove ships aground. One transport sank with its load of horses. Johnson's storage tents were knocked down and torn up and much of his stock was ruined by sand and water. The next day Furber saw bodies of "a hundred or two" drowned animals being washed up on the beach alongside piles of corn, oats, boxes of hard bread and barrels of pork. Some of the food was salvaged, loaded on wagons and carried to other dumps which had escaped major damage.[45]

As the wind died down again, hundreds of men busy as ants worked at assembling wagons and carts from huge piles of wagon bodies, axles, tongues, and bows, and fitting new harness from boxes on uncooperative mules. Pack animals staggered under barrels of hardtack, bundles of tents and mess gear in feverish, chaotic and noisy activity. In the midst of it all, Bushrod Johnson toiled and sweated.

Impatient Hitchcock complained to his diary on March 22: "Here thirteen days without firing a shot." The same afternoon Scott felt he had sufficient guns ready. He sent a summons to surrender to General Juan Morales, the city commandant. Morales refused. At 6:30 P.M., six American mortars led off with a mighty roar, the heavy Paixhans joined in and seven gunboats hauled up near enough to blast at both the city and the castle of San Juan de Ulloa in the harbor. After four 24-pounders and two 8-inch howitzers were emplaced March 25, they added to the chorus of destruction and death.

Results inside the city were appalling. First the houses on the landward side were blown to bits. By dawn on the twenty-fifth, three American shells per minute were bursting in buildings or streets. The ancient city wall was breached, several of its bastions entirely demolished. On the night of the twenty-sixth, the powder storage in Fort Santiago was hit and exploded, blowing the building apart and killing all inside but one sergeant. In an infirmary, nineteen were killed. Seventeen more died in a female hospital. Hitchcock wrote he would never forget the spectacular and terrible fire of the mortars.[47]

The third "norther" to scramble both Johnson's rations and Jordan's gear struck early on Friday, March 26. More than a score of supply ships were dashed ashore. Small boats could not bring in shells and powder to replenish stocks that were being fired away at the city. Sand blew so hard and so heavy it filled up the trenches. Sentries wrapped the capes of their overcoats around their heads and lay in the dunes until sand covered them; then they got up, shook it off and lay down again. More of Johnson's food was saturated with grit.[48]

When the storm ceased and the sun shone brightly the next day, Johnson directed the salvaging of his barrels, boxes and bags all over again. Scott, disregarding the importunities of some of his glory hunting subordinates, Worth and Pillow among them, to make a general assault on the city regardless of cost in lives, offered face-saving terms to Morales. The Mexicans accepted before midnight March 27.[49]

The formal surrender ceremony came Monday, March 29. Four thousand Mexican soldiers, some in green uniforms trimmed in red, blue trimmed in red, and white shakos with red pompoms, marched out with drums beating and bands playing into a plain south of the city. They had suffered 600 casualties. In the city 500 civilians were dead and injured. Scott's 13,000 had only 67 dead and wounded including 14 from the Navy.

The city was a shambles. Shells had fallen thickly in the streets, gouging large holes in pavements, and in exploding had hurled shards and paving blocks through sides of buildings, doors and windows. Broken walls, timbers, planks and plaster, stones and bricks had caved in upon trapped residents. Heaps of rubble blocked numerous streets. Churches were ripped and torn, mosaic aisles pitted and scattered, images broken and splintered. Furber noted that a statue of Christ on the cross had been decapitated.[50] Pestilential smells were overwhelming. Hitchcock moved his tent into the suburbs to escape the "intolerable stench."[51]

Scott named Worth as governor until the army left for Mexico City. Lenient martial law restored order. Scores of Mexican civilians were hired to clean up the debris. Worth ordered 10,000 of Johnson's rations distributed to the poor and his was the task of supervising the dole.[52]

Then ensued a fortnight of feverish preparation for the invasion of the interior. On April 1, a Fools' Day rumor flared that peace was to be declared and everybody would go home. Two days later the first copy of the *American Eagle* newspaper, printed on a Mexican press, appeared as a means of communicating the official word on such matters to the troops and to the gamblers, prostitutes and profiteering enterprisers who came in the wake of the army. It sold for 12½¢ a copy.[53]

The most pressing need was for draft animals to replace those drowned in the "norther," and to augment the few which came from home. Expeditions fanned over the countryside to obtain more. They had some luck. But horses and mules were in such scant supply that when Twiggs started on April 8 along Cortez's road to the capital with Johnson's former company and comrades of the Third, he was limited to only 45 wagons for the entire division.

From Johnson's food stores, each soldier was issued hard bread for four days and enough bacon or pork to cook for two days. He carried this on his back in addition to forty rounds of ammunition. The chief commissary for Scott's army was allotted a hundred wagons with four days' forage for the teams, to carry the food he hoped to obtain en route or to send back empty to Vera Cruz for resupply by Johnson. The laden vehicles sank in the sandy roads, "worse than in New Jersey," Private Oswandel decided, and he noted with horror that barrels of bread and meat were dumped along with discarded knapsacks, clothing and other equipage by Twigg's troops on the route of march.[55]

Johnson's first concern after issuing food for the departing army was to find better storage facilities. He and Staff Captain Jordan, the quartermaster, searched the city for buildings which could be repaired, or, if whole, could be requisitioned. Storerooms which had escaped or survived the shelling, abandoned churches, warehouses and storage buildings were divided between them. Then came the arduous task of shifting the mounds of sand-covered bags, boxes and barrels from the temporary tents and marquees in the dunes into the city.

There were fewer hands to help. The First Infantry left behind by Scott to garrison Vera Cruz was occupied in sentry duty and security. Few of the 1000 sick and wounded left behind were available. Johnson had to depend on hired civilians, adept at pilfering from the most bountiful stock of food they had ever seen. For Johnson, laden with responsibility for the safety and preservation of this valuable government property, it was a time of overwork, frustration and no reward.

In the midst of his labors the word came that Scott had met and defeated Santa Anna in the mountain passes at Cerro Gordo, 35 miles away, on April 17. The Third had fought well. When the honors were passed around a major's brevet went to Captain E. B. Alexander, who had replaced Bainbridge as regimental field chief when Bainbridge was promoted to the Seventh. Johnson's classmate, William B. Johns, back from recruiting duty, and two other first lieutenants won brevet captaincies and three second lieutenants of the class of '45 got brevet first lieutenancies.[56] At Buena Vista, another classmate, George Thomas, had earned his brevet majority.

These stories of glories he had missed further eroded the morale of Bushrod Johnson. So did reports he heard of promotions to staff captain that had come to others of his 1840 class who had been assigned duties similar to his. In addition to Jordan at Vera Cruz, higher rank and more pay came to Joseph L. Folson at San Francisco and William H. Churchill at Fort Polk, neither on duty as important as Johnson's at Vera Cruz.

Johnson could think that he was trapped in an intolerable situation. In May he sent a protest to Commissary General Gibson, who seems to have ignored it.[58] Johnson's military career, the dream of his Quaker boyhood, was on a dead end road.

To his depression of spirit was added a severe attack of the *vómito* late in May. He nearly died. He was prostrated for two weeks and suffered another month of debility. Nobody did anything to help him with his duties, admittedly slacker now that Scott's army was nearing Puebla and its lush resources. Fever-ravaged Johnson came back to his warehouses to find aggravated confusion awaiting him. He got better physically, but not psychologically. Rebuffed, disappointed, discouraged, and resentful, he was ripe for temptation.

Inevitably as in a Greek tragedy, the provocation appeared and it was in his nature to respond with an immaturity almost unbelievable. On July 1, 1847, artless Lieutenant Johnson offered a vague bribe to the wrong man.

Notes

1. *3d. Inf. Ret.*, July 1845; *Hitchcock*, pp. 192–195.
2. Grant, *Memoirs*, pp. 33 f.
3. Major George Deas, "Reminiscences of the Campaign in the Rio Grande," in *Historical Magazine*, sec. ser., pp. 19 f. *Deas* hereafter. Lewis, *Grant*, p. 125.

4. *Hitchcock*, p. 202.
5. Grant, *Memoirs*, p. 30; *McRae*, p. 436.
6. *3d. Inf. Ret.*, Oct.–Dec. 1845; Jan.–Feb. 1846.
7. *Hitchcock*, p. 205.
8. *Ibid.*, p. 212; Grant, *Memoirs*, pp. 30, 56–57; *Deas*, p. 22.
9. *Wilcox*, pp. 72 f.
10. *3d. Inf. Ret.*, March 1846; *Hitchcock*, p. 210; *McRae*, p. 436; Grant, *Memoirs*, p. 38; Lewis, *Grant*, pp. 132 f. Whistler, a senile alcoholic, whose feats as a young officer were an Army tradition, was the uncle of James Abbott McNeil Whistler, the artist. Hitchcock said Whistler was not competent "to give a simple order."
11. Philip Narbourne Barbour, *Journals of the Late Brevet Major Philip Narbourne Barbour and his Wife*, (New York: G. P. Putnam's Sons, 1936), p. 17; *Hitchcock*, p. 221.
12. Details of Cross's death and its aftermath in George G. Meade, *Life and Letters of General Meade*, (New York: Scribner and Son, 1913), I, p. 66.
13. *Wilcox*, p. 46; *Deas*, p. 22.
14. *Wilcox*, p. 49; *Deas*, p. 100.
15. Barbour's journal begins March 28, 1846 with the troops' arrival opposite Matamoros and ends September 20, the eve of his death in battle at Monterrey.
16. *Wilcox*, p. 82.
17. Letter, Grant to Julia Dent, May 11, 1846 quoted in Lewis, *Grant*, p. 145; Grant, *Memoirs*, p. 43.
18. *Deas*, p. 101.
19. *Ibid.*, p. 20; *Furber*, p. 557.
20. *Wilcox*, p. 52; Col. Vincent T. Esposito, *The West Point Atlas of American Wars*, (New York: Frederick A. Praeger, 1959), Map 14a. *WP Atlas* hereafter.
21. Grant, *Memoirs*, pp. 44 f.; *Wilcox*, pp. 54–59.
22. *Wilcox*, pp. 60–64; Grant, *Memoirs*, pp. 45 f.; *McRea*, p. 436; Meade, pp. 78–81, says 182 were killed and wounded.
23. *Barbour*, p. 75; W. T. Sherman, *Memoirs*, (New York: Appleton & Co., 1875), I, p. 11.
24. *Barbour*, pp. 83–86; *Deas*, p. 236.
25. *McKelvey*, pp. 111 f. Company D came home to Belmont County July 22, 1847 without having fought in any battle.
26. Grant, *Memoirs*, p. 48.
27. *Wilcox*, p. 81; Lewis, *Grant*, p. 169.
28. Grant, *Memoirs*, p. 51; Map in *Wilcox*, p. 92. Meade included a sketch map in his description of the battle sent to his wife Sept. 27, 1846 in *Meade*, pp. 132 f.
29. *3d. Inf. Ret.*, September 1846.
30. Grant, *Memoirs*, pp. 52 f.; Wilcox, pp. 94 f. Campbell gave his uncle a graphic description of the assault, calling Worth "the hero of the battle." In the First Tennessee were Lt. Col. Samuel Read Anderson, Nashville banker and postmaster, who was to be Johnson's partner in a real estate firm in Nashville after the Civil War, and Lt. Adolphus Heiman, Nashville architect, with Johnson at Fort Donelson in 1862.
31. *McRae*, p. 437.

32. The terms were repudiated by President Polk, but by the time the word got back to Taylor, seven weeks had expired.
33. *Meade*, p. 128, wrote to his wife on Sept. 3, 1846: "You appear mortified at my having been passed over" in the award of brevets, and added: "There is much heart-burning in the army at the list confirmed . . ."
34. *3d. Inf. Ret.*, November 1846.
35. *Meade*, I, p. 145.
36. Grant, *Memoirs*, pp. 56 f.; *Wilcox*, pp. 164 f.; *Ripley*, I, pp. 498 f.
37. *Furber*, pp. 275–320.
38. *3d. Inf. Ret.*, January 1847. Surviving Third Infantry Returns include only January, March and December for 1847.
39. Grant, *Memoirs*, p. 59.
40. *Wilcox*, p. 244 and Map VII, p. 246; Grant, *Memoirs*, p. 60.
41. *Cullum*, I, p. 619.
42. *Furber*, p. 513 *et passim*.
43. J. Jacob Oswandel, *Notes of the Mexican War*, (Philadelphia: n. p., 1885), p. 68.
44. *Hitchcock*, p. 243.
45. *Furber*, pp. 512 f.
46. *Hitchcock*, p. 244; *Wilcox*, p. 253, says firing started at 4:15 P.M. Philip Young, *History of Mexico*, (Cincinnati: J. A. and U. P. James, 1847), p. 464 says Scott's demand for surrender was made at 2 P.M.
47. *Wilcox*, p. 256; *Hitchcock*, p. 247; *Philip Young*, p. 464.
48. *Furber*, p. 546; *Hitchcock*, p. 246; *Wilcox*, p. 260.
49. *Wilcox*, p. 202.
50. *Furber*, p. 562.
51. *Hitchcock*, p. 248.
52. *Wilcox*, pp. 264 f.; *Furber*, p. 563.
53. *Oswandel*, p. 103.
54. Charles S. Hamilton, "Memoirs of the Mexican War" in *Wisconsin Magazine of History*, XIV, p. 68.
55. *Wilcox*, p. 269; *Oswandel*, p. 108.
56. *Wilcox*, p. 637.
57. Records of the class of 1840 in *Cullum*, I.
58. The letter is indexed as received from Johnson May 10, 1847 in the AG Register of Letters Received but the original cannot be found in Record Group 94, War Dept., AG Files, National Archives. There is no record of any reply.
59. See *supra*, Johnson's letter to Gen. Jones, October 15, 1847.

5
EX-SOLDIER TURNS SCHOOLMASTER

i. "For Sons of the South's Finer Families"

Red and golden leaves were falling along Pennsylvania Avenue and there was a hint of frost in the air as Bushrod Rust Johnson, ex-First Lieutenant of the Third U.S. Infantry, walked to his Washington lodgings from the War Department on October 21, 1847. Out of the Army which had been his livelihood and his shelter for eleven years, he had to make a new start at an age when most men were successfully launched in business or professions as his nephews Nimrod and Lemuel were in Indiana.[1] But what could he do? Besides soldiering he had been only a farm boy and a teenage rural school teacher. He had no present affection for the soil, even if he could raise the money to buy land. He must return to teaching. He would go back to farming in the final activity of his life.

While he pondered ways to salvage his life, he read of the progress of the war in Mexico which he had left so abruptly. The newspapers told of Scott's final assaults on Mexico City and of new honors for gallantry and merit won by so many brother officers with whom he had served or had known at West Point. Fifteen of the thirty-five remaining members of the class of 1840 had won brevets.[2]

His present uncertain situation stood in sharp contrast to theirs.

But the mere fact that he was a former army officer was an asset in his quest for a teaching position. Regardless of politics, Americans were thrilled by the news of victories and the stories told by volunteers returning from Mexico. The general atmosphere was sympathetic to one in Johnson's position, as an officer recently resigned.[3]

Bushrod undoubtedly talked things over with Dr. Nathan in Indiana. He certainly informed him of his resignation from the Army; whether he concealed the circumstances is not revealed. The attachment between the brothers was strong and there is continuous evidence of the abiding concern of Nathan's family with Bushrod's welfare.[4]

A position on the faculty of a military academy seemed to be the best solution for Bushrod. Interest in these schools had been spreading, especially in the South, where the ideal of education stressed character and grace rather than utility. Virginia Military Institute had begun in 1839 and three years later the Military College of South Carolina [The Citadel] had opened its doors. Such institutions needed retired or resigned officers.

Two similar schools recently had started in Kentucky. In 1846, Kentucky Military Institute was founded near Frankfort by Robert T. P. Allen, fifth in the class of '34 at West Point, later a Methodist preacher and teacher at Alleghany College and Transylvania.[5] Its competitor was Western Military Institute, begun in 1847 in Georgetown, Scott County, with the aim of becoming the VMI of Kentucky. Both pitched their appeal to the "South's finer families," but Northerners were welcomed, too.

Founder and promoter of Western Military Institute was Thornton Fitzhugh Johnson,[6] first cousin of Richard Mentor Johnson, vice president of the United States under Van Buren, 1837–1841. Robert Johnson, father of "Old

Dick," came to Kentucky in 1779 from Orange County, Virginia, whence Thornton Johnson, son of Robert's brother William, had gone to West Point October 27, 1818 at the age of fourteen years.

Thornton spent only three years at the Military Academy. He resigned July 15, 1821 after numerous delinquencies punished by 44 "extra duties" because of absence from roll call, tardiness, abusive language, untidy dress and disorderly conduct.[7] Johnson called himself "Colonel" though he had never been in any army, nor in any war nor even in the Kentucky militia.[8] He also claimed a degree of Master of Arts.[9] In catalogues of his military school he always represented himself as "educated at West Point" the inference being that he had graduated.[10] It may be said of Thornton Johnson that he was less than genuine.

He had come to Georgetown in 1829 as the result of a religious rivalry. Two years before, an extensive spiritual awakening, reminiscent of the "Great Revival," had created a demand for religious teaching among Baptists, alarmed at the inroads of Alexander Campbell and his "Reformers," later the Disciples of Christ. Robert Johnson, who had helped found ill-fated Rittenhouse Academy in Georgetown in 1798, was a leader in setting up Georgetown College in 1829, the first Baptist college in the Mississippi Valley. Dr. Joel S. Bacon was its first president.[11] Thornton Johnson, then 24 years old, came to the new college to teach mathematics and civil engineering. He married Margaret, one of the three daughters of William B. Warren, a Virginia lawyer who came to Georgetown about 1794, became a judge, and died in 1824.[12]

Campbellites battled Baptists for control of Georgetown College. Annoyed and perplexed, Bacon quit in 1832. Thornton Johnson joined him and other reformers in a rival institution, Bacon College, opened in Georgetown in 1837. In May 1839, Bacon moved the school to Harrodsburg and Johnson dropped out. Meanwhile in 1837, despite the nationwide depression, Thornton Johnson and his wife started Female Collegiate Institute in Georgetown with himself as principal and professor of mathematics. This boarding school catered to genteel young ladies and offered courses in mathematics, science, literature and languages, with music of harp, guitar and piano, as well as needlework for extra fees. It was housed in a two-story stone building, later known as the "Moore House" in the residential section.[13] Since this girls' school, averaging about a hundred students annually, had been operating for ten years before Johnson started his military academy, his reputation as an educator was well established by 1847.

Western Military Institute began registering students on February 1, 1847. Fifty-nine boys, including three sons or wards of the founder and one grandson of former Vice President R. M. Johnson, signed the pledge of honor printed on each page of a huge volume still in use at Montgomery Bell Academy in Nashville. They promised to observe the rules, to obey orders, to be punctual and to apply themselves and they certified they had delivered to the commandant all private arms and ammunition. All but four of the first cadets were from Georgetown; two others came from Thibodaux, in southern Louisiana, one from Lake Washington, Mississippi and one from Athens, Fayette County, Kentucky. Two cadets died during the initial term—an omen of the recurrent epidemics which were always to plague the school.[14]

In the fall, a new student was William Preston Johnston, son of Albert Sidney Johnston, Kentucky-born West Pointer who had been the Republic of Texas' secretary of war and now resided in Brazoria County, Texas. Young Johnston, later a Confederate colonel, kept a journal describing the Institute's routine, discipline and uniform.[15] First classes were held in a dwelling on North Hamilton Street, but the school soon moved to "Warrendale," the former residence of Mrs. Johnson's family on the edge of

Georgetown where there was room for drill fields and parade grounds.[16]

"Colonel" Thornton Johnson headed the faculty as superintendent. Commandant of cadets was Lieutenant Colonel William Penn Hopkins, born in Connecticut, 1825 graduate of West Point, who also was professor of natural science and instructor of tactics. "Major" William A. Forbes, Virginia Military Institute graduate, credited in the 1847 W.M.I. catalogue with an M.A. degree, was professor of mathematics and civil engineering. Professor of ancient and modern languages was J. J. Wyche, graduate of the University of North Carolina. R. H. Forrester, "a member of the Pittsburgh bar," headed the law department and taught moral science and political economy. In the preparatory department for boys of eight and up, J. R. Swift, Yale Master of Arts, was principal and "Captain" W. W. Gaunt, former city school teacher in Lexington, was assistant.[17]

Listed as tutor was James Gillespie Blaine, Bachelor of Arts, credited in the catalogue with having "graduated first in his class of thirty-three" at Washington College in Pennsylvania in June 1847. Leisurely looking for something to do while visiting at the home of J. N. McKee in Lexington, Blaine learned of a vacancy at Western Military Institute, applied and was accepted. He moved to Georgetown in December, though he was not to begin his duties until January 1848.[18]

Blaine taught algebra, geometry, Virgil, Caesar, and Greek, reviewing continually to keep ahead of his students. Homesick at first, he was reconciled to Georgetown after noting the beauty and charm adorning the female seminary. On its faculty were the three Stanwood sisters from Maine: Harriett, Sarah and Caroline. Blaine's "secret marriage" to Harriett in 1850 after both schools moved from Georgetown, caused some tongue-wagging[19] and echoed in the campaign mudslinging in 1884 when he was the Republican presidential candidate against Grover Cleveland.

Bushrod Johnson, related neither by blood nor marriage to Thornton, joined the school shortly after Blaine, but his name was not included in the 1847–1848 catalogue already printed. How he made the connection is indefinite. He may have read one of the school's advertisements inserted in Northern newspapers by Thornton Johnson in 1847 and applied for a teaching job. Early in 1848 Blaine's letters mention three unnamed "West Point graduates" on the faculty, *i.e.* Thornton Johnson, Hopkins, and Bushrod, who was designated professor of natural philosophy and chemistry with the school rank of major.[20]

Cadets during the first full year totaled 136 from Kentucky, Mississippi, Missouri, Virginia, Arkansas, Louisiana, and Texas, with two from Illinois and one from Iowa. They paid a total of $214, covering $40 tuition; uniforms $54; boarding, fuel, lights and washing for forty-four weeks, $105; books, stationery and incidentals, $15. The school was chartered by Kentucky to grant a bachelor's degree, and a master's degree after two additional years of study. Scott's "Infantry Tactics" was the military text.[21] There was a cadet drum corps which played a crashing accompaniment to parades down Georgetown's Main Street.[22]

Bushrod's compensation was not more than $400 a year plus board and lodging. This was much less than the $1082 yearly pay he received as a first lieutenant. He shared quarters with another teacher and ate at the cadet mess. Schooled in social graces by his army service in St. Louis and Louisiana, "Major" Johnson fitted in well with the upper class element in the Blue Grass. Blaine, thirteen years younger, took a naïve delight in being "perfectly surrounded by great men"—"Old Dick" Johnson only thirteen miles away at Blue Spring; Henry Clay, Robert Wickliffe and General Leslie Combs in Lexington and in Frankfort, John J. Crittenden and Governor Robert L. Letcher.[23]

Bushrod Johnson soon became friendly with the family of Daniel G. Hatch, onetime Virginia schoolmaster, for the past decade a merchant in Georgetown. Of special interest to the new "major" was Hatch's daughter Mary. Born in New Hampshire, Hatch, claiming a master's degree, became principal at nineteen of Wingfield Academy in Petersburg, Virginia. For nearly twenty years he operated it as a boarding school, teaching "all branches of science and literature with success," according to its advertising.[24]

Hatch reached Georgetown about 1837 with his son William, thirteen, an eleven-year old daughter Mary and a son, A. E., aged five. They were the children of his first wife whose place and date of death are not revealed. Three more children were born to him and his second wife, Mary R., in Georgetown between 1842 and 1846. The second wife, fifteen years younger than Daniel, also was born in New Hampshire.[25] Hatch owned five slaves. He also held mortgages on two slave women belonging to his brother William in 1837. He borrowed $2300 from Richard Mentor Johnson in 1838, paid $2300 for a house and lot in 1840 and in 1842 took a $1247 mortgage on Thornton Johnson's residence, furnishings, "chemical and philosophical apparatus, books, globes, maps, 16 beds, four Franklin stoves," etc.,[26] apparently the equipment of the Female Seminary.

Western Military Institute's first commencement was staged July 4, 1848 with parades, speeches and fanfare.[27] Cadets scattered to their homes. The first gala event after classes were resumed in September was the observance of the thirty-fifth anniversary of the Battle of the Thames on October 5. Faculty and students turned out to honor "Old Dick" Johnson, the storied slayer of the Shawnee chief Tecumseh. The aging hero appeared in plain, civilian attire. Blaine thought the sight was "imposing, but ludicrous."[28]

Attacks of measles, malaria and influenza among staff and students delayed class work. One cadet died of "inflammation of the brain" in December. Though more students enrolled in the school's second year, all was not well. By spring of 1849 depressed Blaine was ready to quit although he was now "captain" and school judge-advocate. He considered reading law in Lexington and trying to get a government job.[29]

Hopkins left in January 1849 to join Masonic University in Tennessee.[30] Bushrod Johnson was promoted to commandant of cadets and "lieutenant colonel." Thornton Johnson changed his own title to president. To be superintendent and "colonel" he brought in Edwin W. Morgan, Pennsylvanian, 1837 West Point graduate. Morgan had been a first year man when Bushrod was a plebe. He left the Army in 1839 but returned as a major of the Eleventh U.S. Infantry, a one-year unit, and fought from Vera Cruz to Mexico City with Scott. He was made professor of civil and military engineering at W.M.I. He and his wife, Mary, had no children.[31]

An outbreak of typhoid, scarlet fever and malaria scourged the school in the 1849 spring. Several cadets died. Bushrod Johnson had the melancholy task of arranging their funerals with full military honors. The Order Book designated June 1849 as a "critical period of pestilence."[32]

Thornton Johnson advertised the school extensively in newspapers North and South in the 1849 summer, stressing West Point backgrounds of himself, Morgan, and Bushrod, and Forbes's V.M.I. degree. Blaine was called "adjunct professor of ancient and modern languages." Six other faculty members were listed.

After Western Military Institute began its third full year in September 1849 it added a new and somewhat notable teacher. He was Richard Owen, youngest son of the famous British Utopian Socialist, Robert Owen, who had financed the brief communal experiment in the 1820s at New Harmony, Posey County, Indiana, and had brought to America the "boatload of knowledge" made up of European scientists and educators.

Richard Owen, born in Scotland in 1810 and educated there and in the Emmanuel Fellenberg School in Hofwyl, Switzerland, was older (39) than either Bushrod or Morgan. As a youth at school he learned to admire the liberal educational philosophy of Johann Heinrich Pestalozzi and almost from his birth he had imbibed an equalitarian philosophy that decried caste and class and held slavery to be an unjust and degrading insult to humanity.[33] Now for the first time he was entering an environment based economically upon a social institution he deplored and working in a school whose methods ran counter to his theories of education.

After coming to the United States at the age of seventeen, Owen had tried teaching, brewing in Cincinnati and milling and farming in Pennsylvania and Indiana. He served as a captain in charge of supply in the Sixteenth U.S. Infantry for seventeen months with Taylor in Northern Mexico. The commission had been obtained for him by his brother, Robert Dale Owen, Democrat member of the 28th and 29th U.S. Congress (1843–1847). By the summer of 1849, Richard had finished more than a year's work on a geological survey of the northern shore of Lake Superior with another brother, David Dale Owen. His second wife was Anna Eliza Neef, daughter of Professor Joseph Neef, coadjutor of Pestalozzi, and their two sons were Eugene Fellenberg, nine years old, and Horace Pestalozzi, seven. Mrs. Owen's sister, Caroline, was the wife of David Dale Owen.[34]

Owen was footloose at the end of his geological stint with his brother. Always eager for self-improvement, he reasoned that if he learned civil engineering he might have an active part in some of Indiana's expanding public works. He wrote to Western Military Institute in September 1849 offering to trade his teaching in natural science for instruction in civil engineering. Superintendent Morgan offered him an "adjunct" professorship without salary, but with free board and lodging for himself and his family. Owen accepted. Morgan then wrote that if he would perform "field duty," or drill the cadet battalion, he would be ranked as "major" on the faculty. Owen wanted as much time for his engineering studies as could be spared from school duties, but he reluctantly agreed.

When he reported to Georgetown in October, Owen was amazed to find in the printed catalog that he was listed as a full professor of natural sciences and that he was slated to teach French, German and Spanish, to conduct two classes in chemistry, to give a public lecture on physiology every Friday as well as perform the military chores of roll calls and parades. In return for extra fees he later would teach dancing, fencing and drawing.[35] He never found time for any significant study of civil engineering. For most of the next decade Owen and Bushrod Johnson were to be closely associated in the fluctuating fortunes of the school and in real estate dealings later in Nashville.

Meanwhile chronic financial troubles were haunting Thornton Johnson's female school. A competing institution, the Georgetown Female Seminary, had started in 1846 in a downtown hotel building with more resources than debt-ridden Johnson and he was feeling the pinch.[36] During the fall session of 1849, Thornton Johnson decided to move both of his schools away from Georgetown.

He contracted with Thomas and L. P. Holliday, owners of the resort hotel and cottages in Lower Blue Lick Springs, Kentucky, forty miles northeast of Georgetown, to house and feed his cadets for $2.50 a week after the

Christmas recess. The buildings normally were occupied by health seekers from North and South who came to drink and bathe in the pungent waters credited with fantastic therapeutic properties. Johnson hoped that the students might profit from the waters, esteemed as "diuretic and stimulating to the nervous system"[37] and he hoped the new site at a fashionable resort would be an advertising factor in his favor in competing with Kentucky Military Institute, at Franklin Springs, a less well-known spa.

At the same time, Johnson moved his girls' school to Millersburg, twelve miles south of Blue Lick, and combined it with struggling Millersburg Female Seminary.[38] Blaine rejoiced to know that the Stanwood sisters went to the new location. He was courting Harriett.

The moves were made during the Christmas holidays. Bushrod Johnson and Owen arranged for the reception and billeting of the cadets, a total of 129 of whom reported by January 14, 1850 at Blue Lick. Families of the married teachers, Owen, Morgan, and Gaunt, found quarters in the resort cottages near the hotel building used by the school. The bachelors, including Bushrod, Blaine and two others were housed with the boys.[39] Blaine, now "Major," managed to find a room later at "Forest Retreat," home of Thomas Metcalfe, former Kentucky governor and U.S. Senator, six miles south of Blue Lick and closer to Harriett Stanwood in Millersburg.[40]

The shaky financial condition of the school was forcibly revealed during the removal. Creditors of T. F. Johnson closed in on his property in Georgetown. One of them, Andrew Sheffler, seized the scientific equipment belonging to Owen and used by him in his classes. Owen was compelled to sue in court for its recovery and finally got a judgement for $432.25 which took two years to collect.[41]

Relocation of the school at the health resort brought a new spate of troubles. The constant flow of visitors taking the waters disturbed discipline. Likewise the presence of more than a hundred lively, prank-playing youngsters contributed little to the euphoria of staid and dignified health seekers. The school's order book records numerous cases of neglect of duty, misbehaviour, unauthorized swimming in the Licking River which caused illness and two instances of cadet drunkenness and possession of whiskey, punished by two months' confinement to quarters.

Near the close of the term on June 30, 1850 the little community of the faculty was set agog by what Blaine's biographers call his "secret" marriage to Harriett. All agree on the date, but not the circumstances nor consequences. The following March 1851, facing parenthood in three months and doubting the legality of previous rites, they were married again in Pittsburgh. The female seminary closed for good in March 1851 and Harriett's teaching career ended with it.[42]

Factional strife between the faculty and Colonel Morgan added to the general confusion during the 1850 fall term. Morgan was not on speaking terms with most of the teachers. Feelings between him and Bushrod Johnson were so tense that Johnson requested and was granted release from all military duties on September 21, 1850[43] to lessen his contacts with Morgan. Matters reached a crisis in November when the faculty summoned Morgan to answer to charges of intemperance, inefficiency and conduct subversive to discipline. Morgan did not appear. Owen, now on the payroll at $400 a year, testified against him. The faculty voted to expel the superintendent from the school. He remained at Blue Lick for several months to harass the faculty and proselyte several cadets to join Kentucky Military Institute whose staff he joined in 1854. He continued to carry on a campaign of defamation of T. F. Johnson and his academy.[44]

With the ouster of Morgan, Lieutenant Colonel Bushrod Johnson became acting superintendent with Major

Owen as his chief assistant. In this capacity Owen was sent to Drennon Springs [Lick] in Henry County, another health resort, thirty miles from Frankfort on the Kentucky River about midway between Louisville and Cincinnati, to negotiate with A. O. Smith, the owner, to feed and house the school the following January.

The departure from Blue Lick Springs on Saturday, January 25, 1851 precipitated a wild fight between the faculty and the Holliday brothers and their partisans, who charged breach of contract and tried by force to retain the school. Blaine's biographers credit him with a stellar role in the melee, "employing only his well developed muscles" against guns and knives.[45] The *Covington Journal* on January 30, under the caption "Battle at the Blue Licks" said T. F. Johnson and L. P. Holliday had an angry discussion during which Johnson hit Holliday several times on the head with a pistol. Thomas Holliday joined his brother while Bushrod Johnson and Blaine, (spelled "Blain" in the account), plus the school's drummer, reinforced T. F. Johnson. "Revolvers were freely used," the newspaper said and T. F. Johnson was shot "in the seat of honor! The blood run [*sic*] and so did the Colonel!" The *Journal* reported Blaine and the wounded Johnson fled in a buggy, were overtaken but were permitted to go only after they "begged for their lives." Bushrod Johnson, added the paper, "was last seen making his way into the bushes!" Legal aftermaths of the incident continued for several years. Owen at Drennon Springs missed it all.

Conditions improved a little at Drennon Springs where classes were resumed February 9, 1851 with less than half of the expected 300 boys. T. F. Johnson, having lost his home in Georgetown to his creditors, moved in with the cadets at the resort, but Bushrod Johnson, Owen and the faculty virtually operated the school. Blaine and his wife left at the end of the term in June for a position in a Pittsburgh school for the deaf. His resignation was accepted in

MAJOR GENERAL BUSHROD RUST JOHNSON

Soon after his promotion to major general in May 1864, Johnson had this visiting card portrait made in Richmond. Luxuriant sideburns had replaced the moustache of his brigadier days. (Original in The Confederate Museum, Richmond, Va.)

BRIGADIER GENERAL BUSHROD JOHNSON

Buttons spaced by two on his uniform indicate that this picture of Johnson was made while he was a brigadier general (1862–1864). Cleanshaven while he was an educator, he marked his return to soldiering with a corsair moustache. (Original in Library of Congress)

JOHNSON'S LAST ARMY PORTRAIT

His face showing the ravages of winter in the trenches, this likeness of Johnson probably was made in early 1865. He had restored his moustache. (Original in The Confederate Museum, Richmond, Va.)

TRIBUTE FROM HIS TROOPS

Survivors of the men he led in battle commissioned this portrait by Cornelius Hankins in 1906, years after Johnson's death. It hangs in the Confederate Room of Tennessee's War Memorial in Nashville. (Courtesy Col. W. M. Slayden II, Deputy Director of Conservation, Tennessee)

Vera Cruz Mexico
July 12th 1847

Dr Sir

I venture to inform you of a fact which you may if you think proper turn to your advantage.

If you think proper to Ship me 500 Barrels of Flour, 2 or 3 hundred boxes of Pale Soap (28 & 24 lbs boxes) and about 100 Boxes of Candles Sperm — You can have from me a net proffit of between 1200 & 1500 dollars.

Many of U.S. Ships & Steamers run down here lightly loaded and it would be doing no injustice to U.S. to Ship these articles in Small quantities aboard of them.

If my proposition seems improper or impracticable you will please pardon the liberty I have taken in suggesting it to you. In writing this I repose a certain degree of confidence which your discretion will of course not permit to be injurious. Will you let me hear soon from you. Yours &c.

B R Johnson

To Maj W Seawell

[illegible] you will understand the Stores would have to be Shipped [illegible]

THE LETTER THAT WRECKED A CAREER

7

There are doubtless many other circumstances bearing directly or indirectly on this matter: and many collateral facts might be given in conversation that are not addapted to a written communication; but I must submit the prominent points that I have here hastily seized without order or combination.

I am fully sensible of all the consequences that attach themselves to the letter under consideration: My public and private relations make me feel them as deeply as any other man could do; but I seek no sympathy in the matter and shall at least retain a pride in meeting all the consequences of every act of my life.

The duty I owe to my profession and to my country, as well as my more private duties, prevent me from seeking to abandon a profession in which it has been my pride to serve, at the very moment the country requires new acquisitions to it, and I therefore hope it may not be necessary for me to be cut off from it: but if the foregoing is no deemed sufficient to secure me from further action in the matter I must beg that I be permitted to resign my commission in the army. My previous services and the fact that I have done no injury save to myself will surely entitle me to this privalidge.

I have the honor to be, Sir,

Your most obt. Servt.

B. R. Johnson

1st Lt 3d Infy

PLEA TO A PRESIDENT

Comparison of this letter to President Polk with the "proffit" offer to Seawell suggests that Johnson dictated it to a clerk whose handwriting was more legible than his.

WESTERN MILITARY INSTITUTE, DRENNON SPRINGS, KENTUCKY 1851–1854

Cadet John Bennett Elliott marked his room in the building at right in a letter to his mother in New Harmony, Indiana, September 24, 1853. Though the school functioned in the relaxed atmosphere of A. O. Smith's health resort, Bennett said the dawn-to-dusk routine was "no child's play." (Original letterhead in Elliott Family Papers)

DR. NATHAN AND SARAH HOGE JOHNSON
Twenty-one years older than his youngest brother Bushrod, Dr. Nathan and his wife were his "second parents." Although ardent abolitionists, they sheltered Bushrod's handicapped son, Charles, for seven years while his father fought for slavery. (Courtesy of Meredith Johnson)

DR. LEMUEL RIDDICK JOHNSON

Active in Wayne County Indiana Republican politics, Dr. Lemuel, nephew of Bushrod, risked local repercussions by being guardian for Bushrod's son Charles, who was told his father was fighting for the Union. (Courtesy of Meredith Johnson)

RICHARD OWEN 1810–1890

Scion of a famous family, Owen was associated with Bushrod Johnson for nine years (1849–1858) in Western Military Academy. Divergent ideas of education separated them. Owen later was a Union colonel, first president of Purdue University (1872–1874), and professor of geology in Indiana University (1864–1872; 1874–1879). (Original in Owen Papers)

WESTERN MILITARY INSTITUTE, NASHVILLE, TENNESSEE 1855–1861 1870–1874

The stone building at the right, without the tower, still is in use as Nashville's Children's Museum. Part of the red brick President's House at left, home of Johnson, Owen, and Kirby Smith while on the faculty, was still standing in 1968. (Original in Owen Papers) a faculty resolution written by Owen appreciating the future statesman's "talents and worth" and hoping "his success may be brilliant and his life happy."[46] Nine cadets were graduated on June 28, 1851 with a military ball supervised by Owen, speeches by visiting dignitaries and a bounteous supper.

The Kentucky State Board of Visitors attended and sent a flattering report to Governor John W. Helm. Signed by John M. Harlan, state adjutant general as chairman, John T. Pratt, Humphrey Marshall, William O. Butler and Thomas G. Monroe, the inspectors said the curriculum was "broad and solid," the fare "liberal," accommodations "excellent and comfortable," examinations "competent and satisfactory," the location "salubrious and of incalculable benefit to the health of the cadets" and the faculty composed of "competent gentlemen." Arms and accoutrements belonging to the state were found "in best order." The total corps, they reported, including 45 preparatory students, numbered 216.[47]

In July of 1851, T. F. Johnson, responding to "unprincipled assaults on my character and credit" issued a printed statement to parents and prospects announcing that he had "resigned the whole financial business of the institution" to A. O. Smith, who had by now contracted to supply uniforms to the cadets as well as food and lodging. To Smith, Johnson said, patrons should send pocket money for deposit and issue to the students adding that "Smith will furnish everything needed by the cadets at Louisville retail prices."[48]

Blaine never again touched the life of Bushrod Johnson after he and Harriett left, though he later had contacts with Owen. Reflecting local estimates of Western Military Institute was the comment of Blaine's friend, J. N. McKee of Lexington, in a letter to him five months after his departure:

> You were wise in leaving that institution; it required all

> the energy of such a man as Col. Thornton Johnson to sustain it . . . . the formidable opposition it will have to contend with . . . will be more than the present faculty can uphold. I think you are right not to be buried in its ruins.[49]

McKee's gloomy foreboding followed a few weeks after death came to harassed and ailing Thornton Fitzhugh Johnson at Drennon Springs on October 4, 1851. He was buried from the Christian church in Georgetown and invitations to attend the funeral went to Blue Grass notables.[50] Students voted eloquent resolutions of condolence and wore mourning badges on their uniform for thirty days. The Addisonian Literary Society took the lead in raising funds to erect a gravestone. Owen drafted the faculty eulogies. Notices were sent to newspapers which had carried the school's advertising.[51]

In the uncertainty regarding the school's future after the founder's death, Owen seriously considered quitting and trying for a teaching post at Indiana University. His salary and probably Johnson's were $200 or $300 in arrears, he had lost his scientific apparatus to Sheffler, and he was upset because the name of a new faculty member was listed ahead of his. But he told the faculty that he endorsed Bushrod Johnson to be head of the school "according to the regular order of things."[52]

The faculty agreed. Johnson was named superintendent pro tempore on October 8. Owen was promoted to Lieutenant Colonel and commandant of cadets on October 19 after he had decided to remain.[53] Immediately he was swamped with administrative details: corresponding with tailors making uniforms, hunting bigger stoves for cadet barracks, replenishing the supply of chalk, rewriting regulations on duties of cadet officers and sergeants, supervising and contributing articles to *The Cadet,* the student-edited monthly, caring for ailing youngsters, seeking prospective students, trying to collect delinquent fees, and making personal loans to Johnson.[54]

About this time Johnson and Owen had a clash over a minor matter of method which betokened other variances to come between them over their diverse educational theories: rigid conformity and precision *versus* permissive understanding. Johnson had issued an order putting the resort's kitchen "off limits" to cadets, who occasionally liked to indulge themselves by cooking a turkey and serving the feast to an invited few. Two such permits had been granted. A boy named Straus came to Owen's room asking his signature on a written leave to "eat a turkey." Owen signed it without asking how it was to be cooked. His son, Horace, was invited to partake. Johnson came in. He questioned Owen about Straus's request, reminding Owen of the ban on the kitchen. Then he went out and told the boys there would be no turkey party. Owen was incensed. He demanded a faculty meeting to pass on whether the acting superintendent had authority from the faculty to countermand a permission order given by another officer "thus upsetting the whole system of discipline." No record survives on the faculty's action, if any, but the cadets probably went turkey-less.[55]

In a reorganization after the Christmas recess, early in 1852, Johnson was confirmed as colonel, president, superintendent, professor of mathematics and engineering and co-owner of the school with Owen who became professor of natural sciences, French, German, Spanish, drawing and fencing as well as commandant of cadets.[56] Prospects brightened as enrollment held up. The partners were encouraged.

Both felt discipline improved at Drennon Springs, but they had to deal continually with pranks and more serious misdemeanors. In Owen's talks at cadet assemblies he pleaded for temperance, for "general good conduct and regularity," for older cadets to lead and admonish the less mature mischief makers. He advised new students to strive for "good, physical, mental and moral education." He threatened to expose the names of boys who had plagiarized newspaper articles and palmed them off as themes and he chided those who disrupted study hours by rolling bowling balls which reverberated along the hotel galleries.[57]

In the spring of 1852 Bushrod Johnson felt enough confidence in his future to risk matrimony. Mary E. Hatch rode up from Georgetown with her brother William and she was married to Johnson in Drennon Springs by a local magistrate on April 12, 1852, with Hatch as witness. On the Henry County marriage certificate she gave her age as 24, the same figure listed by the 1850 Census taker two years previously. She said she was born in Dinwiddie County, Virginia. Johnson gave his age as 34, his residence as Drennon's Lick, and his birthplace as Belmont County, Ohio.[58] Owen announced a special holiday for the cadets to mark the event, but forbade any "rabble gatherings usually termed charivari." He told them "even to avoid a round of applause or any shouting," when the couple returned to begin housekeeping in one of the resort's cottages.[59]

There were ten graduates in June 1852, the largest class since the school began. The *Louisville Daily Times,* June 21, 1852 devoted more than a column to a special correspondent's account of the day. Present were Governor Lazarus Whitehead Powell of Kentucky, Generals William O. Butler, John T. Pratt and John M. Harlan, Colonel Ben Selby and others. They came by steamboat from Frankfort and Louisville. One coach upset "as the gay party approached the scene of the festivities," and two ladies and a gentleman were hurt. Johnson's baccalaureate address "was characterized by clearness and force" paying tribute to the memory of the school's "deceased and distinguished" founder. At night the barracks and grounds "were brilliantly illuminated," dancing continued until 12:30 A.M. when a "magnificent and sumptuous" supper was "partaken by 500 or 600 persons," and "champagne corks popped" afterward.[60] Owen stage-managed the affair. During his years with the school he appears to have directed the rather frequent balls and dancing parties, aided by student boards of managers. Preparatory to some of these fêtes he gave extra dancing lessons to Mrs. Johnson and other faculty wives.[61]

The school year 1852–1853 began auspiciously with 230 boys. Health and disciplinary problems were no more serious than usual. The co-owners could hope their enterprise was moving into a period of prosperity. But on April 20, 1853 the sheriff called regarding the claim of the Holliday brothers for $1500. He was ready to levy an execution unless a return was made by May 9. Johnson and Owen hastily consulted an adviser in Louisville, Owen went to Paris, seat of Bourbon County, to see a lawyer and they sold "some additional things" to A. O. Smith to raise $500. Apparently some settlement with the Hollidays was reached, because Owen spent two days subsequently at the state arsenal in Frankfort to arrange for 85 small percussion muskets to be loaned by Kentucky for cadet use.[62] He wrote enthusiastically about the school in May to his father, Robert Owen, in Scotland, telling him there were sixteen graduates, a record number, and that Brigadier General Thomas L. Jesup, Quartermaster General of the United States Army, had visited the place, told him he knew his father and "was pleased at what he saw" at Western Military Institute.[63]

Right after commencement Johnson sent Owen on an extensive trip to the East to contract for books and equipment, to visit other schools and sources of information and to recruit students. Owen reported by letter to Johnson while on his way back to New Harmony by Ohio river steamboat. He said he "bought on sixty days time" in Boston, paid cash with his own money in New York and Philadelphia, decided against purchasing a theodolite and transit. He said he called at Yale, Harvard, West Point, the Academy of Science and the Patent Office in Washington. He had garnered one cadet and promises of two others. He regretted hearing of the deaths of four boys and hoped Drennon Springs "is now healthy."[64]

A description of Johnson, known to the cadets as "Old Bush" has come from the memories of two students in the school in 1852. Writing in 1906, when a portrait of Johnson was presented for display at George Peabody College of Teachers in Nashville,[65] R. M. Tunno, Savannah, Georgia, told the *Confederate Veteran*:

> As a student at Western Military Institute at Blue Lick Springs and Drennon Springs, Ky., I knew General (then Colonel) Johnson. . . Gen. Johnson was dignified yet his heart was filled with fatherly kindness to his "boys" as he called us. He was . . . strict, but easily approachable by us, sympathetic and eminently just. I never heard a cadet complain of harshness or injustice at his hands, and when we left the institution to take our places as men, we felt we had left behind us a true friend and one who had our highest respect.[66]

On the same occasion, Colonel R. Bogardus Snowden, a New York-born cadet from Nashville at Drennon Springs who later served as Johnson's adjutant in the Confederate Army, also testified to the respect and affection the boys had for "Old Bush."[67] Even allowing for the fact that a golden glow hazes the past in the mind of the aged, these tributes, 55 years after their association with Johnson, reflect his influence as a mentor of youth.

The usual friction between the school and its landlord flared in the fall of 1853. The partners were dissatisfied with the performance of A. O. Smith's employes in the resort buildings used by the faculty and cadets. Smith, in turn, argued that the $2.50 weekly per person paid to him was inadequate. Owen complained that the servant's attendance "falls short," beds were not made nor rooms cleaned until late afternoon, fires were not lighted in sleeping or recitation rooms, shoes were not blacked, washing was not done, the coffee was bad and meat was too scant.[68] Cadet John Bennett Elliott, son of an Owen neighbor in New Harmony, wrote to his mother that all the servants were Irish immigrants who brought clean towels only every other day.[69]

Disaster struck soon after the 1853–1854 term began in September. One rash of illness followed another; infirmary and medical facilities were overtaxed. Some cadets clamored to leave for their homes lest they, too, join the ailing. Two faculty members decided in November to permit those boys to depart who wanted to go, after two cadets died. Classes were suspended. Two more boys succumbed in December. The full burden of handling the crisis fell upon Owen because Johnson had taken his wife to Covington to her family pending childbirth, and he was away from the school in November and December.[70] The co-owners finally decided by correspondence to send all the cadets home and close the Institute.

It appeared that McKee's doleful prophecy had come to pass and that Johnson and Owen were about to be "buried in the ruins."

ii. Sumter's Guns Dismiss Classes

Their school wrecked in the midst of a Kentucky winter, owners Johnson and Owen refused to quit. Johnson had an added incentive to make another try when Mary gave birth to a son about the time classes were suspended. He was named Charles Corling Johnson and was to be their only child. Tragically he was sickly and mentally retarded. Troubles seldom came singly to Bushrod Johnson.

The partners began casting about for a new location for

the Institute, if and when classes could be resumed. On December 5, Owen wrote his brother David about New Harmony, Indiana as a site and later asked about renting David's house there, keeping Johnson informed by letter. He collected and packed boxes of guns for return to the state arsenal in Frankfort. Then he was stricken and spent ten days in bed.[71] By January 10, 1854 he recovered enough to write an article on the concept of the military school which he sent to W. Jackson, Nashville, Tennessee. He explained in these terms:

> The military system is effective in developing physical energies, inducing habits of order and obedience and in placing the student under supervision of those who represent his parents and guardians, but the cadet must be convinced of the necessity and propriety of these rules and that they are administered impartially and kindly for his benefit . . .
>
> Physical, moral and intellectual faculties are equally cultivated.[72]

This literary effort, in a sense, was propaganda and advertising, because Johnson and Owen had agreed to try to transfer Western Military Institute to Tennessee. Owen spent the rest of January in Jeffersonville, Indiana at the home of his wife's sister, Caroline, who was Mrs. David Dale Owen. He and Johnson continued to exchange views by mail. Early in February Owen went on a missionary trip to the Tennessee capital. Here he called on leading citizens including Andrew Ewing, Samuel D. Morgan and Dr. D. T. Scott who were trustees of the University of Nashville. He discussed money matters with them, as well as a possible location at Tyree Springs, a health resort in Sumner County a dozen miles north of Nashville, and a Tennessee charter to replace the one from Kentucky which the school would relinquish. By February 4 he met such encouragement that he telegraphed Johnson to join him and wrote him a long letter on the success of his interviews. The next day, on Sunday, he went to Tyree Springs and found its owner, William Roberts, "disposed to board us at $3 per week if we furnish our own lights."[73]

He returned to Nashville, spent a day in the state House of Representatives completing arrangements for the Tennessee charter and devoted another day to a close inspection of the geological collection of Gerald P. Troost, the Dutch savant who had taught Owen geology in New Harmony in the 1820s and who had been state geologist of Tennessee until his death in 1850. With Owen was Dr. John Barrien Lindsley, chancellor of the University of Nashville, who soon would be considering the possibility of joining the Johnson-Owen institute to the University. Johnson arrived the same day, February 8, 1854, and they spent a week together completing details.[74]

To Owen fell the task of composing, printing and mailing 1000 circulars to parents and prospects, announcing the relocation of the school at Tyree Springs and soliciting patronage. Part of this chore he did in New Harmony in mid-February; he then went by steamboat with his family from Mount Vernon, Indiana to Nashville. The trip took from 2 P.M. Thursday to 9 A.M. Saturday. He hired a buggy and brought his wife and sons to Tyree by 8 P.M. February 25 for their first supper in their new home.[75] Some of the cadets already had arrived, including young Elliott, who thought the new location better than Drennon Springs.[76] As classes began in makeshift quarters and in the hotel ballroom, Owen hired bricklayers and carpenters to make repairs and adjustments. He also gave Johnson a $2000 loan to meet mounting bills. He began drilling the boys on March 13 and ten days later had things well enough in hand that he could give dancing lessons to "Miss R and Mrs. Johnson,"[77] now fully recovered from her childbirth.

Unseasonable snow and cold in late April halted drills and caused illness. Cadet Elliott, perturbed because his expenses had reached $300, caught a cold and probably a touch of typhoid at a dance in May, was cared for by the Owens in their quarters and came home several weeks before the term ended in June.[78] There were three graduates of a total of 138 cadets.

Their sad experiences with the transient character of the Institute convinced the co-owners that a permanent location was an essential for survival, as the first full term in Tyree Springs began in September 1854. A military academy and a health resort simply could not coexist on the same premises. Roberts had been reluctant to make a new contract for boarding the cadets, especially after the members of the Seventh Mess, as each table of a dozen boys was designated, became enraged one evening at dinner and turned everything on the table upside down: plates, food, butter, sugar bowls, etc., and another lad threw all the spoons out of the window at another time.[79] Owen had to placate and mollify the landlord and chide and punish the offenders.[80] It was manifest that Western Military Institute could not abide long at Tyree Springs.

Happily, an opportunity for a change came in the spring of 1855. Chancellor Lindsley of the University of Nashville was anxious to rehabilitate its sagging "literary" or collegiate department; all of its professors recently had quit. He told his trustees that a military school was the solution because its discipline and regulation were best suited for dealing with southern students, who "are, as a matter of fact, boys and not young men as in colleges north" and because of the "strictness of its government, the cheapness, comfort and healthfulness of its system of living and the thoroughness and efficiency of its institutions."[81] Lindsley knew Johnson and Owen were looking for a permanent location, for he had started discussing the chances of a merger with them as early as February.

The university had existed since 1826, but its antecedents went back to 1795 and from these it had inherited considerable real estate in land grants and city lots. In

1853, aided by an $18,000 subscription campaign among Nashville citizens, it had erected a substantial two-story stone building as its central hall, named John Berrien Lindsley Hall, but its curriculum consisted of little more than a medical school which Lindsley had headed prior to 1855.[82] Its seventeen-acre campus called "University Place" was on South Second Street in the Seventh Ward about a mile from the public square.[83]

Johnson and Owen reached an agreement with the trustees April 4. Western Military Institute would retain its name and would become the "collegiate" department of the University of Nashville which gave it the free use of the ground and buildings and little else. Johnson and Owen were elected to university professorships, but without salary. Instead they would split the fees of their students on the basis of $1750 apiece for each 100 cadets and not less than $2500 for each 200. There would be four professors for each hundred students, to be named by Johnson and Owen. Johnson and Owen also would divide ten percent of the profits from the stores and shop services which sold uniforms, textbooks, stationery and incidentals. The university would not be responsible for an old debt of $16,000 of the Institute.[84]

Cadet fees were set at $160 a year for tuition, board, lodging, washing, fuel, lights, services, field music and furniture. Extras included: surgical fee, $10; graduation fee, $5. The West Point style uniform was a flashy brass buttoned blue frock coat and red striped trousers. Daily routine began at dawn with reveille and ended with taps at 10 P.M. Each boy was graded daily in each subject, examinations were oral, and monthly reports went to parents.[85]

Colonel Bushrod Johnson was superintendent and professor of civil engineering. Lieutenant Colonel Richard Owen became secretary and treasurer of the collegiate department, professor of geology and commandant of cadets.

He continued to instruct in drawing and fencing; part of his modern language chores went to another teacher.[86] Each moved his family into the President's House, a brick building originally erected to shelter only one family, but ultimately crowded with five faculty households. Irish immigrants were hired to attend them and the students. Only one professor, Major James H. Hamilton, Kentucky-born mathematics teacher and adjutant, owned a slave, an eighteen-year old house servant; the school surgeon, Dr. C. K. Winston, who taught in the medical school and also was a university trustee, owned five.[87]

The Northern antislavery backgrounds of the two educators seem to have been no barrier to an initial rapport with the trustees of the university who were members of leading Tennessee families; they were: Andrew Ewing, president, Aaron V. Brown, Return Jonathan Meigs, Samuel D. Morgan, John M. Lea and James Woods, all of Nashville; Andrew Jackson [junior] and Dr. D. T. Scott of Hermitage; General William G. Harding of Belle Meade; Colonel Joseph C. Guild, Gallatin; Gideon J. Pillow, Columbia; Lewis P. Williamson, Somerville; John H. Crozier, Knoxville and Edward S. Cheatham, Springfield. Most of these were owners of varying numbers of slaves, up to 156 for Harding.[88] Sons of some of the trustees were students.

When these trustees were asked by Johnson and Owen for an advance of $40,000 to build the barracks and mess hall for which W.M.I. was obligated to pay under the merger terms, the board gave them $30,000 for a starter and work was soon under way.

The first session of the merged school opened Monday, September 10, 1855 with around 200 students including Owen's sons, Eugene and Horace.[89] Ten were graduated in June 1856. Despite the usual illnesses and the inconvenience of unfinished buildings, the first year of union was hailed enthusiastically by Chancellor Lindsley. He told the trustees in April:

> The gentlemen who were formerly proprietors of Western Military Institute . . . have laid hold of the enterprise here with a thoroughgoing zeal and disposition to carry out the plan of the board . . . . The Collegiate Department has opened with success as encouraging as its best friends could wish.

He said the school had faced "doubt and suspicion on the part of many of our citizens" but it was affording a "sound classical and literary training as well as mathematical in which the military feature is merely the means of promoting health, exercise and good government."[90]

For Johnson and Owen the initial year in Nashville had been financially successful. True, they had received no salaries as professors and had spent their own money on furniture and fixtures; but their shares in the student fees and the profits of the stores and shop services had been substantial. On March 17, 1856, their partnership called "Johnson-Owen" paid $5000 cash and gave notes for $5000 more for an undivided tenth interest, five acres, in the town of McGavock, a real estate development in Nashville's northwest suburbs promoted by Moses Wetmore and Dr. David McGavock, member of a family prominent in society, business and politics. They later divided the land into eighteen town lots, each retaining nine.[91]

Owen busied himself in two other directions. In addition to his duties at the school, he attended classes in the university's medical college which adjoined W.M.I. in University Place. Applying himself diligently, he was able to pass the required examinations in 1857 to obtain a medical degree at the age of 47. He could add M.D. after his name in the 1857–1858 catalog which listed him as a lieutenant colonel, commandant of cadets, professor of geology and chemistry and secretary-treasurer of the collegiate department.[92] At the same time he completed writing and had published his *Key to the Geology of the Globe,* which attracted wide attention in the scientific world including that of Alexander von Humboldt, the Prussian physical geographer.[93]

But these were disquieting days for Owen, however much his financial and professional situations were improving. He saw his sons rounding out their formative years in the climate of slavery, closely associated with boys whose parents regarded the institution of human bondage as a mainstay of their way of life. In the commencement ball and graduation festivities in June 1857, Eugene Owen, now sixteen years old, officiated as manager alongside scions of the prestigious Pillow, Cheatham and Cockrell clans, and Mrs. Owen's name appeared in programs with the *grandes dames* from plantations whose slaves numbered in scores.[94]

Owen's dilemma was that faced by many Northern professional men domiciled in the South, where attractive environment and favorable economics confronted old loyalties and principles in a setting of partisan passion, emotion and pressure. He was not reassured by an address of General Pillow to the Agatheridan and Eurosophian literary societies of the university in June 1856. The controversial politico told the students:

> No matter what your country's cause of quarrel, it is enough for the patriot to know she is in a war. Be her cause right or wrong, it is your duty to espouse it, and if she calls on you to command her armies, to lead them to victory or to death.[95]

A committee of the societies asked Johnson to get a copy of the address for publication. Pillow furnished the text. The cadets had it printed at their own expense. Their action indicated an agreement with Pillow's sentiments and if his phrase "your country" meant the South, as it usually did, the conclusion was disturbing to Owen.

His misgivings may have grown as the trustees moved at the end of the second year to catalyze the school's success and its southern military orientation. Chancellor Lindsley saw as "highly encouraging" that the public was "becoming acquainted with the character of the school" and "our numbers are daily increasing." Johnson and Owen had shown zeal and confidence, he told the trustees in June 1857, by spending $6000 of their own on furnishings and equipment, though they had gone another year without salaries and had made themselves liable to see that others were paid first. The partners submitted a memorial from the faculty asking for another $40,000 loan to expand housing for the faculty, five families of which were still crammed into the President's House, and for a new brick barracks and a "cheap building" to be used as an infirmary.[96]

A new trustee, Sterling Robertson Cockrell, whose ancestry went back to the founding of Tennessee, was named on a committee to look into the partner's request. His report on June 25, 1857 concurred in the committee's recommendation that $30,000 be spent. He went on to voice what he thought should be the aim of Western Military Institute in this gestation period of the Civil War. He said:

> There is a large field for patronage in the South among the Cotton States. Alabama, Mississippi, Louisiana, Arkansas and Texas may be relied on to furnish 200 regular students, provided assurances can be given that they will be taken care of and *governed.* The uniforms, the fife and drum, the musket and reveille, taps, drills and sundry calls of the roll during the day constitute a division and filling up of time, which combined with the supervision and presence of officers and professors, make up a plan of control peculiarly fitted for the youth of this day and this region of the country.

> The South with its great staples of cotton and sugar, its climate and the institution of slavery, makes up a new character different from ancient or modern and no parallels to it exist. A physical training in drills and in gymnasium are a necessary part of the education of young men who are not trained to labor at home which is the case in the South and may never be altered.[97]

The university sold a 300-foot lot from its South Field near the Franklin Pike for nearly $30,000 which was earmarked for the building expansion. The trustees also decided to ask the state legislature for money to build an arsenal on the campus for storing arms and military equipment and to be used as a training school for officers of the state's volunteer companies.[98] This project never materialized.

For Bushrod Johnson the school year 1857–1858 loomed auspiciously. He had put a decade behind his disrupting removal from the Army. After so many vicissitudes as a military school administrator he may have thought that, finally, he was riding a floodtide of good fortune. He was making money. He had standing and acceptance in the community. He had a wife and small son to share his advancement. At the age of 41 he could savor the satisfaction of achievement after an era of frustration and disappointments. The future looked rosy, despite the rising national tumult over slavery which soon was to disrupt Western Military Institute. Johnson's serene euphoria was not to continue.

A few days after the 1857–1858 term began, there occurred a *cause célèbre* in which neither Johnson's nor Owen's part is entirely clear. Owen definitely was involved as commandant of cadets and was supported by Johnson and the faculty. The case was touched off by Cadet William Early Benson, eighteen and a half years old, from Grayson, Arkansas on a "point of honor based on sentiment growing out of the institution of slavery and common to the South" according to a vague statement by Trustee Cockrell to whom the matter was submitted later.[99] Other cadets from Georgia, Texas, Mississippi and Louisiana, ranging in ages from ten to twenty-one, supported Benson.[100] The school faced a major revolt. The faculty united in declaring discipline had to be maintained. It expelled seventeen boys for insubordination. Seven or eight others resigned in sympathy. The ousted ones appealed to Cockrell who owned several hundred slaves in Tennessee and Arkansas plantations and two of whose eight children were cadets, not involved in the controversy. His proslavery attitude was well known.

At a trustees' meeting October 4, 1857, Cockrell read a paper signed by the seventeen explaining the "causes of misunderstanding between themselves and the faculty." Chancellor Lindsley countered with a statement of the faculty's "reasons for action." Cockrell argued that a mistake had been made on both sides and suggested that expulsion be modified to suspension. Other trustees did not concur. They approved a resolution by Dr. Winston that the expulsions stand but that the boys might be received back "upon proper acknowledgement," not otherwise defined. The trustees, however, took from the faculty the right to expel, reserving it to themselves in the future.[101] There is no evidence that any of the expelled students returned.

The incident showed that the convulsion over slavery and states' rights, stoked by the Dred Scott decision the previous spring, had risen to an emotional pitch that penetrated even this quiescent academic environment. Though Owen called for tolerance and dispassionate discussion on both sides and characteristically advocated "gentlemanly language and courtesy," he made no truce with the "blight that debased the master and degraded the slave."[102] He expressed his views before a select audience of leading citizens gathered in the new state capitol on December 4, 1857.

Speaking on "Honor to the Illustrious Dead" on behalf of the Mount Vernon Ladies Association of the Union, he made an impassioned plea to "quell all angry passions, dissentions, jealousy and hatred" and "implore Divine Providence to crush the seeds of discord," so that there would be "no civil war with brother butchering brother and the bullet of the father reaching the heart perhaps of an only son." His peroration:

> Instead of discord and bloodshed, party strife and murder, the struggle shall be who shall acquire the most wisdom, who lead the most virtuous life, who best promote virtue by rewarding the "Distinguished Living", who most honor virtue by rendering "Honor to the Illustrious Dead."[103]

Love and understanding, emphasized in the Pestalozzian system of education to which Owen gave his undiminished allegiance, influenced not only his political opinions but also a reappraisal of the military system of education. Earlier in 1857 Trustee Cockrell had voiced the accepted aim of the school. With this exacting format Bushrod Johnson, as a graduate of West Point, agreed. It ran counter to the philosophy of Owen, trained at flexible Hofwyl. He pondered long on the differences between their views and when the school was forced to suspend for six weeks in December 1857 by an epidemic of typhoid, he had more time to consider his course. Both Johnson and Owen were alarmed enough by the outbreak of illness to send their families away to safety. Owen's wife and sons went to Indiana. Johnson hired a slave girl, Fanny Brown, to accompany Mary and small Charles to Cincinnati by steamboat and thence to Covington, Ky., where the Hatch family had moved from Georgetown. Owen made out and signed the passport as commandant of cadets for the girl to return alone to Nashville after she had delivered her charges.[104]

The school reopened in February after Dr. Winston as its surgeon certified that no new cases of typhoid had developed within four weeks. Johnson inserted an advertisement in the Nashville *Daily Union and American,* January 28, 1958 stating that the barracks had been thoroughly renovated during the cadets' absence and "students could return in safety." Owen wrote and Johnson signed a circular that went out to parents in February with Winston's reassurances.

Serenity returned to the classes but not to the co-owners. The academic issue between them over how the school should be oriented rapidly reached a point of no return. It has been long believed that the separation of the partners, who now were in the most prosperous phase of their nine-year association, came over a divergence of their opinions on slavery; it is said that Owen's never concealed antipathy to the institution clashed violently with the sympathy for it that ex-Quaker Johnson had acquired along with his desirable economic status. But a study of the papers of Richard Owen clearly shows that the burning social question of the day had no part in their differences. Rather the rift seems to have been widening for some time entirely over the stubbornness with which two dedicated men held to their pedagogic philosophies: a liberal permissiveness versus martial regimentation.

By the spring of 1858 Owen reached a decision that he and Johnson must part. He wrote out and gave to Johnson a proposal that one buy out the other and sever his connection with the Institute at the close of the term. He began thus:

> It appearing very evident that we conscientiously differ in our views regarding the best means of bringing a college into the highest state of perfection, I think it decidedly best for us not to impede each other in views and systems so opposite. I therefore propose the following, to which I would like an answer as soon as convenient, say within a week or thereby, so as to allow me the necessary time to carry out my arrangements.

> I propose to sell out to you, or if you prefer it, I will accept the offer I now make to you if you will make it to me. Should I sell out to you and leave, you would still be Superintendent. Should you sell out to me and leave, I would have to run the risk of being appointed superintendent (by the Institute). Therefore I should prefer leaving, but in a pecuniary point, the chances are as fair as I know how to make them.

Owen said he would take Johnson's lots in McGavock in lieu of all his claims against the University, with an arrangement for another endorser of his notes; he would ask $150 worth of goods from the school store operated by Johnson-Owen; $150 for apparatus to be agreed upon; $200 for furniture; a division of books jointly owned in common, plus $300 in cash. He offered to select and leave an exhibit of geological specimens and display cabinets he owned to be appraised later.[105]

Owen's offer to sell out or to buy Johnson's interests was submitted to Chancellor Lindsley by the partners. For a month this moving spirit behind the University of Nashville pondered the proposal, talked to trustees and discussed their positions with Johnson and Owen. Then he signified his desire that Johnson should remain. The co-owners signed an agreement dissolving Johnson-Owen on April 12, to become effective July 1, 1858 after the spring term. The deal involved a total in excess of $10,000 including the shuffle of five McGavock lots to Owen besides the cash payments. Owen explained to the trustees his reasons for resigning:

> After a trial of several years I am compelled to conclude without desiring to attach blame to anyone, that my views regarding education are neither understood nor appreciated by my colleague and partner and that we are consequently likely by remaining together to impede each other . . . I therefore some months since made him a proposition . . . concluding by offering to sell out or buy out his interests.

> At the close of a month's deliberation, Dr. Lindsley having signified his desire that Colonel Johnson should remain, he decided to buy me out. . . I am well aware that by this step I sacrifice a very considerable pecuniary claim besides my chances of profit from the store and that I resign a most agreeable position sufficiently remunerative under ordinary success to satisfy my modest desires and a position which affords facilities for completing the education of my sons free of expense.
>
> Such being the advantage of remaining, you will readily understand that the feelings which impelled me to resign without any knowledge or prospect of another position must have been sorrowful. These motives were love of peace and harmonious action, a feeling which I hope and believe *never* trenches on the rights of others, but as carefully guards any encroachment on mine.[106]

If his antislavery convictions had been a paramount reason for the severance, one might expect the forthright Owen to have said so at some time during the prolonged parleying. The fact that he remained silent on the issue and that instead he voiced regret that his sons could not finish their education in the South would dispute the theory that in 1858 he felt it was high time to remove them from this undesirable situation.[107]

There may have been another reason for Owen's action, not mentioned in his letter to the trustees. A hint of this appeared in the September 1858 issue of the Nashville *Journal of Medicine and Surgery* which was reprinted in the New Harmony *Advertiser* September 11. It said:

> Desiring to found an agricultural college near his former home with a view of increasing his field of usefulness, Dr. Owen has resigned his chair in the University of Nashville and returned to Indiana. We part with a learned and accomplished colleague with unfeigned regret . . .[108]

A month later the *Advertiser* editorially hailed the appearance of a circularized prospectus of "The Indiana School of Practical Sciences, New Harmony, Posey County,

Indiana" with a faculty including David Dale Owen, M.D., professor of geology applied to agriculture and mining and Richard Owen, M.D., professor of descriptive geology and mineralogy.[109] The school did not materialize. Instead Richard joined in a geological study of Indiana with his brother David, who had become the state's geologist for the second time as well as for Arkansas and Kentucky. Richard would complete and publish the results of this study in 1862 after David's death.[110]

Johnson and Owen did not part in anger, nor did Owen leave behind any animosity at the school nor in the community. In Chancellor Lindsley's annual report in July 1858, he referred to the "withdrawal" of Owen "for reasons known to most." He added:

> His kind and gentle, but manly deportment rendered him no small favorite with both students and professors, but as harmony of views between two of the chief officers of the institution are [*sic*] indispensible to the well being of all concerned, it can not be regretted. The dissolution of the relations so long existing between him and Colonel Johnson had been perfected in a kind and friendly way throughout.[111]

The *Journal of Medicine and Surgery* September issue spoke for Nashville, in these terms:

> We will not take leave of our late colleague without a public tribute to his heart as well as his head. Never was there a man of warmer and kinder feeling. In all the relations of life he was the bland, conscientious, frank and elegant gentleman. He carries away with him the best wishes for prosperity of a host of the wisest and best of our citizens and every student, medical and military, that attended the university during his connection with it.[112]

Later in the spring of 1858 a greater calamity befell Johnson. His wife, Mary, contracted an illness diagnosed as "nervous fever." She lingered a few weeks and died May 23, 1858.[113] She and Bushrod had been married only six years and their retarded son, Charles, was just past four. The grief-stricken husband bought a lot in Nashville's Old City Cemetery, where the great and lowly had been laid to rest since 1822. Above Mary's grave in the center of the plot a five-foot high, urn-adorned marble shaft was raised later, appropriately inscribed.[114] Members of the Hatch family came from Covington, Ky., for the funeral.[115] If the maternal grandparents offered to take care of the little boy, the father declined. Little Charles was looked after by an immigrant Irish girl servant, Bridget Farley, in Johnson's apartment in the faculty house for the next two years.[116]

Johnson and Owen continued a friendly correspondence, somewhat intermittently for the next seventeen years. They met again only once in September 1862 when Colonel Owen and his men of the Sixtieth Indiana Volunteer Infantry were taken prisoner at Munfordville, Kentucky.[117]

Departure of Owen did not interrupt the profitable progress of Western Military Institute, now calling itself only the Collegiate Department of the University of Nashville in its newspaper advertising. Lindsley assured the trustees in July that Owen's withdrawal had not divided the faculty. "They all understand the character and prospects of the university," he said. "They have identified their interests and reputation with its prosperity and are determined to leave nothing undone to build it up." He added:

> One very encouraging feature is the largely increased patronage from our immediate vicinity which shows that the distrust and suspicion under which the faculty labored at the commencement of this enterprise is fast disappearing.[118]

Lindsley took over Owen's teaching duties as professor of chemistry and geology without pay.[119] French and drawing went to F. L. J. Thyssens, A.M., while nobody was listed as teaching Spanish and German, though both subjects were still offered in the catalog. Colonel Johnson, the superintendent, professor of civil engineering, assumed Owen's duties as commandant of cadets. J. H. Stewart, South Carolinian, professor of Greek and Latin, was named treasurer. Major Hamilton continued as adjutant in addition to instructing in astronomy, mathematics and natural philosophy. Only Hamilton and Johnson now bore school-awarded military titles. Others on the faculty were George S. Blackie, A.M., M.D., born in Scotland, the librarian and botany and natural history teacher. The Reverend J. W. Hoyte, A.M., M.D., taught mental and moral philosophy and Biblical literature and Dr. C. K. Winston was the school surgeon.[120]

Including the preparatory department, a total of 219 boys enrolled for the 1858–1859 term and eight were graduated in June 1859.[121] Among the graduates was George Washington Gordon, 23 years old, of Giles County, Tennessee, destined to be the last Confederate brigadier to sit in the U.S. Congress in 1911.[122] As a sequel to the insubordination furor of the previous year, the student body testified to its high regard for Johnson by giving him a sword bearing this inscription:

> Presented to Colonel Bushrod Rust Johnson by the cadets of 1858–59 as a token of appreciation of his talents as an instructor and gentlemanly bearing as superintendent.[123]

The progressive well-being of the school was generally unaffected by the unsettled state of affairs in 1859 throughout the South, whose "finer families" continued to consign their sons—192 of them in September 1859—to the care and tutelage of Colonel Johnson. The Institute was paying $1000 annually to the university toward retiring its building debt and spending a like amount in permanent improvements.[124] The Nashville directory spoke glowingly of the seventeen-acre campus with "four large buildings, large fine and convenient residences of professors and steam heated dormitories. The entire property is valued at $500,000."[125]

Johnson continued to harvest a healthy income from his share of the student fees and the profits of the store. His 1858–1862 book of receipts, expenditures and accounts with Treasurer Stewart shows he made nineteen periodic settlements in the 1858–1859 school year ranging in amounts from $259.00 to $4251.00 and finished the term $4661.14 ahead. He was never again in his life to savor such a prosperous period.[126] He added to his real estate holdings by buying on October 10, 1859 a tract of 320 acres of prairie land in Osage County, Kansas, thirty-five miles south of Lawrence for $300.[127] His real estate venture in McGavock was not nearly as flourishing. In the summer of 1859 Johnson had to send bad news to Owen in New Harmony regarding their shares in the development. Some $10,000 in notes taken from purchasers of some of the lots were no good and the property was repossessed. Street making had been costly. To settle their remaining joint portion of $1013, Johnson proposed that one of them take his share in land and the other in a "good note" plus a cash difference. Owen apparently agreed to let the land go to Johnson, as this was the subject of further correspondence between them ten years later.[128]

The fall term began in September 1859 with 164 students. The tremors in the nation forecasting the impending upheaval were further agitated by the John Brown raid at Harper's Ferry during the term, and his subsequent trial and hanging. Studies got short shrift from the young cadets arguing passionately the merits and principles of the political factions girding for the 1860 campaigns. In spite of the excitement, a class of thirteen was graduated in June 1860, the largest number since 1853.[129]

The frenzied oratory of the fateful political contest echoed across the land in September 1860 when the cadets, in diminished numbers, came back to classes. Joining them on January 5, 1861 was young Sam Davis, son of C. L. Davis of Smyrna, Tennessee, eighteen and a half years old. He would attain immortality in Confederate hagiography when the Federals caught and hanged him as a spy in Pulaski, Tennessee in 1863.[130]

The days of the school were numbered as soon as Abraham Lincoln was elected. Almost every issue of any Nashville newspaper thereafter told of some portentous development: seizures of U.S. arsenals and military installations by Southern states, secession of South Carolina, resignation of Southerners from President Buchanan's cabinet and from Congress. Cadets from the deep South went home for Christmas vacation and stayed there. Most of those who returned for the second term left again before it was many weeks under way.

Some pretence of operating the school continued, while Tennessee, torn among neutrals, Unionists and Secessionists, steered a hectic course. The attack on Fort Sumter, April 11–12, 1861, and Lincoln's call upon the states for troops, changed the entire face of things in Tennessee and on the campus of the University of Nashville. Cadets resigned and rushed to volunteer back at their homes or in Tennessee's provisional army of 55,000 authorized in May by the state legislature. The boys traded their gleaming uniforms for Confederate gray. Some faculty members, hoping to capitalize on whatever military knowledge they had ever had, importuned the authorities for commissions as officers. Entries in the school's Order Book cease after April 12, 1861 except for one dated January 24, 1862, dismissing two boys for disciplinary offenses.

Colonel Bushrod Rust Johnson, West Point graduate, Mexican War veteran, military institute superintendent, joined the throngs seeking to barter their talent and experience for preferment in the state's armed forces. He did not have long to wait. On May 28, Governor Isham G.

Harris offered him and he accepted a commission as a militia major to act as engineer on Harris's staff.[131] A month later he was promoted to colonel of engineers in the Provisional Army of Tennessee, still separate from the Confederacy.

The schoolmaster resumed his role as a soldier and was off to a last tryst with adventure along the only path that was left for him to follow. Fortune was offering him a cause and a duty and he accepted both.

Notes

1. Nimrod had been practicing law in Wayne County, Indiana since 1843, and soon would be prosecutor; Lemuel, studying medicine with his father, Dr. Nathan, shortly would enter Starling Medical College in Columbus, Ohio.
2. *Cullum,* I, pp. 600–619; *Wilcox,* pp. 631 f.
3. Walter Millis, *Arms and Men,* (New York: G. P. Putnam's Sons, 1956), pp. 106 f.
4. *Robert Johnson,* p. 12. He says: "Bushrod . . . was much at my grandfather's house and one day when he and my father were walking with an uncle of mine, Lemuel Johnson, who was tall and slender, someone called out 'There go Bushrod, Nimrod and Lightning-rod!' "
5. *Cullum,* I, p. 446.
6. B. O. Gaines, *History of Scott County,* (Georgetown, Ky.: Printed by author *ca.* 1905), II, p. 291.
7. Record of Cadet Thornton F. Johnson in WP Archives, *USMA List of Cadets,* (Washington: no publisher, 1887), for 1818–1821.
8. Letter to author, February 4, 1962 from Major Eugene P. Reynolds, records custodian, Adjutant General of Kentucky.
9. Source of the M.A. degree is not revealed. It was not granted by William and Mary or the University of Virginia, a check in 1961 revealed.
10. *Catalogue and Regulations of Western Military Institute for 1847,* (Cincinnati: Herald of Truth Print, 1848).
11. Leland Winfield Meyer, *Life and Times of Col. Richard Mentor Johnson of Kentucky,* (Ph.D. dissertation, Political Science, Columbia University, 1932), p. 388. Georgetown College absorbed Rittenhouse Academy.
12. William Henry Perrin, editor, *History of Bourbon, Scott, Harrison and Nicholas Counties,* (Chicago: O. L. Baskin & Co., 1882), p. 182.
13. Advertisement on back cover of WMI 1847 catalog; location in *Gaines,* p. 294.
14. *Register of Cadets, Western Military Institute,* still in use by Montgomery Bell Academy, Nashville, begins on February 1, 1847. In

the *Western Military Institute Order Book,* 340 pages, now in the library of George Peabody College for Teachers, Nashville, Order No. 1 is dated May 25, 1847, leading some writers to assume this date was the beginning of the school. The May date is followed by Mabel Altstetter and Gladys Watson, "Western Military Institute, 1847–1861" in *Filson Club History Quarterly,* X, pp. 100 ff.; James G. Rule, *History of Montgomery Bell Academy,* (Nashville: n. p. 1954), and Isabell Howell, "Montgomery Bell Academy" (unpublished MS thesis, Department of History, Graduate School of Education, George Peabody College for Teachers, June, 1940). *Altstetter and Watson, Rule* and *Howell* hereafter.

15. Johnston's Journal, "Student Life at Western Military Institute" is transcribed by Arthur M. Shaw in *Filson Club History Quarterly,* XVIII. *Register* omits the "t" in his father's name.
16. *Gaines,* II, p. 292 shows photos of these buildings as they appeared ca. 1900. Thornton Johnson's photo in *ibid.,* p. 291.
17. *WMI 1847 catalogue*; For Hopkins, *Cullum* I, 275. Hopkins left W.M.I. in 1849, taught at William and Mary and the U.S. Naval Academy and died in 1859 while U.S. consul in Jamaica.
18. Edward Stanwood, *James Gillespie Blaine,* (Boston: Houghton Mifflin, 1905), p. 14.
19. *Gaines,* II, p. 294.
20. Letters of Blaine to college classmates quoted in Gail Hamilton, *Biography of James G. Blaine,* (Norwich, Conn.: Henry Bill Publishing Co., 1895), p. 86.
21. *WMI 1847 catalogue.*
22. *Gaines,* II, p. 294.
23. Letter quoted in *Hamilton,* p. 86.
24. Advertisement in *The Intelligencer and Petersburg Commercial Advertiser,* December 15, 1826 quoted in WPA Federal Works Agency, *Dinwiddie County,* (Dinwiddie County School Board, publisher, 1942), p. 181.
25. *1850 U.S. Census* and *Slave Schedule,* Georgetown, Scott County, Ky.
26. Scott County, Ky., *Deed Record,* Book O, pp. 124, 284; Book Q, p. 37; Book R, p. 392.
27. Data in *Order Book,* July 1848.
28. Letter to Thomas Seabright, October 28, 1848, quoted in *Hamilton,* p. 94.
29. Letter to Seabright in *Ibid.,* p. 96.
30. *Cullum,* I, p. 275.
31. *Ibid.,* p. 420.
32. *Order Book,* April 19, June 29, 1849.
33. Victor Lincoln Albjerg, "Richard Owen" in *The Archives of Purdue,* No. 2, ([Lafayette, Ind.] March 1946), p. 23. *Albjerg* hereafter. Owen expounded his theories of education in a series of articles in the *South West Sentinel,* Evansville, Indiana newspaper in 1841.
34. *National Cyclopedia of American Biography,* (New York: J. T. White Co., 1893–1962), XIV, p. 276; Arthur H. Estabrook, "The Family History of Robert Owen" in *Indiana Magazine of History,* XIX, pp. 63 f. Owen's first wife was Martha Chase, who died soon after their marriage in New Harmony, Indiana.
35. Details from undated holographic memorandum of remarks by

Owen to the WMI faculty, probably in October 1851 in WMI Folder No. 1 *Richard Owen Papers*, New Harmony, Indiana. *Owen Papers* hereafter with specific folder location given. *Albjerg*, p. 21 says Owen joined the school at Drennon Springs, repeating the error of Thomas R. Johnson and Helen Hand, writing on Owen in *Archives of Purdue* No. 1 (November 1940), p. 402 and *National Cyclopedia of American Biography*, XIV, p. 276. The school did not move there until 1851.

36. *Gaines*, II, p. 295.
37. *Perrin*, p. 330.
38. *Altstetter and Watson*, p. 104; WPA Federal Works Agency, *Kentucky, A Guide to the Blue Grass State*, (New York: Hastings House, 1954 revised ed.), p. 370. *Ky. Guide* hereafter.
39. *1850 U.S. Census*, Nicholas County, Ky., shows cadets' birthplaces as follows: La., 35; Ky., 30; Tenn., 7; Iowa, 7; Ohio, 6; Texas, 6; Ga., 5; Miss., 5; Pa., 5; Ark., 4 and N. Y., 4.
40. *Ky. Guide*, p. 370.
41. Statement of judgement in case of Richard Owen *vs.* Andrew Sheffler, March 11, 1850 and costs of suit and execution to July, 1852 in WMI Folder No. 2, *Owen Papers*.
42. *Stanwood*, pp. 23 f., infers a connection between the marriage and the death of Blaine's father in June, 1850. Russell H. Conwell, *The Life and Public Service of James G. Blaine*, (Augusta, Me.: E. C. Allen & Co., 1884), p. 68 mentions only the Pittsburgh nuptials. Charles Edward Russell, *Blaine of Maine*, (New York: Cosmopolitan Book Corp., 1931), p. 28, says Blaine left the school "almost at once" after "the secret marriage"; *Gaines*, II, p. 294 tells of the excitement and gossip in both schools over the "secret marriage."
43. *Order Book*, Special Order No. 43.
44. Printed statement by T. F. Johnson in circular dated July 1851 in WMI Folder No. 1, *Owen Papers;* undated holographic memorandum titled "Testimony of Richard Owen re: Edwin W. Morgan" in Miscellaneous Folder, *Owen Papers*. Morgan did not return to the Army during the Civil War. He taught mathematics for years after 1866 at Lehigh University. (*Cullum*, I, pp. 520 f.)
45. Walter R. Houghton, *Early Life and Public Career of the Hon. James G. Blaine*, (Chicago: Union Publishing House, 1884), p. 30.
46. Draft of resolution in WMI Folder No. 2, *Owen Papers*. In 1869 at Owen's request Blaine wrote letters of introduction for Owen to use on a trip to Europe and inquired about Bushrod Johnson and other colleagues of his WMI teaching days. Blaine letter in Correspondence Folder No. 10, *Owen Papers*.
47. Roster of all graduates after 1850 is in *Catalogue of the Collegiate Department, Western Military Institute, School Year 1854–1855*, (Nashville: Cameron and Fall, 1855). Printed copy of Board of Visitors' Report, dated June 26, 1851 included in printed prospectus of school in Miscellaneous Folder, *Owen Papers*.
48. Printed copy of T. F. Johnson statement in WMI Folder No. 1, *Owen Papers*.
49. Letter to Blaine in Pittsburgh, December 4, 1851 quoted in *Hamilton*, p. 96.
50. Included in Marie Dickoré collection of Kentucky funeral invita-

tions in Ohio Historical Society Library, Columbus. Death date in *Gaines*, II, p. 291. He says "... Johnson was involved in a difficulty at Dremon [*sic*] Springs where he lost his life."

51. Copy of notice signed by James Dacres, adjutant, Western Military Institute saying T. F. Johnson died "after painful, protracted illness, resulting from a complication of diseases Saturday October 4, 1851" in WMI Folder No. 1, *Owen Papers*. Mourning badge order in *Order Book*, October 9, 1851.
52. There are two undated memoranda of statements to the faculty, covering similar ground in WMI Folder No. 2, *Owen Papers*, but they probably refer to only one session of the faculty.
53. *Order Book* entries on these dates.
54. Notations in Owen's *1849 Journal*. Letter, probably from Bushrod Johnson to Owen in Louisville, December 21, 1851 in Miscellaneous Folder, *Owen Papers*.
55. Undated holographic memorandum in WMI Folder No. 2, *Owen Papers*. Owen had a penchant for saving the notes he wrote on all occasions.
56. *Order Book* entry January 4, 1852; *Altstetter and Watson*, p. 108.
57. Draft texts of "Addresses to Cadets" in Owen's handwriting in WMI Folder No. 2, *Owen Papers*.
58. *Henry County, Ky., Marriage Records, 1852*. Copy in Kentucky Historical Society Library, Frankfort.
59. Undated drafts in Owen's handwriting in WMI Folder No. 2, *Owen Papers*.
60. *Louisville Daily Times*, June 21, 1852.
61. Notations in Owen's *1853 Journal;* programs of social events in Miscellaneous Folder, *Owen Papers*.
62. Owen's *1853 Journal*, entries on pp. 33, 34 and 42.
63. Copy of letter to Robert Owen, May 28, 1853 in Correspondence Folder No. 2 (1851–1859), *Owen Papers; Altstetter and Watson*, p. 109 and *Rule*, p. 27, say thirteen were graduated.
64. Copy of letter to Johnson from steamboat "Badger State" June 14, 1853 in Miscellaneous Folder, *Owen Papers*. The date seems to be in error, since in his *1853 Journal* Owen notes he left Drennon Springs for the East and New Harmony on June 24.
65. The portrait painted by Cornelius Hankins now in the Confederate Room of the Tennessee War Memorial in Nashville is mismarked "brigadier general."
66. *CV*, XIV, p. 109. James D. Tillman, student in 1859–60, wrote in 1906 Colonel Johnson "was a quiet, studious and courteous gentleman ... just in all things."
67. *Ibid.*, p. 13. Snowden commissioned the portrait and Sumner Cunningham, editor of *The Confederate Veteran*, spoke at the presentation.
68. Copy of Owen letter to Smith, September 27, 1853 in WMI Folder No. 2, *Owen Papers*. Another on March 23 said cadets were forced to bring in their own coal and water.
69. Letter of John B. Elliott to his mother, September 24, 1853, in possession of his granddaughter, Miss Helen Elliott, New Harmony. Elliott marked his room on the second floor of a three-story building named "The Cincinnati" engraved as a letterhead on the school's stationery. He called the daily routine "no child's play", starting

at 6 A.M. and ending with taps at 10 P.M. He said the cadets "have a bad name abroad" but termed this "slander."

70. Owen's *1853 Journal,* pp. 113–117.
71. *Ibid.,* p. 118
72. Nashville directories of the period throw no light on the identity of W. Jackson. No Nashville newspaper printed the letter.
73. Owen's *1853 Journal,* pp. 120 f.; for charter see *Acts of the Tennessee Legislature 1853–54,* chap. 124.
74. Owen's *1853 Journal,* p. 121.
75. *Ibid.,* pp. 121–124.
76. Letter from H. Hundsen, New Harmony, March 31, 1854 to John B. Elliott, Tyree Springs, in John B. Elliott letters.
77. Owen's *1853 Journal,* pp. 127–129.
78. Letters, Elliott to his mother, April 21, May 13, 1854; letter, Richard Owen to John Elliott, father of the cadet, June 9, 1854 in John B. Elliott letters.
79. Letter from E.A.C. (Edwin Cooper) cadet at Tyree Springs to John B. Elliott, New Harmony, [May] 27, 1854 in John B. Elliott letters.
80. Letter, Owen to John Elliott cited *supra* fn. 78; undated memorandum of address to cadets on "forgetting pledges of honor and imagined injury" in WMI Folder No. 2, *Owen Papers.*
81. Lindsley's recommendations to trustees in *University of Nashville Trustees Minute Books,* I, pp. 73–91, March 9, 1855. *Minute Books* hereafter.
82. John G. Frank, "Adolphus Heiman, Architect and Soldier," in *Tennessee Historical Quarterly,* V (March–December 1946), pp. 43 ff. Heiman later was colonel of the Tenth Tennessee at Forts Henry and Donelson. Lindsley Hall is still in use as the Nashville Childrens' Museum.
83. Rev. John P. Campbell, *Nashville City and Business Directory, Vol. IV, 1859,* (Nashville: n.p., 1859), p. 89.
84. *Minute Books,* I, pp. 97 ff., April 4, 1855.
85. *Regulations of the Military College, The Literary Department of the University of Nashville,* (Nashville: John T. S. Fall, 1859), p. 21.
86. *Minute Books,* I, pp. 97 ff.
87. *1860 U.S. Census Slave Schedules,* Davidson County, Tennessee.
88. *Catalogue, University of Nashville Collegiate Department, Western Military Institute,* (Nashville: Cameron and Fall, 1855); *1850 U.S. Census Slave Schedules,* Davidson County, Tennessee.
89. There are discrepancies in figures on total enrollment in most writers on W.M.I. Some returning students did not sign the Register again; preparatory and day students are not always included in reported totals. Figures in this work are estimates drawn from all sources.
90. Statement in *Minute Books,* I, pp. 117 ff. The "doubt and suspicion" may have been based on the Northern antislavery backgrounds of the two partners or on the reputation for disorderly antics acquired by the cadets at previous locations.
91. Davidson County, Tennessee, *Warranty Deed Record,* Book 24, pp. 174, 175; Book 27, pp. 231, 608, 609. McGavock, now part of Nashville is six blocks northeast of Fisk University. Owen's heirs sold the last of the lots in 1904.
92. *Western Military Institute Announcement for 1857–1858.* Photostat in Tennessee State Library. *Albjerg,* p. 21, says Owen got the degree

in 1858; *National Cyclopedia of American Biography,* XIV, p. 276 calls the degree a Master of Science.

93. Letters in French from von Humboldt in *Owen Papers.* Owen's book was published by A.S. Barnes & Co., New York, 1857.
94. Program of Commencement Ball, June 11, 1857 in Miscellaneous Folder, *Owen Papers.*
95. Gideon J. Pillow, *Address Delivered Before Agatheridian and Erosophian Societies of the University of Nashville,* (Nashville: Cameron and Fall, 1856).
96. *Minute Books,* I, pp. 135 ff.
97. *Ibid.,* pp. 159 ff. Cockrell's name also appears as Cockrill.
98. Ibid., p. 144.
99. *Ibid.,* pp. 172 ff.
100. Names in *Register* and in *Minute Books,* I, p. 174.
101. *Minute Books,* I, pp. 172 ff. Neither the students' nor the faculty's statements are included in the trustees' minutes.
102. *Albjerg,* p. 23.
103. Owen had the lecture published for sale for the benefit of the association which was raising funds to buy and restore Mount Vernon, the home of Washington. *Honor to the Illustrious Dead,* (Nashville: A. A. Stitt, 1857).
104. Copy of "Passport for Slave" made out and signed by Owen in WMI Folder No. 2, *Owen Papers.*
105. Undated and unsigned four-page proposal in Owen's handwriting filed with agreement of dissolution signed by Owen and Johnson April 12, 1858 in Business Papers Folder No. 4, *Owen Papers.*
106. Text in Owen's handwriting in WMI Folder No. 1, *Owen Papers.* Italics are his. The *Minute Books* have no reference to the letter.
107. This thesis appears in a letter of Robert Dale Owen to Secretary of War Edwin M. Stanton in 1862 urging Richard's promotion to brigadier general in the Union Army. Letter in *Owen Collection,* Lilly Library, Indiana University.
108. New Harmony *Advertiser,* September 11, 1858, page 2, column 3.
109. *Ibid.,* October 10, 1858. Copy of circular in Professional and Scientific Papers, Social Science Education Folder No. 2, *Owen Papers.*
110. *Dictionary of American Biography,* VII, p. 116.
111. Lindsley's report in *Minute Books,* I, pp. 178 ff.
112. *Journal of Medicine and Surgery,* Nashville, September, 1858 reprinted in New Harmony *Advertiser,* September 11, 1858. No news stories on Owen's resignation were carried by Nashville newspapers at the time.
113. *Interment Records,* May 1858, Old City Cemetery, Nashville.
114. The inscription was no longer legible in June 1962. The lot is No. 14, Section 12, corner of City and Mulberry Streets in the cemetery.
115. Scott County, Ky., *Deed Records,* Book 4, p. 329, shows Daniel and Mary Hatch on January 1, 1860 sold at a $1500 loss a Georgetown lot bought by them in 1849 for $5500. They had moved to Covington in the meantime. Mary's brother, William is listed in the 1860 U.S. Census in Georgetown.
116. *1860 U.S. Census,* Seventh Ward, Nashville, p. 88.
117. Letter, Richard Owen to Mrs. Owen, Brandenburg, Ky., September 26, 1862 in Correspondence Folder No. 4, *Owen Papers.*
118. *Minute Books,* I, p. 180.

119. *Ibid.*, pp. 189, 190.
120. School advertisement in *Campbell's Directory*, p. 249; slaves listed in *1860 U.S. Census Slave Schedules.*
121. *Catalogue of Literary and Medical Department of the University of Nashville, 1858–59,* (Nashville: John T. S. Fall, 1859).
122. *Warner*, pp. 109–110.
123. Tracy M. Kegley, "Bushrod Rust Johnson: Soldier and Teacher" in *Tennessee Historical Quarterly*, VII, p. 257.
124. *Altstetter and Watson*, p. 114.
125. *Nashville City and Business Directory, Vol. V, 1860–61,* (Nashville: n.p., 1860), p. 22.
126. Colonel Bushrod R. Johnson's Cash Receipts and Expenditures, 1858–1862 Account Book in *University of Nashville Records*, Vol. XVI. Microfilm in Tennessee State Library and Archives, Ms. Section.
127. Osage County, Kansas, *Deed Book*, A, p. 127.
128. Letters, Johnson to Owen, June 25 and July 11, 1859 in Business Papers Folder No. 4, *Owen Papers.*
129. *Altstetter and Watson*, p. 112.
130. *Register*, January 5, 1861.
131. E. C. Bearss, "The Construction of Fort Henry and Fort Donelson" in *West Tennessee Historical Society Papers*, XXI, 1967, pp. 26–29.

6
EX-TEACHER RETURNS TO THE SWORD

i. Fatal Folly at Fort Henry

Months before Bushrod Johnson elected to fight for Tennessee, he had been keenly aware that he faced the ordeal of making a fateful decision. His impassive temperament was unlikely to be influenced by the perfervid emotionalism crackling in the air; he was not to take any rash or unconsidered action. Rather he made a careful estimate of the factors involved on both sides. He was a widower, 44 years old, with a small handicapped son. He was acutely conscious of the attitude and deep seated convictions of his closest relatives in abolitionist Wayne County, Indiana. He must have recalled the antislavery Quaker tenets of his heritage.

On the other hand, he had become definitely identified with the Southern *mores* as an educator of the youth of the land in a military school. He was the associate of many who argued, with sincerity and eloquence, for the philosophy of Southernism: slavery and states' rights. His continued economic welfare was linked to theirs. With the deterioration of the academic retreat from which he had surveyed the situation, he well knew he would be expected to cease being a mere spectator and become a participant. Conforming to the mystique of the military profession to which Cadet, Lieutenant and "Colonel" Johnson had subscribed for twenty-five years, he saw no alternative but to join the armed phase of the conflict. He was a "West Pointer" and such a title in the popular view implied a certain magic competence.

Calmly and deliberately, in plenty of time, he plotted the measures he felt he must take. In the summer of 1859 he spent six weeks in visits to kinsmen and others in Ohio, Indiana and Kentucky.[1] Something in the nature of a Johnson family conclave could have taken place in Cambridge City, Indiana in the home of Nathan and Sarah Johnson. Their daughter, Ruth Hoge Williams, wife of Alfred B. Williams, recently had moved to Cambridge City from St. Louis. Alfred had been a well-to-do trunk manufacturer, but in 1859 he sold his factory to become a land agent.[2] Hedging against the hazards of their future in slave-holding Missouri, the Williams family had been buying property in Cambridge City and other farmland in Wayne County, among the abolitionists and Quakers. They paid $9500 cash for such real estate in 1859. Early in 1860 they added more farm acreage and a city lot.[3] Come what may they had assured their security.

Living at home and practicing medicine with his father was unmarried Dr. Lemuel Riddick Johnson, 37 years old. He was active in Republican party councils and would later be named the city's postmaster by President Grant. Ten miles east in Centreville lived Judge Nimrod Johnson and his wife, Catherine Coyle Underwood Johnson, and their two sons, Henry Underwood, born in 1850 and Robert Underwood, born in 1853, the first destined for fame in law and in Congress and the other in letters and diplomacy. They were a companionable age to Bushrod's son, Charles. Judge Nimrod, one-time law partner of Oliver P. Morton, Indiana governor, had a law office in Cambridge City. Two miles west, in Dublin, dwelt David

Spencer, maternal first cousin of Bushrod and Nathan. His son, David, Jr., would fight in the Second Indiana Cavalry and die of wounds in 1863.[4] Among these who were closest to him by blood and family feeling, Bushrod discussed his own and little son's present and future welfare. Apparently some tentative plan was made which was carried out in the summer of 1860.

In Ohio in 1859, Bushrod may have paid his last visit to the scenes of his boyhood in Belmont County, whence he had gone to West Point nearly a quarter-century before. His sister, Aletha, 53-year old widow of Thomas Leslie whom she had married in 1826, lived near Bethesda in Goshen Township with her daughter Lucretia and son Francis. Her other sons, Nathaniel, a wagon-maker like his father, and Bushrod, twenty years old, named for his uncle, were married and in their own homes. Young Bushrod, a farm laborer, had a wife and two daughters.[5]

Most of the Spencers and Johnsons had gradually drifted from the Society of Friends during the Hicksite and later doctrinal differences. Most of them had moved away from Eastern Ohio. They had scattered over Ohio, Indiana and as far west as Iowa. One maternal cousin, William Windom, found political success in Winona, Minnesota. In 1860 he was reelected to his seat in Congress; later he would become a Senator and Secretary of the Treasury in the cabinets of Presidents Garfield and Harrison.[6] Bushrod's brother Joseph had gone soon after he married Sarah Stillwell in 1822. His sister Mary with whom Bushrod had grown up in Norwich, married an aged, wealthy widower in St. Clairsville in 1833. He died in 1837 and there was a court contest over bequests to a daughter by his first wife. In 1838 while Bushrod was at West Point, she was married to John Galbeth and they moved away.[7]

In Covington, Kentucky, across from Cincinnati, Johnson might have visited his parents-in-law, the Daniel Hatch family, also for the last time. Daniel would die during the war and his widow would survive to 1883.[8]

In the summer of 1860, Johnson went back to Indiana. He took Charles with him and gave the lad into the care of Mrs. Williams, who had a family reputation for grace and dignity. Throughout the war the boy remained in the North, allowed to think that his father was fighting for the Union.[9] His cousins Henry and Robert, the sons of Judge Nimrod, thought him a bit odd, but tolerated him with sympathy and compassion. A family tradition says Bushrod sent a diamond ring as a token of appreciation for giving the boy affectionate care for the next seven years.[10]

To provide for Charles in case anything happened to his father, Bushrod arranged for Dr. Lemuel Johnson to become Charles's legal guardian. He next bought, on July 19, 1860 from Alfred and Ruth Williams, two tracts of farm land, north of Brighton in Macoupin County, Illinois, totaling 227 acres, for $6000. He was to pay for this in a series of notes: $1000 in ninety days; $1334 in fourteen months; two more for $1333 each in three years. Johnson then transferred title to Lemuel as guardian for Charles. Somehow, Bushrod managed to pay off the notes in spite of war and separation and on January 4, 1866 the land was declared free of debt.[11] On one of these parcels was the farmhouse to which Johnson came in 1874 with his son when his second school venture failed in Nashville.

To add further to his provision for Charles, in July 1861, Bushrod deeded to him the 320 acres in Osage County, Kansas he had acquired in 1859, in consideration of "love and affection." This gave the boy a substantial investment in Northern property likely to enhance in value as he grew older.[12]

By these arrangements, Johnson freed himself of the problem of keeping a home in Nashville for the retarded boy and at the same time provided him with a fair stake in the North months before the firing started. These actions need not be taken as evidence that he was still struggling within himself as to what course he would take. He had made up his mind. Sometime during the summer of 1860 he had a conversation with his classmate, W. T. Sherman, like himself the head of a Southern military school. Sherman was on his way back to Louisiana after leaving his family in Lancaster, Ohio until their house was completed on the campus near Alexandria. Sherman had been there since December 1859 and had been harassed by undisciplined and insubordinate cadets as Bushrod had been.[13]

Sherman was disturbed and angered by Johnson's attitude toward the impending crisis. Bushrod, he wrote five years later, had joined "in the popular sneer at Yankees, when he knew better."[14] Sherman, at this time, also had reached his decision and early in 1861 he resigned from his academy and returned to the North.

Johnson had a larger financial stake in the South than Sherman. He told the 1860 census taker on June 18 that he owned $5000 in Nashville real estate and $12,000 in personal property[15] which would have included riding horses, carriages, jewelry, household effects, stocks and securities, and his interest in the school store. For comparison, at the same time, his nephew Nimrod, on the common pleas bench in Indiana, listed only $1800 in real and $1000 in personal property, while Dr. Nathan, after practicing medicine in Indiana since 1839, had been able only to go from $600 in 1850 to $3500 real and $400 personal property by 1870.[16] The South had made Bushrod the wealthiest of the Johnson clan.

Johnson had almost three times as much property in the South as he held in the North—a potent economic motive for choosing the side he did. Only one apologist for him, writing a half-century after the war and decades after his death, credits him with being inspired by a belief in the constitutionality of states' rights, and recognizing "a paramount duty to the state."[17] No expression of Johnson's has come to light to support this thesis. Nor is there evidence for crediting any persuasion of logic, philosophy or instinctive allegiance to Tennessee. He had no sentimental or romantic ties to his adopted state; his wife was dead, his son was in the protective hands of northern kin; his school was suspended indefinitely; his faculty colleagues and his "boys" were gone.

But time and events demanded that he become a participant. Any return to the "Old Army," into whose ranks flocked Sherman, Grant, Halleck, McClellan and others, was barred to Johnson, who still may have cherished a smouldering resentment over his forced resignation. The murky story of his separation from the Army was a readily available threat to him in the files in Washington. His 1847 nemesis, Seawell, now a colonel, was on duty in neighboring Kentucky as chief mustering officer. He could be expected to return to the attack. But in this new army of the South and in this new war against those who had been preferred and promoted over him and who had cast him out for his "mistake" Johnson might look for the martial distinction which had eluded him in Mexico.

Tennessee itself had undergone considerable soul searching before resolving upon a course. Governor Harris, Democrat in office since 1857, called a special session of the legislature in January. While it sat, Mississippi, Florida and Alabama seceded. At Harris's behest the legislature set February 9, 1861 for a popular vote on the question of calling a secession convention. Voters defeated the call for such a convention, 69,675 to 57,798 with only cotton-growing West Tennessee counties in favor.[18] But the firing on Fort Sumter and Lincoln's call upon the states to supply troops reversed opinions in Tennessee. Demands for cooperation with the South swamped the governor, backed now by even the Conservative Unionists, who included several trustees of the University of Nashville.[19]

When the General Assembly met again April 25, Harris asked for an ordinance declaring Tennessee a separate sovereignty, independent of the Federal Union. Then, he said, the state must unite with the Confederate States whose constitution had been adopted March 11 in Montgomery, Alabama. The lawmakers authorized Harris to make a military alliance with the Confederacy, as between two independent nations, which was ratified May 7. Tennessee agreed to turn over all her military resources and all public property taken from the United States. The Southern "nation" was to reimburse the state for all military expenditures made before the state joined the Confederacy, which it did not do formally until June 24, 1861. Meanwhile on June 8, a popular vote of 104,913 to 47,238 approved an ordinance of secession passed by the legislature on May 6.[20]

Johnson's opportunity came with the enactment of measures to raise and equip a Tennessee Provisional Army of 55,000 and to appropriate $5 million for this purpose. To receive, process and train these men required the services of anybody with any military background and to these were added those numbers who made up in political influence and enthusiasm for what they lacked martially. First, state commissions as major generals went in June to politicians Pillow, Benjamin F. Cheatham and ex-Congressman Felix Kirk Zollicoffer, Nashville Postmaster Samuel Read Anderson and Memphis Postmaster William Henry Carroll. Daniel Smith Donelson, 60 years old, West Point 1825, speaker of the Tennessee House of Representatives and nephew of President Andrew Jackson, also was made a brigadier general. To West Pointers Johnson, class of '40, John Porter McCown, '40, and Alexander Peter Stewart, '42, went colonelcies.[21] Devotion to a cause and dedication to duty compensated for ignorance and inability in many cases of lesser officers, but chaos long endured. In crowded and confused "camps of instruction," such as

Camp Trousdale in Sumner County, northeast of Nashville, bewildered civilians, self-conscious in unfamiliar uniforms, lived and fumbled in misery and disorder trying to learn the trade of the soldier.

Senior Major General Gideon Pillow headed Tennessee's Provisional Army. Acting for him as a mustering officer, Bushrod Johnson on May 5 inducted the First Tennessee Infantry, commanded by Colonel George Earl Maney, University of Nashville graduate in 1845.[22] Johnson gave special attention to the First's adjutant, Robert Bogardus Snowden, New York-born former student at Western Military Institute, who would become Johnson's adjutant at Shiloh and remain his admirer and defender until his death in 1909.[23] Son of a prominent merchant in Nashville where he had lived since the age of three, Snowden had been a cadet at Drennon and Tyree Springs. He had been operating a wholesale grocery in Nashville since 1858.[24]

While his legislators debated, his citizenry volunteered and his brand new officers became accustomed to their roles, Governor Harris turned an anxious eye down the natural avenues of approach into his heartland, the Tennessee and Cumberland rivers. He had no doubt that the Yankee invaders would use these streams despite Kentucky's optimistic illusion that she could stay neutral and deny her soil to armies of both sides. Harris wasted no time. In April he appointed a prominent civilian engineer, Adna Anderson of Nashville, who was operating the Edgefield and Kentucky Railroad as receiver, to locate and construct defensive works on the two rivers. Aged General Donelson was detailed as his military adviser and Major, later Colonel, Bushrod Johnson, head of Tennessee's Army corps of engineers, sat in final judgement on their decisions.

Anderson also had the services of Major Wilbur F. Foster, another civilian engineer who had volunteered for the First Tennessee Infantry Regiment and had been commissioned in April. Anderson and Foster organized a surveying party to pick sites on the rivers for earthworks strong enough to mount guns to resist Federal gunboats and large enough to house infantry to repel ground assaults. They began reconnoitering May 10. On the basis of their studies, Anderson located the site of Fort Donelson, named for his colleague, on the Cumberland River a mile west of Dover in Stewart County, less than a dozen miles south of the Kentucky state line. Donelson and Johnson approved. Foster's surveyors laid out the works and a large force of men began felling trees and moving earth.

A dozen miles west on the Tennessee River the story was different. Anderson first picked a point five miles upstream from the final location, between the mouth of Standing Rock Creek and the Paris road nearly opposite the mouth of the Big Sandy River. Foster concurred. But Donelson, sent by Harris to examine the site and report back to the governor, disagreed. He favored a location downriver across the border in Kentucky. Since this view collided with Tennessee's determination to respect Kentucky's neutrality, it got no approval in Nashville. So Donelson decided on Kirkman's Old Landing on the east bank of the Tennessee, twelve miles due west of Fort Donelson on the Cumberland. This site was across from high ground on the Kentucky (west) side of the river and therefore was about as close to the border as geographically possible. Foster and Anderson objected. The place was on a lowland, they said, dominated militarily by the heights on the opposite bank.

Johnson visited the disputed spot. He listened and considered. Then he agreed with Donelson. A fort on the bottom land, he rationalized in his report, had a better command of the river, being on a bend in the Tennessee and at the head of a straight stretch of two miles—an excellent "field of fire" for defensive guns. To the lasting disgust of Foster and Anderson he rejected their arguments and directed Foster to begin surveying and planning the walls and gun emplacements.[25]

Certainly better defensive works could have been erected on both rivers farther north, downstream in Kentucky. But Harris and those charting Tennessee's course felt they had no right at this time to encroach into Kentucky which they believed ultimately would become one of the Confederate states anyhow. This hindrance and Johnson's lack of perception of the vulnerability of Fort Henry combined to hamper Tennessee's defenses with an Achilles' heel. By September when the first movements of Leonidas Polk and U. S. Grant shattered the dream of Kentucky's neutrality, it was too late to salvage Johnson's error of judgement at Fort Henry.[26]

In mid-June, the Tenth ("Irish") Tennessee began building the works and positions for seventeen guns at Fort Henry. The colonel of the Tenth was versatile Adolphus Heiman, Prussian-born Nashville architect and slave owner who had built the University of Nashville's Lindsley Hall and who was a veteran of the First Tennessee Volunteer Infantry in the Mexican War. He pushed the digging and building so that the first gun was emplaced and test-fired with a blank shell on July 12. Initially six smooth-bore 32-pounders and one 6-pounder were set up. Ammunition was so poor it was necessary to add special quick burning powder to each charge, creating the hazard of a premature blast to endanger the gun crews.[27] Foster left to rejoin his regiment in Western Virginia.

Repercussions began to mount over Johnson's approval of Fort Henry's site. In September, Captain Jesse Taylor was sent there at Governor Harris's request to command and instruct the gun crews. He was dismayed at what he found. The fort was nearly at water level below hills on both sides of the river from which rifle fire could reach the garrison and gunners.

"I was convinced by a glance at its surroundings that extraordinarily bad judgement, or worse, had selected the site for its erection," he decided. He complained at once to state authorities in Nashville. He got a tart reply that the selection had been made by competent engineers. Knowing, he wrote later, that his "crude ideas concerning fortifications would receive little consideration when conflicting with those entertained by a 'West Pointer,' " he first resolved to acquiesce quietly. Then he noticed high water marks on trees above, below and in the rear of the fort, convincing him that the normal winter floods would put the works under two feet of water.[28]

Taylor sent another protest to Nashville. He was curtly notified that the state's forces had been transferred to the Richmond government and he should do his complaining to General Leonidas K. Polk in Columbus, Ky. Stubbornly determined to get some action before it was too late, Taylor wrote several letters to the headquarters of the bishop-general. Here the buck was passed finally to Polk's superior, General Albert Sidney Johnston, commanding all Confederate forces from Arkansas to Cumberland Gap. By now the days of September and October had slipped away.

General Johnston took action. To investigate, he dispatched his chief engineer, Major Jeremy F. Gilmer, fourth in the West Point class of '39. Gilmer hurried to Fort Henry early in November. He noted its deficiencies but realized it could not be shifted to any other location. He conferred with Taylor and Heiman on what could be done to strengthen the place. All agreed that fortifications and gun emplacements should be built across the river on the high ground in Kentucky, now no longer neutral. This was done. The new fort on the hill was named Heiman for the Fort Henry commander.[29]

Armament in Fort Henry was gradually increased to 17

smooth bores of various calibres. Six 12-pounders were added, but these were made of such poor metal that two burst on test-firing and the rest were discarded.[30] The uneasy garrison watched the downriver horizon anxiously for the first smoke columns that would mean the Federal fleet was coming. They knew the invaders could outrange their weapons and make easy targets of their low lying positions.

When Brigadier General Lloyd Tilghman, Maryland-born 1836 graduate of West Point, took command of both Forts Henry and Donelson he was as alarmed as Taylor at what he called the "wretched military position" of the Tennessee River bastion. Later, after he was forced to surrender the place he wrote:

> The history of military engineering records no parallel to this case. Points within a few miles of it, possessing great advantages and few disadvantages were totally neglected and a location fixed upon without one redeeming feature or filling one of the many requirements of a site such as Fort Henry . . . the enemy had but to use their common sense in obtaining the advantage of high water . . . to have complete and entire control of the position.[31]

Johnson escaped official blame for his unwise choice. Amid the flurry of protests about it, he tried to present Fort Henry in the best possible light. In listing Tennessee's fortifications on September 15, 1861 he called Fort Henry a "good enclosed work" with bastion fronts, mounting six 32-pounders and two 12-pounders "requiring about 1,000 men to man it."[32] This finished his engineering duty and he went to other tasks. Those bemused with the "ifs of history" might speculate on how different the outcome of Grant's invasion of Tennessee in February 1862 could have been had Johnson sided with Anderson and Foster, the civilian engineers, against Donelson, the sexagenarian brother alumnus of West Point, in approving their Big Sandy river mouth site. Realistically, the conclusion is inescapable that Johnson's first vital decision as a Confederate officer was an inept and tragic mistake.

ii. Two Tries Finally Make a General

In the letter he wrote on October 1847, trying to explain his offer of a "proffit" to Major Seawell, Bushrod Johnson argued that his military service "might be found as faithful and bright as some that have been more glaring and been more fortunate in rewards." He had been unnoticed and unhonored in Mexico. Fame and promotion had come to classmates, juniors and subordinates, but none to him. And now in this frenetic summer of 1861, events were shaping up that indicated the pattern might be repeated for Johnson.

In July, after Tennessee's troops had been incorporated into the Provisional Army of the Confederate States, status in the forces of the central government became the goal of every man's desire. The political generals led the pack. Postmaster Anderson, 57-year old Mexican War veteran, was commissioned brigadier general on July 9. He had been a major general in the state's army. He took over as a brigade the First Tennessee of Maney, the Seventh, Colonel Robert H. Hatton, Ohio-born Lebanon lawyer and ex-Congressman, and the Fourteenth, Colonel W. A. Forbes, and went with them to Western Virginia.

Another state major general, farmer-politician Benjamin Franklin Cheatham, 40 years old, became a brigadier on July 9. He had been a colonel in Mexico. Brigadier's rank on the same day went to Gideon Pillow, 55, senior major general in the state's army, university trustee and law partner of President Polk who had sustained him in Mexico in a long quarrel with Winfield Scott. To Donelson, Johnson's colleague as a river fortifications expert, also went a brigadier's wreath and stars and he left for troop duty in Western Virginia.[33]

The fifth July 9 brigadier was Editor and ex-Congressman Zollicoffer who had served for a year as a volunteer against the Seminoles in 1836. He supported the Bell-Everett ticket in 1860 and was credited with having influence among dissident Unionists in East Tennessee.

The political overtone of these appointments was not lost on Bushrod Johnson, restive and anxious in Nashville. The furor over Fort Henry had not reached full force in August when he carefully laid a campaign to impress the Richmond government with his qualifications and his availability for a general's rank.

First, Johnson importuned Governor Harris to write to the Secretary of War, Leroy Pope Walker of Alabama, introducing Johnson and endorsing him for promotion to general. This went forward on August 15. Next, Johnson persuaded five Tennessee members of the Confederate Congress to write to Walker supporting Johnson's candidacy for brigadier. This was dated August 21 and should have impressed the bothered and fumbling Walker with the amount of influential backing Johnson was able to muster. It also shows that the Northern antecedents of Johnson were not being held against him by his friends and associates in Tennessee's circles of power.

On the same day, Johnson addressed a letter to Walker, enclosing another from Governor Harris commending Johnson's services as chief of engineers in the state's forces. Johnson told Walker:

> . . . I entered West Point in 1836 and graduated in 1840. Served as an officer of the 3d Infantry for seven years in the Florida and Mexican wars and participated in four battles. During the last 6 months of my service . . . I was Depot Commissary at Vera Cruz with very heavy responsibilities.

> Since I left the army I have been constantly connected with a military college and for the past six years I have been superintendent of the Military College of the University of Nashville . . .
>
> At present I hold from the state of Tennessee a commission of colonel commanding the Corps of Engineers of the Provisional Army of that state and as such have been mainly engaged in fortifying the Tennessee river. Herewith I take the liberty of enclosing a letter from Governor I. G. Harris commendatory of my services . . .
>
> Perhaps I am most thoroughly at home in the infantry arm of the service. It will be for you to determine whether you can do better than place me in the Engineer Corps or the Artillery Service.[34]

All of this should have impressed Walker. It radiated political pressure, the "faithful and bright" service Johnson felt he had performed, and the laudatory appraisal of it from an influential governor. At this stage, unfortunately, Walker was tottering mentally and physically from the burden of his duties and the tremendous demands upon his inadequate abilities and resources. He quit September 16. His successor was Judah P. Benjamin, Louisiana ex-Senator. In the changeover, Jackson's drive for preferment came to nothing. The letters and endorsements were swept into the files.

Johnson had another iron in the fire. This was an effort to make himself known to the Confederate Army leaders with whom he would serve if his ambitious hopes were realized. He wrote on August 5 to Polk in Memphis, listing and appraising the dozen officers in Tennessee's Corps of Engineers. He included himself as colonel commanding, said he had been last on duty at Fort Henry and now resided in Nashville.

In mid-September he duplicated the report he had sent to Polk, forwarding it this time to Johnston, who had been made a full general a few days before and put in command of all Confederate troops west of the Alleghenies. Johnson signed himself as colonel commanding a corps of twelve engineer officers including one major, five captains, five lieutenants and himself. It was no accident that he wrote to Johnston on stationery of the Military College of the University of Nashville—a subtle effort to insinuate his background into the consciousness of the commanding general whose word could bear weight on his behalf in Richmond.[35] Johnston's attention had not yet been called to Fort Henry's deficiencies, so Bushrod Johnson risked no adverse reaction to his attempt to attract attention, but the effort brought no results.

Johnson was not inclined to bide his time awaiting the whims of fortune. He felt the state of affairs called occasionally for prodding fate toward his aims. He wrote to Owen in New Harmony a few weeks after the firing on Fort Sumter expressing this belief. In a letter in May from Memphis where he was studying the city's defense requirements, Johnson told his former business partner that while he was "disposed to trust all things to providence and take the evil as well as the good . . . in these troublesome times" one might feel inclined to "attempt to assist Providence." To that end he proposed some exchange of their property interests separated from each other by the war.

"I have two quarters of sections of land in Kansas," Johnson continued. "You have lots and claims in Nashville and doubtless we both occasionally feel that our property may give us much trouble. Are there any terms upon which we can exchange? . . . If you have a proposition that you are disposed to make on this exchange I will carefully consider it . . . Write to me here or in Nashville."[36]

If Owen ever responded his reply has been lost. He probably dismissed the matter without action because in three weeks he was commissioned a lieutenant colonel of the Fifteenth Indiana Volunteer Infantry and had scant time to worry about his lots in Nashville.[37]

While he nursed his hopes, Johnson's engineering tasks

diminished. In the late summer of 1861 he was shifted to the command of Camp Trousdale, the concentration point for the volunteer companies being formed in Middle Tennessee. After a few weeks of recruit training, ten companies would join themselves into a regiment, elect a colonel, and offer their services formally to the Confederate government for twelve months. Assisted by Lieutenant J. P. McGuire as temporary adjutant,[38] Johnson drew upon his experience as a supply officer in the 1840s to feed, house and equip these men from Johnston's army supply depots in Nashville. He knew how rapidly hungry soldiers devoured food stocks and that the problem of keeping the supply pipelines filled never diminished. On November 10 he complained to Colonel William Whann Mackall, Johnston's adjutant general, who had been a first classman at West Point when Johnson was a plebe. He had on hand only six days' rations of salt meat and fifteen days' supply of other stores, he said. He continued:

> The Chief of Staff states he has no funds to buy *fresh meat*. I apprehend we cannot make purchases here on credit.[39]

While Johnson fretted over inadequate supplies and resources at Camp Trousdale, he must have noted with envious disappointment that Alexander Peter Stewart, his ex-colleague on the university faculty, had been appointed a brigadier general on November 8. Stewart, an East Tennessee Whig anti-secessionist, was graduated from West Point in '42. He had been a lowly underclassman to Cadet Sergeant and Cadet Captain Johnson in '38 and '39. He resigned from the Army in 1845 after serving the bare minimum requirement and missed any battle experience in Mexico, being out of the service. While Johnson had fought four battles and had fourteen years as a military academy educator, Stewart taught mathematics, natural and experimental philosophy at Cumberland University in Lebanon from 1845 to 1861 with a brief interlude in 1855 when he headed the "scientific department" of the University of Nashville as professor of mathematics and engineering.[40] As any passed-over officer has always done, Johnson probably stacked his own record and qualifications against Stewart's and wondered why he had not been "more fortunate in rewards."

Stewart's promotion was the second affront to Johnson's sense of what he believed was his due. On October 12 a brigadier's rank came to his classmate John Porter McCown, another East Tennesseean, who had graduated tenth in 1840 and won a brevet at Cerro Gordo. McCown had served nearly 21 years in the "Old Army" before resigning his captain's commission on May 17 to enter the Southern service.[41] In five months he had become a general.

In the office of Tennessee's adjutant general, W. C. Whitthorne, to which he was transferred in December from Camp Trousdale, Johnson renewed his drive for promotion. His target widened this time to include Colonel Mackall, who as General Johnston's adjutant saw all the papers and reports coming to the Western area commander. As "Acting Brigadier General," a rank he assumed with his new desk job, Johnson on November 29 and December 2 sent Johnston and Mackall a report that 127 companies had been organized in Tennessee and that Governor Harris had ordered more volunteers to rendezvous at Camp Trousdale until a total of 5000 were there. Then regiments would be formed and inducted into the Confederate service.

"This is for the information of the commanding general," Johnson added.[42] The inference was plain. Additional regiments meant new brigades and these required generals to command them.

On Christmas Day, Johnson followed up this theme in another letter to Johnston, repeated to Mackall. He had received word, he said, from Congressman Thomas M.

Jones in Richmond that Secretary Benjamin had informed Jones that Bushrod Johnson's appointment as brigadier general would be made "as soon as the necessity for additional generals from Tennessee" existed. Johnson expressed the hope that General Johnston "may think the necessity now exists and may be disposed to set forth that fact to the War Department."

Johnson "ventured to lay the statement" before Johnston that from 10,000 to 12,000 troops "have gone forward from our defensive lines in Tennessee under the late call for 30,000 and 5000 more are in camp ready to receive arms." He added:

> I should be pleased to receive the appointment and be ordered to duty at once with the army advancing from Bowling Green. However, I will cheerfully render services wherever it is deemed most appropriate.

Petitions had gone to Richmond from five Tennessee regiments, Johnson wrote, asking for his appointment "with a view to my command of them." Somewhat lacking in sincerity, he continued: "Of course I do not anticipate such a command, although the petitions were made by voluntary and unsolicited action on the part of the petitioners."[43]

Johnson may have exaggerated a little in stating that five regiments were asking for him. Surviving documents show only three: Officers of the 32d, 44th and 54th signed statements endorsing Johnson for brigadier general. The 53d did not add its assent from Camp Weakley until January 17, 1862.[44]

The next day, December 26, Johnson dispatched two more letters to Johnston and Mackall to try to clinch his argument. "Since I wrote yesterday," he said to Johnston, "Gen. Whitthorne, adjutant general of Tennessee, says Tennessee has 50 regiments of infantry in the field all duly organized and that there are sufficient companies to organize two regiments at Jackson, two at Camp Weakley, two at Fort Donelson, one at Camp Trousdale, one at Knoxville and one at Columbus, Ky., making 59 regiments of infantry for Tennessee. The legislature will be told after the holidays that Tennessee has 60 regiments besides 12 battalions of cavalry and two regiments of artillery.

"I would be pleased if the general recommended my immediate appointment."[45]

To Mackall he wrote much the same story with one difference, the number of regiments. "Gen. Whitthorne assures me he will be able to report to the state legislature after Christmas that Tennessee has 65 regiments of infantry, 12 battalions of cavalry and two regiments of artillery. I should be pleased if the general finds it consistent with his duty in view of these facts to recommend my immediate appointment by the War Department . . . It seems the Department will wait till he indicates the necessity."[46]

All of this labor seemed to be in vain. The New Year 1862 came with Johnson still behind a desk in Nashville, shuffling papers in the adjutant general's office.

Meanwhile Johnson was providing shelter in Nashville to a kindred Northern soul espousing the cause of the South. He was George Jones, grandson of George W. Jones of Iowa, former member of Congress from Michigan and Wisconsin, U.S. surveyor general, first U.S. Senator from Iowa and U.S. Minister in Bogota, New Granada. The elder Jones, born in Indiana, was a Transylvania College classmate of Jefferson Davis. He had been recalled from South America by President Lincoln in July 1861 after he wrote to Davis, his "noble and dear friend," expressing sympathy with the Confederate president and his cause. In December 1861, ex-Minister Jones was arrested on arrival from South America by order of Secretary William E. Seward after he expressed the purpose of going South and joining Davis.

From Dubuque in July, Jones's son, C. S. D. Jones,

wrote his father in New Granada an account of the Federal debacle at Bull Run. He continued: "George went to Nashville about May 26 with my approbation. He was engaged for a little time in drilling recruits but is now staying with Colonel Bushrod Rust Johnson."[47] Johnson's connection with the Jones family is vague, unless the grandson was a cadet at Western Military Institute prior to 1860. Governor Harris also had a personal interest in the young man. When Lieutenant George Jones was captured at Fort Henry, the governor was informed personally of the fact by private letter.[48] Grandfather Jones ultimately was freed from Fort LaFayette in New York harbor after 64 days imprisonment and lived in retirement in Dubuque until his death in 1898.[49]

As the year 1861 ended, all eyes in Nashville were turned down the Tennessee and Cumberland rivers whence would come the Federal gunboats and Grant's invading thousands. To oppose them were only the defenses of Forts Henry and Donelson which Tilghman was trying to man with 5000 raw troops. The 43,000 in Albert Sidney Johnston's Army of the West were spread across more than 400 miles from the Mississippi River above Memphis to Bowling Green, Ky., with the two fateful rivers piercing the center of his extended front. Polk at Columbus, Ky., with 12,000 men, warily watched Grant's increasing force at Cairo, Ill., and Paducah, while William Joseph Hardee, West Point '38 and author of the standard *Rifle and Light Infantry Tactics,* divided 22,000 among Simon Bolivar Buckner, West Point '44, John Buchanan Floyd, ex-Secretary of War, and John Stevens Bowen, West Point '53, at Bowling Green, with some 2000 under Charles Clark, Ohio-born Mississippian at Hopkinsville, soon to join another smidgen under Pillow, 25 miles southeast at Clarksdale, Tenn.[50]

Johnson had serious doubts of the forts' ability to hold back the Federals. In mid-January Governor Harris sent him to Fort Donelson to inspect it after a force of slaves, guarded by troops, came from Alabama to labor on additional works.[51] Johnson took temporary command of Fort Donelson on January 21 for a week while Tilghman was absent at Fort Henry. His gloomy appraisal of what he found prompted two telegrams and a letter to Harris. The enemy was moving from Murray, Kentucky to the Tennessee River with a good road thence to the Confederate forts, he wired on January 22. "Forces weakened here by detachments withdrawn," he said. "Cavalry and infantry ought to be sought. Can arm temporarily 500 more infantry. Need field artillery." Two days later he telegraphed the governor asking "equipment for 536 sporting rifles and 35 muskets." In a letter on January 26 he reported the arrival of the balance of Colonel A. H. Abernathy's Fifty-third Tennessee, which he somewhat disparaged by the statement: "One more regiment of new troops will be as many of that description as will be desirable here. Should still be pleased to get one good regiment of old troops." Ominously he added: "Fort Donelson is now our weakest point. I trust it will be duly strengthened."[52]

Johnson came back to Nashville a few days later to find good news awaiting him. On January 25, I. I. Hooper, secretary of the Confederate Congress had informed President Davis that on the previous day, that august body "did advise and consent to the nomination of B. R. Johnson to be brigadier general." These gladsome tidings were wired from Richmond to Johnson. He finally had reached his goal after five months of trying. Without regret he bade farewell to the pile of papers in the adjutant general's office and reported for duty by telegram to Mackall at Johnston's headquarters.

Another strange role awaited him.

Notes

1. Letter, Johnson to Owen, July 11, 1859 in Business Papers Folder No. 4, *Owen Papers.*
2. Data from St. Louis city directories for 1857, 1859 and 1860 furnished by Marie H. Roberts, St. Louis Public Library, Jan., 1962.
3. Wayne County, Indiana, *Deed Record,* Vol. 26, pp. 223, 645, 682.
4. Family data from Meredith Johnson and *Jenkins,* pp. 139, 215; *1860 U.S. Census,* Wayne County, Indiana; *Sutherland and McEvoy's Richmond and Cambridge City Directories,* 1860, 1861, pp. 91, 92, 97, 99.
5. *1860 U.S. Census,* Belmont County, Ohio.
6. *Congress Directory,* 1836. Windom was the son of Mercy Spencer, daughter of Nathan Spencer, Jr., brother of Rachel, mother of Bushrod.
7. Belmont County, Ohio *Probate Court Record,* Case No. 1352.
8. Data from Covington, Ky., city directories supplied by Mary Ann Morgan, Librarian, Kenton County Public Library, August 9, 1968.
9. *Robert Johnson,* p. 13.
10. Statement of Meredith Johnson to author.
11. Macoupin County, Illinois *Deed Record,* Vol. RR (1858–1861), p. 358; Vol. AO, p. 154.
12. Osage County, Kansas, *Deed Book,* A, p. 127.
13. Lewis, *Sherman,* pp. 116–141.
14. Letter of Sherman to Sewall L. Fremont, April 21, 1865 in *OR*, XLVII, pt. 3, p. 271.
15. *1860 U.S. Census,* Seventh Ward, Nashville.
16. 1850, 1860, 1870, *U.S. Census,* Cambridge City and Centreville, Ind.
17. Col. J. D. Porter in *CV*, XIV, p. 13.
18. James Walter Fertig, *The Secession and Reconstruction of Tennessee,* (Chicago: University of Chicago Press, 1898), p. 15.
19. Ralph A. Wooster, *The Secession Conventions of the South,* (Princeton, N. J.: Princeton University Press, 1962), pp. 173 f.
20. *Ibid.*, p. 188; *Fertig*, pp. 24 f.
21. *Warner*, pp. 44, 47, 74, 157, 199, 241, 293, 349.
22. *Ibid.*, p. 210.
23. *CV*, XIX, p. 211.
24. *NCAB*, XXXII, p. 46.
25. Foster says Johnson selected the final site of Fort Henry in his account in Bromfield L. Ridley, *Battles and Sketches of the Army of Tennessee 1861–1865,* (Mexico, Mo: Missouri Printing and Publishing Co., 1906), pp. 64 f. William Preston Johnston, *Life of Albert Sidney Johnston,* (New York: Appleton & Co., 1878), p. 407 says sites of both forts were picked by Donelson and approved by Johnson. This view is followed by Edwin C. Bearss, "The Construction of Fort Henry and Fort Donelson" in *West Tennessee Historical Society Papers,* No. XXI (1967), pp. 24 f.
26. *WP Atlas,* Map 25.
27. Capt. Jesse Taylor, "The Defense of Fort Henry" in *Battles and Leaders of the Civil War,* (New York: Thomas Yoseloff, Inc., 1956), I, pp. 368 f. *B&L* hereafter.
28. *Ibid.*, p. 369.
29. *Ibid.*

30. *Ibid.*
31. Tilghman's report after surrender of Fort Henry in *OR*, VII, pp. 138 f.
32. *OR*, IV, p. 408.
33. *Warner*, pp. 44, 47, 74, 241, 349.
34. Originals of all correspondence in *B. R. Johnson File* in CSA Staff Papers, National Archives.
35. Originals of reports in *ibid.* Gen. Johnston forwarded the letters from Gov. Harris and Johnson to Richmond on November 29, 1861 noting he had only "a very slight" acquaintance with Johnson, but adding that his "education qualifies him for the office sought," *OR*, VII, p. 718.
36. Letter Johnson to Owen, May 22, 1861 in Business Papers Folder No. 4, *Owen Papers.*
37. *Heitman*, p. 763.
38. J. P. McGuire, "Thirty-Second Tennessee Infantry" in *Military Annals of Tennessee*, p. 469.
39. Letter Johnson to Mackall, November 10, 1861 in *B. R. Johnson File*, CSA Staff Papers. Italics are his.
40. *Warner*, p. 293; *Minute Books*, I, p. 97. Stewart returned to Cumberland when the scientific department of the university failed.
41. *Warner*, p. 299.
42. *OR*, LII, pt. 2, p. 226; letters Johnson to Johnston in *B. R. Johnson File*, CSA Staff Papers.
43. *OR*, LII, pt. 2, p. 244.
44. Originals of petitions in *B. R. Johnson File*, CSA Staff Papers.
45. *OR*, LII, pt. 2, p. 245.
46. *Ibid.*, p. 227.
47. *OR*, Ser. 2, II, p. 1298; *Congress Directory*, p. 1136.
48. Private letter, John C. Burch, aide-de-camp, to Harris from Fort Donelson, February 9, 1862 in *Harris Papers.* In *OR*, Ser. 2, II, p. 1298 Lt. Jones is called "son of Senator Jones of Iowa" instead of grandson.
49. *Congress Directory*, p. 1136.
50. *WP Atlas*, Map 25.
51. Gilmer's report in *OR* VII, p. 132. Gilmer says the slave force was expected in the fall but was not sent until after January 1, 1862.
52. Telegrams, January 22 and 24 and letter, January 26, 1862, Johnson to Harris. Originals in *Isham G. Harris Papers*, Tennessee State Archives; reproduced in *Fort Henry and Fort Donelson Campaigns, February 1862*, (Fort Leavenworth, Kansas: Command and General Staff School, 1923), pp. 273, 276, 277. *Source Book* hereafter.

7

THE MEASURE OF COMBAT

i. Forgotten Man at Fort Donelson

All day Friday, February 7, 1862, Bushrod Johnson, with new general officer's wreath and stars shining brightly on his uniform collar, restlessly paced the deck of a steamboat, en route down the Cumberland River from Nashville. He was on his way to his first field assignment as a brigadier. The previous midnight a telegram was delivered to him in Nashville from Bowling Green, Ky., headquarters of Albert Sidney Johnston's Western Department, ordering him to assume command at once at Fort Donelson.[1] Only a few hours before, Fort Henry had surrendered to Federal Flag Officer Andrew H. Foote's gunboats. Lloyd Tilghman, the only Confederate general in the two defensive works, was a prisoner of war.

Johnson boarded the first boat that left Nashville on Friday morning. Some 65 miles downstream at Clarksville, the craft halted to take on the Second Kentucky Infantry of Colonel Roger W. Hanson, which had come by train from Russellville, Ky., earlier in the day and was ordered by Brigadier General Gideon Pillow to embark immediately for Fort Donelson.[2] While these troops and their gear were being crowded aboard, Johnson took the time to report to Pillow, who gave him an additional order to take command at Donelson.[3] In late afternoon the steamer got off again for the final 35 miles to Dover, the tiny courthouse town just over the hill from Fort Donelson. Long after dark Johnson led his horse down the gang plank and rode through the mud 150 yards to the Dover Hotel, a two-storied, unpainted frame building being used as headquarters.

Pursuant to his two orders, as a brigadier general of a fortnight's seniority, Johnson assumed command of a garrison force of the 30th, 49th, 50th and 53d Tennessee regiments, three artillery batteries and in addition the two brigades salvaged from Fort Henry by Colonel Adolphus Heiman on the previous day when the folly of Johnson's selection of the site had been demonstrated by Tilghman's fate.

As Grant's forces approached Fort Henry on both banks of the Tennessee River (on the left the division of Charles Ferguson Smith, mentor of Johnson and Grant at West Point, and on the right the division of John A. McClernand, Kentucky-born Democrat politico-general), Tilghman gave up Fort Heiman on the Kentucky heights on February 4. Then because Tilghman and a few score of stalwarts stayed behind, sacrificing their freedom, and because rain and bad roads delayed McClernand, Heiman had been able to get away from Fort Henry, plodding through clinging mud into Donelson at midnight on the sixth. He abandoned his artillery; it could not have been pulled through the quagmires. Tilghman gave up in two hours after Foote's gunboats began shooting up the flooded works. Now as Johnson began his duties at Fort Donelson late Friday night, Grant's 20,000 Federals were bivouacked 13 miles away, catching their breath until the flotilla moved around to the Cumberland River to support their move against all that stood between them and middle Tennessee and the vital center of Johnston's Western Department.[4]

Bushrod Johnson had only a few hours to exercise any command. These were filled with concerns over unloading and storing rations and munitions brought by steamboat from Nashville, evacuating the sick by river craft to hospitals in Clarksville or beyond, and assigning and moving troops to defensive positions without any definite idea of what reinforcements were yet to come. On Sunday, February 9, Pillow arrived from Clarksville with what had been the brigade of Charles Clark, who had resigned in a fit of pique, then regretted it[5] and led his 2800 men from Hopkinsville, Ky., to Clarksville on a 26-mile forced march on the sixth. But Major General William J. Hardee, with whom Clark had been disputing, took away his command and gave it to Colonel T. J. Davidson of the 8th Kentucky under Pillow's overall direction. Clark loaned Pillow one of his horses as a personal mount.[6] Pillow brought it to Donelson with him.

As ranking general, Pillow assumed command. In his first order, issued a few hours later, he made Johnson commander of a division composed of Heiman's brigade—the 10th (Irish), 42d, 48th and 53d Tennessee, plus the 27th Alabama, Davidson's brigade of the 15th Arkansas, Fourth Mississippi and two battalions from Alabama and Tennessee.[7]

This was only temporary. On Tuesday, Brigadier General Simon Bolivar Buckner reported with two brigades he had brought by train from Russellville, Ky., to Clarksville and thence marched to the fort. Buckner had been a general since September 14, 1861 and hence outranked Johnson, who had graduated four years ahead of him. Pillow gave Buckner command of the right sector and Johnson of the left and set them to building rifle pits and earthworks as laid out by Major Jeremy Gilmer, the engineer who had tried too late to correct Fort Henry's deficiencies. Gilmer had come afoot to Donelson with Heiman on the night of the sixth. Pillow asked him to

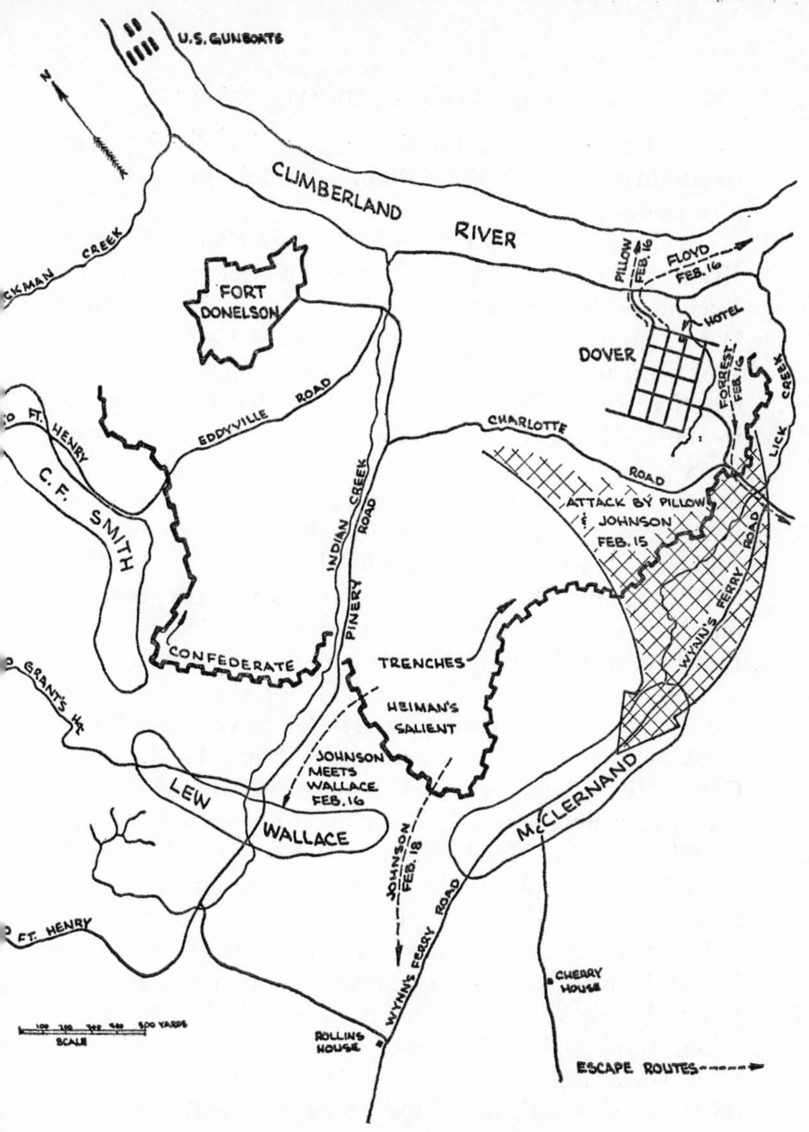

FORT DONELSON
February 12–16, 1862

Ignored by his superiors in moments of crisis, Johnson leads a successful attack on Grant's left until he is halted and recalled by Floyd and Pillow. He carries word of the surrender to Lew Wallace. Then he hides from his captors, leaving the sad chores of defeat to Buckner, and strolls away two days later. (From B&L, *I, p. 402)* stay and help prepare for the coming siege.[8] Gilmer had spent three years at West Point with Johnson and knew him well.

On Thursday the thirteenth, John Buchanan Floyd arrived. Secretary of War in the cabinet of President Buchanan, he was under Federal Court indictment in Washington. He was a brigadier general since May 23, 1861 with military experience limited to a few inglorious months in the Virginia mountains under Robert E. Lee in the 1861 fall. He was senior to the three other brigadiers present, albeit the least experienced, but he bore orders from Johnston to take command. He and Pillow both were 56 years old. He probably had no more than a slight acquaintance with Bushrod Johnson.

Within an area roughly 2000 by 1800 yards, bordered on three sides by the river and two unfordable creeks, Floyd mustered nearly 15,000 men in 28 regiments from Tennessee, Mississippi, Virginia, Kentucky, Alabama, and Texas. Many were poorly armed. Some carried flintlock muskets. Few had ever been under fire. The Tennessee Cavalry Regiment, led by Colonel Nathan Bedford Forrest, still a neophyte at his trade, had been present since Monday evening the 10th, sent ahead by Clark when he started from Hopkinsville. There were six light batteries of artillery and 17 heavy guns.[9]

In a wide irregular arc, making best use of ridges, timber and moat-like streams, more than two miles of rifle pits and shallow trenches had been built hastily from logs, fallen trees and yellow mud with pitifully inadequate tools since Pillow's arrival. Johnson and Forrest took off their coats and joined their men in wielding axes and shovels on Thursday.[10] Into these defenses Floyd put most of his force. On his right to include the bastioned 25-acre irregularly sided fort, he assigned Buckner with six regiments and two batteries between unfordable Hickman Creek on the north and Indian Creek which bisected the defense area. To the left on the south, between Indian Creek and barely fordable Lick Creek and including the town of Dover, went Pillow and Johnson with the brigades of Heiman, Davidson, G. C. Wharton, John McCausland and William E. Baldwin, all colonels.

The generals were a strangely assorted quartet. Floyd, a civilian politician in uniform, timorous, unsure and unskilled in his role, was in command. Pillow, arrogant egocentric, insubordinate and perverse, was dominantly assertive. He had Mexican War experience, however varicolored. Buckner, brevetted twice in Mexico for gallantry and eleven years in the "Old Army" was the most professionally competent. Between him and Pillow were unresolved hard feelings going back to the Mexican War. Johnson, displaying his usual self-effacing, unassertive traits of character, was definitely outclassed in this confrontation of personalities. During the hectic hours ahead he stayed mostly in the shadows, forgotten or ignored by his colleagues. When the farce was ended he faded into the mists and even his captors seemed not to remember he existed.

Grant's thousands began moving from Fort Henry before daylight Wednesday, February 12. Smith's division with some of McClernand was on the Eddyville Road. McClernand moved on a parallel road two miles south. By sundown both forces were assembling in front of Buckner's wing. Pillow while in command for four days had done nothing to meet or oppose them. On Thursday Grant told McClernand to move farther to the Federal right, along the Wynn's Ferry Road, opposite Pillow and Johnson. Again the defenders remained in their trenches, content to shell the Blue marchers with two ineffectual batteries.[11] At dusk on the twelfth, Johnson's pickets and a working party in front of his center near the Wynn's Ferry Road, preparing to extend their abatis, were fired on by a sizeable body of the enemy. Two were killed. This action showed how the Federals were moving around the Confederate left.

Johnson seemed unimpressive almost from the start. A low opinion of him as a leader was acquired by one young Virginian as soon as he arrived Thursday afternoon. Johnson was on his horse near the Dover landing when Captain John H. Guy was directing the unloading of the four guns of the Goochland Light Artillery from a steamboat. Two Federal shells hit the vessel as the cannoneers struggled to take off their plunging horses and roll the limbers and caissons up the step street from the water's edge. Guy saluted Johnson who had been watching the debarkation, and inquired where he should take his battery.

Johnson was very affable and gentlemanly, Guy recorded in his journal, "but he made no impression on me as an officer." While they rode together along a good portion of Johnson's lines, reconnoitering and considering where to place the guns, the newly made general solicited and listened to the opinions of the youthful captain instead of directing.

"In doing this we were more or less exposed to the enemy's fire," Guy recorded, "and I did not see that he was overanxious to avoid danger. But I saw no manifestation of generalship."

Finally Johnson made up his mind and gave orders where the battery was to be located. Guy left him and trotted back to Dover to bring up the guns. They had moved only a short distance when Pillow rode up. He halted the battery and asked Guy who he was and where he was going. Guy told him. Pillow's volatile temper flared. He heatedly told Guy that Johnson had presumed in giving such an order to him without authority. He ordered Guy to halt the movement and report back to Pillow's headquarters in the home of Major Rice of his staff in Dover. The upshot was an order by Pillow to Guy to take the Goochland guns to Buckner on the right wing, in reserve. By this time darkness was so near that Guy moved only to a ravine outside of town to bivouac until morning.[12] Johnson was left to find out for himself that his directions had been overruled and countermanded.

On spring-like Thursday night, the thirteenth, a Federal brigade from Don Carlos Buell's army landed three miles downstream from the fort. This unit with some troops left at Fort Henry was collected into a division under Lew Wallace. Grant sent him into the center of his line on the night of the 14th, between Smith and McClernand, opposite the brigades of Heiman, Colonel Joseph Drake and Davidson. The Confederates now were surrounded on the land side, except for an area from Dover east along the river, toward which McClernand was moving. The weather suddenly turned bitterly cold with temperatures near 10°. Sleet and snow fell. Inadequately sheltered men on both sides suffered intensely. Many were frostbitten, especially the Confederates who had few blankets or overcoats.[13]

Johnson definitely was overshadowed in the first conference of the generals, called by Floyd on Friday forenoon. They met to decide how to react to the Federal encirclement. Floyd seemed overwhelmed by his responsibility; Pillow and Buckner asserted their views; Johnson contributed little. He had already been shown by Pillow that he was to take, not give, orders. But he joined in the unanimous decision to attack with Pillow's force against Grant's unbalanced right, to try to break out and retire toward Charlotte and Nashville. Buckner was to cover the rear if the sortie succeeded.[14]

It was obvious that bold action must be taken at once before the Federals unloaded more reinforcements. So it was with a sense of urgency that Johnson rode back to the trenches on the left on the high ground between Dover and swollen Lick Creek. He sent his four aides to the five brigades and twenty regiments of Pillow's force with orders to move out at once toward the Charlotte Road.

Johnson's efficient young staff officers were Major Powhatan Ellis, Jr., and Captain W. T. Blakemore, both of whom had been with Tilghman at Fort Henry and had escaped; Lieutenant Frank J. McLean of George Gantt's Tennessee Cavalry Battalion; and a volunteer artilleryman, Lieutenant George Triplett Moorman, a former secretary to Thomas C. Reynolds, lieutenant governor of Missouri.[15] Moorman had made a last minute trip to Nashville to find a pintle and pintle plate missing from the one rifled gun in the fort capable of throwing a 128-pound conicle shell. He finished installing the parts on Tuesday, the eleventh.[16]

Pillow's troops had marched scarcely more than 500 yards toward the Federals when Johnson got an order to halt the men and return them to the trenches. Pillow had suddenly decided that not enough daylight remained for making the attack.[17] Johnson's aides made their second round of the units with this word about midafternoon.

Then Johnson joined the spectators crowding on the high ground above Indian Creek west of Dover to watch the duel which opened at 3:30 P.M. between Foote's flotilla of four ironclads and two wooden gunboats and the dozen guns of the fort's water batteries.[18] Young Captain Guy was there, too. Again he was struck by Johnson's attitude. While the others excitedly followed the firing through their glasses as best they could through the smoke and haze and cheered the effective marksmanship of the Confederate gunners, Johnson sat silently on his horse in obvious depression of spirits. Nor did his mood change when the sight of the battered Federal warships' withdrawal set off exultant jubilation among the watchers. He did not join in the happy shouting. "He was as gloomy and wore as anxious a look when it was known that the boats had been driven off as when the fight was hottest," Guy wrote in his journal.[19]

Johnson was summoned to the council of the beleaguered brigadiers in the Dover Hotel Friday night. He wrote later that it was decided "to cut our way out of the fort and unite with the army in Nashville," to which Johnston had withdrawn from Bowling Green as the Federals came up the rivers. Plans were made, he said, "for every contingency" but nothing specifically for a retreat after the way was opened, "only a resolve to attack the enemy right."[20] He took part until after midnight in assigning positions to the units after most of the brigade and regimental commanders were sent for. These were told that Pillow's and Johnson's troops would hit McClernand's thinly stretched line along heavily wooded Wynn's Ferry Road at 5 A.M., two hours before sunrise.

In the smothering darkness of the frigid night, Johnson and his staff labored to move hundreds of tired, half-asleep and half-frozen men out of their earthworks across the crunching snow in the heavy underbrush and over the icy waters of Lick Creek's feeders. They moved so quietly the nearby Union pickets were not alerted. By 4 A.M. most were standing in a shivering line along the Charlotte Road ready to crash down upon the unsuspecting foe.

A final check showed Davidson's brigade was missing. Johnson rode posthaste back to the trenches. Why were two Mississippi and one Texas regiment still bivouacked in their paltry shelters? The regimental commanders protested they had received no orders to move. Johnson found Davidson's adjutant, Captain R. B. Ryan who told him that his colonel was "severely indisposed." Johnson hurried to Davidson. Prostrate with illness, the Kentuckian had not told anybody about the attack plan. Johnson sent this word to Pillow who named Colonel John M. Simonton of the First Mississippi to take over the brigade. Then

Johnson and his aides scurried along the earthworks to arouse and prod the laggards into line. An hour was lost until they fell in at the rear of the brigades of Baldwin, McCausland and Wharton, led by Pillow in the advance. He told Johnson to bring up Simonton and Drake on his left flank, beyond which Forrest's eager troopers were poised to strike at first light.[21]

After the sudden attack caught the awakening Federals and sent them reeling back in shock, Johnson spent most of the morning hours with Drake's brigade. Repeatedly warning the men to aim low, sometimes he personally directed their short charges through the brush-filled hollows and sloping woods. The crouching, firing and rushing Southerners kept up a slow but steady advance against McClernand's stiffening and stubborn right. The unrelenting pressure was gathering momentum about 9:30 A.M.[22] By nearly noon Drake and Simonton's men had pushed an agonizing mile across the rugged terrain from hill to hill while Forrest swinging his horsemen wide through the clawing thickets, hit the Federal flank and rear in repeated assaults. As more and more of the overcoated Blue infantry began to give way, Forrest was sure he could sniff a rout in the making. He galloped up to Johnson and pleaded for an order that would send all five of Pillow's brigades plunging forward in a general rush against the faltering Federals. Pillow had ridden off a few moments previously with Gilmer to see why Buckner was not supporting Pillow's right and rear.[23] In his absence, hesitant and deferential Johnson held the power of decision.

Two days before, Johnson had roused Pillow's wrath by assuming authority in such a minor matter as locating Guy's battery. Now Forrest was urging him to move most of an army in the absence of its leader. Johnson pondered while Forrest impatiently and forcefully argued for action. In a characteristic rationalization, Johnson considered that the Federals would not withdraw so rapidly of their own accord after their obstinate stand unless they were trying to draw the Confederates into an ambush. Thus he persuaded himself to avoid the responsibility for giving the order Forrest wanted. He compromised by telling the cavalry leader he would continue to advance Pillow's troops slowly and cautiously rather than with a smashing charge all along the line. Keenly disappointed, Forrest gave up and speeded away in a fruitless search for Pillow and then, frustrated again, went back to his troopers, convinced for the rest of his life that a golden opportunity for victory had been lost by a "West Pointer's" reluctance to presume.[24]

By 1 P.M. Johnson's two brigades had reached a point where the Wynn's Ferry Road slanted up over a hill through heavy timber. Many companies were out of ammunition. Simonton's men were scrounging cartridges from the enemy dead. Resistance seemed to be stiffer. Units of Lew Wallace's division were shifting from the Union center to help McClernand's disintegrating Illinoisans.[26] Johnson continued to urge Drake's men forward until he suddenly noted that he no longer had any support on his right, between his troops and the trenches to the west. Without informing Johnson, irresolute Floyd had agreed to a decision by Pillow to break off the attack and return the men to the trenches, ostensibly to pick up rations and equipment before continuing along the breakout road to Charlotte. So ordered, Pillow's three brigades on Johnson's right were falling back. Simonton's regiments were following them.

Entirely unaware of this drastic change in the battle plan, Johnson hurried an aide to Floyd to ask for reinforcements. The aide came back with an order for Johnson to report in person to Floyd. Johnson left the front and cantered back along the Wynn's Ferry Road toward Dover. He found Floyd. He asked for help in pressing the attack

Forrest had urged two hours previously. Floyd, committed now to Pillow's withdrawal, refused. It was one of the few times in his life that Johnson argued with a superior; he "hazarded the suggestion" (in his words) that the enemy in front of Drake should be pressed. Floyd said "No!" and told Johnson instead to "display" Drake's two regiments and two battalions in sight of the Federals to cover the recession of the other brigades to the nearest trenches about a half-mile away.

Reluctantly, Johnson went back to a task which nullified all the efforts and sacrifices of the morning. Sensing shortly that the Confederates had thrown away their initiative, the bluecoats in rallied and strengthened numbers advanced on Drake. Johnson sent orders to Forrest to cover the infantry withdrawal. The troopers' charges blunted the menace and Drake's force, as the rear guard for Pillow's disastrous tactic, made it to the safety of the earthworks. As before, Johnson had not been informed of a decision which blighted the Confederate advantage; he had been left to find it out for himself.[27]

Johnson spent the rest of the short winter daylight and on into the night trying to reassemble and reform the bewildered and resentful survivors of Pillow's five brigades, to direct the recovery of the scores of wounded from the snow and slush of the woods into shelters in Dover, and to salvage weapons and ammunition from the Federal dead. The exhausted and hungry Confederates were shaken and disturbed. Many had been fighting for more than seven hours in their first major engagement. They had thrilled to the pursuit of a retreating foe and now, frustrated, wet, cold, and tired, they were back where they had started. More than a thousand were dead, hurt or missing.[28]

His brother brigadiers did not include Johnson in their embittered council that met late Saturday night in Pillow's headquarters in the Rice home.[29] While they heard conflicting reports on the progress of the Union re-encirclement and argued over tactics, Johnson was out in the frigid night with the demoralized and weary troops. At 1 A.M. orders came to him announcing that the defenders were going to evacuate Fort Donelson and Dover and retreat toward Charlotte. He was told to see that the men supplied themselves with cooked rations for three days, with ammunition, blankets, and knapsacks, and that they be ready to go at 4 A.M. in the positions and formations outlined in the order.[30]

As Johnson presided over these hectic preparations, the other generals around the fireplace in the comfort of the Rice parlor were wrangling over what to do. The minutes ticked away while Pillow advocated fighting their way out in accordance with the order already sent to Johnson and Buckner argued for his gloomy view that the troops, outnumbered, exhausted, hungry and out of ammunition could neither attempt a sortie nor march 60 miles to Nashville. Forrest sent men to check on whether McClernand had moved back up the Wynn's Ferry Road to close possible escape routes. Their reports gave him confidence that he could not only get through but also could protect any accompanying infantry. Floyd was not moved. He was convinced by Buckner and by further reports of Federal movements that the situation was hopeless and he decided that surrender was the only thing left. Forrest would have none of this. He assembled 500 of his men and some 200 straggling infantry and led them before dawn across a hundred yards of Lick Creek's icy floodwater at Smith's Ford. Not until after eight o'clock did the Federals block that point and by then Forrest was safely on his way to Cumberland Iron Works, six miles upstream.[31]

Fearful of what he faced if captured, Floyd first thought he would try to escape with Forrest, then changed his mind and decided to leave by steamboat taking his Virginia division with him. He turned over his command of the fort to Pillow. Equally concerned with his individual safety, Pillow passed the responsibility to Buckner. Floyd sent orders to McCausland, Brown and Wharton to bring their men at once to the steamboat landing in Dover. While Major W. N. Brown's 20th Mississippi stood guard to make sure nobody else got on board,[32] Floyd ferried the Virginians across in several trips on the steamboat *General Anderson*. At 3 A.M. Pillow invited Gilmer, who had slept through the council session in an upstairs bedroom, to go with him.[33] Major Rice rowed them across the Cumberland in a small flatboat. Pillow recovered Clark's horse which had been carried across by Floyd with his troops and everybody headed for Clarksville either afoot or afloat. They reached Nashville Tuesday morning.[34] Left in command by the default of his seniors, soldierly Buckner wrote the note to Grant that brought the famous "unconditional surrender" reply.

Johnson, goading miserable and bone-weary men into formation along the Charlotte Road as the hours passed, had no inkling of what was being debated and decided in the Rice parlor. At 2 A.M. Moorman, his aide, brought word to Heiman to move out without noise and follow the unit on his left, prepared to fight at daybreak through the enemy whose widening arc was outlined by his campfires glowing through the brush and trees a few hundred yards away on their right. Colonel John W. Head of the Thirtieth Tennessee already had moved his garrison force into the confusion of Dover's few crowded streets.[35] The men of Simonton and Drake stood in profane wretchedness along the Charlotte Road in the muddy slush, churned by the tramping feet of thousands for the past two days.

Shivering and waiting with them shortly after 3 A.M., Johnson was astounded to observe that the Virginia brigades had left the assembly area and were moving toward the Dover landing, 800 yards away. He rode over and asked why. On orders of Floyd, he was told. Deferential as always,

Johnson sent an aide to the Dover Hotel, not to question whether there had been a change in the plan to fight a way out at 4 A.M., but simply to report that all of Pillow's brigades were in line and ready to go wherever they might be directed. The messenger returned with a note from Buckner saying he was now in command and to await further orders. Meanwhile the men of Wharton, Brown and McCausland left Johnson's area and jammed into Dover to get aboard the ferry.

Completely in the dark, literally and figuratively, Johnson learned from a courier shortly afterward that Buckner was looking for him. Johnson forced his horse through the milling hundreds in the streets to the Dover Hotel. Buckner was not there. But a staff officer told Johnson that surrender had been decided upon, that Floyd and Pillow had given up command to Buckner and had gone. The staff officer asked Johnson to contact the nearest Union outpost by flag of truce and ask for a cease fire until the troops along the Charlotte Road could return to their trenches. Johnson rode back to his field headquarters and began instructing his staff on what he finally had learned.

Within minutes, a written message came from Buckner, officially verifying what Johnson had been told at the hotel. Buckner added that he had sent a note to Grant and that, until further orders, all hostilities should be suspended. The message also said that Johnson's truce party should ask the Federals where Grant was located.[36]

Johnson may have been chagrined that he had been ignored and not informed on developments, but he wasted no time on regrets. He had never been ultra-optimistic regarding the possible outcome; he had expressed his fears to Governor Harris days before Grant's force had appeared and he had manifested his pessimism to such observers as young Guy. Now he went briskly about his new task and sent his staff, reduced to three after Ellis fled with Floyd, at once to Heiman, Baldwin, Drake and Simonton to tell them to bring their men back into their trench bivouacs and stack their arms.

With his aides absent on such business, Johnson picked Major W. E. Rogers of the Third Mississippi to improvise a white flag and fasten it to a pole to be carried like a lance. He decided to accompany Rogers. They rode their horses over the parapet in the graying dawn toward the nearest Union troops which were Colonel John M. Thayer's Third Brigade of Lew Wallace's division. Wallace chanced to be there, saw them approach and had them halted and questioned at a distance. Then he rode over himself.

Introductions were stiffly formal. Johnson told Wallace why he and Rogers carried the white flag. Wallace asked if the surrender were "perfected." Johnson replied he did not know if a formality would be required, but except for that, it was a surrender. He said his troops were drawn up with their arms stacked and were ready to give up possession of their earthworks.

Thrilled Wallace yielded to an impulse to be the first Federal inside the defenses. He told his aide, Lieutenant James R. Ross, to guide Rogers to Grant's headquarters in Mrs. Crisp's log house, nearly two miles away. He sent other aides to his brigade commanders with orders to move their lines forward to "take possession of persons and property." Johnson looked at him gratefully, he wrote later, when he strictly forbade any taunts or cheering by his men.

Wallace asked Johnson if he would guide him to Buckner, an old friend, at the Dover Hotel where Johnson said he might be found. Johnson agreed. He took the flag from Rogers, telling him "You won't need it" and added to Wallace, "Our people are in a bad humor, but I will be glad to have you go with me."

Carrying the flag, Johnson led Wallace and his small

staff back across the trenches and through Dover's commotion to the hotel. He went through a door at the far end of the shallow hall, saw Buckner and told him Wallace was outside. Buckner asked him to send in the Union general. Johnson did not follow Wallace into the dining room for a breakfast of coffee and corn bread but went back to the trenches.[37] This probably was the last time Johnson and Buckner saw each other until August when Braxton Bragg mounted his invasion of Kentucky and Johnson led a brigade in Buckner's division.

Back at his post in the field, Johnson found Heiman's men had not returned to their salient between the Pinery and Wynn's Ferry roads, but were milling around in the turbulent Dover area. The other units followed orders, went back to their camp areas, stacked arms and waited sullenly for the next episode.[38]

Grant arrived at the hotel in mid-morning, talked with Buckner, heard estimates of numbers of captives and amounts of materiel and then began planning for the removal of surrendered men and officers. He directed that the prisoners be collected as rapidly as possible near Dover under their own officers and get two days rations preparatory to being embarked for Cairo, Illinois. He sent a jubilant telegram to Henry Wager Halleck, his chief in St. Louis:

> We have taken Fort Donelson and from 12,000 to 15,000 prisoners, including Generals Buckner and Bushrod Johnson.[39]

The wire touched off a hilarious flight of telegrams because "Johnson" was misread for "Johnston" and the Federal high command succumbed to the wishful hope that Grant's quarry was Albert Sidney Johnston. Orders on what to do with him flew back and forth between Washington, St. Louis and Norfolk, Virginia until it gradually became clear to all the reluctants that the prisoner was not the Confederate general-in-chief of the West, but only diffident Bushrod Johnson just as Grant had reported in the first place.

But where was Bushrod Johnson? The answer to this focuses a revealing light on his concept of duty and ethical responsibility. It is expressed in the disingenuous rationale by which he tried to justify what he did—an echo of the July 1847 "proffit" offer to Seawell and his defense of it. Unobtrusive after he left Wallace and Buckner on Sunday morning, Johnson kept out of sight. He did not report personally but sent one of his aides to Buckner on Sunday afternoon with a list of his surrendered troops. In it, he included himself, his aides Moorman and McLean, the brigades of Heiman, Drake, Davidson (Simonton), Baldwin and Head,[41] a total of sixteen regiments and two battalions; some fragments of Forrest's cavalry left sleeping when the bulk got away, parts of the 20th Mississippi and three other regiments.[42] Then Johnson faded into the confused background.

He indulged in no social amenities with the victors. Until they left for Northern prisons the leading Confederate officers messed with their Federal counterparts,[43] in the Dover Hotel and elsewhere. Johnson did not join them. He especially avoided Grant who had known him at West Point when Johnson was Cadet Captain and Grant was a yearling, and later when they were in adjacent regiments in Louisiana, Texas and Mexico. He also shunned Charles F. Smith, adjutant and instructor at the Military Academy in Johnson's cadet days. For three days he covertly watched his Tennessee friends and acquaintances loaded aboard crowded steamboats for Cairo and St. Louis. His presence among them until they left went entirely undetected.

Why the Union command made no consistent effort to check on their second most important captive, asked no questions of Buckner or others concerning him, nor pushed any search for him when they noted his absence from the joint mess is unexplained. The Federals appear simply to have forgotten Johnson existed. The chaotic situation may be blamed. Not since Saratoga and Yorktown had an entire army been captured on American soil. Neither side quite knew how to act. Victors had not yet adopted the policy of paroling the vanquished and sending them home to await exchange. Scores of the surrendered men, convinced the war was over, walked away unchallenged. Grant admitted that his sentries became so familiar with the sight of Confederates passing to and fro on burial or fatigue details that many got beyond their sight and went on unimpeded.[44]

So did Bushrod Johnson. By Tuesday afternoon, February 18, all of the men he had led in battle were on the way to Northern prisons. He concluded it was unlikely that he "could be of any more service to them," though it is not clear what he had done since Sunday either for the men or for conscientious Buckner who had to bear the brunt of the disastrous situation without support. Realistically, departure of the troops and his aides Moorman and McLean would have put an end to Johnson's hiding place among them. Near sunset on Tuesday he walked westward with Captain John H. Anderson[45] of the Tenth Tennessee, starting from the rifle pits so recently occupied by Heiman's men. No pickets or other Federals challenged them, so they kept going to Nashville, sixty miles away.

The morality of the exploit posed doubts even in Johnson's mind. He must have been aware how his conduct compared with Buckner's. That stalwart character felt that both his own and the Confederacy's honor required that everything under his command should be turned over to the Federals after he agreed to Grant's terms of surrender. He had even sent a threat to Floyd that he would shell the *General Anderson* at dawn if it did not leave the Dover landing immediately with the crowded escapees.[46]

There was no question in Buckner's concept of his duty regarding his soldierly obligations and he did not feel called upon to explain. Johnson attempted to justify his actions in his report, written in Huntsville, Alabama on March 4 and sent to Pillow, his immediate superior, then in Decatur, Alabama under suspension from command pending inquiry into his performance at Fort Donelson.[47] Johnson said:

> . . . Almost immediately upon discovering that steps had been taken toward surrendering our forces, the question occurred to me whether the example of our commanding general was an appropriate one, under the circumstances in which I was placed, to be followed, especially as I had no part in the surrender and had only on an emergency taken command of the troops with which I had not been previously identified. I, however, concluded to stay with the men, promote their comfort as far as possible and share their fate.
>
> By Tuesday, Feb. 18 the troops in my command had been separated from me, having been sent down the river on board of steamers and I concluded that it was unlikely that I could be of any more service to them. I, however, formed no purpose or plan of escape.

When he argued that he had no part in the surrender, Johnson carefully overlooked the fact that he had escorted the flag of truce to Wallace and had guided the Federal general back through the lines. He added that he had received "no orders or instructions from the Federal authorities," that he "had not been recognized or even seen by any of the general officers," forgetting again his liaison with Wallace, and that he "had given no parole and had made no promises."[48]

In protesting that he made "no purpose or plan of escape," Johnson would make it appear that he and Anderson, strolling casually into the wintry dusk away from any food or shelter with chill night coming on apace, suddenly had the whim to keep on walking for 60 miles. There were only two habitations within a thousand yards of Heiman's salient. Both of these dwellings, the Rollins and Cherry houses, were in use as Federal hospitals,[49] offering no haven nor help to the fugitives. To avoid Union patrols, Johnson and Anderson would have had to trudge across broken country or snow covered fields for more than a mile to find any sympathetic farmer from whom a hurried transaction might procure mounts for the two-day trip to Nashville.[50] The conclusion is inescapable that young Anderson, probably a former student of Johnson's, had cached horses and food in the thick woods prior to their twilight ramble, that both removed or concealed their insignia of rank to avoid detection by the relaxed sentries and once beyond them followed a planned beeline to freedom.

Johnson sought absolution for his misdeed after he confessed it. He said: "If my escape involves any question of military law, duty or honor I desire it to be thoroughly investigated and I shall submit with pleasure to any decision of the proper authorities."[51] Nothing ever came officially. Pillow was too occupied trying to answer Richmond's questions. Buckner bore no resentment that his chief lieutenant had avoided sharing his fate. Johnson later served under him and Buckner always had high praise for his service. He also endorsed Johnson's periodic pleas for promotion to major general during the next two years.[52]

The charge that Johnson had violated a parole of honor was widely circulated. Back home in Belmont County, Ohio, the *Chronicle,* after first printing on February 20 that "Gens: Pillow, Floyd, Johnston and Buckner were taken" on February 27 said on page two, first column:

> The rebel Gen. Johnson captured at Ft. Donelson has

violated his parole of honor and escaped. The next time he is captured a drum head court martial will speedily dispose of him in a manner that will effectively prevent another escape.

On the same page, column three, in a dispatch from Columbus, the *Chronicle*'s correspondent said: "Three hundred sesech prisoners, officers, captured at Ft. Donelson, I learn, are to arrive here today to go into quarters at Camp Chase. Among them is a Brig. Gen. Bushrod R. Johnson, said to be formerly a citizen of Belmont County and a native of the village of Belmont."

The St. Clairsville *Gazette* on February 27 was more specific, and the Johnson and Spencer relatives of Bushrod still in the area could read the following on page four, first column:

AN OHIO RENEGADE

A Columbus correspondent of the Cincinnati *Commercial* says:

Brig. Gen. Bushrod Johnson, captured at Fort Donelson, was born in Belmont County, Ohio. He was appointed a cadet to West Point in 1836 by Hon. Wm. Kennon, graduated 23d in his class and was appointed 2d Lieutenant in the army, was promoted 1st Lieutenant in 1844, subsequently was professor of mathematics at West Point, then principal of a military school at Nashville and finally a rebel general and a Federal captive. Those who knew him in Ohio regarded him as an able man.

In Wayne County, Indiana, where bonfires were lighted in the streets to celebrate the Union victory and where other Johnsons and Spencers may have hoped to avoid the scornful gossip of their neighbors over the defection of their maverick relative, the Richmond *Palladium,* while giving normal news coverage to the capture of Fort Donelson, neglected by chance or choice, any reference to Bushrod Johnson. The *Palladium* was politically Republican and thus would have been friendly toward Judge Nimrod Johnson and Abolitionist Dr. Nathan Johnson of Cambridge City.

The Democrat organ, the Richmond *Jeffersonian* was not so chary. On Thursday, February 27, on page two, column three, this appeared:

> The Captured Gen. Johnson
>
> The Gen. Johnson captured at Fort Donelson is not Gen. A. S. Johnson [*sic*] as at first supposed but a Tennessee general of that name. Of the captured Gen. Johnson, the Lafayette *Courier* says:
>
> "The rebel Gen. Bushrod Johnson, taken prisoner at Fort Donelson and concerning whom there has been so much inquiry is a brother of Dr. Nathan Johnson of Cambridge City, an uncle of Judge N. H. Johnson of Wayne County and, we are proud to say, a relative of Tom Underwood of this city. His little son is now with his relatives in Cambridge, having been sent there when the rebellion first broke out. Gen. Johnson received his education at the expense of the government and is a graduate of West Point and his case, like many others, involving the basest ingratitude and treachery admits of no extenuation.
>
> He has been until the last few weeks superintendent erecting batteries on the Potomac at Aquia Creek but was lately transferred to the Western Department and commissioned a brigadier general just in time to receive the benefits which the unenviable distinction will now confer upon him."
>
> DR. NATHAN JOHNSON of this city, is one of the most extreme anti-slavery men and has been active in the Abolition movement in this region.[53]

The parole violation charge against Johnson got additional publicity from the exiled Tennessee Unionist, William Gannaway Brownlow, in his book published in Cincinnati shortly after Fort Donelson fell. He said that Johnson "violating his parole, escaped."[54] The Indiana Johnsons took umbrage at the attacks on their rebel relative, according to Robert U. Johnson, and "went to great trouble to vindicate his honor," even to the point of getting Grant to admit, twenty years after the war, that Bushrod Johnson had given no parole.[55] Grant could say this in all truth, since none of the surrendered Confederates was asked, and consequently none gave, any parole of honor. What "great trouble" was taken by the Indiana Johnsons is not disclosed by their literary descendant. Nothing in print appeared from them in the newspapers at the time.

There were no reproaches regarding Johnson's conduct during the engagement, albeit praise was scanty. Floyd reported: "Gen. Johnson led his command with firmness and spirit in the conflict," and Pillow wrote, almost as an afterthought in his report: "I must acknowledge my obligations to Gen. Bushrod Johnson who assisted me in command of the forces with which I attacked the enemy and who bore himself gallantly throughout the conflict."[56] Buckner did not mention Johnson in his two reports.[57] Nor did Albert Sidney Johnston in a personal letter to Jefferson Davis on March 18 when he said: "Floyd, Pillow and Buckner were high in the opinion of officers and men for skill and courage, and among the best officers of my command."[58] Johnson also got the silent treatment from Personne, special correspondent of the Charleston *Courier* in his florid account of the battle. He wrote: "During the entire engagements of three days" Floyd, Buckner and Pillow "behaved with a gallantry which excited the admiring cheers of their entire command."[59] But Johnson's performance lingered long in the memory of Colonel W. N. Brown of the 20th Mississippi. In 1880 he wrote to Jefferson Davis at Beauvoir, Mississippi, this acclaim:

> It gives me great pleasure to bear testimony to the gallantry, efficiency and generalship of General Bushrod Johnson who assumed command of the left during the engagement of the day preceding the surrender. He seems to have been

without a special command, but on that occasion his presence and labors were invaluable.[60]

Floyd and Pillow may have ignored or forgotten Johnson on the night before their flight from Fort Donelson, but they were more than eager to get his testimony into the record when Richmond began questioning their judgment and generalship. Equally anxious to read Johnson's version was Judah P. Benjamin, Secretary of War, who ordered General Johnston on March 11 to direct Johnson "to make a full and detailed report as promptly as possible." Two weeks later the new Secretary of War, George W. Randolph, told Pillow he was still awaiting Johnson's report.[61] Johnson had already written his version on March 4, but it took nearly a month to go through Pillow and up to the War Department. Eight months later Johnson wrote a supplemental report to buttress Pillow's defense that the breakout and withdrawal to Nashville could not have been made on the day of the fight without food and blankets.[62]

If Johnson had any morbid thoughts on the inglorious results of his first campaign as a general, no evidence has survived. Even though his brother brigadiers several times seemed unaware he existed he had played a creditable part in a tragi-comedy of martial ineptitude. But his dubious action in walking away clouded the finale. His temperament and character compelled him to undergo the catharsis of the letter to Pillow seeking official remission. This never came and it made little difference. Soon this worry was replaced in Johnson's consciousness by the disturbing reality that his adopted home and his properties in it were perhaps irrecoverably in the hands of the enemy.

ii. Shiloh's Wound; Perryville's Mischance

Without a command, spare horses or personal baggage, Bushrod Johnson came back for a few frenzied hours in Nashville after his escape. From the stunned capital Albert Sidney Johnston's army was withdrawing South, only a few steps ahead of the 50,000 Federals of Don Carlos Buell. The Confederate rear guard marched out on the night of February 23 and the next day Union troops occupied Edgefield, across the river. Johnson would have had time only to acquire new mounts, gather a few belongings and hasten 32 miles to Murfreesborough, where Johnston's 17,000 halted until the 28th. In Huntsville on March 4, Johnson found enough leisure to write a report of his roles at Fort Donelson. He would not be back in Nashville for nearly four years.

On March 9 he was cheered by a telegram from Colonel Mackall in Decatur, Alabama, one of the way stations on Johnston's month-long march to join Beauregard at Corinth, Mississippi. The message said: "Come here at once prepared to take the field." An order the next day told him to report to Beauregard's headquarters at Jackson, Tennessee.[63] Thence he was posted to the army of Polk, moving south from Columbus, Ky., through western Tennessee to the concentration of Confederates in the Corinth area.[64]

With Polk's force was B. F. Cheatham, Johnson's Nashville acquaintance, politician, horse fancier and militia general who at 40 years old, ranked Johnson, 45, as a brigadier. On March 10 Cheatham was made a major general and he and Charles Clark, the Ohio-Mississippian who had finally resolved his contretemps with Richmond over his resignation threat, led the two divisions in Polk's Corps as reorganized in Johnston's "Army of the Mississippi." Bushrod Johnson took over the first brigade in Cheatham's Division. It contained the Second Tennessee, Colonel J.

Knox Walker; the Fifteenth Tennessee, Lieutenant Colonel R. C. Tyler; the 154th Senior Tennessee, a former militia unit, Colonel Preston Smith; and Colonel A. K. Blythe's Mississippi Battalion with Captain Marshall T. Polk's Tennessee Battery.[65] For a brief time Johnson also was assigned duty as fortifications officer for the corps in charge of building defenses at Bethel Station, 21 miles north of Corinth. He vainly tried to get 100 picks and 500 shovels he needed for his task.[66] Cheatham's Division was left at Bethel Station when the rest of Polk's troops joined Johnson's assembly at Corinth.

There approximately 40,000 Confederates gathered: Johnston's 17,000 from central Kentucky closed on March 22; Braxton Bragg brought 10,000 from the Mobile area; Massachusetts-born Daniel Ruggles added 5000 from Memphis in late February and Polk's 8000 were on hand. These were organized by Johnston into three corps under Polk, Bragg and Hardee with a two-brigade reserve under John Cabell Breckenridge, once Vice President of the United States. General P. G. T. Beauregard, sent from Richmond several weeks earlier and put in charge of the western half of Johnston's Western Department, was designated second in command. Bragg was named Johnston's chief of staff in addition to running his corps.[67]

On March 11 the first of more than 80 Federal transports began unloading Grant's bluecoats at Savannah, 31 miles north of Corinth. On the same day, President Lincoln put Halleck in command of all troops between Knoxville and the Mississippi River. This included Buell's 50,000 in Nashville. Halleck told Buell to take them to Savannah, too. General C. F. Smith, commanding Grant's army because Halleck was jealously displeased with the victor of Donelson, moved nine miles upstream to Pittsburg Landing to camp while awaiting Buell's lagging thousands. By March 17 Grant was back in command after Smith was disabled by a leg injury that later killed him. He had five divisions: McClernand, W. T. Sherman, W. H. L. Wallace, Stephen A. Hurlbut, and Benjamin M. Prentiss, bedded down in an irregular triangle formed by the Tennessee River and Snake Creek with its branch Owl Creek as the triangle's sides and an open base toward the South across which flowed Lick Creek and its branch Locust Grove Creek. There was no system about the location of the division camps, no defensive works and no cavalry outposts. A sixth division, Lew Wallace's, was stretched between Crump's Landing, about five miles downriver, to Adamsville, five miles west along the Crump-Purdy Road.

During the last half of March, scouts and pickets of Wallace and Cheatham warily eyed each other. Bushrod Johnson personally checked on reports that the Federals were building a road from Pittsburg Landing toward the Pea Ridge Road and found them true.[68] Preston Smith ordered 300 bales of cotton burned after his scouts reported increased enemy activity.[69] Wallace told Grant the rebels were in strength at Purdy, causing Grant to conclude that any attack would occur in Wallace's area.[70] Cheatham sent word to Polk that he was being menaced by Wallace and this dispatch, reaching Beauregard about 10 P.M. on Wednesday, April 2, precipitated the decision at Johnston's headquarters in Corinth to move forward against Grant before Buell's reinforcement arrived.[71]

Sometime Thursday afternoon Cheatham's division of the brigades of Bushrod Johnson and Colonel William H. Stephens began moving out of Bethel Station with three days' cooked rations in haversacks, two additional days' food in wagons, 100 rounds of small arms ammunition and 200 rounds for field pieces.[72] Ahead of them stretched twenty miles of hiking along a narrow mud road through heavy woods to Mickey where they would join the rest of Polk's I Corps, now marching thirteen miles north from Corinth behind Hardee's III Corps. Bragg's II Corps and

Breckenridge's Reserve Corps traveled the Corinth-Monterey (Pea Ridge) Road, two miles to the east.

Through the night and all the next day, Friday, April 4, Johnson's troops and wagons toiled slowly forward. A torrential rain and thunderstorms on Friday night added to the general confusion resulting from poor maps, terrible roads, inexperience and inefficiency. The showers soaked the Federals, too, and Grant's horse slipped and fell on him, injuring his ankle and putting him on crutches for a week.[73] Bragg's Corps was especially laggard, Jones Mitchell Withers's division taking thirty hours until Friday night to tramp twelve miles from Corinth to Monterey.[74] At Mickey, on Saturday, three corps funnelled into one eastward road in a column of corps: Hardee first with a brigade of Bragg, next the rest of Bragg, then Polk with Cheatham bringing up the rear and finally Breckenridge. Johnson's men had a chance to catch a little sleep beside the road as other troops plodded through the bottle neck to reach their places in the order of battle. When darkness fell on Saturday, April 5, Johnson's Tennesseeans and his Mississippi regiment got into position and bivouacked for the night, two and a half miles from the Federals of Sherman and McClernand, extending east and west behind Oak Creek in the vicinity of a little log chapel in the middle of the woods called Shiloh Church.[75]

Sunday's dawn found Johnson and his troops astir in the rear of Colonel R. M. Russell's brigade, which was the left wing of Clark's division. Ordered to deploy on Clark's left, they moved out in this order: Second Tennessee, Fifteenth Tennessee, Polk's Battery, Blythe's Mississippians and the German and Irish ex-militiamen of the 154th Senior Tennessee.[76] Already they could hear the rising crescendo of battle in the woods ahead as Hardee's line crashed and routed first Sherman's left regiment and then two others of Colonel Jesse Hildebrand's brigade and hammered at the right of Prentiss. At 7:30 A.M. Beauregard ordered Polk to hurry a brigade of Cheatham to support Bragg's left where McClernand, coming forward at Sherman's call for help, temporarily stalled the Gray onrush. Polk sent in Colonel W. H. Stephens's Seventh Kentucky, First, Sixth and Ninth Tennessee and Captain Melancthon Smith's Mississippi Battery. Major General Cheatham rode at their head.[77]

Soon Polk got another call to send in Johnson's and Russell's brigades to bolster Bragg's center. Clark led Russell's three Tennessee and one Louisiana regiments. Polk, a corps commander performing a brigadier's duties, personally took Johnson's men forward. Either the bishop-general lacked confidence in Johnson or he was over-eager to get close to the fighting. The time was 8 A.M. Johnson's untried troops under enemy artillery fire, were marched first to the left then by the right flank for fifteen minutes before they were put into line of battle to move to the front and get into action.

Hampered by marshy ground and a small stream which held them up, and unnerved by the bursting shells and searing bullets, men began wavering and straggling. Tyler of the Fifteenth Tennessee drew his pistol and by threats and commands restored his lines and pressed forward. Johnson rode along the lines urging, prodding and driving the units forward toward the woods bordering the road passing Shiloh Church. Captain Polk's guns moved forward, set up and began blasting at the stubborn, but slowly withdrawing Ohio and Illinois regiments of Sherman and McClernand.

Soon Johnson discovered that the 154th Tennessee, Blythe's Mississippians and a section of Polk's Battery were detaching themselves from his lines and moving toward the right. He hurried an aide to find out why. He was informed that Bragg himself had ordered the move through a staff officer. Chagrined and disturbed to find he had lost control of half of his troops, Johnson moved the Fifteenth Tennessee to the ground first taken by Blythe and put the Second Tennessee in the rear of Polk's remaining guns. Under a heavy fire, the Fifteenth advanced 200 yards. Tyler was shot from his horse and forced to quit. Major John F. Hearn took over for him.[78]

Under the anxious eyes of General Polk, Blythe drove a Union battery and its supporting infantry from its position. Moments later he was killed.[79] Lieutenant Colonel D. L. Herron and Captain R. H. Humphreys of the same regiment were mortally wounded. Command went to Major James Moore.[80] The 154th with the section of Polk's guns crossed an open field and waded a muddy stream 300 yards from a Federal battery. As the guns got off a half-dozen rounds, a new order came from Bragg to push the unit forward. Preston Smith led a charge which captured four Union guns, but his losses were murderous.[81]

Federal musketry and artillery were taking a frightful toll of the Second Tennessee, trying to protect the rest of Captain Polk's guns, a few hundred yards north of Shiloh Church. Half of the regiment were casualties. The disorganized survivors milled around in a state of shock. Twice Johnson with Colonel J. Knox Walker formed them into line but each time when ordered forward the men wavered and broke for shelter. Captain Polk's leg was broken by a Union shell and half of his guns were disabled. Soon only one was able to continue firing. Johnson ordered it withdrawn.

He tried again to form the Second and lead it ahead. He succeeded in bringing the men forward to the ground they had occupied before the wavering started. Then an exploding shell knocked him to the ground. His horse was killed.[82] Members of his staff carried him to the rear. First reports to the high command said his wound was mortal, then "severe" and disabling. General Polk sent word to Preston Smith to take command of the brigade.[83] This was about 11 A.M. and a day and a half more of bloody fighting were ahead. Before it was over, both division commanders Clark and Cheatham were wounded, five regimental commanders were dead and Polk's Corps posted a ghastly total of 2,376 in killed, wounded and missing, of which 740 came from Johnson's Brigade.[84]

Perverse fate, as at Donelson, had limited Johnson to a secondary role. Polk personally supplanted him in leading his brigade into action; Bragg ignored him in moving half of his troops. In action less than four hours, he had shown a degree of professional competence under fire and a bold courage that seemed to be rallying and inspiring his men just as he was disabled. He could take consolation from the praise of his superiors. Beauregard called him "most meritorious," Polk felt "greatly indebted" to him and Cheatham said Johnson "displayed the soundest judgement and skill and the temporary loss of his services is very unfortunate."[85]

By the end of the week, on April 12, Johnson had recuperated enough in Columbus, Mississippi, nearly 150 miles south, to write his report, probably with the help of some of his staff: Major C. G. Rogers, adjutant; Captain William T. Blakemore who had been with him at Fort Donelson; and Captain L. D. Moore, volunteer aide. At Shiloh Johnson also had the services of Captain J. H. Anderson who had walked away with him from Donelson. Anderson had two horses shot under him and had been slightly injured by a shell at Shiloh.[86]

For Bragg's action in abruptly taking half of his brigade from him without any notification, Johnson had this aspersion in his report:

> I have to regret that, from orders apparently given to subordinates of my command, I was prevented from bringing the whole brigade handsomely into action. To this object all my efforts had been most zealously and carefully directed.

> Had I accomplished my purpose I am convinced I would now have to report much more satisfactory results.[87]

While he was recovering from his wound, Johnson kept a close eye on his surroundings. He reported what he observed to Colonel Thomas Jordan, Beauregard's adjutant general, who had been his classmate at West Point, and was quartermaster in Vera Cruz when Johnson was acting assistant commissary of subsistence. On April 21, Johnson wrote Jordan that 800 infantry and 300 cavalry in Columbus were without weapons, that 300 guns were ready for issue in the local gunsmiths where "good cannon" was being made. He added a bit of political intelligence:

> The northern counties of Alabama, you know, are full of Tories. There has been a convention recently in Winston, Fayette and Marion counties, Alabama [50 miles northeast of Columbus] in which people resolved to remain neutral; which simply means they will join the enemy when they occupy the country. Since Mississippi seceded, people from these counties have been in this state carrying the U.S. flag. There are suspected men even in this county. Fayette County, Alabama, joins this county. The enemy can approach through that county without being exposed, make a dash for this place and in a few hours destroy all the public property and shops in the town.[88]

In May, after a bout with illness which kept him off duty for several days, Johnson was back with Beauregard's army in Corinth, heavily fortified focus for reinforcements from Arkansas, South Carolina, East Tennessee and the Gulf Coast. When Beauregard, on the night of May 29–30, re tired 60 miles south to Tupelo in the face of 120,000 Federals of Halleck and Grant approaching from the Shiloh area, Johnson, under Hardee, commanded the Third Division in acting as the rear guard, holding river crossings and watching for any pursuit. He had a few brushes with Union reconnaissance parties for two days, but thereafter Halleck gave up the chase.[89]

Bragg replaced Beauregard at Tupelo, June 27. In reorganizing the Army of Mississippi in July, Hardee got command of the Left Wing. He designated Bushrod Johnson on July 7 to lead the Third Brigade of the Third Division which temporarily went to Brigadier General S. A. M. Wood, seventeen days senior to Johnson.[90] Command of this division later was taken by Buckner, finally released in August from Fort Warren by exchange for Union General George A. McCall, and promoted to major general August 16. Wood got Buckner's Fourth Brigade.

Five Tennessee regiments made up the Third Brigade, Johnson's new command. They were the Seventeenth, Colonel A. S. Marks; Twenty-third, Lieutenant Colonel R. H. Keeble; Twenty-fifth, Colonel J. M. Hughs; Thirty-seventh, Colonel Moses White; and Forty-fourth, Colonel John S. Fulton. The Fifth Confederate Infantry, Colonel J. A. Smith and Captain Putnam Darden's Mississippi Battery, called the Jefferson Artillery, made up the rest of the brigade. For nearly two years henceforth, the fortunes of Johnson and these Tennessee regiments rose and fell together and such was the rapport and mutual loyalty among them that the regiments continued to call themselves "Johnson's Brigade" until Appomattox, months after his connection with them had ceased.[91]

Johnson and his brigade were a part of Bragg's week-long rail movement of 30,000 men from Tupelo to Chattanooga, via Mobile, July 21–28. This was the start of a grand design for Bragg to invade Kentucky in connection with Kirby Smith's 19,000 based in Knoxville. Both were to move across mountains with poor roads, Bragg toward Louisville and Smith toward Lexington, then to unite.[92]

Smith started first on August 14, passing to the left of the Federal division of George W. Morgan at Cumberland Gap, routing an improvised Federal force at Richmond and reaching Lexington August 30. He kept the Cumberland mountains on his left between him and Buell who withdrew from McMinnville, through Murfreesborough to Nashville and then north to his supply base in Bowling Green, Kentucky. Late on September 16 he pointed his 16,000 for Munfordville, 40-odd miles away. But Bragg won the footrace, though he had not started until August 28.

Bragg's advance brigade under James R. Chalmers reached Munfordville early September 14. The Federal garrison there included Colonel Richard Owen's Sixtieth Indiana, the Seventeenth Indiana of Colonel John T. Wilder, industrialist turned soldier, who commanded the fort, and two other regiments, a battery and miscellaneous detachments aggregating 4000 men. Chalmers rashly assaulted the place and was bloodily repulsed. On the 16th, Wilder's and Owen's force was surrounded by Bragg's army and the next day it surrendered. The two colonels were paroled with their men.[93] Before the Federals left, Johnson had a long, cordial reunion with his former colleague in Western Military Institute. Two former students, Major I. B. Johnson and Captain Harry Flack accompanied Johnson on the visit. Owen also was the recipient of courtesies from Bragg, Hardee and Buckner who had served with him in Mexico.[94]

Bragg cut Buell's supply line from Louisville. Instead of pursuing his advantage he moved to Bardstown permitting Buell to pass to the west into Louisville. As rainless September turned into equally drought-parched October, Buell, reinforced, sent two divisions toward Frankfort to contain or watch Smith in Lexington and moved the balance of his army, the corps of Alexander McCook, Thomas L. Crittenden and Charles C. Gilbert toward Bardstown to attack Bragg. Polk was left in Bardstown while Bragg went off to Frankfort to assist in the futile installation of a provisional Confederate governor. Unaware of the size of the Union force moving against him, Bragg told Polk to hit Buell's flank. Polk, better informed, began retiring to the southeast.[95] Bragg then directed the bishop-general to go to Harrodsburg to protect the route to a large stock of supplies Smith had stored in Lexington. Polk's left wing under Hardee reached Perryville, ten miles southwest of Harrodsburg on October 7. Cheatham's division, which had started for Salvisa, twenty miles northeast, to reinforce Smith, was recalled in time to support the divisions of Buckner and James Patton Anderson of Hardee the following day. Johnson's Brigade was in Buckner's Division.

Thirsty soldiers hunting water brought the collision near Perryville. Federal brigades as they arrived after dawn on Wednesday October 8, occupied high ground above a few pools of stagnant water in nearly dry Doctor's Creek, northwest of the town. The Confederate cavalry brigade of Colonel John A. Wharton and Cheatham moved out opposite and beyond these bluecoats who were McCook's left flank. Buckner's four brigades: Johnson, St. John R. Liddell, Patrick R. Cleburne and S. A. M. Wood were in the center of the Southern lines and Anderson was on the left. Polk had selected the positions although Bragg was present, but the Union leader Buell, two and a half miles away, was not aware of the fight until it was nearly over.[96]

To McCook's right was Gilbert with the division of Phil Sheridan in front. Crittenden's corps was on the Federal right, too far away to get into the action, opposite Anderson.

Cheatham hit McCook's left (north) flank soon after 1 P.M. He routed a green brigade, killed two brigadiers and drove nearly half a mile before being slowed. Buckner, beefed-up with brigades from Anderson, probed for a weak spot between McCook and Gilbert on the right of Lovell H. Rousseau's division and began hammering in a wedge.[97]

The point of the wedge was Johnson's Brigade. He had moved down the Macksville Pike, west of Perryville, at 11 A.M., thence to the brow of a hill sloping 600 yards down to Doctor's Creek and its precious pools. Along the breast-

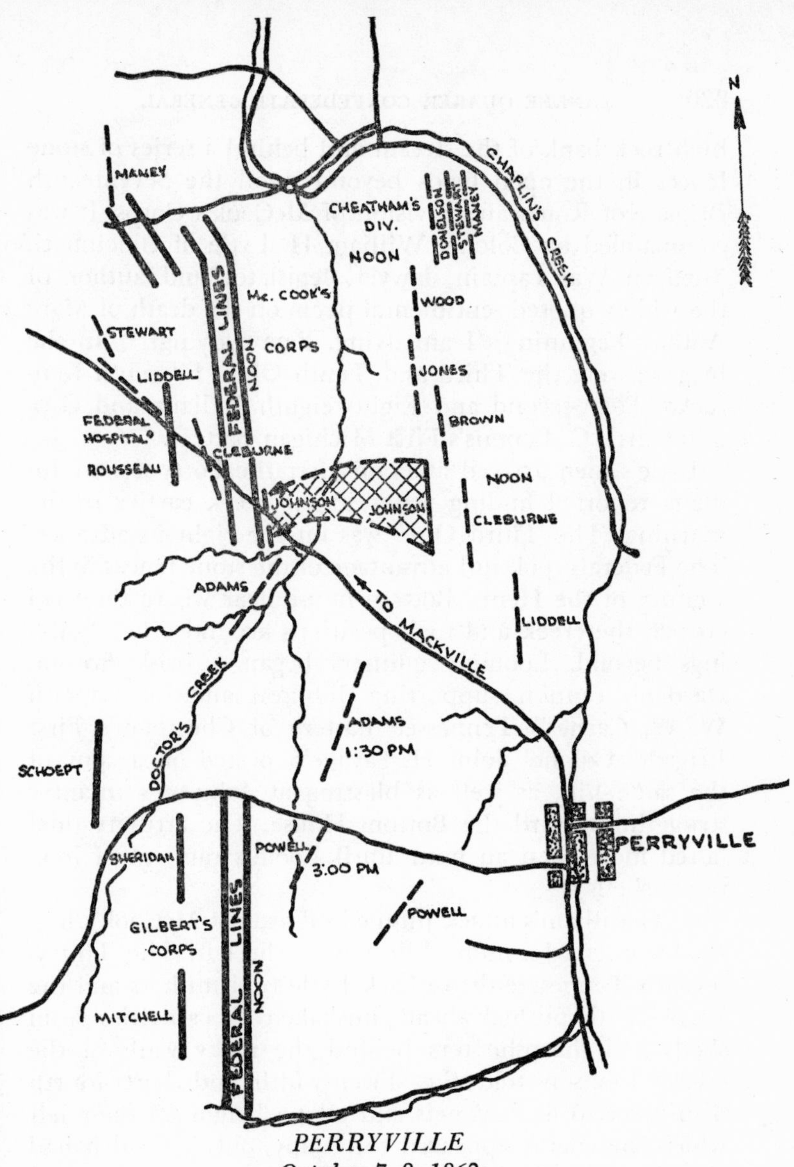

PERRYVILLE
October 7–8, 1862

Five horses are shot under Johnson as he spearheads Buckner's wedge into the Federal center. At the moment of triumph his troops run out of ammunition and flashier Cleburne and his men replace Johnson's Brigade. (From OR *Atlas Plate XXIV)* high rock bank of the stream and behind a series of stone fences in the open fields beyond stood the Seventeenth Brigade of Rousseau's division of McCook's Corps. It was commanded by Colonel William H. Lytle of Cincinnati, Mexican War captain, lawyer, legislator and author of the widely quoted sentimental poem on the death of Marc Antony beginning "I am dying, Egypt, dying!"[98] In the brigade were the Third and Tenth Ohio, Fifteenth Kentucky, Forty-second and Eighty-eighth Indiana and Captain Curtis O. Loomis's First Michigan Battery.

Lytle's men arrived at noon after the Forty-second Indiana reported finding water in the creek earlier in the morning. The Third Ohio was on the right in advance. The Federals took full advantage of the stone fences in the vicinity of the Henry Bottom house near where the road crossed the creek and took positions around other buildings beyond. Loomis's gunners began a brisk fire on Darden's cannon supporting Johnson and on Captain W. W. Carnes's Tennessee Battery of Cheatham's First Brigade, Colonel John H. Savage's, posted on a spur of the same hill, as well as blasting at Johnson's infantry struggling toward the Bottom House. The artillery duel lasted more than an hour until Loomis ran out of long range shells.[99]

As Cheatham's attack jumped off against McCook's left, Buckner sent Johnson obliquely to the left. The Thirty-seventh Tennessee drove back Lytle's skirmishers and the Forty-fourth pushed ahead, unshaken by casualties from shells and sharpshooters behind the rocky walls of the creek. Johnson told the Twenty-fifth and Forty-fourth Tennessee to fix bayonets and take a height on their left which the enemy appeared to occupy, only to find it had already been seized by troops of Brigadier General Daniel W. Adams of Anderson's Second Brigade. The Fifth pressed on in spurting charges against the series of stone walls, pouring in a deadly fire, setting a barn and houses afire. Resistance was stubborn. Three times a Federal flag was cut down by bullets.

Adams asked for and Johnson loaned him the Twenty-fifth and Forty-fourth to protect Captain C. H. Slocomb's Washington (Louisiana) Battery in the face of a threatened Federal counterattack. Buckner put them in position in the cover of a small woods. The Thirty-seventh, Seventeenth and Twenty-third joined the Fifth Confederate in flushing Ohioans and Hoosiers from behind the fences as they retreated slowly into the open fields across the creek and along the Macksville Road. The Union Fifteenth Kentucky was badly shattered. Rallying his obstinate defenders, Lytle was knocked from his horse by a creasing head wound. Before he could remount he was surrounded and captured. Colonel Curran Pope of the Fifteenth Kentucky took command of Lytle's brigade. A short time later Pope was carried from the field, mortally wounded.

Johnson was unscathed, but five horses were shot under him. Blakemore and Snowden of his staff also lost mounts.[100] Johnson was pressing the Twenty-third and Thirty-seventh, small regiments of 230 men each, and the Seventeenth and Fifth athwart the Macksville Road toward the Russell House, a half-mile away when Lytle was brought to him by a soldier guard. Johnson saw the blood-smeared head of his foe, called one of his adjutant's clerks and told him to take the Union colonel back to Johnson's brigade surgeon. His wound cleaned and bandaged, Lytle was escorted to Harrodsburg the next day and paroled. He hired a buggy and drove by way of Danville back to the Union army, reporting on Friday to Buell.[101]

For more than four hours the vicious fire fight had been raging. It was about 5 P.M. and Johnson's four regiments in the wedge were running low on ammunition. They had progressed to where Darden's shells were bursting dangerously close to them. Johnson sent an aide to the rear to bring up more rifle ammunition and to tell the left section of Darden's guns to cease fire, lest they hit their own comrades. He retrieved the Twenty-fifth and Forty-fourth, which had remained near Adams's position until the Federal attack threat passed, and sent them up the hill to the left of the Russell farmhouse. On Buckner's order he directed the Seventeenth and Thirty-seventh to the right of the house to support the remaining guns of Darden, Slocomb's four cannon and a section of Calvert's Arkansas Battery from Cleburne's Brigade.

Cleburne's two Arkansas and one Tennessee regiments, making up the second brigade of Buckner's division, were sent in by Buckner to take over Johnson's position as his fire slackened and his drive stalled for lack of ammunition. In the gathering darkness, Lytle's brigade, which had suffered 822 casualties, braced on the heights above Wilson's Creek west of the Russell House, which had been its original position in the morning. Johnson's men fell behind Cleburne's, drew back to the creek bed and at midnight got orders to withdraw.[102] He had lost 204 men killed, wounded and missing.

Elsewhere along the Union front, Sheridan held his ground and in counterattacks pushed Anderson back toward Perryville. Bragg ordered a general withdrawal on the night of the battle. He linked up with Smith at Harrodsburg on Friday and began a long, unpursued retreat through Cumberland Gap to Knoxville. Johnson's Brigade, hailed by Hardee as the one at Perryville which "gallantly led the advance"[103] reached there in less than two weeks in good condition considering their 170-mile march over rough roads and deep fords. Johnson wrote his report on October 23.

During November, when Bragg was regrouping his army in Murfreesborough, Johnson's Brigade was sent from Hardee's Corps at Tullahoma, 16 miles northwest to Shelbyville "to secure supplies of all kinds" and ship them by rail to depots along the Nashville-Chattanooga Railroad.[104] While his men were foraging through the rich farms of the area, Johnson lost the Fifth Confederate by transfer to Cleburne's Brigade.

If he was disturbed to find his command shrinking, Johnson was due shortly for a greater disappointment. In December Buckner was transferred from his division to take charge of fortifying Mobile. To succeed him the Irish-born Arkansan, Cleburne, was promoted major general, December 13, 1862. A druggist in Helena, Arkansas who had studied and practiced law with considerable success in the 1850s, Cleburne had served three years in the British army before purchasing his discharge and coming to America in 1849.[105] On the list of brigadiers in Joseph E. Johnston's western armies on November 27, Cleburne stood sixteenth to Johnson's eleventh,[106] and his elevation ahead of West Point graduates and political figures, some of whose combat records compared favorably with his must have caused an epidemic of heartaches and fancied injustice. But in Cleburne's favor were his youth—he was 34—and his aggressive fighting qualities of which his cause stood in dire need.

Bushrod Johnson had proved himself a proficient and skillful leader in two bloody battles, but in neither had he found the complete success that is the measure of merit in the profession of arms. He had served well at Shiloh until his wound removed him from the scene prematurely; at Perryville he had aggressively led Buckner's spearhead until the ill luck to run out of ammunition took him out of action just short of his goal and replaced him with a more colorful figure. In both battles he had demonstrated a high degree of bravery and coolness under fire, prime requisites of leadership. His star was still ascending, but its pace was slow. The new year, 1863, would bring its zenith.

Notes

1. Johnson's report in *OR,* VII, pp. 385 ff.
2. *Ibid.,* p. 345. Hanson was killed at Stones River.
3. *Ibid.,* p. 358.
4. *WP Atlas,* Map 26.
5. Originals in *Charles Clark Papers,* Mississippi Department of Archives and History, Jackson.
6. Pillow letter to Randolph, May 15, 1862 in *OR,* VII, p. 305.
7. General Order No. 1, HQ Fort Donelson, Feb. 9, 1862 in *OR,* VII, p. 868.
8. Gilmer's report, *OR,* VII, p. 261.
9. *OR,* VII, p. 288.
10. Andrew Nelson Lytle, *Bedford Forrest,* (New York: Minton Balch & Co., 1931), p. 58.
11. *WP Atlas,* Map 27.
12. John H. Guy, *The Diary or Prison Journal of John H. Guy,* Mss. Coll., Virginia Historical Society, Richmond. Entry of April 21, 1862 on p. 20.
13. *OR,* VII, pp. 296, 362.
14. *Ibid.,* VII, p. 330.
15. *OR,* Ser. 2, III, p. 864. Roster of aides in *ibid.,* VII, p. 363. Ellis had the task of writing the dispatch on February 7 to Polk announcing the fall of Fort Henry (*OR,* VII, p. 135). He escaped from Fort Donelson with Floyd on February 16 (*OR,* VII, p. 428). Blakemore from Christian County, Kentucky, continued to serve with Johnson until he lost a leg in the Petersburg campaign in 1864.
16. *OR,* VII, p. 410. One of the rifle's shells hit the U.S.S. Carondelet on the thirteenth.
17. *Ibid.,* VII, p. 330.
18. Henry Walke, "The Western Flotilla at Fort Donelson, Island Number Ten, Fort Pillow and Memphis" in *B&L,* I, pp. 433 f.
19. *Guy Diary,* p. 21, entry April 21, 1862. Forrest's report (*OR,* VII, p. 384) says "Never were men more jubilant; old men wept, shout after shout went up, the Army was in the best possible spirits."
20. *OR,* VII, pp. 263, 360, 365. Johnson does not say definitely that he was present and Gilmer also does not name Johnson with himself, Floyd, Pillow and Buckner as attending, but apparently Johnson was there.
21. *Ibid.,* VII, p. 360; Maps 27, 28 in *WP Atlas.* The Charlotte Road, at right angles to the Wynn's Ferry Road southeast of Dover, was also known as the Forge Road.
22. *OR,* VII, pp. 263, 361, 381.
23. *Ibid.,* VII, p. 282.
24. General Thomas Jordan and J. P. Pryor, *The Campaigns of Lt. Gen. N. B. Forrest and of Forrest's Cavalry,* (New Orleans, Memphis and New York: Blelock & Co., 1868), p. 74; John Allan Wyeth, *That Devil Forrest,* (New York: Harper & Bros., 1959), p. 45; *Lytle,* 66. Neither Johnson nor Forrest mention the incident in their after-action reports.
25. *OR,* VII, pp. 374, 381.
26. Lew Wallace, "The Capture of Fort Donelson" in *B&L,* I, p. 422.

27. *OR*, VII, p. 361. Buckner in *ibid.*, p. 332 says Pillow sent him "reiterated orders" to return to the trenches early in the afternoon. When Buckner later met Floyd, the latter "seemed surprised at the order," Buckner says, but after consultation with Pillow, Floyd sent Buckner an order to go back to his former position in the works as soon as possible. McCausland in *ibid.*, p. 277 says his brigade was ordered back by Pillow.
28. *OR*, VII, p. 288.
29. A graphic detailed account of the midnight council, based on reports and recollections of participants is Edwin C. Bearss, "Unconditional Surrender: The Fall of Fort Donelson" in *Tennessee Historical Quarterly*, XXI, Nos. 1 and 2 (March and June 1962). *THQ* hereafter.
30. *OR*, VII, p. 365.
31. Forrest's report, *ibid.*, VII, pp. 383 f.
32. *Ibid.*, VII, p. 381.
33. *Ibid.*, VII, p. 264.
34. Captain Guy and his men, abandoning their guns, clambered aboard the steamboat on its second trip and rode all the way to Nashville. McCausland's regiments were ferried across the river, then hiked through ice and mud to Clarksville, where they were taken aboard again. *Ibid.*, VII, pp. 288, 302 f.; *Guy's Diary*.
35. *OR*, VII, pp. 369, 370, 378.
36. Details in Johnson's reports, *ibid.*, pp. 358 ff. and 365 ff.
37. Details in Lew Wallace, *An Autobiography*, (New York: Harper & Bros., 1906), p. 426. In the story text Wallace refers to "General ———" but identifies Roger's escort as Bushrod Johnson in fn. 2, p. 426. He does not mention Johnson in *B&L*, I, p. 428, nor does Johnson make any reference to the incident in his report because he justifies his later walkaway with the thesis that he had taken no part in the surrender.
38. *OR*, VII, pp. 363, 370.
39. *Ibid.*, VII, pp. 336, 635.
40. *Ibid.*, Ser. 2, III, pp. 269, 275 f., 310, 312.
41. Head already had escaped by boat, leaving his men, because he was suffering from exposure and feared imprisonment meant death. He reported later to Johnson's headquarters at Murfreesborough, asking for duty. None was assigned and he resigned. *OR*, VII, p. 378. Since Johnson did not list Blakemore with his staff, he may have escaped with Ellis. He was back with Johnson at Shiloh.
42. *Ibid.*, p. 363.
43. Foster in *B&L*, I, p. 372.
44. U. S. Grant, *Personal Memoirs of U. S. Grant* 2 vols. (New York: Chas. L. Webster & Co., 1885–1886), I, pp. 313–14.
45. *OR*, VII, p. 364. Anderson is identified in Johnson's report on Shiloh in *ibid.*, X, pp. 444 ff. He is not named in Johnson's report on Fort Donelson. Anderson later, as colonel, commanded the 8th Tennessee at Stones River, Chickamauga, Atlanta and Nashville.
46. *Ibid.*, VII, pp. 275, 382.
47. *Ibid.*, VII, p. 254.
48. *Ibid.*, VII, p. 365.
49. Map No. 29 in *WP Atlas*; Fort Donelson map in *B&L*, I, p. 402.
50. *OR*, VII, p. 365.

51. *Ibid.*
52. Originals in *B. R. Johnson File,* CSA Staff Papers.
53. Capitalization of Dr. Nathan Johnson in original.
54. William Gannaway Brownlow, *Sketches of the Rise, Progress and Decline of Secession,* (Cincinnati: Applegate & Co., 1862), p. 190.
55. *Robert Johnson,* p. 13.
56. Floyd's report in *OR,* VII, pp. 255 ff; Pillow in *ibid.,* pp. 285 ff.
57. Buckner's report in *ibid.,* VII, pp. 327 f.
58. *Ibid.,* VII, p. 259.
59. *Source Book,* p. 1110.
60. Letter, Brown to Davis from Victoria, Texas, August 24, 1880 in Dunbar Rowland, ed., *Jefferson Davis, Constitutionalist,* (Jackson, Mississippi: Printed for Miss. Dept. of Archives and History, 1923), VIII, p. 487.
61. *OR,* VII, pp. 256, 304.
62. *Ibid.,* VII, p. 365.
63. *OR,* LII, pt. 2, p. 286; X, pt. 2, p. 304.
64. General Order No. 2, HQ, Army of Mississippi, Jackson, Tennessee, March 13, 1862. Original in *B. R. Johnson File,* CSA Staff Papers.
65. Opposing Forces at Shiloh in *B&L,* I, p. 539.
66. Requisition for picks and shovels signed by Johnson as fortifications officer in *B. R. Johnson File,* CSA Staff Papers.
67. Map 33, *WP Atlas*; Matthew F. Steele, *American Campaigns,* (Washington: U.S. Infantry Association, 1935), p. 171.
68. *OR,* X, p. 359.
69. *Ibid.,* p. 374.
70. *Steele,* p. 175; Map 33, *WP Atlas.*
71. G. T. Beauregard, "The Campaign of Shiloh" in *B&L,* I, pp. 569 ff.
72. *Ibid.,* p. 579.
73. U. S. Grant, "The Battle of Shiloh" in *B&L,* I, pp. 466 f.
74. Beauregard in *ibid.,* p. 582.
75. *OR,* X, p. 444.
76. *Ibid.*
77. *Ibid.,* X, p. 407; *Steele,* p. 176.
78. *OR,* X, p. 444.
79. *Ibid.,* X, p. 408.
80. *Ibid.,* X, p. 440.
81. *Ibid.,* X, p. 446.
82. Voucher for payment of $180 for "large chestnut sorrel horse killed in the public service" at Shiloh in *B. R. Johnson File* in CSA Staff Papers. As late as May 22, 1862 the Morgan County Ohio *Herald* included Johnson's wound in a "List of Confederate Generals and Calamitous Happenings to Them."
83. *OR,* X, pp. 408, 440, 444, 451.
84. Opposing Forces at Shiloh in *B&L,* I, p. 539.
85. *OR,* X, pp. 390, 412, 440.
86. *Ibid.,* X, p. 445.
87. *Ibid.*
88. *Ibid.,* X, pt. 2, p. 431.
89. *Ibid.,* X, pt. 2, pp. 563–568. Johnson's illness reported by Hardee to Beauregard, *ibid.,* p. 537.
90. *OR,* XVII, pt. 2, p. 642.
91. *CV,* XIV, p. 545.

92. *Steele,* p. 309; Maps 75, 76, *WP Atlas.*
93. Joseph Wheeler, "Bragg's Invasion of Kentucky" in *B&L,* III, p. 9.
94. Letter, Owen to Mrs. Owen, Brandenburg, Ky., September 26, 1862 in Correspondence Folder No. 2, *Owen Papers.*
95. *Steele,* p. 311.
96. Map 76, *WP Atlas.* Buell's isolation was due in part to "acoustic shadow," an atmospheric condition which silenced the noise of battle in Buell's vicinity.
97. Charles C. Gilbert, "On the Field at Perryville" in *B&L,* III, pp. 52 ff.; Don Carlos Buell, "East Tennessee and the Campaign of Perryville" in *ibid.,* pp. 31 ff.; Wheeler in *ibid.,* p. 16; map in *ibid.,* p. 24.
98. Ruth Brill, "Cincinnati's 'Poet-Warrior' " in *Bulletin of the Historical and Philosophical Society of Ohio,* Vol. 21, No. 3 (July 1963), pp. 183 ff.
99. Johnson's report in *OR,* XVI, pp. 1124 ff.; Lytle's testimony before Buell commission in *ibid.,* pp. 67–75.
100. Original of claim for $325 for bay stallion paid December 4, 1862 in *B. R. Johnson File* in CSA Staff Papers. Therein also are original claims for $325 for a dapple gray; $300 for a sorrel horse; bay mare $300 and another bay mare $200 all lost at Perryville. A board of officers was designated Oct. 11, 1862 to appraise these claims and those of Snowden and Blakemore. The board decided $1485 was due Johnson, $250 to Snowden and $290 to Blakemore. Since the pay of a Confederate brigadier was $301 a month, the casualties to Johnson's personal mounts represented a considerable financial drain. There is no extant record of payments.
101. *OR,* XVI, p. 71.
102. *Ibid.,* XVI, pp. 1108, 1127; Cleburne's report, *OR,* LII, pp. 51 ff.; Captain Irving A. Buck, *Cleburne and His Command,* (Jackson, Tennessee: McCowat, Mercer Press, Inc., 1959), p. 112.
103. Hardee's report, *OR,* XVI, p. 1121.
104. *OR,* XX, p. 413.
105. *Warner,* p. 53.
106. *OR,* XVII, p. 765. Bragg endorsed Cleburne for promotion as "young, ardent, exceedingly gallant but sufficiently prudent . . . the admiration of his command."

8

"A GALLANT AND ZEALOUS OFFICER"

i. "Inexplicable Panic" at Stones River

Christmas Day 1862 was celebrated by Bushrod Johnson's brigade as well as any men could when they had to keep a constant eye on a bigger enemy only twenty-five miles away. In their cheerless camp with the rest of Cleburne's Division of Hardee's Corps at College Grove, twenty miles southwest of Murfreesborough, Johnson's veterans of two desperate battles and hundreds of miles of marching made the best of what they could gather in the way of festive food and drink. At least most of them could rejoice that they were still in their home state, Tennessee, among friends.

The next day the holiday ended abruptly. Cavalry outposts reported that the Federals, now led by William Stark Rosecrans who had replaced Buell October 24, had started south from Nashville. Cleburne broke camp at once. Johnson and his troops were on the road to Murfreesborough early Saturday, December 27, marching by way of Eaglesville, 6 miles south and 13 northeast to evade the bluecoats. They got to Salem Turnpike, within a mile of Stones River, by nightfall. On Sunday Polk and Hardee met with

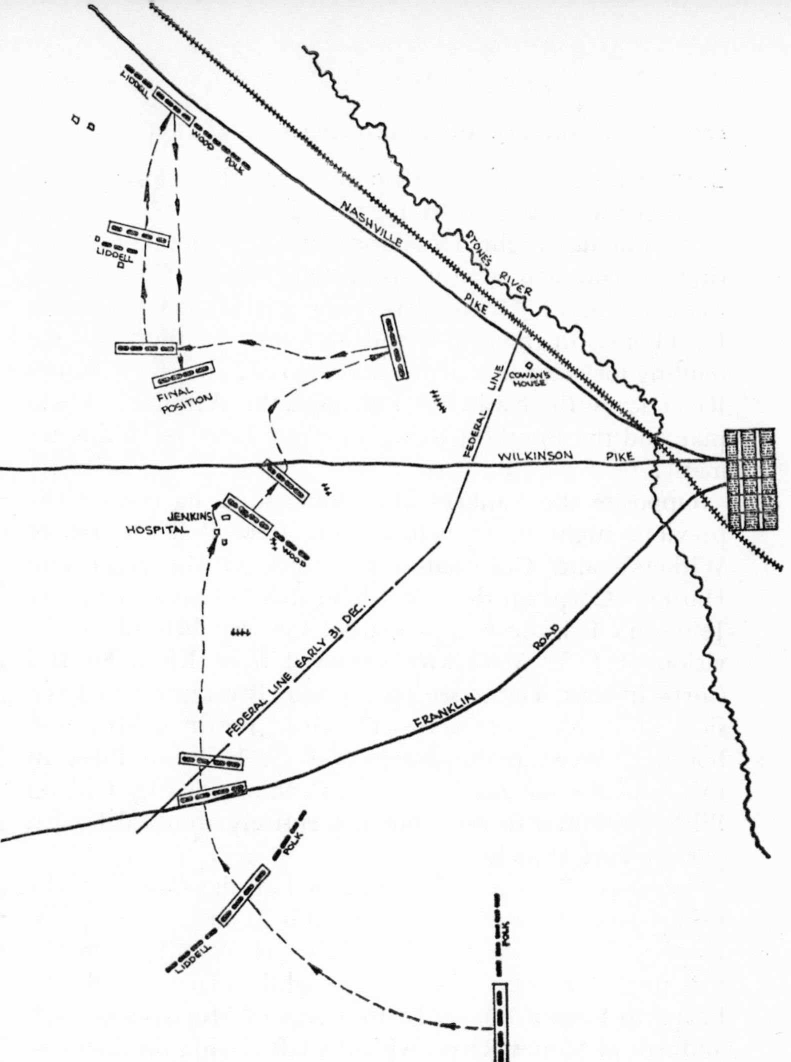

STONES RIVER (MURFREESBOROUGH)
December 31, 1862–January 3, 1863
Unreasoning panic among his troops robs Johnson of complete victory after seven hours of fighting. He rallies the runaways beneath their regimental colors. He joins the outcry against Bragg for giving up his advantage and retreating. (From map accompanying Johnson's report in OR, *XX, pt. 1, p. 882, in* OR Atlas, *Plate XXXI)*

Bragg who directed the disposition of their forces. The weather was bitterly cold, foggy and rainy.[1]

By Tuesday night, December 30, the Union concentration was complete, a mile and a half from the Confederate lines. Thomas L. Crittenden's wing was on the left, George H. Thomas in the center and McCook's on the right, extending for more than three miles to the South from Stones River across the Nashville Turnpike, the Wilkinson Turnpike and the Franklin Road, (Triune Road on Johnson's map).

Opposite the Yankees after some shuffling during the previous night in drenching rain, were Polk's Corps of Withers's and Cheatham's divisions on the right and Hardee's Corps on the left. Cleburne's Division including Johnson's Brigade was in Hardee's center, behind the division of J. P. McCown, borrowed from Kirby Smith's Corps in East Tennessee on the left. Breckinridge's Division, of Hardee, was across the river, north of Murfreesborough, between the stream and the Lebanon Pike. In this unit, the second brigade was commanded by Gideon Pillow, restored to duty but not entirely absolved for his part at Fort Donelson.[2]

Johnson's 2016 men had marched all day Saturday, the twenty-seventh, over miserable roads in an icy downpour. Hardened now, they made nearly twenty miles. On the morning of Sunday, the twenty-eighth, Hardee told Cleburne to form a line of battle north of Murfreesborough and east of Stones River, with the left resting on the river and the right on the Lebanon Turnpike, about 800 yards behind Breckinridge. The troops remained on the alert, drawn up in battle array, but inactive until the evening of Tuesday the thirtieth. At nightfall, they were ordered across the river to the west. Stumbling in the dark cedar brakes for five miles, 6000 men waded across the ice cold water at a ford south of the Franklin Road and bivouacked 450 yards behind McCown at what they guessed was a prolongation of Cheatham's line, judging by the glowing campfires.

Johnson's men were stretched north and south with his left on a lane leading to the McCulloch house. After midnight, orders came from Hardee. Cleburne sent the word to his brigadiers: Johnson, St. John R. Liddell, L. E. Polk and S. A. M. Wood to be ready to move against the Federals at 4:30 A.M., "without signal of bugle or drum" to achieve surprise.[3] Bragg planned to hit Rosencrans's right. Hardee was to direct the main attack and envelop McCook's right flank.[4]

Before first light on Wednesday, the last day of 1862, line of battle was formed. Cleburne put Polk, with Calvert's Battery, on his right, Johnson with Darden's guns in the center, and Liddell and the Warren Light Artillery on the left. Wood, in reserve, had no cannon. His artillery had been detached the day before and sent to Breckinridge.

On the Federal side, across from McCown and Cleburne in the cedar thickets, were the divisions of Kentuckian Richard W. Johnson, West Point '49, Jefferson Columbus Davis of Indiana, who had shot and killed Major General William Nelson in the Galt House in Louisville the previous September 29 and had never been tried,[5] and Phil Sheridan of Ohio, building his reputation as a fighting foot soldier. Rosecrans intended that these elements of his right wing would hold the Confederates in check or fall back slowly while Thomas and Crittenden struck and drove back Bragg's right.[6]

Clear day had not yet appeared about 6 A.M. when Hardee's order to advance came to Cleburne. The footsloggers moved out. Fences and matted thickets made it almost impossible to stay in line of battle. Men bunched up in some sections to get around obstacles and left gaps in and between units. Johnson rode feverishly through the brush shouting orders to companies to march by the flank or make other corrections to keep a solid formation. As the whole division advanced, a gap developed between Cleburne and Cheatham. Hardee called Wood from Cleburne's reserve to plug it. Then Cleburne, who thought he was following McCown, found that he had "unaccountably disappeared" from his front.[7] McCown had slanted on a left oblique against R. W. Johnson, caught his men at breakfast and was crunching into three Union brigades after a brief resistance. Cleburne at once moved abreast of McCown's right to keep up the momentum of the attack.

The men on the left of Johnson's Brigade, in Cleburne's center, began to be hit by Federal bullets from a tangle of trees along the first Franklin Road. He sent out his skirmishers. Before they had a chance to shoot, a heavy volley of enemy fire wounded Colonel Moses White and Lieutenant Colonel R. D. Frayser of the Thirty-seventh Tennessee. Mayor J. T. McReynolds took over the regiment. Later in the day he was killed and the Thirty-seventh fought the rest of the battle under Captain C. G. Jarnagin.

Unshaken by losing first blood, Johnson's men pushed forward against Jefferson C. Davis's Federals. A Michigan battery of four guns on the flank of the Twenty-fifth Tennessee on Johnson's left began ripping into it with a heavy fire of shells and grape. Johnson sent the Seventeenth Tennessee on a plunging charge which captured the battery, killed eight of its crew and most of its horses and damaged the guns,[8] but not without loss. Colonel A. S. Marks of the Seventeenth was severely wounded and carried to the rear. Captain John Overton, volunteer aide to Johnson, was also hit. Captain J. H. Vanleer, another volunteer aide of Johnson's, lost his horse to enemy fire. Afoot, he grabbed a rifle from a disabled soldier and fought the rest of the day in the ranks.

To add firepower to the mounting impetus of his attack,

Johnson ordered Darden to displace his guns forward with the Seventeenth, now led by Lieutenant Colonel Watt W. Floyd.[9] The Twenty-third rushed up to help push the enemy from the protecting wood. After a few bloody minutes, the Tennesseeans cleared the enemy from the evergreens and gained the open fields beyond, ahead of the rest of the brigade. The Twenty-fifth, Forty-fourth and Thirty-seventh on the right found the going rougher. Major H. C. Ewin of the Forty-fourth was mortally wounded.

This was the first phase of the battle. It had lasted less than half an hour. But the brigade's losses were heavier than in all subsequent fighting of the day. Nine field officers had been killed or wounded in three of the five regiments.[10] Each unit counted its toll during a brief interlude when the men replenished their ammunition supply in a line running north and south between the Franklin Road and the Wilkinson Turnpike.

The next act began as soon as the fired-up Tennesseeans had filled their pockets with cartridges. Their objective was a cotton gin which was a Union strong point. It was seventy yards from the Griscom, also called Gresham, house (labeled Jenkins on Johnson's map) being used by the Federals as a hospital. One gun to the left of the buildings and four to the right battered at the Seventeenth, advancing along a lane between two cotton fields without much cover from the shrapnel and canister. An acre or so of undulating ground finally furnished some shelter as the regiment split, ten companies to the right and three to the left, to envelop the farm dwelling. Soon a white flag signalled the hospital's surrender. Its patients and personnel, totaling 250, were taken prisoner. Many Union wounded were lying in tents in the farmyard in the winter's cold.[11]

Among the Federals in the area was the First Brigade of Sheridan's Division, commanded by 31-year old Ohioan

Brigadier General Joshua W. Sill, West Point '53. Sill was killed not far away, near a fence bordering a lane which passed the Griscom House. After the battle, a long and acrid controversy raged between Johnson and Liddell over whose troops captured the hospital and killed Sill. Liddell argued that Colonel Daniel C. Govan's Second Arkansas had reached the place ahead of the Tennesseeans.[12] But Floyd of the Seventeenth Tennessee asserted his men were there thirty minutes before any others,[13] and Lieutenant Colonel Reuben F. Harvey of the Second Arkansas agreed that the place had surrendered a half-hour before he reached it, but he insisted that he had encountered heavy Federal fire, right and left, from nearby buildings before his arrival. Liddell admitted the Tennesseeans had gravitated between him and his brigade in the hospital area. He became separated from his troops and had been forced to ask Johnson, whom he met nearby, where his (Liddell's) brigade had gone.[14]

Johnson demanded the case be submitted to the Secretary of War, declaring he wanted "justice done to those who have a right to expect it at my hands."[15] Liddell retorted Johnson was glory hunting, but conceded there might have been a mistake in the identity of the hospital.[16] Cleburne wisely sidestepped the issue in his report, stating only that the Seventeenth Tennessee and the Second Arkansas were contending for the honor of first taking the hospital and killing Sill.

By noon, Johnson's Brigade had driven more than two miles to the north of the Franklin Road. Cleburne ordered it to shift right across a corn stubble field, and then front to support Polk in an attack across the Wilkinson Pike to drive the enemy from behind limestone rocks and natural earthworks in another cedar brake. After correcting some gaps that resulted, the division hammered at Sheridan's force which had been bent, but not broken like R. W. Johnson's and Davis's and Rousseau's, sent in from the reserve by Rosecrans. After the woods were cleared, Cleburne told Johnson to move back toward the left and link up with Liddell. Johnson pushed through the trees to the brow of a slight hill where Liddell yielded ground and reformed *en echelon* to Johnson's left rear under the crest. Then Johnson's men went on with their grim chores.[17] Cleburne's Division was now aligned by brigades thus: Polk, right; Preston Smith of Cheatham, right center; Johnson, left center; Liddell, left.

Across an open field, 400 yards away, an enemy battery zeroed in on Johnson, now surging forward in an arc to his right. The Tennesseeans charged toward the battery and after a 20-minute fire fight drove off its protecting infantry and captured four Parrott guns.[18]

It was nearing 3 P.M. Johnson's and the other brigades of Cleburne had been fighting for nine hours. They had forced back a stubborn enemy for nearly three miles, had crossed over McCown's axis of advance and were now the extreme left of Bragg's army. The men were exhausted, thirsty and hungry. They had little ammunition left. Artillery had not kept pace with the rapid infantrymen, so some of the driving punch was lacking. Hardee had ordered Johnson to leave Darden's guns in reserve in the rear near the Wilkinson Pike.[19] The Federal divisions of Davis, Sheridan and R. W. Johnson with their backs to the Nashville Turnpike, had a chance to reorganize behind the division of 54-year old Horatio Van Cleve, brought from the east side of the river, and the brigade of Colonel Charles G. Harker of Thomas J. Wood's division.[20]

Calamity entered at this point to reverse the tide. Fatigue diluted the aggressive spirit of the Confederates. Federal resistance stiffened and heavy artillery fire increased. A wild report suddenly spread that Cleburne's division had been flanked on the right where McCown was supposed to be fighting. Smith's brigade, led by Colonel A. J. Vaughan, faded back in the mounting confusion. Then

Polk's men, on his right, caught the contagion. Next Johnson's force felt the fire of the revived Federals. Captain N. R. Allen of the Twenty-third was mortally wounded; Captain F. M. Orr of the Seventeenth was killed; Major J. C. Davis of the same regiment was captured; the Forty-fourth lost two officers; the Twenty-fifth lost two lieutenants, a color bearer and its flag. Johnson's adjutant, his former student, Captain R. B. Snowden, was hit twice and his horse was disabled but he remained at Johnson's side.

With his confidence rising that victory was near, Johnson was dumbfounded when his surging troops, within less than a rifle shot from the Nashville Turnpike, broke ranks and nearly ran him down in a wild scramble for the rear. "The movement was totally unexpected" he wrote in his report a fortnight later, "and I have yet to learn there existed a cause commensurate with the demoralization that ensued." Johnson led his staff and other officers as they rode among the scrambling men, pleading and shouting in a desperate effort to stem the panicky stampede. Johnson caught up with regimental color bearers and sent them, flags waving, into a sheltering woods, 400 yards away, to act as gathering points for confused men who needed to find something familiar in the chaos. Discipline returned. Most of the fugitives formed up again though some scampered back as far as the Wilkinson Turnpike.[21] By sundown the situation was beginning to be stabilized around Liddell's Brigade which had not taken part in the final phase of the fight. Fresh supplies of ammunition were brought up and the weary men dug in for the night. They ate whatever cold food they had in their haversacks.[22] For what remained of Johnson's Brigade, the fighting was about over.

The next morning, New Year's Day, rumors spread that Rosecrans was retreating. To check on the situation, Hardee ordered Cleburne to reconnoiter in force without bringing on a renewal of the previous day's bloody business. Wood's Brigade was sent forward cautiously and Johnson put out skirmishers *en echelon* on Wood's right flank. Proof that the Federals were still in strength on Cleburne's front came quickly and convincingly. Wood's men were badly roughed up before they were withdrawn to their former place in the line.[23]

During the next thirty-six hours, until 10 P.M. Friday, January 2, while the battle raged to a standstill elsewhere, Johnson's regiments with the balance of Cleburne's held their positions. Men savored what rest they could get in the cold, always alert to the enemy within musket range. Between the lines lay hundreds of dead and moaning wounded. No truce enabled either side to give help or comfort. One of Johnson's men, trying to aid a wounded foe, was hit in the arm by a Union sharpshooter.[24] Friday afternoon Southern salvage parties ventured out to the skirmish lines to pick up discarded Union weapons. They gathered up 160 Enfield rifles, minié and percussion muskets and supplied them with ammunition from a four-horse Union wagon loaded with fifteen boxes of cartridges captured during the drive on Wednesday.[25]

Friday night, Cleburne's Division was withdrawn from Hardee's left wing and sent five miles around to the east bank of Stones River to support Breckinridge, who had made a vigorous, but futile attempt on Friday to drive Rosecran's left wing back across the stream. Miserable in heavy, freezing rain, Johnson's Brigade remained a mile behind Breckinridge's lines until near midnight Saturday, January 3, when Bragg's retreat began. All day Sunday in the rain and sleet the troops plodded southward toward Manchester, 32 miles away. Many of the men straggled or fell by the roadside from exhaustion or illness due to exposure.[26]

Losses in Johnson's Brigade during the fighting were appalling. He had taken 2106 men into action; 623 were killed, wounded or missing, nearly one man in three.

Cleburne lost 2081 of 6045 in the division.[27] Cleburne's report said the "country is indebted" to Johnson and his brother brigadiers "for their great exertions." He praised Liddell's "skill, courage and devotion."[28] Johnson personally felt there might have been more exertion by Cleburne and Hardee and said as much in his report. During the inactive lull during the night of December 31–January 1, he said, he "suggested planting heavy artillery on my left and front but my suggestions seemed not to be approved either by the artillery officers or my seniors. My own convictions still approve this suggestion, convinced as I am, that on the field of battle there should be no repose and that energetic, judicious, persistent action affords the only reliable means of success."[29]

Johnson was not the only critic of what had happened. Most of Bragg's command seethed with discontent, especially over the Confederate retreat. His army had battled a superior force to a standstill, had suffered some of the severest losses of the entire war and then had given up any advantage by withdrawing to a position which was vulnerable to a replay of the same ghastly tragedy. Bragg's chief lieutenants, Polk and Hardee, were especially bitter. Less that a fortnight after the fight, Hardee sounded out Breckinridge and Cleburne after Bragg, smarting under the criticism, asked that a survey be made of opinions among the generals of his army. Hardee reported:

> I feel frankness compels me to say that the general officers whose judgement you have invoked are unanimous in opinion that a change in command of this army is necessary.

Cleburne was equally blunt. He talked to Johnson, L. E. Polk, Liddell, and Wood, his brigadiers, and then told Bragg that they "see with regret, and it has also met my observation, that you do not possess the confidence of the army . . . in that degree to secure success."[30]

Bragg withstood the assault for the time being and

nothing came of it. The issue did not die, however. Johnson had a further small part in it again nine months later, after Chickamauga, when the situation reached a boiling point requiring the personal intervention of President Jefferson Davis.

In the Shelbyville-Wartrace area northeast of Tullahoma, which was Bragg's new base, Johnson's Brigade and other troops of Hardee's Corps fretted out the rest of the winter. Recuperated after Stones River and the retreat, they were kept busy building fortifications and entrenchments against the inevitable day when Rosecrans would resume the offensive from Murfreesborough.[31] When work with pick and shovel was finished, Johnson had his regiments on the drill grounds. Colonel William Preston Johnston, one time Western Military Institute cadet, inspecting Bragg's Army for President Davis, watched an exhibition on March 23 and wrote a laudatory report to Richmond:

> . . . on Monday, March 23 . . . I saw Brig. Gen. Bushrod R. Johnson drill his brigade and witnessed a match or trial battalion drill. . . . The Tennesseeans' fine stature, manly bearing, steadiness of movement and rapidity and accuracy with which the battalion executed every manuever at the double quick was unequalled.[32]

Fifteen months a brigadier general, Johnson felt something more than praise was his due for the professional competence he had demonstrated in and out of combat. A campaign for his promotion got under way, oddly enough not through Cleburne and Hardee under whom he had fought at Stones River, but through Cheatham in whose division he had served nearly a year previously at Shiloh. Cheatham sent a strong recommendation for Johnson's raise in rank to Secretary of War James A. Seddon. Lieutenant General Leonidas Polk endorsed it: Johnson "has the qualities and attainments that fit him for command of a division." A month later, even though Johnson had concurred with his critics, Bragg added:

> General Johnson has served nearly a year under my command and has uniformly borne the reputation of a gallant and zealous officer. In all engagements with the enemy he has received high commendation.

Nothing resulted. In June, Cleburne, promoted to major general over the head of Johnson, revived the matter in a letter to Adjutant General Samuel Cooper. "None more richly deserve it," he said. On July 15, Hardee added: "It would afford me pleasure to have him promoted."

Seddon sent the papers to President Davis, July 28. The following penned on the back of the file, tell the fate of the effort:

> To Seddon—
> For what division?
> JD
> To President—
> I know no vacant division
> JAS
> Aug 10
> Returned for file
> JAS

While these papers moved in the official labyrinth in Richmond, Johnson himself started a new series. On July 22 he wrote to Joseph E. Johnston, commanding the Western Department. Somewhat inaccurately, he said:

> . . . Hitherto I have abstained from presenting any claim to position. I desire to command rather than solicit a place in the military service of the country and confess I now make the application with extreme reluctance, but with thorough and profound conviction as to its justice.

This petition went the rounds of the commanders, too.

Bragg wrote on it he had no vacant command, but would be willing "to see him assigned elsewhere if he could be employed in a larger and more useful sphere." Other endorsements were:

Cleburne: "I know of no officer . . . who excels him."

D. H. Hill, fresh from Lee's Army and now the new corps commander replacing Hardee: "I have no doubt he will make an excellent division commander."

Polk: "Well qualified for division command."

J. E. Johnston: "No vacancies . . . exchange of Vicksburg prisoners makes an excess of major generals."

Seddon sent the array to Davis on September 5 and this colloquy ensued:

> To JAS—
> Is there a vacancy?
> JD
> To President—
> I know no vacant division
> JAS

So into the limbo of the files went Johnson's second try.

There had been a vacancy in June when A. P. Stewart was promoted to major general and this may have spurred Johnson's effort in July. A new division was created for Stewart from Johnson's Brigade and those of two Tennesseeans: William Brimage Bate, ex-steamboat clerk, editor and legislator and John Calvin Brown, captured at Fort Donelson, plus Henry DeLamar Clayton, Alabama lawyer and politico. Johnson lost the Thirty-seventh Tennessee Regiment to Bate's Brigade where its diminished numbers were combined with the Fifteenth Tennessee.[34]

Johnson had little time to nurse his chagrin. Rosecrans came alive in Murfreesborough. In late June he started the corps of Thomas and Crittenden through the rugged country to the southeast in the direction of Manchester; McCook came down the center through Liberty Gap and

Stanley pointed for Shelbyville, simulating a main effort. Their moves had the objective of maneuvering Bragg from behind his formidable defensive entrenchments in the Shelbyville and Tullahoma areas.[35] Johnson's Brigade had been moved forward to Wartrace on April 20 and later to Fairfield, four miles farther toward Hoover's Gap when the bulk of the corps concentrated at Wartrace.[36]

Mud-covered by hard riding on a dark and rainy day, two boys dismounted at Johnson's headquarters in Fairfield on the afternoon of Wednesday, June 24. They brought word that the enemy was advancing on Hoover's Gap, less than ten miles away. Stewart's new division with Johnson's Brigade marched until dark, deployed in position and waited. Early in the next forenoon the shooting started. It continued for the rest of the day. Company A of the Forty-fourth Tennessee, armed with long-range Enfields, went forward as skirmishers but ran out of cartridges by 10 A.M. Johnson replaced them with 100 men from the Twenty-third Tennessee and the brisk fight went on. The next day, June 26, Stewart rode up about noon and told Johnson he would have to fall back to the main body. By 7 P.M. Saturday, the twenty-seventh, the brigade had tramped twenty-five miles back to Tullahoma.[37]

Johnson's Brigade had been opposed by the mounted infantry of John T. Wilder, the Indiana industrialist who had surrendered with Richard Owen at Munfordville nine months before. Wilder's men were armed with the new Spencer seven-shot breech-loading repeating carbine. He personally had financed the purchase of this weapon by his men and later was reimbursed by the Washington government. The resultant extra firepower created the illusion of numerical superiority.[38]

In mortal danger of being isolated by Rosecrans's moves, Bragg pulled his army back toward Chattanooga, leaving Tullahoma July 1. Johnson's Brigade resumed maneuvering and fighting rear guard actions from June 30 to July

6 when its part of the Confederate evacuation of middle Tennessee ended at Wauhatchie Station, 11 miles west of Chattanooga. Heavy rains fell incessantly, lowlands were flooded, roads were quagmires and horses and mules died, imprisoned in the mud.[39]

During the balance of July, Johnson's Brigade was detached and stretched for 70 miles along the East Tennessee and Georgia Railroad between Chattanooga and Loudoun, guarding the vital bridges linking Bragg with Buckner in Knoxville.[40] In mid-July Hardee left for Mississippi and Daniel Harvey Hill, recently of Lee's Army, was promoted lieutenant general and took over Hardee's Corps of Cleburne's and Stewart's divisions.[41] Bushrod Johnson was now subordinate to two West Pointers of 1842 who had been underclassmen when he was Cadet First Sergeant and Captain. When the rest of Stewart's Division was sent to join Buckner's Corps in Knoxville, Hill acquired Breckinridge's division from Mississippi to replace it.

In August, as Burnside advanced from the northeast toward Knoxville and Rosecrans was sliding McCook and Thomas plus Stanley's cavalry through Alabama and Georgia around Bragg's left flank to the south, Buckner was pulled in from Knoxille toward Chattanooga. Johnson's Brigade led Buckner's Corps south from Loudoun back to the east side of Chickamauga Creek, east and south of Chattanooga,[42] evacuated by Bragg on September 8. Bragg hoped to strike Rosecrans's separated and isolated corps, but was frustrated twice by the caution and lassitude of Hill, Polk and Thomas Carmichael Hindman, recently joined. As a result the Union army was able to reunite on the west side of Chickamauga Creek by September 17.

While Bragg fumed at his tardy corps chiefs, he was strengthened by the division of W. H. T. Walker and was soon to get Evander McNair's brigade, both from Mississippi. Longstreet's Corps was coming by rail from Lee in Virginia. Bragg reshuffled his cohorts again into four corps of two divisions each: Polk with Cheatham and Hindman; Hill with Cleburne and Breckinridge; Walker in reserve with his own and Liddell's divisions; Buckner with Stewart and William Preston. Later Longstreet brought Lafayette McLaws and John Bell Hood. Forrest mustered the cavalry divisions of Frank C. Armstrong and John Pegram and Joseph Wheeler's horse soldiers included the divisions of John A. Wharton and William T. Martin.[43]

To Bushrod Johnson a golden opportunity came at last. On September 14 he was given command of a provisional division made up of his own Tennessee brigade, McNair's six Arkansas and one North Carolina regiments and John Gregg's six Tennessee and one North Carolina. These 3500 were the largest number he had ever led. Assigned on paper to Buckner's Corps, the division was to fight the battle of Chickamauga under Hood and Longstreet, linked with the troops they brought from Virginia, 843 miles in seven days and ten hours over sixteen different railroad lines with varying track gauges.[44]

As the summer of 1863 had passed without fulfillment of his promotion hopes, Johnson now welcomed the chance to prove, in a sphere of greater responsibility in the inevitable battle shaping up, his total dedication to his adopted country and her cause. This should have been an antidote for any gnawing vexation of spirit over his failure to progress.

In a few days he would do better than he had ever done as a soldier. But there would be no rewards.

ii. "Ahead of Everything" at Chickamauga

Dour Braxton Bragg, target of criticism by his generals and of disdain by his soldiers, in turn felt himself frustrated by their sloth and reluctance in carrying out his

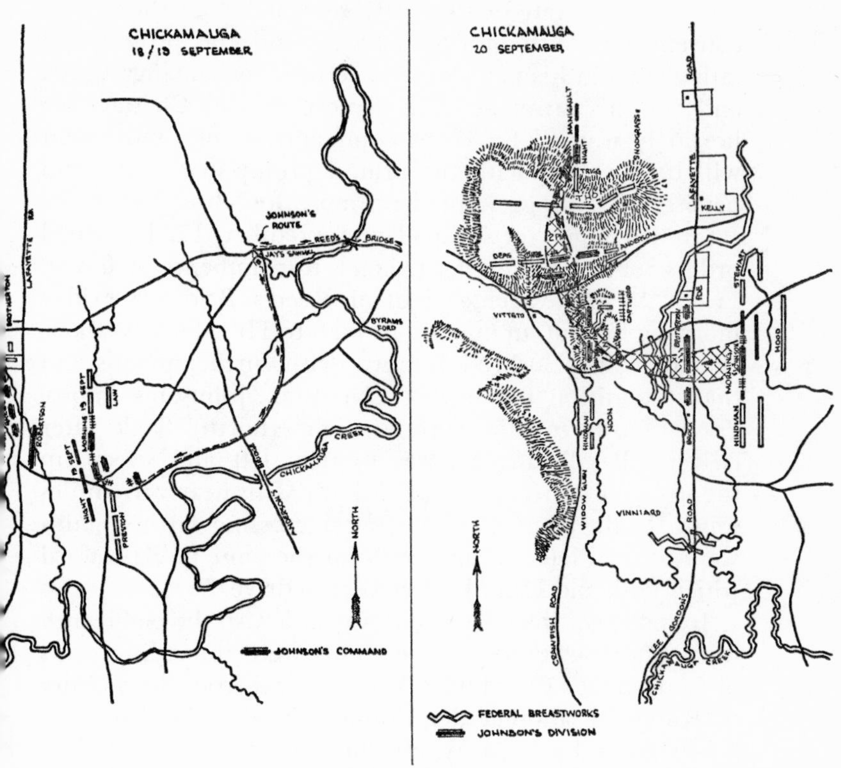

CHICKAMAUGA
September 18–20, 1863

Johnson's perceptive, aggressive reaction to the gap in Rosecrans's line at the Brotherton House brings him his greatest day in battle on Sunday, September 20. The day before, Bragg thought him laggard and sent Hood to take over command of the right wing Johnson had led. (From maps in Johnson's report in OR, XXX, *pt. 2, pp. 468–69)* orders. Hill and Polk had moved tardily, if at all, between September 9 and the thirteenth in executing his plan to crush the separated corps of Rosecrans before they could concentrate south of Chattanooga, and the project had failed.[45] So in his new design to cross Chickamauga Creek and put his army between Rosecrans and Chattanooga he tartly warned his corps commanders the "movement will be executed with the utmost promptness, vigor and persistence." Bragg wanted no more foot-dragging.

On the night of Thursday, September 17, he issued orders for a crossing of the creek to commence at 6 A.M. Friday by his extreme right at Reed's Bridge.[46] Friday morning he sent an operations plan to Hill, Polk, Walker, Buckner, and Bushrod Johnson with further details and the admonition for speedy execution. Johnson's improvised division on the extreme right (north) flank, after crossing Reed's Bridge, was to turn left and sweep up the stream toward Lee and Gordon's Mills nearly five miles south. Walker and Buckner, after crossing farther south were to turn left also and push for the same target toward which Polk and Hill likewise were to drive.[47]

Johnson got his men under way at 5 A.M. the eighteenth from Catoosa Station where trains were unloading units of Longstreet's Corps from Virginia and from the vicinity of Ringgold, another detraining point for the reinforcements from Lee's Army. By the time the march began, Johnson's original force of McNair's, Gregg's and his own Tennessee brigades had been augmented by three of Longstreet's brigades: Henry L. Benning's four Georgia regiments, Evander McIver Law's four Alabama regiments led by Colonel James L. Sheffield, and Jerome Napoleon Robertson's three Texas and one Arkansas regiments. In numbers, Johnson was leading a corps. He left Benning and the Georgians in Ringgold to guard Bragg's army supply depot. Colonel Sheffield was told to have his men cook rations first and then follow as soon as possible.[48]

Acting on a previous order which sent him in the direction of Leet's tanyard, Johnson moved out in a long column of four brigades: his own under Colonel John S. Fulton, then McNair, Gregg and Robertson. The Texas physician-soldier's men must have been grateful to take to the road again to get the kinks out of their legs, cramped from ten days of inaction on flatcars. Because artillery had not arrived with Longstreet's troops, Johnson had only three batteries: Lieutenant W. S. Everett's Georgia Battery with Fulton; Bledsoe's Missouri Battery with Gregg and Captain J. F. Culpeper's [*sic*] South Carolina Battery. Each brigade was followed by its wagons, stringing out the marching men, cannon and vehicles for miles. On the right and front flanks rode the screening and protecting horsemen of Forrest, including 300 dismounted remnants of the raiders John Morgan had led to catastrophe in Ohio.[49]

Johnson's column had marched three miles toward the tanyard when a dispatch rider galloped up with orders from Bragg to turn around and go back to Ringgold and thence take a direct road to Reed's Bridge, cross the creek and "make a lodgement"[50] on the west bank. This was the previous night's order just now catching up with Johnson. The grumbling marchers about-faced and started back to Ringgold. Then another courier brought Bragg's operations plan issued earlier that morning. Johnson was told to take command of the right column of Bragg's Army, cross the creek at Reed's Bridge, turn left and push south.

From Ringgold to Reed's Bridge is about seven miles. The long column had marched and countermarched five miles or so and still had seven to go. But Bragg, in fretful anxiety at his headquarters in Leet's tanyard, seemed to feel that Johnson was affected with the same lassitude that had foiled the previous week's operations. Impatiently, he sent a special written order by a staff officer before 11 A.M. to "proceed without delay" and at 1 P.M. he dispatched another urging Johnson to "push on vigorously and engage the enemy regardless of the force on your front."[51]

Bragg never forgot that Johnson had not moved as rapidly as he desired. In his after-battle report he was critical of Johnson, indicating that because of his tardiness "his crossing of the creek was not effected until late afternoon."[52] Months later he endorsed a promotion appeal for Johnson with the indictment: "Gen. Johnson is slow."

What Bragg did not know when he sent the prodding note at 11 A.M. was that Johnson was meeting resistance. When the column halted for a breather at 11 A.M. near Peller's Mill on the Graysville-LaFayette Road, four and a half miles from Graysville, several sympathetic farmers in the area told Johnson the Federals were about a mile ahead of him. Johnson hastened orders along the files to deploy into a line of battle across the road with McNair, Fulton and Gregg and their artillery in front and Robertson in reserve. Sensing impending action, Forrest and his staff rode with Johnson as the advance resumed toward Pea Vine Creek, a tributary of the Chickamauga. Opportunely, eight guns had just arrived from the direction of LaFayette, brought up by Major Felix H. Robertson commanding the reserve artillery of Bragg's Army. Some of these were parceled out to the Seventeenth Tennessee which was told to take the lead in clearing the way to Pea Vine Creek. This was briskly done with effective help from some of Forrest's troopers. The four brigades waded across the little stream preserving their classic battle formation: three brigades in front in line, one in reserve. Time necessarily was lost in forming, fighting and moving forward again. Meanwhile Bragg sent his second heckling prod.

The opposing Federals were several horse regiments of Colonel Robert H. G. Minty trying to delay the creek crossings by fighting at the fords or destroying the bridges.

A furious charge by a hundred dismounted cavalry of Forrest and by the Twenty-third Tennessee chased Minty's men from Reed's Bridge around two o'clock before they could set it afire. About 3 P.M. the main body of Johnson's force reached there and began crossing the Chickamauga, some at the bridge, others wading across a nearby ford. In an hour all of the more than 4000 men, their artillery and wagons were on the west side.[53]

Restive and impatient Bragg, still concerned over Johnson's progress, sent Major General John Bell Hood to take over the command of Bragg's entire right column almost as soon as Hood get off the train at Ringgold about 3 P.M. and reported to the army commander. Hood's arm, pierced by a bullet at Gettysburg was still in a sling, but he rode at once to Johnson, seven miles away. The 32-year old, sad-eyed Kentucky-born Hood had been only nine years old when Johnson left West Point in 1840 and Johnson had been out of the army seven years when Hood finished near the bottom of the class of 1853. But Johnson obeyed without demur when Hood directed him to change his march formation back into a column of brigades, with only one of Gregg's regiments in advance in line of battle as soon as they reached Jay's steam sawmill a mile west of the bridge. While the march continued for two and a half miles southwest Johnson briefed his unfamiliar new chief on the situation. They were interrupted by a flurry of firing from Federal skirmishers that forced a halt while Gregg, McNair and Fulton deployed back into the former formation of three brigades abreast. By darkness the force had reached a line 800 yards east of the Vinniard House on the LaFayette Road. There the weary men bivouacked, sleeping on their arms by turns, with one-third required to stay awake.[54]

By Saturday's dawn, September 19, all of Bragg's infantry was on the west side of the creek except Cleburne, Hindman and Breckinridge. Hood stood now in left center instead of far right. The Federals across from him were Wilder's rapid firers and behind them Joseph J. Reynolds's division of Thomas's Corps. At Hood's right rear was Walker, facing toward John M. Brannan and Absalom Baird of Thomas. Cheatham's Division of Polk was moving in between Hood and Walker. On Hood's left was Buckner's Corps, opposite whose left was Crittenden holding the creek crossing at Lee and Gordon's Mills.[55]

Johnson formed line of battle at 7 A.M. Saturday in a curve around the crest of an elevation in a woods 1000 yards east of the LaFayette Road. Union Colonel John T. Croxton's brigade of Brannan's division on a reconnaissance in force toward Reed's Bridge, collided with Forrest's dismounted men at Jay's Mill and then with Walker. Baird came to Brannan's support. Thus began a day of bloody confusion with the advantage wavering alternately between the armies. Each rushed fresh units into the front lines without much plan and then fought each other until both were spent.[56]

Johnson's division was drawn into the maelstrom after a series of fights on its north raging since morning. Liddell of Walker rolled over two brigades of Baird and then was flanked by R. W. Johnson. Cheatham came to help Liddell and was hit on the flank by John M. Palmer's division of Crittenden. Stewart's division of Buckner attacked Palmer and drove him back, R. W. Johnson retrograding at the same time. Stewart crashed into Van Cleve. The fresh Federal divisions of J. C. Davis, Sheridan, Thomas J. Wood and James S. Negley were moving up.[57]

About 2 P.M. an enemy advance drove in Johnson's skirmishers. Johnson ordered artillery to fire in the direction of Vinniard's. The Federal attack was halted on the right of Gregg and left of Fulton but continued on the left of Gregg. The Fiftieth Tennessee lost a dozen killed and 45 wounded. Half an hour later by Hood's direction Johnson ordered a general advance by his division to engage the enemy and wheel slowly to the right. Progress was slow. From a wood in front of Gregg, Federals of Reynolds and Van Cleve hotly disputed his course while Fulton on the right made 600 yards before being fired on. Johnson leapfrogged his artillery by sections of two guns to keep up with the infantry. Into the gap developing between Gregg and Fulton he sent two of McNair's regiments. Robertson's Texans came up, too and the attackers pushed across the LaFayette Road north of the Vinniard House.[58]

Gregg boldly rode out ahead of his troops to reconnoiter the enemy position. Union skirmishers fired at him. As he turned to go back to his lines he was shot through the neck and knocked from his mount. Union soldiers ran forward and grabbed his sword and spurs. Some of Robertson's Texans rushed out and chased them away, picked up Gregg and caught his horse.

Fulton, leading Johnson's Brigade, pushed steadily ahead, across the LaFayette Road and into the cover of a woods. The Twenty-fifth Tennessee commanded by Lieutenant Colonel R. Bogardus Snowden, former student and adjutant of Johnson's, with part of the Twenty-third Tennessee captured an enemy battery in a nearby field. Suddenly Federals from Negley and Brannan appeared on the left and rear of the Third and Forty-first Tennessee of Gregg's Brigade which had moved ahead of Fulton. In the fighting and shifting that resulted, the division was forced to fall back east of the LaFayette Road. The captured battery was lost. Johnson sent his aide, Captain W. T. Blakemore, to put the Third and Forty-first in position and their countercharge halted the pursuit.

At sunset, Johnson reformed his lines in the cover of some trees several hundred yards east of the LaFayette Road. Losses had been heavy. About 50 were dead and 250 wounded including the Forty-fourth Tennessee's leader, Lieutenant Colonel John L. McEwen.[59] Hood ordered temporary breastworks be set up and long into the night tired men cut trees and brush and scooped out hollow trenches with any tools they could get. To the west in the darkness they could hear the enemy doing the same, piling up logs, rocks, fence rails—anything from behind which they could fight off an assault.[60]

At the end of a dozen days of the long journey from Lee's Army, Longstreet got off the train at Catoosa at 2 P.M. Saturday. He waited two hours until his horses came on another train. Neither greeted nor guided by any aide of Bragg's, he mounted and with two lieutenant colonels of his staff, G. Moxley Sorrel, his adjutant general, and P. T. Manning, he lost the next seven hours riding in the dusk and moonlight in search of Bragg's headquarters. At one point they were almost shot or captured by Union pickets. It was 11 P.M. when he found the army commander asleep in an ambulance. At a midnight conference, Bragg reorganized his army into two wings without regard to existing corps. He gave Longstreet the left wing composed of the corps of Hood and Buckner, including Johnson's division, Hindman's division and Joe Wheeler's horsemen. Polk's right wing took over the corps of Hill and Walker, Cheatham's division and Forrest's cavalry.[61] Bragg's battle plan called for successive attacks from right to left, beginning at daylight.

As the fateful Sunday, September 20, dawned in a thick fog blanketing the valley of Chickamauga Creek, the opponents were lined up roughly opposite each other by divisions from north to south thus: Breckinridge and Cleburne, backed by Walker, faced Baird, R. W. Johnson and Palmer with Negley in reserve; Stewart in front of Law (Hood's), Joseph B. Kershaw's and Benjamin G. Humphrey's Brigades of McLaws newly come from Virginia plus Cheatham opposite Reynolds and Brannan backed by Van Cleve; Bushrod Johnson, Hindman and Preston in line across from Sheridan and Davis.[62]

The right wing attack, ordered by Bragg for daylight, was delayed until 9:30 A.M. Polk was painfully slow, Hill was not properly briefed, Breckinridge was sluggishly tardy. Breckinridge finally began the planned assault, had some partial success but was stalled. Cleburne tried next with like results. Stewart and Walker in turn made no headway. By 11:30 all of Polk's divisions were virtually stalemated against the Federal left wing. Longstreet's wing and the Union right across from him had scarcely pulled a trigger.

Bushrod Johnson formed his division at 7 A.M. with McNair on the right, Fulton center, then a scratch brigade of the Fiftieth Tennessee, First Tennessee Battalion and the Seventh Texas on the left and the balance of wounded Gregg's Brigade, led by Colonel C. A. Sugg of the Fiftieth, as a second line. Each brigade had a four-gun battery in support. Hindman's Division was on Johnson's left and Stewart was on his right as Longstreet had shifted them after his arrival on the scene early in the morning. Behind Johnson now were Law (former Hood), Kershaw and Humphreys of McLaws with Preston in reserve at his left rear. This built a formidable battering ram of fire power and forceful numbers. Across the LaFayette Road from them, north to south, were the Federal divisions of Reynolds, Brannan, Wood, Davis and Sheridan, some of them crouching behind makeshift breastworks of timber, brush, fencerails and rocks extending from the Brotherton House on the north to the Vinniard House on the south.[63]

All morning Johnson's skirmishers crept toward the Union lines on the west side of the road, potshotting at anything that moved within range. The day was hot, dry and dusty. The rest of Longstreet's wing, eager to go, awaited the word. Shortly after 11 A.M. the order to begin the attack went from Bragg directly to the division commanders, bypassing Hood and Longstreet. Lee's chief lieutenant was irked by this cavalier treatment but he did not let his affronted pride dilute his energy. Hood gave Johnson the word to move. As his brigades burst out from their cover on the double quick, the Federals opened up with every cannon and rifle available. The division raced 500 yards westward and plunged across the LaFayette Road toward the Brotherton farm. The left brigade split, passing on both sides of the house. The drive gathered momentum and Bluecoats who did not run out of the way were killed or captured at the farmyard fences and outbuildings. In the center Fulton's and Snowden's Tennesseeans shattered the 100th Illinois of Wood, shot and captured its colonel, one-armed F. A. Bartleson. They rejoiced at the number of fine swords, belts and pistols yielded up by the Illinois officers.[64]

Just at the time when Johnson's men were storming ahead, fate played into his hands. In the Federal defensive lines, Wood received an order written by Major Frank S. Bond, Rosecrans's aide, directing him to "close up on Reynolds as fast as possible and support him." Brannan was between Wood and Reynolds. Earlier in the day Rosecrans had tongue-lashed Wood for what he regarded as tardy compliance with an order to shift his division, so this time Wood did not question nor hesitate. He pulled out his troops, leaving a 400-yard gap between Brannan and Davis at the Brotherton House.[65]

This astounding opportunity quickly became apparent to Johnson as his men routed the Union skirmishers, chased defenders from their improvised breastworks and overran a battery of Davis's in a field south of Brotherton's. Beyond the house, in a wood of small pines, McNair came under heavy fire. Sugg rushed three regiments to help and the pressure began again, the yelling Confederates exploding into long open fields across which the Federals were withdrawing under cover of their artillery.

Johnson's report now takes up the story in lyrical and exultant prose quoted for years afterward:

> The scene now presented was unspeakably grand. The resolute and impetuous charge, the rush of our columns sweeping out of the shadow and gloom of the forest into the open fields flooded with sunlight, the glitter of arms, the onward rush of artillery and mounted men, the retreat of the foe, the shouts of the hosts of our army, the dust, the smoke, the noise of firearms—of whistling balls, grapeshot or bursting shells—made up a battle scene of unsurpassed grandeur.
>
> Here General Hood gave me the last order I received from him on the field:
>
> "Go ahead and keep ahead of everything!"[66]

Go ahead and keep ahead Johnson did! Credited by D. H. Hill with "the coolness and judgement for which he was always distinguished," Johnson "took in the situation at a glance" and began a flank movement to the right to deepen and widen the gap against Brannan's right. Nine pieces of artillery were captured and Sugg and McNair disputed later over whose troops had done it. McNair was wounded and Colonel David Coleman, Thirty-ninth North Carolina, led his brigade. An elevation of open ground beyond the fields was taken with small resistance. A pile of abandoned Union knapsacks there was speedily appropriated.[67]

Then the brigades of Z. C. Deas, J. M. Manigault and J. Patton Anderson of Hindman widened the gap in the Union line on Johnson's left (south) against Davis and Sheridan, cutting them off from the rest of the Federal army. On Johnson's right, Henry L. Benning, Robertson and Colonel Sheffield of Law's division, angled to the north against Brannan and Van Cleve. George P. Buell's Union brigade of Wood, marching on its misconceived errand to support Reynolds, was hit broadside with its flank and rear exposed. In moments, 35 artillery horses were destroyed, the battery captured, skirmishers shot up and scattered. The brigade disintegrated.[68]

From the high ground he had just taken, shortly after

noon Johnson sent Captain Blakemore to report the situation directly to Longstreet, bypassing Hood, and to bring the artillery forward. Longstreet and Johnson knew each other well from West Point, Jefferson Barracks and Mexico. In a nearby gap through which passed the Crawfish Spring Road and the telegraph lines from the field to Rosecrans's headquarters, Johnson spied through his field glasses a Union wagon train parked like a sitting duck within shelling distance. He sent Lieutenant W. S. Everett's guns into a position between Fulton and Sugg on the high ground. They began blasting at the vehicles. During the instant panic among the wagoneers, Johnson's skirmishers dashed forward and captured not only the convoy but an adjacent battery of four guns, thirty wagons and seven caissons full of ammunition distributed at once to Johnson's artillery. One of the Napoleons taken by the Federals on the nineteenth was returned to its original owner, Lumsden's Battery.[69]

Longstreet rode to Johnson's area. He ordered a line of skirmishers be advanced to keep the enemy busy while the triumphant Confederates had time to take a breather and eat whatever they carried in their haversacks. An aide brought up Longstreet's lunch of Nassau bacon and Georgia sweet potatoes and spread it at a convenient spot, not entirely out of range of Union rifle fire. Johnson was invited to share the food. Longstreet was unaccustomed to the potatoes on which one of his staff nearly choked. Drinking water was scarce, most canteens had been drained during the morning's heat and no resupply was handy.

Halfway through the lunch Bragg sent for Longstreet. The army commander had ridden up behind the new position. Longstreet rode back to Bragg and explained the changed situation. Bragg was disturbed by the failure of his right wing attack which had upset his battle plan and was in no mood to hear Longstreet's proffered suggestions. After a few minutes he rode back to his headquarters at Reed's Bridge and Longstreet returned to his meal.

After eating, Longstreet told Johnson to realign his brigades and those of Hindman for a renewed push toward Snodgrass Hill. Johnson turned Sugg on his right from facing west to north, leaving Fulton headed west with Coleman in reserve on the right. Then he rode to the left and rear looking for Hindman, whose brigades in pressing toward the Vinniard House had fragmented Davis and Sheridan. Deas's men had killed Brigadier General William H. Lytle, the Ohio poet-soldier who had been Johnson's prisoner at Perryville. Hindman had taken a thousand prisoners including three colonels, salvaged 1400 small arms and 165,000 rounds of ammunition, seventeen guns with caissons, wagons and animals in abundance, with an ambulance to boot.[70] He had sent the Union Army leader, Rosecrans, flying from his headquarters at the Widow Glenn's along with two corps commanders, Crittenden and McCook. Shaken and stunned, convinced the day was lost the Federal chiefs rode all the way back to Rossville, six miles behind the firing.

As he jogged cross-country hunting Hindman, about 1:30 P.M. Johnson met Kershaw and Major E. H. Cunningham, Hood's inspector general. They told him Hood had been severely wounded and had been taken to the rear. A minié ball pierced his right leg, shattering the thigh bone an hour earlier, shortly after Johnson's men broke the enemy defense at Brotherton's. One of McLaws's staff officers who had brought the news suggested that Kershaw as senior brigadier assume command of the two brigades of McLaws which were fighting on his right. Johnson at first demurred. Precious time was lost while a comparison of rank was made by him and Kershaw "which seemed to satisfy" Johnson, the South Carolinian said later.[71] Actually Johnson ranked from January 24, 1862 which was twenty days ahead of Kershaw, but deferential as usual, he gave in. Wisely, Major Cunningham suggested that Longstreet be informed of the issue. He also told Johnson that Kershaw could not support him because his force was needed for a frontal attack ahead of his position.

While this discussion was going on, Johnson sent his faithful Blakemore to find Hindman. A short time later Johnson resumed his search for the East Tennessee ex-Congressman who could afford to be generous now since all opposition, except for Wilder's mounted riflemen, was fading from his front. He soon found Hindman who was looking for Johnson after Blakemore's visit. With Hindman was Anderson, whose brigade was immediately put at Johnson's disposal. Hindman said Deas would support Johnson's left while Anderson swung around to bolster his right.[72]

Johnson again reformed his front line: Sugg on the right, Fulton on the left extending through a cornfield south of the Vittetoe House[73] to the Crawfish Springs Road. He told Deas to move up to align with Fulton and then press forward. When Fulton's men took the Vittetoe farmhouse, filled with wounded Federals, the women of the family who had hidden in the cellar on Saturday and Sunday "burst forth and greeted our soldiers with clapping hands, presenting an impressive scene," Johnson wrote later.[74]

An hour was used up in relocating artillery and replenishing ammunition from captured wagons. Then the drive was resumed about three o'clock toward a crest a thousand yards distant on the left. Sugg gained the summit after a sharp fight. But he had no support on his right and the Federals sharply counterattacked. He began falling back. Johnson sent orders to hold the hill and said he would send help. Manigault of Hindman soon was coming up on the left and Deas reported to Johnson after sweeping the enemy from a ridge west of the Crawfish Springs

Road. Johnson sent both brigades to his left and his alignment now, left to right, was Deas, Manigault, Fulton, Sugg and Anderson with Coleman in the rear of Fulton.

Riding to the rear a little after three o'clock Johnson reported his situation to Hindman who was beginning to feel the effects of a wound suffered three hours before when he was hit by a shell fragment. He had been ill the previous day, unable to go back to duty until afternoon. Hindman believed that a Federal counterattack was in the making and he had sent to Longstreet and Buckner for reinforcements. He also believed a "concert of action was necessary," therefore as the officer of highest rank present he assumed overall command of Johnson's division as well as his own and directed an "immediate and vigorous attack on the enemy in our front." He told Johnson to take over the left wing of this effort and wheel to the right aiming for Snodgrass Hill where Thomas, last senior Union commander on the field, was stoutly resisting the battering of Kershaw, sent in by Longstreet to deliver the *coup de grâce*. Kershaw agreed to conform to Johnson's movements which began at 3:30 P.M.

Acting now almost as a corps commander with his own and most of Hindman's division under his control, Johnson rode along his front, commencing with Deas, to put the new assault in motion. At the same time Thomas was being reinforced by the division of James Blair Steedman from the Reserve Corps at McAfee Church, four miles north. The reserves were commanded by Gordon Granger who took the initiative without orders from Rosecrans to speed "Old Steady" and his five Ohio regiments to the front at Brannan's right. Their counterattack was sudden and fierce. Deas and Manigault fell back to the foot of the ridge and Anderson still farther. Johnson strove mightily to hold the high ground and stem any sudden retreat like that at Stones River which would cheat him of a triumph. Vigorously he rode among the faltering men, shouting orders and appeals to them to rally and not abandon their gains. Officers joined him "with every energy and zeal," he said later. Skulkers were persuaded or pummelled from behind trees or booted erect from prone positions on the ground to go back to their places and resume the pressure. But the flaming drive of battle was petering out. Only two regiments of Manigault out of Hindman's three brigades responded and reentered the fight. By 5 P.M. Deas and Manigault told Johnson's aide they had decided "it was not safe to put their commands in the same position without fresh troops."[75]

Longstreet in later years estimated his troops made all of twenty-five assaults on Snodgrass Hill. He brought up three fresh brigades of Preston from his reserve and passed two through Sugg and Fulton to the front for an attack coordinated with Johnson, to no avail. Thomas "The Rock" was not to be budged.[76]

At dusk Johnson pulled back 250 yards to a good location near the top of the ridge still held by his classmate Thomas. Pickets were sent to the front and patrols went out to feel out the Union dispositions. A line for the night was formed of Manigault, Fulton, McNair (Coleman) and Gregg (Sugg). Tense and worn out men bivouacked, ate what they could and fell asleep. A drowsy third was prodded into staying awake and alert. Johnson saw to that.

By 8 P.M., his troops set for the night, Johnson abandoned hope of any further action. Then he did a strange thing. Still exhilarated by the day's successes, he quit his usual quiescent role and set off alone on his horse to find Bragg and pridefully "report his position," hopefully to hear his praises. His heady mood led him to bypass Longstreet under whose eye he had done the day's work and to whom such a situation report normally should have been made. He wandered along the cluttered roads and across fields and thickets in the warm darkness made frightful by the screams of hundreds of neglected wounded. Until 11 P.M. he hunted in the rear for the army commander, never finding him. Disappointed, he went back to his division bivouac "worn out with the toils of the day." The next morning the enemy was gone, drawn back to Chattanooga.[77] Monday's only tasks were to salvage weapons, bring in the injured and bury the dead.

If he reviewed Sunday's achievements before he fell asleep, Bushrod Johnson had many reasons for feeling pride and satisfaction. He had ably led a division and at times had functioned proficiently as an acting corps commander. He had displayed the professional competence requisite for leadership and command. Ordered to spearhead an attack, he had done so with determination and fortitude, using his artillery skilfully and shifting his infantry with judgement and imagination. Especially he had been sensitive to the gap in the Union lines and responsive to its opportunity by taking aggressive and resourceful advantage of the chance.

D. H. Hill lauded his perception and initiative. Longstreet acknowledged Johnson "thought he had the key of battle,"[78] and obviously was more impressed in his afterthoughts than the perfunctory mention in his report of Johnson as "distinguished for conduct and ability."[79] A score of years later he told Robert Johnson that Bushrod's "quickness of decision as a leader" of the attack on September 20 "won for the Southerners their greatest advantage" at Chickamauga.[80] Hindman praised his "signal gallantry and efficiency."[81]

Johnson had demonstrated those elements of character deemed essential in a commander: courage, diligence and resourcefulness. He had been alert and tenacious, proficient and resolute to a degree he never attained again. He had tried to take care of his men. He had ridden to all parts of the field and to all units to inspire, to counsel and guide. To admiring Snowden of the Twenty-fifth Tennessee, Johnson was "our ubiquitous general, early in the saddle."[82] Above all, Johnson had been able to elicit the best and greatest effort from his Tennesseeans and from some of those who had joined him at the last minute: Gregg's (Sugg), and McNair's (Coleman) brigades.

But not without tremendous cost. Out of his total strength of around 3500 his casualties were more than 1400 killed, wounded and missing. Some of his units were pitifully reduced, never to recover.[83]

One laurel for Johnson came from the Federal side. The former Czarist staff officer, Brigadier General John B. Turchin (né Ivan Vasilevitch Turchininoff), commanding the Third Brigade in Reynold's Division, writing of the battle twenty-five years later, called Johnson "one of the best, if not the best, officer in Bragg's army."[84] The praise was not wholly exaggerated. On that ghastly Sunday, September 20, 1863 Bushrod Johnson reached his military zenith.

Notes

1. David Urquhart, "Bragg's Advance and Retreat" in *B&L,* III, p. 605 and n.
2. Map 78, *WP Atlas*; *Steele,* p. 315.
3. Cleburne's report, *OR,* XX, pp. 843 ff. All citations in this volume are in Part 1 unless otherwise noted.
4. *Steele,* p. 316.
5. Buell in *B&L,* III, p. 43 n., p. 44 n.
6. *Steele,* p. 317.
7. *OR,* XX, p. 844; G. C. Kniffin, "The Battle of Stone's River" in *B&L,* III, pp. 613 ff. The spelling "Stones River" without an apostrophe in this biography of Johnson follows Steele and most modern writers.
8. *OR,* XX, p. 876.
9. *Ibid.,* XX, pp. 977 f.
10. *Ibid.,* XX, p. 844.
11. *Ibid.,* XX, p. 860.
12. *Ibid.,* XX, p. 857. Govan's report says a soldier gave Sill's gloves to Captain E. G. Brasher of his right company after the body was brought to the hospital at 11 A.M. He adds that he would have taken Sill's

uniform at the time except that it was too large. Actually Sill's uniform jacket was Sheridan's donned mistakenly the night before during a visit by Sill to Sheridan's tent.

13. *Ibid.*, XX, p. 885.
14. *Ibid.*, XX, pp. 858, 863.
15. *Ibid.*, XX, p. 857.
16. *Ibid.*, p. 865. Johnson says the place his men captured was called the Jenkins house and not "Griscom" as on the maps. He argued that Liddell's troops had taken the "Widow Smith's."
17. *Ibid.*, XX, pp. 846–848, 879.
18. *Ibid.*, XX, p. 878.
19. *Ibid.*, XX, p. 848.
20. Map 82, *WP Atlas.*
21. *OR*, XX, p. 879. Johnson blames an unnamed unit on the right for touching off the panic. Vaughan's report, *ibid.*, pp. 743 f. indicates he had outstripped Polk on his right and started to fall back when he came under heavy Union enfilading fire. This apparently triggered the rush to the rear by adjacent troops.
22. *Ibid.*, XX, p. 849.
23. *Ibid.*
24. *Ibid.*, XX, p. 880.
25. *Ibid.*, XX, p. 882.
26. *Ibid.*, XX, p. 881.
27. *Ibid.*, XX, p. 852 for Cleburne's figures; pp. 780, 881 for Johnson's. Bragg's report, *ibid.*, p. 674 puts Johnson's losses at 606.
28. *Ibid.*, XX, p. 850. Liddell's troops were Cleburne's fellow Arkansans in whom he had a special interest.
29. *Ibid.*, XX, p. 880.
30. *Ibid.*, XX, pp. 683 f.
31. Gilbert C. Kniffen, "Manœuvering Bragg out of Tennessee" in *B&L,* III, pp. 635 ff.
32. *OR*, XXIII, pt. 2, p. 757.
33. Originals of all promotion correspondence in *B. R. Johnson File* in CSA Staff Papers.
34. *OR*, XXIII, pt. 2, p. 867.
35. Map 108, *WP Atlas.*
36. *OR*, XXIII, pt. 2, pp. 601 ff.
37. *Ibid.*, XXIII, pt. 2, pp. 601 ff.; *Kniffen*, p. 636.
38. Glenn Tucker, *Chickamauga, Bloody Battle of the West*, (Indianapolis: Bobbs Merrill, 1961), pp. 115 f.; Fairfax Downey, *Storming the Gateway*, (Garden City, N. Y.: David McKay, Inc., 1960), pp. 36 f. After the war, Wilder had a distinguished career in Tennessee industry and was elected mayor of Chattanooga.
39. *OR*, XXIII, pt. 2, p. 608; *Kniffen*, p. 637.
40. *OR*, XXIII, p. 905.
41. Daniel H. Hill, "Chickamauga, the Great Battle of the West" in *B&L*, III, pp. 638 ff.
42. *OR*, XXX, pt. 4, p. 620.
43. Opposing Forces at Chickamauga in *B&L,* III, pp. 673–675.
44. *Downey*, p. 87.
45. Maps 111a, 111b, *WP Atlas.*
46. *OR*, XXX, pt. 2, pp. 31, 467, 470.
47. *Ibid.*; Hill in *B&L,* III, p. 647 n.

48. *OR*, XXX, pt. 2, p. 451.
49. *Ibid.*; *Wyeth*, p. 221; Forrest's report, *OR*, XXX, pt. 2, pp. 523 ff. Darden's Mississippi Battery, usually with Johnson's Brigade, was in Buckner's Corps reserve.
50. *OR*, XXX, pt. 2, pp. 31, 467.
51. *Ibid.*, XXX, p. 467.
52. *Ibid.*, XXX, p. 31.
53. *Ibid.*, XXX, p. 452; *Lytle*, p. 207.
54. *OR*, XXX, pt. 2, p. 453.
55. *Steele*, p. 432.
56. Map 113a, *WP Atlas.*
57. *Steele*, p. 433; Text, Maps 113a, 113b, *WP Atlas.*
58. Johnson's report, *OR*, XXX, pt. 2, pp. 451 ff.
59. *Ibid.*, XXX, pt. 2, p. 456.
60. *Ibid.*, XXX, pt. 2, pp. 455 f.; *Steele*, p. 434.
61. Longstreet's report, *OR*, XXX, pt. 2, p. 287; Longstreet, *From Manassas to Appomattox*, (Dallas, Texas: Dallas Publishing Co., 1896), p. 438; Hill in *B&L*, III, p. 652; *Steele*, p. 435; Map 113b, *WP Atlas.*
62. *Steele*, pp. 434 f.; *OR*, XXX, pt. 2, p. 288.
63. *OR*, XXX, pt. 2, p. 456.
64. *Ibid.*, XXX, pt. 2, p. 288; Fulton's report, *ibid.*, p. 474; Snowden's report, *ibid.*, p. 490.
65. Emerson Opdycke, "Notes on the Chickamauga Campaign" in *B&L*, III, p. 670; *Steele*, p. 436; *Tucker*, pp. 254 ff.
66. *OR*, XXX, pt. 2, p. 458.
67. *Ibid.*, XXX, pt. 2, p. 459. Four three-inch rifles belonging to the Federal First Missouri Battery were turned over to the Confederate First Missouri Battery (Bledsoe's).
68. *Tucker*, pp. 266, 286.
69. Details in Johnson's report. Since Fort Donelson, Blakemore had served with Johnson who acclaimed his "honor and ability" which "merits more than I can say." *OR*, XXX, pt. 2, p. 466.
70. *Longstreet*, pp. 450–452; Hindman's report, *OR*, XXX, pt. 2, p. 304.
71. Kershaw's report, *OR*, XXX, pt. 2, p. 503. Archibald Gracie, *The Truth About Chickamauga*, (New York: Houghton Mifflin, 1911), pp. 54 ff., 294 f., charges Johnson with "inertness for two and one-half hours" after noon on September 20 before starting the northward attack. "Questions of rank and procedure" which could have been settled by Longstreet's presence, he also blames for delays. Gracie, a wealthy New York broker, who was the son of Brigadier General Archibald Gracie in Preston's Division, died in the Titanic sinking, April 14, 1912.
72. *OR*, XXX, pt. 2, p. 460.
73. Spelled "Videto" in Johnson's report and "Villetoe" in map, *B&L*, III, p. 648. The spelling "Vittetoe" here follows modern writers.
74. *OR*, XXX, pt. 2, p. 461.
75. *Ibid.*, XXX, pt. 2, pp. 304, 463 f.
76. Map 114b, *WP Atlas*; J. S. Fullerton, "Reenforcing Thomas at Chickamauga" in *B&L*, III, pp. 665 f.
77. *OR*, XXX, pt. 2, p. 465.
78. *Longstreet*, p. 450.
79. *OR*, XXX, pt. 2, pp. 288 ff.
80. *Robert Johnson*, p. 12. In John B. Hood, *Advance and Retreat*, (New

Orleans: Published for Hood Orphan Memorial Fund, 1888), pp. 62 f., Hood makes only casual mention of Johnson and nothing about his attack while he speaks of "Kershaw's splendid division" and "Hindman's advance."

81. *OR*, XXX, pt. 2, p. 305.
82. *OR*, XXX, pt. 2, p. 490.
83. *Ibid.*, XXX, pt. 2, p. 467; Longstreet's report, *ibid.*, p. 291 gives Johnson's total casualties as 950.
84. John B. Turchin, *Chickamauga*, (Chicago: Fergus Printing Co., 1888), p. 209.

9
"JUSTICE TO HIS GREAT MERIT"

i. To the Rescue of Perturbed Pickett

What followed the glories of Chickamauga was a morale-eroding anticlimax. During October 1863 there was nothing more than desultory shooting between Rosecrans's hungry, listless, discouraged and besieged men and Bragg's shaken, lethargic and vegetating forces investing Chattanooga. Grant, named overall Federal commander between the Mississippi and the Alleghenies, came to Chattanooga on October 23 and replaced Rosecrans with Thomas. Crittenden and McCook already had been relieved and were on the road to oblivion. Vindictive Bragg also did some purging and got rid of critics such as D. H. Hill, Bishop Polk and Buckner. Reorganized, the corps commands went to Breckinridge, Hardee and Longstreet.[1]

Bushrod Johnson remained in the Army of Tennessee as Buckner's replacement in divisional command but he definitely put himself again on Bragg's black list. Along with Polk, Hill, Longstreet, Buckner, Preston, Cleburne and others on October 4, Johnson signed the round-robin appeal to President Davis to relieve Bragg from command, an action he previously had supported after Stones River.[2] The letter brought Davis by special train from Richmond to Bragg's headquarters. In the presence of Bragg, Davis asked all of the senior officers to give their opinions of their commanding general. Stepping forward were Longstreet, Hill, Buckner, and Cheatham, but not Bushrod Johnson, either ignored as at Fort Donelson or too reticent to attend and speak up. Polk, already relieved, had been interviewed in Atlanta. Longstreet was vigorously critical. He had urged Bragg to take the offensive on September 21 when Rosecrans's dismayed fugitives were still disorganized after Chickamauga. Bragg had delayed, then went to Missionary Ridge instead of Chattanooga, failing to harvest the fruit of his success. Longstreet felt, and said, that considering the low state of morale in the Army of Tennessee, Bragg could be of greater service elsewhere. The other signers concurred.[3]

There probably was no surprise among the Bragg faction at headquarters on November 4 when Longstreet was detached with 12,000 men of the divisions of McLaws and Hood (now commanded by Micah Jenkins), and sent against Burnside in Knoxville. The move set off a flap in Washington. Under pressure from there Grant stepped up his activity in Chattanooga, especially after he was joined by Sherman and his Army of the Tennessee on November 15.[4] On November 22, Johnson was told to join Longstreet threatening the Federals in Knoxville.

The division Johnson had taken over as Buckner's successor included his old brigade, now Fulton's. It was an emaciated shadow. The Seventeenth and Twenty-third Tennessee had been combined into one regiment as also had the Twenty-fifth and Forty-fourth Tennessee. Later the Sixty-third Tennessee was added to the brigade. What had been Johnson's Brigade at Perryville and Stones River now consisted of three tiny regiments. New to the division was the Alabama brigade of Archibald Gracie, Jr., New York-born West Pointer of '54, only member of his family to espouse the South. He also had signed the anti-Bragg round robin. Gracie had four regiments: the Forty-first, Forty-third, Forty-ninth and Sixtieth Alabama. The third brigade in Johnson's Division was Alexander W. Reynolds's, West Point '38, captured at Vicksburg and recently exchanged. It had two Virginia and two North Carolina regiments. The entire division counted 3886 effectives, poorly clad, meagerly equipped and badly shod.[5]

During Bragg's doldrums after Chickamauga, the scratch division Johnson had led to glory there was dissolved. During the next few weeks his shriveled Tennessee brigade first was assigned to Stewart's Division in Breckinridge's Corps, then to Buckner in Hardee's. When he got the order to join Longstreet, Johnson and his men were part of Cleburne's Division, encamped on the crest and eastern slope of Missionary Ridge. Cleburne was first designated to take the reinforcements to Knoxville, then Bragg changed his mind and picked Johnson instead.

While he was getting his men aboard the train starting just after dawn on November 23 in Dalton, Georgia, Johnson lost a third of them. About noon an order from Bragg through Cleburne told Johnson not to take any troops who had not yet entrained. Reynolds's Brigade, therefore, got off the cars without its gear which had gone ahead with Johnson's and Gracie's brigades. Cut to 2625 effectives, Johnson required four days to make the 115 miles to Longstreet.[6] Infantry, artillery gear and baggage went by rail from Dalton to Charleston, then unloaded and marched until picked up by a train from Loudoun. Horses and empty wagons traveled entirely by road. Many men, especially Tennesseeans, deserted on the way, Johnson said.[7] He reported to Longstreet on Friday, November 27. Unknown to either, Bragg had been badly beaten two days before on Missionary Ridge and had fled with his army twenty-five miles to Rocky Face Ridge, near Dalton.[8]

Burnside had withdrawn behind his fortifications in Knoxville while Longstreet had been reconnoitering, feinting and waiting for Johnson. Early on the wet, foggy and cold Sunday, November 28, Longstreet mounted an assault on Fort Sanders, the main Union bastion west of the city. Two of McLaws's brigades, W. T. Wofford, led by Colonel S. Z. Ruff, and Benjamin G. Humphreys, advanced in column of regiments. The attack was to be made with fixed bayonets and no shooting, under the covering fire of sharpshooters.[9] Johnson, supporting Humphreys, moved Gracie along the south side of the East Tennessee & Georgia Railroad tracks and Fulton along the north side of the railroad to within 250 yards of the fort.[10] Longstreet stayed with Johnson to watch the action through the gray morning light.[11] The Federals waited inside, behind a wet ditch. The Southerners had no fascines nor scaling ladders to cross this obstacle. Entanglements of telegraph wire, used extensively for the first time in combat history, were stretched between stumps, creating a further hazard for the attackers.

The assault was quickly repulsed with 129 killed, including Colonel Ruff, 488 wounded, and 226 captured.[12] Major Goggin of McLaws's staff told Longstreet it was impossible to take the fort without axes to cut through the wire. Longstreet ordered recall sounded. Since he was not actively engaged, Johnson's loss was two killed and nineteen wounded. He pleaded with Longstreet to let him renew the attack with his fresher troops, but Lee's lieutenant told him to take his men back to camp.[13]

Longstreet was ready to try again a few days later. Then a telegram from President Davis told of Bragg's debacle.[14] Longstreet called a council of his generals, including Johnson, to decide whether to rejoin Bragg or retire toward Virginia. McLaws argued for Virginia and nobody dissented. At dark, December 4, Johnson took his men from the rifle pits they had manned since the November 28 failure and they began a bone-freezing trudge on muddy roads via Strawberry Plains toward Russellville. Johnson and his men with Darden's Battery led the force. For two days, December 6–8, they halted at Russellville, 35 miles from Knoxville and scoured the countryside to find enough food to sustain them further on the march. The effort was almost fruitless. Many East Tennessee Unionists were actively hostile. Many other Tennesseeans in the division, unhappy over the prospect of moving farther away from home, took advantage of being detached as foragers to desert. Flour rations were cut in half.

At Cloud's Creek, 5 miles west of Rogersville and 32 agonizing miles farther on the march, Johnson ordered a four-day halt between December 9 and 13 while several tanyards and shoe cobbler shops were taken over. Tanners and shoemakers among the soldiers were put on extra duty to prepare hides and make shoes. The need far exceeded the supply and many were still left barefooted.[15]

Shod or not, Johnson's division was on the road again early Monday, December 14. The weather was bitterly cold and the road was soupy after heavy rains. Sixteen miles of deep mud on the road back toward Knoxville were Bean's Station and three brigades of Union cavalry under James M. Shackelford, Kentucky-born captor of John Hunt Morgan and his raiders in Ohio. The Federals were too eager in their pursuit and had outstripped their supporting infantry. Longstreet sent four cavalry brigades under William T. Martin down the south side of the Holston River and two more horse brigades under William E. ("Grumble") Jones around the mountains to cut off the Federal retreat. The infantry, including Johnson, moved directly on Bean's Station.[16]

By 3 P.M. Johnson and Jones found enemy pickets three miles east of the town. They chased them back into it. Johnson brought up Gracie who deployed the Fifty-ninth Alabama with the Forty-third Alabama behind it. Gracie was hit severely in the arm. Shackelford had turned a three-story hotel in the center of the village into a fortress, firing from loopholes cut in the walls of the second and third floors. Johnson ordered up the Virginia Batteries of Captains Osmond B. Taylor and William W. Parker to fire almost pointblank into the building. Covered by the shelling, the Sixtieth Alabama raced into the shelter of a stable, fifty yards from the hotel. Two Confederate shells fell short and hit the stable, killing two men. Johnson lost 30 killed, 180 wounded including Gracie, and 12 missing from his shrinking force which now numbered only 1135 effectives.[17]

Martin's cavalry mismanaged its task and the Union troopers managed to streak out of Bean's Station without much loss to personnel but they had to leave 68 supply wagons, about 40 of which were laden with coffee, sugar and other stores, gleefully welcomed by their short-rationed captors. Longstreet's report praised Johnson for "his fine march from Cloud's Creek to Bean's Station over very bad roads and for his handsome attack upon the enemy's cavalry, driving him steadily back."[18]

A week later, early in the morning of December 21, Johnson moved his depleted force into Morristown, 41 miles from Knoxville, and built temporary shelters against the woes of winter. The work was interrupted on December 28 by another 16-mile march in the mud to Dandridge Station to discourage another Federal pursuit from Knoxville. Then the grim routine was resumed of trying to feed off the country when erratic supply lines failed and to live under constant harassment by anti-Confederate Tennessee bushwhackers. Morale was low, desertions were high. Misery was a condition of life.[19]

In a midwinter report to Longstreet, Johnson voiced the bleak despondency and disappointment of his own low spirits as he wrote of his suffering troops:

> The highest mead of praise is due to the men of this command, who have toiled faithfully on amid privations

> and discouragements, and who have, half-clad, braved alike the winter's rains and the bullets of the invading foe, while they have been abandoned by less determined comrades, who have hitherto borne their part in this cruel, iniquitous war and who have bravely fought at their side on the most bloody fields of battle. In view of the services of these faithful men I feel that there are no other instances of courage or valor necessary to be specified. These have all nobly performed their duty to their suffering country and to the cause of liberty. May God give them what men may never be able to bestow upon them—an adequate reward. They enjoy at least the proud consciousness of arduous duties nobly performed.[20]

The dreary season was somewhat enlivened by Longstreet. He filed charges against three commanders: McLaws for neglect of duty in the assault on Fort Sanders and for want of faith in the efforts and plans of Longstreet; Law, for obtaining a leave of absence under "false pretences"; and Robertson, the Texas doctor-soldier. for conduct prejudicial to good order and military discipline in voicing lack of confidence in the campaign at Bean's Station and expressing resentment at the condition of his shoeless and foodless men.

The disputes were symptomatic of the state of morale. Buckner came from Bristol, Virginia to preside at the courts-martial and the cases dragged on until spring, with long wrangles by letter between Longstreet and Richmond. McLaws ultimately was exonerated by President Davis, whereat Longstreet threatened to resign; the War Department would not uphold the charge against Law; Robertson appears never to have been tried but later was transferred back to Texas.[21]

As 1864 made its bleak and dismal entrance, the wretched lot of Johnson and his men grew no better. The shelters built at Morristown were scarcely finished in December when the division had to leave them and get moving, first across the French Broad River, then back to Dandridge, thirty miles east of Knoxville, thence to Bull's

Gap, thirty miles farther up the valley between Morristown and Greeneville in vain efforts to plug mountain gaps through which the Federal cavalry and guerillas were passing at will.[22] Before leaving Dandridge, Johnson made a speech to his troops assuring them the Confederates were not going to fall back farther than Greeneville.[23] His effort at boosting morale was futile.

The stream of desertions never halted. The disaffected ones compounded their offenses in many cases by telling the Federals who caught them later how destitute was the condition of Johnson's and Longstreet's troops. In March, two of the defectors were lieutenants from the Seventeenth Tennessee.[24] In April Johnson had to report to Joseph E. Johnston that a runaway had given the enemy the key to the code used in the Confederate Signal Corps.[25] Concerned over his dwindling numbers, Johnson sent a plea to Secretary of War Seddon for the return to him of Reynolds's brigade which had been taken off the train in Dalton by Bragg's order in November. Reynolds, now an orphan unit in Carter L. Stevenson's division with J. E. Johnston in Georgia, bereft of wagons, horses or cooking utensils which had gone off with Johnson's trainload, made the same plea. Both were refused.[26]

In March Longstreet moved to Bristol, Virginia and in April he took back with him to Eastern Virginia what was left of the thousands sent to Chickamauga from the Army of Northern Virginia six months previously. At Greeneville Buckner assumed the hollow command of the Department of East Tennessee which had no more troops than Johnson's feeble hundreds, based at Zollicoffer. These were shifted with Buckner's headquarters to Abingdon, Virginia late in April,[27] and thus ended Johnson's war service in his adopted state and in the western armies.

Buckner sent a gloomy report of the situation to Adjutant General Samuel Cooper. The area was stripped bare of any food or forage; late spring brought almost no grass for cavalry mounts; horses generally were "unfit"; conditions were "lamentable." Buckner also protested against being bypassed by Bragg, now President Davis's military adviser who was sending tactical orders to Johnson to "throw his cavalry forward."[28] Cooper, of course, was in no position to remedy anything. He was facing a two-way crisis. The Union politico-general Benjamin F. Butler was ready to move against Richmond along the south bank of the James while Grant, now with Meade's Army of the Potomac, was poised to bulldoze a path through the Wilderness toward the Confederate capital from the northwest.[29]

The next thing Buckner got from Cooper was an order, dated April 28, assigning him to duty in the Trans-Mississippi Department,[30] and a telegram two days later: "Send Johnson's brigade without delay to this place," i.e. Richmond.[31] The destinies of Johnson and his Tennesseeans henceforth were to be tied in with the fate of the Confederate capital.

Before he parted company with him, Longstreet agreed to revive Johnson's dormant promotion hopes. He wrote Cooper April 12, pointing out that Johnson had commanded a division both at Chickamauga and since then in Eastern Tennessee. "I have found him to be one of the ablest division commanders that I have ever had with me," said Longstreet. "He has courage, skill and ability to an eminent degree and most excellent ideas of action and strategy."[32]

Prior to leaving for the West, Buckner added his weight to the effort. He wrote Cooper May 3 inviting his attention to Johnson's services: "distinguished at Fort Donelson, Shiloh, Perryville, Murfreesboro, Chickamauga and Bean's Station, on the last two occasions in command of divisions." He added:

> By education a soldier, he has steadily gained reputation in

> every action in which he has been engaged. He has been recommended for promotion on several occasions. He has been repeatedly under my command and whenever called upon for the discharge of important duties, he has discharged them with gallantry and ability. I consider it but an act of justice to his great merit as a soldier to make this recommendation for his promotion, a recommendation which is altogether unsolicited by him.[33]

Johnson may not have importuned him as Buckner said. But it was no happenstance that President Davis got a letter on May 5 from Humphrey Marshall of Kentucky, former brigadier general, now Confederate Congressman, stating he had known Johnson before the war and recommending his promotion. Another endorsement of Johnson was signed by the entire Kentucky and Tennessee delegations in the Confederate Congress.[34]

Despite this impressive array of military and political backing, the matter at first seemed doomed to follow previous efforts into the files. Cooper told Secretary Seddon he knew of no division open except possibly McLaws's, whose conviction by court-martial on Longstreet's charges had been rejected by the War Department and who was being considered for a post in Savannah, Georgia. Seddon then said, in effect, "Hold it up!" Events were to overrule him very soon.

Johnson's men, variously estimated between 800 and 1168, were on the way to Richmond by train from Bristol on May 2. The next day[35] Grant's 119,000 began moving South toward the fords of the Rapidan River, west of Chancellorsville, and Lee put his 64,000 in motion to counter him.[36] Beauregard, recently named to command the Departments of North Carolina and Cape Fear, was at Weldon, North Carolina, forty-five miles south of Petersburg.[37] Major General George Edwards [*sic*] Pickett, since September 1863 in command of the Department of North Carolina, was in Petersburg under orders to return to Lee's Army.[38] The South Carolina brigade of Johnson Hagood was traveling northward from Charleston to reinforce Lee and the Virginians of Henry A. Wise's brigade prepared to follow.

Reports of extensive enemy activity aimed at the Petersburg–Richmond area were pouring in on Pickett on May 4 and 5. Federals were landing at Bermuda Hundred, less than ten miles east of the vital Richmond and Petersburg Railroad. They were elements of the Union Army of the James, led by Benjamin F. Butler.[39]

Friday May 6 brought some help to Pickett. First, Daniel H. Hill came as a voluntary aide to Beauregard.[40] Next, Pickett was authorized to use 300 of Hagood's Brigade, just arriving in Petersburg under Colonel R. F. Graham of the Twenty-first South Carolina.[41] Pickett sent them toward Port Walthall, five miles below Petersburg on the Appomattox River.[42] Graham shortly was joined by 300 more of his regiment. With these skimpy numbers Graham twice beat off Federal assaults by part of the XVIII Corps.[43]

When Johnson's thousand men climbed stiff-legged from the rickety railroad cars in Richmond after their 200-mile trip from Bristol, they had time only to gather up their gear and start marching toward the defenses on the James River below the capital. By the afternoon of May 5 they were ten miles away at Chaffin's Farm. That night they went on to Drewry's Bluff. By 3 A.M. Friday, May 6, they occupied Fort Stevens. Two hours later part of the Twenty-first South Carolina of Hagood's Brigade arrived. Johnson assigned them and his men to positions. As soon as it was daylight he rode off on reconnaissance and while he was gone, orders came from Major General Robert Ransom, commanding the Department of Richmond and thereby Johnson's immediate superior, telling him to rush Hagood's men via the Richmond and Petersburg Railroad if possible to Port Walthall Junction, about ten miles south. No train was available. The Carolinians started afoot. Then another order came to Johnson to dispatch his own men to the same place. This gave him the first intimation, Johnson said later, that the enemy was menacing the vital rail line running south from the capital. Within two miles of his target Johnson got a frantic message from Major F. W. Smith, left in command at Fort Stevens, saying that the enemy was six miles away at Ware Bottom Church and beseeching Johnson to turn around and come back. Johnson ignored the plea, continued on, and found Graham had twice repulsed the enemy. As senior officer present, Johnson assumed command and extended the defense lines to the right.[44]

During the night the balance of Hagood's Brigade arrived with its commander. He was junior to Johnson who retained control. The next morning, Saturday May 7, Johnson got a report from Roger A. Pryor, erstwhile prewar secessionist "fire-eater," Confederate brigadier and Congressman and serving now as courier and scout, that the enemy was at Ware Bottom Church. An advance was decided upon. Before it started, D. H. Hill arrived. He had been sent by Pickett, to whom Johnson was a stranger. Hill made a personal reconnaissance, found enemy cavalry only 300 yards away and then helped Johnson and Hagood deploy their men, now totaling 2668.[45]

The main Federal attack by three brigades of W. T. H. Brooks, West Point '41, came at 2 P.M. It fell heaviest on Hagood and lasted two hours. Before they were repelled, the Federals cut telegraph lines and tore up a length of the rail spur running from the junction to Port Walthall. Union casualties were 289; Hagood's 177; Johnson's 7.[46] After dark another unit of Hagood's reported, boosting the defenders to around 3500.

Perturbed Pickett began to heckle Johnson with dispatches suggesting, then ordering, a withdrawal two miles south to Swift Creek where entrenching tools would be sent. Fearful of the consequences to the vital railroad if he left, Johnson delayed moving until Saturday midnight.[47] The next day, May 8, Pickett directed D. H. Hill to march the troops back to Port Walthall Junction. An amiability existed between Hill and Johnson going back to Chickamauga and they agreed to comply only partially by retaining the main body at Swift Creek and sending detachments to the Junction. While the troops dug themselves in on the 8th and 9th, Johnson took a part of Hagood's Brigade, on Pickett's order as he interpreted it, and made a reconnaissance in force to the north side of the creek. He found the Federals were there in strong numbers. Later the enemy tried to cross the creek, but were driven back.[48]

Tuesday, May 10, more troops came from the South. First to arrive was tall and handsome Robert F. Hoke, North Carolinian former cadet at Kentucky Military Institute, the rival of Bushrod Johnson's school, and a major general since April 24. He was twenty years younger than Johnson,[49] who yielded the command to him. With Hoke were his own old brigade, three regiments of Wise, two of Matt Whitaker Ransom and, due shortly, Thomas L. Clingman's four North Carolina regiments.[50] Beauregard, recovered from illness in Weldon, came to Petersburg, too. He began organizing for an offensive.

Beauregard replaced Pickett as military district commander with Brigadier General Henry A. Wise, 58-year old former governor of Virginia. Pickett was assigned to command one division and Hoke to lead the other made up of the heterogeneous brigades on the ground. Johnson and his brigade went to Hoke, along with Hagood, Clingman, and Montgomery D. Corse's Virginians.[51] They were told to march north to Drewry's Bluff to link up with Robert Ransom's force made up of the brigades of Gracie, who had been with Johnson at Bean's Station, Seth M. Barton, and Eppa Hunton, totaling almost 5000.[52]

Pickett, senior major general in the Confederate armies,

suddenly was out of all of this. The anxieties and anguish of the past week had laid him low. In a state of nervous collapse, he reported sick on Tuesday night and kept to his quarters on Wednesday, cared for by his adoring young wife.[53] Beauregard wired William H. C. Whiting in Wilmington, North Carolina, to come to Petersburg. Whiting, first in the class of '45 at West Point, ranked Hoke as a major general by two days.[54] By Friday he was on hand and Beauregard told him to concentrate the troops in the Petersburg area while he hurried north to Drewry's Bluff.

Beauregard's plan called for an assault by Whiting from the South at daylight, May 19, while the Drewry's Bluff force, reshaped into three divisions of Hoke, Ransom and Brigadier General Alfred H. Colquitt, would try to cut Butler off from his base at Bermuda Hundred. Colquitt had his own Georgia brigade and Matt Ransom's.[55] D. H. Hill stayed in Petersburg to help Whiting.[56]

In a dense fog at 4:45 A.M. May 16, Robert Ransom jumped off and in an hour captured the first line of Union rifle pits and breastworks, one general and 400 prisoners. He asked for help. Beauregard sent Colquitt's Brigade.[57] In the center of Beauregard's line, Hoke's left brigade, Hagood, advanced with Johnson on his right. Hagood took five Federal guns. Hoke then ordered him to tie in with Ransom on the left. The maneuver left Johnson's flank exposed and this was set upon by the enemy.

"Johnson was heavily engaged," Beauregard said later in his report. "The line of the enemy bent around his right flank subjecting his brigade for a time to fire in front and flank. With admirable firmness, he repulsed frequent assaults of the enemy moving against his right and rear. . . . The brigade, holding its ground nobly, lost more than a quarter of its entire number. . . ."[58]

This was most of the battle. A heavy rain started. Whiting never moved north and his inaction was variously blamed on state of mind, narcotics or whisky.[59] D. H. Hill took informal command and brought the division North on the morning of the seventeenth. By this time the Federals had given up and retired behind their Bermuda Hundred lines.

Bushrod Johnson and his men had been in Eastern Virginia less than a fortnight and had definitely established themselves as worthy of status among the bravest and best. Whether the easterners would acknowledge or appreciate this fact was yet to be seen. After their losses at Drewry's Bluff there were not many of the Tennessee strangers left to make a numerical impression. Among the losses was Captain Blakemore. On May 20 a shell shattered his leg, later amputated.

Beauregard was stirred enough by Johnson's performance to do more than reward it with the words of praise in his report. In the brief lull after the fighting, he asked Richmond to promote Johnson. On May 19 he telegraphed Bragg, who had the sympathetic ear of Jefferson Davis:

> . . . I respectfully request that Brigadier General Bushrod R. Johnson be made a major general, or that an officer of that rank be ordered to report to me.

Aside from his desire to recognize Johnson, Beauregard also may have felt that as a full general commanding a department actively engaged in a decisive operation separate from Lee's Army, he was entitled to higher ranking subordinates than the brigadiers who were being given to him with their units and then taken away almost capriciously. An immediate aftermath of Drewry's Bluff was a shuffling of command: Robert Ransom went back to his desk in the Department of Richmond; Whiting's Division was taken from D. H. Hill, who also was to be relieved and lost to Beauregard.

After two days passed without a reply from Bragg, Beauregard prodded him again by wire on May 21:

> One or two major generals are indispensible to this army. Gen. Hill will be relieved today when I shall remain with one only [Hoke]. Gen'ls Johnson and Colquitt would suit well. May I request prompt action.

Bragg had not forgotten the round-robin letter with Johnson's name on it criticising him after Chickamauga. He could also recall Johnson's concurrence with Cleburne, Polk, and Hardee after Stones River that he was unfit for further command of his army. He forgot that he had once written that Johnson had a reputation as a "gallant and zealous officer." He reluctantly endorsed Beauregard's request to Davis, agreeing that Beauregard had eight infantry brigades which should be formed into two divisions with Hoke in command of one. He added a grudging lukewarm estimate of Johnson:

> Brig. Gen. Henry A. Wise is the senior brigadier general. I know nothing of the qualifications of Brig. Gen. Colquitt, but have heard him well spoken for gallantry and vigor. Brig. Gen. Johnson is slow, but an educated soldier who has long served, with some distinction, as a brigadier.

President Davis, sensitive to the weight of political pressure backing Johnson's promotion papers in Secretary Seddon's files since May 5, did not write his usual laconic deathblow to Johnson's hopes. He directed Adjutant Cooper: "Nominate Brig. Gen. Johnson for promotion as recommended."

Cooper acted with unwonted speed. He made the nomination the same day. On the back of the sheaf of Johnson papers in his "suspend" file, Seddon wrote, "Has been appointed and file."[60]

And thus, after two years of rebuffs and disappointments, Bushrod Johnson was promoted to major general to rank from May 21, 1864. The honor came not as a reward for his notable achievements in six battles, which Bragg denigrated as service "with some distinction," not in recognition of demonstrated competence and professional ability which his superiors often had acknowledged, but as the result of political pressure coincidental to a chance exigency that left the Richmond authorities with scant alternatives except to name him. This was not a circumstance likely to make a proud spirit soar with the gratification and satisfaction of being recompensed for work well done. But at last, at the age of 47, far behind his classmates, his juniors and his civilian associates turned soldier, Bushrod Johnson had made the grade.

ii. Breakfast Comes First at The Crater

To most of the troops in the new division which he commanded as a major general, Bushrod Johnson was an unknown quantity, probably resented as a stranger from the West. He had no previous acquaintance with Henry A. Wise nor with the four Virginia regiments in his brigade: the Twenty-sixth, Thirty-fourth, Forty-sixth and Fifty-ninth. He had fought a few days beside Matt Ransom's five North Carolina regiments which he was soon to lose without replacement. The brigade of William S. Walker came without its chief, wounded and captured May 20. It also soon would leave Johnson's division and be replaced by Stephen Elliott's five South Carolina regiments who also did not know Johnson.[61]

Hoke's Division of four brigades returned to Lee's Army on May 30. Johnson's men were stretched to cover the vacated defenses, corking Butler in the Bermuda Hundred bottle and extending south from Petersburg.[62] Just as Ransom and his Tar Heels started to leave on June 3, a heavy skirmish began on his front. Beauregard protested the departure, but Ransom was sent to Drewry's Bluff anyhow. Then Wise was detached to Petersburg, but

Gracie's Alabamans of Knoxville and Bean's Station memory came to Johnson as replacements on June 11.[63]

Beauregard's defenses on the east side of Petersburg consisted of a chain of strong redans, which were artillery positions set up for both frontal and flanking fires. There were plenty of guns but insufficient crews. These strong points were connected by trenches with approaches obstructed by ditches and felled trees. Against these at 7 P.M. Wednesday, June 15, an assault was mounted by W. F. Smith's Federal XVIII Corps, which had come by steamer down the York River and up the James to Bermuda Hundred and then marched westward. The attack tore a mile-wide gap in Beauregard's forts. But a rumor that Lee was nearing with his army caused Smith to halt and wait for reinforcements. That saved the game for Beauregard.[64]

At 10:20 P.M. Johnson was ordered to direct the immediate evacuation of the Bermuda Neck and hurry to defend Petersburg, where Hoke, recalled from Lee's Army and rushed south, and Wise, the military district governor, were sorely beset. Johnson directed the burial of heavy guns, carriages and chassis at Fort Danzler and left pickets and skirmishers who were told to stay until 6 A.M.[65] The rest of the division quick-marched through the soft, spring night to a position behind Redans 12, 13 and 14 on a ridge near the Shand House, between Hoke's Division and Wise's Brigade,[66] which had been led by Colonel P. R. Page since Wise's transfer to command the district.

Wise left his office in Petersburg and rode out to be with his Virginians. He felt Johnson was making a mistake in not filling a gap between his division and the Twenty-sixth Virginia on the Confederate left where the pressure of the Federals was mounting hourly. Never reticent about his own views, Wise went to Johnson at 11 P.M. Thursday, the sixteenth, and warned him he was courting disaster before sunrise unless the hole was plugged. Wise said later that Johnson "professed to have issued the proper orders, but they were not executed" and the next morning "the Twenty-sixth was flanked on the right and Colonel Page and Captain George D. Wise fell in a few minutes of each other."[67]

This was the start of the Wise family vendetta against Johnson which endured through two more generations until the 1900s, two decades after Johnson was dead. The erratic ex-governor scarcely ever made any effort to conceal his abiding hatred for Johnson who was regarded by the Wise clan as an interloping, incompetent, indolent ex-Yankee promoted to major general ahead of a distinguished Virginian who outranked him by six months as a brigadier.[68]

At 6 P.M. Thursday, June 16, a heavy assault by elements of Winfield Scott Hancock's II and Ambrose P. Burnside's IX Corps forced the defenders from four more redans. Lieutenant Colonel Snowden of the 25/44th Tennessee was wounded. Counterattacks by the Confederates failed to regain the strong points. A strong Federal assault at first light the next day pushed back Johnson's right on the Shand House ridge. Other Union drives were beaten off. Firing continued until 11 P.M.[69]

During the fighting on Friday, the seventeenth, Beauregard and his chief engineer had selected the site of another, shorter defense line, staked it out and showed it to staff officers of Hoke and Johnson so they could guide their units to their proper places in the dark. About 12:30 A.M. Saturday, the eighteenth, behind a decoy of numerous, blazing campfires and sentinels thrown out near the enemy, both divisions pulled back almost a mile and began digging trenches.[70]

All night, Johnson's and Hoke's men worked themselves into a state of dazed exhaustion. When Kershaw's Division, sent by Lee, arrived before dawn, they were greeted with feeble cheers. Two hours later came the division of Charles W. Field of the First Corps and before noon Lee appeared.

The day's attacks by the Federals were hasty and uncoordinated; gains were minor and losses heavy.[71] Petersburg had been saved again and for the nonce the crisis was passed.

Johnson had extracted the ultimate in endurance from his men in marching, fighting and digging. Beauregard called their resistance "almost incredible." New to the Virginia scene and proud of the showing made in six weeks since he left Bristol, Johnson jealously husbanded whatever honors accrued to his Tennesseeans and to himself. Consequently he was disturbed when he read, in the Richmond *Examiner* of June 20, the following:

TROPHIES OF THE FIGHT

> There were deposited temporarily in this office on Saturday [June 18] two flags taken from the enemy in the battle of Petersburg by General Wise's brigade. One from the 113th N.Y. State Volunteers with the motto "Excelsior" is bullet torn and blood stained silk with the painted illustrations of the Revolutionary War. The other is an artillery bunting flag emblazoned with the "ace of clubs"... We understand General Wise has presented the Excelsior banner to the state and it will be hung in the state library with other trophies.

Johnson fired off a letter to Beauregard's headquarters. The colors referred to, he said, had been captured on Thursday by Johnson's Tennesseeans and had been carried to the rear by a wounded corporal of Company I, Forty-fourth Tennessee. He had left it temporarily with the acting druggist at Poplar Lawn Hospital. Johnson enclosed a statement from the druggist saying he had "turned the flags over to General Wise." Johnson added:

> This communication is not intended to emblazon the achievements of Johnson's Brigade nor detract from the just credit of any other troops. My object is simply to insure that a body of gallant and meritorious men are not bereft of the reward of their heroic deeds and to procure the restoration

of trophies that belong rather to the Confederate government than to any particular state.

Beauregard, who had his own reasons for being unenthusiastic about Virginians and their ways, agreed with Johnson and sent the letter to General Lee recommending that Colonel G. W. Munford, secretary of the state of Virginia, be asked to return the flags. The governor of Virginia was asked for his remarks and he ordered the trophies delivered to Adjutant Cooper. Wise was asked for an explanation. He replied in hot fury that the hospital druggist had given the flags, not to him, but to one of his couriers who brought them to Wise's headquarters.[72] No shrinking violet, Wise had sent the colors to the newspaper office without any explanation as to their origin.

Before the letters, statements and endorsements subsided, the army high command, the executive branch of the Virginia government, and Confederate officialdom had become involved. The result was to make Wise look foolish in his own eyes and stoke his burning resentment of Johnson. He got his revenge ten months later in Johnson's abasement after Sayler's Creek, an incident he and his descendants gloried in retelling.

By the end of June the Petersburg defense front gravitated into static trench warfare. Johnson's Division took its place opposite Blandford Cemetery, between Mahone on the right and Hoke on the left in the center of a three-mile arc extending east of Petersburg from the Appomattox River to beyond west of the Jerusalem Plank Road.[73] Johnson and Hoke were part of Beauregard's departmental command; Mahone answered to Ambrose Powell Hill, chief of Lee's Third Corps.

Mysterious activity in the Union lines opposite Johnson's trenches became apparent early in July. The division of James H. Ledlie of Burnside's IX Corps manned the Union works at this point and coal miners of Lieutenant

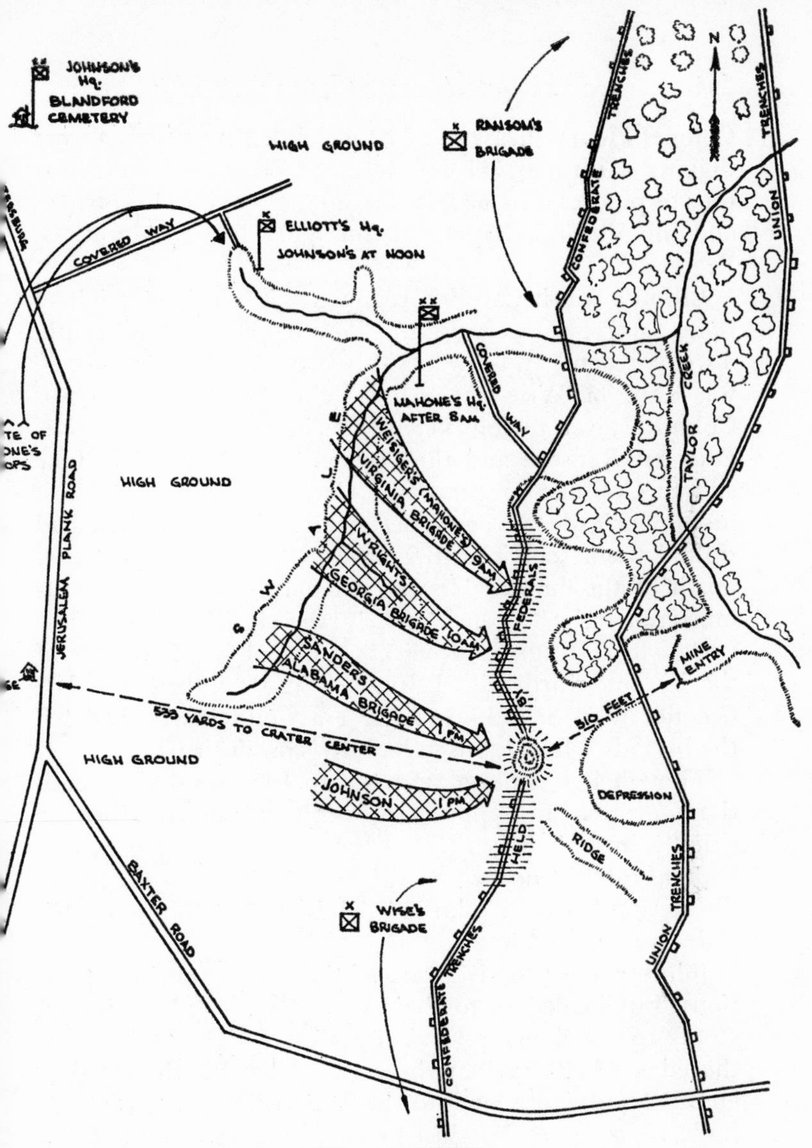

THE CRATER
July 30, 1864

Inexplicably torpid in meeting his command responsibilities when the Federal mine blows up his troops, Johnson makes a poor showing under the eyes of Lee for the first time and energetic Mahone gets all the credit for saving Petersburg. (From map by T. F. Rives, Dinwiddie County, Va., surveyor, Sept. 3, 1892)

Colonel Henry Pleasants's Forty-eighth Pennsylvania were digging a tunnel, 511 feet long, to be loaded with four tons of powder beneath the brigade of Stephen Elliott, Jr., and the Virginia Battery of four guns of Captain R. G. Pegram.[74]

Elliott's South Carolina regiments, aligned from left to right were: Twenty-sixth, Seventeenth, Eighteenth, Twenty-second and Twenty-third. On his left on July 30 was Ransom. Wise was on his right. At Wise's right was Colquitt, given to Johnson July 28 in exchange for Gracie. Between Ransom and the Appomattox River was Hoke and to Colquitt's right was Mahone.[75] Johnson had lost his old brigade of Tennesseeans July 7. Beauregard had shifted them to Richard S. Ewell, commanding defenses north of the James.[76] Its sad remnants of five regiments mustered only 385 effectives. In the trenches it had lost two of its distinguished officers: Colonel R. H. Keeble of the Twenty-third, killed June 30 and on the next day, Colonel John S. Fulton of the Forty-fourth who had led the brigade when Johnson had division duties.[77]

Though it was never returned to Johnson despite petitions, protests and appeals, the unit proudly retained its title "Johnson's Brigade"[78] as long as it could, perplexing Federal intelligence which at first did not comprehend the distinction between Johnson's Division and Johnson's Brigade in separated locations.[79]

Johnson was acutely aware of the Union mining operations, but baffled as to their exact location. He ordered scouts to crawl out several times each night to listen at the edge of the ravine where the mine mouth was situated.[80] Men were sent into the Union lines, ostensibly to trade newspapers, but instructed to look around.[81] Johnson suggested a listening gallery be run from the right of Wise's Brigade to check on tunnelling progress.[82] He drove his troops to help bore a half dozen counter-mines in his sector, using some sixty toilers each night. The task of lengthening the pits a few feet in the dark was so hard, some disgruntled soldiers deserted to the enemy and tattled about the countermining, the hard work and the short rations.[83] One-third of the whole division was required to be awake at all times and the entire command was routed out and mustered under arms at 2 A.M. daily.[84] Johnson directed that sentry posts be set up in the rear of his lines to keep men at their work and to prevent stragglers without passes from hiding in deserted houses in the east part of Petersburg.[85]

In view of the vigilance, enterprise and diligence Johnson manifested during July, his amazing lack of dash and decision on the morning of July 30, when the mine exploded, is difficult to understand, much less explain. The perspective of a century tends to discount some of the feverish charges made in 1870 by supporters of Mahone's claims to all the glory for saving Petersburg[86] and the 1900 venom of John Sergeant Wise, son of General Wise who was absent at the time.[87] Arguments over who got where and when and who did what, including some that were flamboyant and inaccurate,[88] continued in the Southern Historical Society Papers and at veterans' reunions down to 1909. But the inescapable conclusion, even now, is that Johnson failed to show the initiative and leadership to be expected in a commander whose troops had been blown up and in whose defensive lines a gap had been ripped for fifty yards[89] exposing an entire army to possible disaster.

The explosion came at 4:44 A.M. beneath the salient occupied by Pegram's battery and the Eighteenth and Twenty-second South Carolina regiments of Elliott. Eight men were working in Countermine No. 2 under Pegram's position at the time. They were blown to bits. Two guns, five companies of the Twenty-second and four of the Eighteenth were tossed into the air or buried under huge chunks of clay, wood, metal and debris. At least 278 men were killed or hurt.[90] Three companies of the Twenty-third and Company A of the Seventeenth also suffered casualties.

Elliott got to the scene of indescribable horror, turmoil and confusion in fifteen minutes, followed by Colonel A. D. Smith of the Twenty-sixth. Elliott sprang to the crest of a small hill west of the smoking hole and tried to form the Seventeenth and Twenty-sixth for a charge on the milling Federal hundreds crowding into the pit. He was shot down in five minutes. Colonel F. W. McMaster of the Seventeenth took over the brigade, countermanded Elliott's orders and tried to form some of the troops in the shelter of the double line of Confederate trenches.

McMaster said later he sent "courier after courier"[91] to Johnson's headquarters in a dwelling on a road just off the Jerusalem Plank Road a short distance north of the first entrance to Blandford Cemetery, less than a mile from the site of the blast.[92] Johnson hurried off an aide with the news to Beauregard's headquarters in Petersburg. He dispatched orders to Ransom and to Colonel J. T. Goode, Thirty-fourth Virginia, commanding Wise's Brigade in the ex-governor's absence, telling them to extend their lines toward Elliott's flanks and reinforce the shaken and shattered South Carolinians. With pleas for help at once, he sent Captain John E. Saunders to Hoke, a mile away on his left, and Captain Eugene R. Smith to Mahone in the Branch House, just west of the Willcox Farm, two miles distant on his right.[93]

Then as the minutes ticked away, while his area of command responsibility seethed in a frenzied, desperate melee, Johnson remained in his headquarters, entirely unperturbed according to his critics, calmly awaiting developments. He told his orderly to prepare breakfast.[94]

Soon Beauregard came to Johnson's headquarters. His dark creole face alight with excitement, he rode forward to the Gee House, 533 yards west of the crater. He had already sent a staff officer, Colonel Samuel B. Paul, to inform Lee at his headquarters on the lawn of Violet Bank, the Shippen family home, across the river, so that by 6:10 A.M. the army commander knew something of the extent of the catastrophe.[95] From a bedroom window on the second floor of the bullet- and shell-pierced Gee House, Beauregard saw some of the surviving Carolinians blocking the trenches at each side of the gap, while others were forming under cover of a marshy ravine, or swale, 200 yards northeast, and the Confederate artillery from three sides was crashing canister and shrapnel into the jam-packed, disorganized Union black and white troops in the hole.[96] He watched for a short time and then rejoined Johnson in the house back at the cemetery. He may have shared some of Johnson's meager breakfast.

Lee had acted quickly when he got the news. He sent Lieutenant Colonel Charles S. Venable with orders directly to Mahone, bypassing A. P. Hill, the corps chief, to save time. Mahone was told to rush two of his brigades from the Willcox farm, two miles southeast of the crater, into the ravine, or swale, behind the blast site and form for a counterattack.[97] Mahone, already highly energized by the visit of Captain Smith, Johnson's aide, flashed into action. His 120-pound figure in a tent-cloth suit with a civilian "round about" jacket, bristled with vigor as he directed David A. Weisiger's Virginians, formerly his own brigade, and Ambrose ("Rans") Wright's Georgians, to fade back from their trenches into a stream valley and then move northward, discarding knapsacks, blankets and other gear in order to go faster. He first told them to report to Johnson, then he decided to go with them rather than let some strange general command his troops. Venable told this to Lee later and the commander-in-chief "expressed gratification." Lee knew Virginian Mahone; to him Johnson was a western newcomer.[98]

Ahead of his quick-stepping infantry, Mahone galloped to Johnson's headquarters about 8:15 A.M. He had never met Johnson before. He had been told his corps commander, A. P. Hill, might be found in the house, but he expected Johnson would be at the scene of the crisis in the trenches. Consequently Mahone was amazed, as he told it later, to find Johnson "absorbed in looking after his breakfast and apparently oblivious to what was going on in his front. He was talking unconcernedly with Beauregard."[99]

Mahone saluted Beauregard and reported his two brigades near at hand. Beauregard turned to Johnson and told him he "had better turn over any outlying troops" to Mahone and "let him make the attack." Johnson agreed quiescently; too readily, Mahone thought, instead of rising to his obvious responsibility as the major general commanding the area and claiming overall supervision and direction of the action by a brigadier general. Mahone asked Johnson a few excited questions about the extent and location of the Federal thrust. Johnson's vague replies irked and disgusted him. When he wanted Johnson to show him the way to the scene, Johnson passed up another chance to share the leading role in the bloody drama about to be staged. He called a young aide, Lieutenant Harris, to guide Mahone to Elliott's salient.[100]

Johnson's lethargy in the face of the desperate situation had also impressed others unfavorably. Almost an hour earlier, before 7 A.M., Captain W. Gordon McCabe, adjutant of Colonel William Pegram, who was bringing up two batteries from his Third Corps reserve artillery to support the counterattack, was shocked to learn Johnson "knew nothing of the extent of the disaster" and had not been to the front or even as far forward as Gee's and could not answer McCabe's or Pegram's questions.[101]

Into the fog of indecision at Johnson's headquarters around 8:30 A.M. came General Lee. He quizzed Beauregard. With him and Johnson he rode to Gee's to watch from the shattered upstairs windows. Mahone's troops were beginning to assemble in the swale. Elliott's survivors and Goode's Virginians, after more than three hours, were still confining the Federals to the area originally taken. Lee estimated the situation, turned to Johnson and asked if other reinforcements were available. Johnson did not think so, aside from the Sixty-first North Carolina coming belatedly from Hoke, plus some of Elliott's survivors gathered in the ravine.[102]

At this point, Johnson again might have risen from his sluggish languor to suggest he could lead Hoke's men and Elliott's fragments in the coming assault. But he said nothing and Lee could contrast his torpor with Mahone's initiative when that bolder spirit dashed in to report he had sent for his third brigade, the Alabamans of 24-year old Brigadier General John G. S. Sanders. Lee told him he must charge with what he had as soon as they were formed and not wait for more.[103]

Mahone's Virginians first hit the Federals about 9 A.M. They swept the stubbornly resisting enemy from some of the parallel trenches north of the hole.[104] Then they bogged down. In the second assault about 11 A.M., Wright's Georgians surged out of their assembly area in the swale, drifted north under heavy fire and still failed to clean out the crater.[105] At ten o'clock, nearly six hours after the blast, Johnson bestirred himself. He moved to Elliott's brigade headquarters 260 yards from the crater and sent for Mahone and McMaster. They met in the ravine. Johnson turned over the remnants of the Seventeenth South Carolina, led by Captain Steele, to Mahone. It was agreed that Johnson would coordinate an attack at 1 P.M. by Elliott's and Wise's brigades south of the crater, while Mahone directed Sanders's Alabamans and the Sixty-first North Carolina from Hoke from north and west of the pit. Johnson hurried south to collect his men.[106]

A ghastly, demoniacal melee ensued when the two forces hit the crowded mass of blacks and whites in the bloody hole. By 3:25 P.M. the long, fearfully hot day of frenzy was over and Lee was able to report to Secretary Seddon that the salient had been retaken and that the enemy had been driven back with appalling loss.[107]

Johnson wrote the only report of the action extant in the Official Records and however much he adorned the façade of his faulty achievement and acknowledged his thanks to others, the hero of the day was little Billy Mahone. This was obvious to all, especially to Lee, who recommended his immediate promotion to major general, Weisiger to brigadier general and Mahone's aide, French-born Victor Jean Baptiste Girardey, from captain to brigadier, the only instance of such a jump in Confederate Army annals.[108]

For Johnson there was neither praise nor rewards. He was ignored entirely in the *Petersburg Express* accounts of the battle on Monday, August 1 and subsequently.[109] The manifest disparity in the performances of Mahone and Johnson was pointed up in the statistics of their trophies. Johnson's men took three Union flags and 130 prisoners; Mahone's troops harvested seventeen colors, two guidons and 1101 captives. Johnson sent his flags to Beauregard who forwarded them to Lee; Mahone's impressive bag went to Lee through A. P. Hill.[110] Comparisons were inevitable, then and now.

The image of Billy Mahone as the "Hero of The Crater" was firmly fixed in Confederate legend. It still endures long after his death in 1895 in Petersburg where he spent the final quarter-century of his life. It is perpetuated in his grave in Blandford Cemetery, not far from the site of the house where Johnson dallied at his breakfast on that fateful morning.[111]

A century later, oblivion still shrouds Johnson's part in the battle. Time and nature have reduced the crater in the Petersburg National Park to a fraction of its original size and the Gee House and Johnson's headquarters vanished long ago. A tall monument honors Mahone's Virginians. South Carolina's Confederate daughters later erected a stone to memorialize the men who were blown up.

But in the maps and mementoes in the park's museum and in the tape recorded broadcast account of the bloody event there is no mention of Bushrod Johnson. It is just as if he had never been there. Only a set of drawing instruments, said to be his, and the original copy of his post-action report in the park library, link his name to the epic Battle of The Crater.

Notes

1. Map 115, *WP Atlas.*
2. *OR*, XXX, pt. 2, pp. 65 f. Photocopy in Hal Bridges, *Lee's Maverick General,* (New York: McGraw-Hill, 1961), p. 237.
3. *Longstreet,* p. 465.
4. Text, Map 116, *WP Atlas.*
5. *OR*, XXXI, p. 531; *B&L,* III, p. 752. All citations in *OR*, XXXI are in pt. 1 except as noted.
6. *OR*, XXXI, p. 531. Johnson's report, written in January 1864, details the move.
7. *Ibid.*, XXXI, p. 533.
8. Map 145, *WP Atlas.*
9. Orlando M. Poe, "The Defense of Knoxville" in *B&L,* III, p. 741.
10. *OR*, XXXI, p. 531. Johnson's report called the objective "Fort Loudoun" and the railroad "East Tennessee and Virginia." The fort's name had been changed by the Federals to "Sanders" to honor Brigadier General William P. Sanders, killed November 8. For a detailed description of the battle see Digby Govan Seymour, *Divided Loyalties,* (Knoxville: University of Tennessee Press, 1963), pp. 191–203.
11. *Longstreet,* p. 505.
12. *Steele,* p. 450. E. Porter Alexander, *Military Memoirs of a Confederate,* (New York: Chas. Scribner's Sons, 1907), p. 489, says Johnson pleaded with Longstreet to be allowed to renew the attack, but Longstreet, giving full faith to an exaggerated report of the wire entanglement, forbade.
13. *Longstreet,* p. 505.
14. *Steele,* p. 461.
15. *OR*, XXXI, p. 533.
16. Longstreet's report in *ibid.*, XXXI, pp. 455 ff.

17. *Ibid.*, XXXI, p. 536.
18. *Ibid.*, XXXI, p. 465; XXXI, pt. 3, p. 837.
19. *Longstreet*, p. 532.
20. *OR*, XXXI, p. 535.
21. Charges in *ibid.*, XXXI, pp. 470 f., 498. Best account of the cases and results is in Douglas S. Freeman, *Lee's Lieutenants*, (New York: Chas. Scribner's Sons, 1944), III, pp. 299 ff.
22. *OR*, XXXII, pt. 2, pp. 556, 610, 790, 812, 818. These are letters and dispatches between Johnson and Longstreet relating to operations.
23. *OR*, XXXII, pt. 3, p. 9.
24. *OR*, XXXII, pt. 3, pp. 9, 61, 98, 106. Two pro-Union Tennesseeans, arrested by the Confederates in Blount County and held in jail in Greeneville, were forcibly enlisted in Johnson's Sixty-third Tennessee from which they deserted to the Union Army with information on strength and conditions of Johnson's troops.
25. *Ibid.*, XXXII, pt. 3, p. 795.
26. *Ibid.*, LII, pt. 2, p. 577; XXXII, pt. 2, p. 556.
27. *Ibid.*, XXXII, pt. 3, p. 852.
28. *Ibid.*, XXXII, pt. 3, pp. 803, 854.
29. Map 120, *WP Atlas.*
30. *OR*, XXXII, pt. 3, p. 838.
31. *Ibid.*, XXXIII, p. 1330.
32. Original in *B. R. Johnson File*, CSA Staff Papers.
33. Original in *ibid.*
34. Originals in *ibid.*
35. *OR*, LII, pt. 2, p. 664.
36. Map 120, *WP Atlas.*
37. *OR*, LI, pt. 2, p. 872. Beauregard renamed it the Department of North Carolina and Southern Virginia.
38. *Ibid.*, LI, pt. 2, p. 886.
39. *OR*, XXXVI, pt. 2, p. 958. A detailed study of these operations appears in Clifford Dowdey, *Lee's Last Campaign*, (Boston: Little, Brown & Co., 1960), pp. 234 ff.
40. *OR*, XXXVI, pt. 2, pp. 960, 965. Hill had been jobless since Bragg removed him after Chickamauga.
41. *Ibid.*, XXXVI, p. 255.
42. *OR*, LI, pt. 2, p. 895.
43. *Ibid.*, LI, pt. 2, pp. 251–256 *et passim.*
44. Johnson's report, *OR*, XXXVI, pt. 2, pp. 239 ff.
45. *Ibid.*
46. *Ibid.*, XXXVI, pt. 2, pp. 240 f. Johnson reported 1000 Union losses.
47. *Ibid.*, XXXVI, pt. 2, p. 242.
48. *Ibid.*, XXXVI, pt. 2, p. 244.
49. *Warner*, p. 140.
50. *OR*, LI, pt. 2, p. 915.
51. *OR*, XXXVI, pt. 2, p. 1004.
52. *Ibid.*, XXXVI, pt. 2, pp. 985, 988.
53. *Ibid.*, XXXVI, pt. 2, p. 992.
54. *Warner*, p. 334.
55. *OR*, XXXVI, pt. 2, p. 200; G. T. Beauregard, "The Defense of Drewry's Bluff" in *B&L*, IV, pp. 200 ff.
56. Freeman, *Lieutenants*, III, p. 485.
57. *OR*, XXXVI, pt. 2, pp. 201, 212.

58. *Ibid.*, XXXVI, pt. 2, p. 203.
59. Freeman, *Lieutenants,* III, pp. 490–493, summarizes the case.
60. Originals of these papers in *B. R. Johnson File* in CSA Staff Papers. Beauregard's May 19, 1864 wire to Bragg in *OR*, LI, pt. 3, p. 947.
61. *OR*, XXXVI, pt. 3, pp. 821, 891; *Warner,* p. 324.
62. *OR*, XXXVI, pt. 3, p. 857.
63. *Ibid.*, XXXVI, pp. 872, 879; LI, pt. 2, p. 1004.
64. Maps 137, 138a, *WP Atlas.*
65. *OR*, XL, pt. 3, pp. 657, 677. The buried armament and materiel was recovered undamaged when Confederates re-occupied the area.
66. Map 138b, *WP Atlas.*
67. *SHSP*, XXV, p. 14.
68. John S. Wise, *The End of an Era,* (Boston: Houghton Mifflin, 1900), pp. 358 ff.
69. G. T. Beauregard, "Four Days of Battle at Petersburg" in *B&L*, IV, p. 543.
70. *Ibid.*
71. Text, Map 138, *WP Atlas.*
72. *OR*, XL, pt. 1, pp. 769 ff.
73. Map 139, *WP Atlas.*
74. Details in William H. Powell, "The Battle of the Petersburg Crater" in *B&L*, IV, pp. 545 ff.
75. Johnson's report, *OR*, XL, pt. 1, pp. 787 ff.
76. *OR*, XL, pt. 3, p. 748; XLII, p. 1266.
77. *Ibid.*, XL, pt. 1, p. 773.
78. *CV*, XIV, p. 545.
79. *OR*, XL, pt. 3, pp. 293, 554, 562.
80. *Ibid.*, XL, pt. 3, p. 745.
81. *Ibid.*, XL, pt. 1, p. 779.
82. *Ibid.*, XL, pt. 1, p. 765.
83. Burnside to Meade, July 17, 1864 in *OR*, XL, pt. 3, pp. 300 f.
84. *OR*, XL, pt. 1, pp. 775, 788; pt. 2, p. 714.
85. *Ibid.*, XL, pt. 1, p. 776.
86. Gen. J. Watts DePeyster, "A Military Memoir of William Mahone Major General in the Confederate Army," in *Historical Magazine,* VII (June 1870), pp. 390 ff.
87. *Wise*, 358 ff.
88. W. H. T. Squires, *The Land of Decision,* (Portsmouth, Va: Printcraft Press, Inc., 1931), p. 172.
89. Length of the gap is variously reported: 135 feet by Johnson; 170 feet by Powell in *B&L*, IV, pp. 545 ff.; 500 yards including trenches from which survivors fled after the blast in Map 139, *WP Atlas.*
90. *OR*, XL, pt. 1, pp. 557 f.
91. *SHSP*, X, p. 121.
92. *Ibid.*, X, p. 125 and *ibid.*, XVIII, p. 6. George S. Bernard, *War Talks of Confederate Veterans,* (Petersburg, Va: n.p., 1892), pp. 152, 213. Map of explosion area with location of Johnson's headquarters in *OR Atlas*, pt. 2, plate LXXVIII, No. 5.
93. Johnson's report in *OR*, XL, pt. 1, p. 789.
94. *SHSP*, XVIII, p. 6.
95. *Ibid.*, II, p. 289; Douglas S. Freeman, *Lee,* (New York: Chas. Scribner's Sons, 1935) 4 vols., III, pp. 457, 467 f.; *OR*, XL, pt. 1, p. 557.
96. *SHSP*, X, p. 123.

97. *Ibid.*, XVIII, p. 5; *Bernard*, p. 150. Bernard was a member of Company E, Twelfth Virginia in Weisiger's Brigade and a Petersburg newspaper writer after the war.
98. *SHSP*, XVIII, p. 5 fn.
99. *DePeyster*, p. 391; Mahone's account in letter August 10, 1892, quoted in *Bernard*, pp. 213 ff.
100. *Bernard*, p. 215; also in *SHSP*, XXVIII, p. 218.
101. *SHSP*, XVIII, p. 35 fn.; *Bernard*, pp. 177 f.
102. Freeman, *Lee*, III, pp. 470 f.
103. *Ibid.*, p. 472.
104. *SHSP*, XXVII, pp. 305 f.
105. *Ibid.*, II, p. 292.
106. *OR*, XL, pt. 1, p. 792.
107. *Ibid.*, XL, pt. 1, p. 752.
108. *Ibid.*, XLII, pt. 2, pp. 1156 f.; *Warner*, pp. 106, 208, 330. Girardey was killed seventeen days later.
109. *Petersburg* [Virginia] *Express*, issues of August 1, 2, 3, 1864.
110. *OR*, XL, pt. 1, pp. 753, 755. Henry Goddard Thomas, "The Colored Troops at Petersburg" in *B&L*, IV, p. 567.
111. *Squires*, pp. 169, 177, 203.

10

DEFEATISM BREEDS IN STAGNATION

i. Spring Brings Only Death to Hope

The honors he might have had, but missed at the Battle of The Crater seem to have troubled Bushrod Johnson not at all. Of more pressing concern to him was the future of the little brigade of Tennesseeans he had led at Perryville, Stones River, Chickamauga and Bean's Station. When Beauregard took them from him and gave them to Ewell on the north bank of the James River in July, the officers and men looked forward confidently to their return to Johnson. Six weeks went by. Then the rumor spread that their attachment to his brigade had been applied for by Brigadier General James Jay Archer,[1] Maryland-born graduate of Princeton and ex-captain in the U.S. Army who had recently returned to the Army of Northern Virginia after a year of captivity on Johnson's Island, off Sandusky, Ohio, since Gettysburg.[2]

Archer commanded a brigade combining the units he had led at Gettysburg and the three Virginia regiments of Henry Harrison Walker, severely wounded at Spottsylvania Courthouse in May. With Archer were the First Tennessee (Provisional Army), the Seventh and Fourteenth Tennessee, and his talking point was that Johnson's

Tennesseeans belonged with comrades from their own state.

The application, made August 27, 1864, was approved by Henry Heth, division commander and by A. P. Hill, III Corps chief and sent to Lee. "Circumvolution" might describe the course of the paper thereafter. Lee sent it to Beauregard who returned it because the brigade was under Ewell. Lee fired it back to Beauregard because, on paper, "Johnson's Brigade" was still a part of Johnson's Division, now under Beauregard. He gave it to Johnson who sent it to the commanders of the 17/23d, 25/44th and 63d. All objected to any transfer from Johnson's command.[3] Nothing happened. The unit stayed with Ewell for the time being.

Johnson tried again. On September 20 he sent Ewell a remonstrance from officers of the brigade: Colonel John M. Hughes and Major William H. Fulkerson of the Sixty-third; Captain U. C. Harrison and Lieutenant Colonel Horace Ready, 17/23d; Lieutenant Colonel R. Bogardus Snowden and Major J. E. Spencer, 25/44th. They protested against Johnson's Brigade losing its identity. They promised to try to recruit fillers and replacements to bolster their numbers, reduced to 47 officers and 341 enlisted men on the strength returns of September 20, 1864, if permitted to return to Johnson.[4] The paper died in Ewell's files.

One last attempt, a personal appeal to Lee, was made by Johnson. He wrote to Lee October 19 that he had heard with regret some reports that morale and discipline in his cherished brigade were bad and growing worse and that "discord and dissatisfaction are likely soon to prevail." He reminded Lee that he had recommended Snowden, his former student and adjutant, for promotion to brigadier to head the unit and since no action had been taken he offered the names of three others. They were Colonel A. S. Marks, formerly of the Seventeenth Tennessee, now with

Forrest's staff, but obtainable if President Davis would wire for his return; Isham G. Harris, fugitive ex-governor of Tennessee now serving as an aide in Hood's army in the West; and Major G. C. Brown, a Tennesseean who was Ewell's adjutant.[5] Johnson suggested to Ewell that Harris take over both the old brigade and that of Archer[6] who was dying in Richmond from the effects of his long confinement.

All this came to naught. Shrunk to the size of half a regiment by its battle casualties, Johnson's Brigade was integrated into Archer's. He died in October. Six months later, by the time of the surrender at Appomattox, the sparse remnants had been buried in the brigade of William McComb, Pennsylvanian by birth, Tennesseean by residence.[7]

Psychologically, Johnson sorely needed his Tennesseeans. Between him and them existed an affection born of shared hardships and dangers, of comradely achievement, of mutual respect and confidence, and friendly understanding. All of these vital elements were missing in Johnson's present situation. His troops were Virginans, Carolinians, Alabamans. They never had shared any experience with Johnson except at The Crater where he was a singularly uninspiring figure. Their officers accepted Johnson because it was their duty to do so, but without faith, assurance or trust. Wise, volatile and frenetic, but politically influential and therefore somewhat privileged, detested Johnson.[8] McMaster who had taken Elliott's place at the head of the blast-wrecked South Carolina brigade, always felt Johnson failed to give him leadership, counsel or support when he asked for it in the hideous hours after the mine exploded.[9] With Colonel Paul F. Faison of the Fifty-sixth North Carolina in Ransom's Brigade, Johnson had constant friction in July over failure to send out details to work on mortar pits and covered ways,[10] continuing into the winter when Johnson reported Faison was absent without leave, "dissatisfied" and "not disposed to return to duty with this command."[11] Johnson's relations with Gracie, killed December 2 in the trenches[12] may be indicated in the attitude of his son who wrote disparagingly of Johnson at Chickamauga in 1911.[13] Johnson knew he had few friends in his new division. It was a severe blow to him to be denied the company of the ones he had known and led for so long.

In attaining the coveted rank refused to him in the heyday of his fortunes, Johnson had lost some of the essentials of the craft of command. The aggressive valor of Perryville, Chickamauga and Stones River was strikingly diminished at The Crater. In the dismal corrosion of the trenches, it would ebb further. There would be no more bright flashes of beckoning glory to inspire the heart and lift the spirit.

Something of the tranquil Quaker may have survived in Johnson, even in the atmosphere of Southern hate inflamed by the Federal use of Negro troops at The Crater.[14] During the truce on August 1 when the dead in the frightful hole were being buried, Colonel Henry G. Thomas of the Nineteenth U.S. Infantry, a Negro unit, made a wrong turn and walked into the Confederate lines. Caught and blindfolded he was taken to Johnson. Though known to be the leader of the loathed blacks, his treatment by Johnson was "civil, even cordial," he said later, in contrast to that of others "less considerate." He was told that thirty-six of his men were prisoners and had been put to work as headquarters servants and on similar duties. On orders of Beauregard, to whom Johnson referred the matter, Thomas was freed.[15]

Late in September Beauregard was transferred to the Military Division of the West, comprising the armies of Hood in Georgia and Richard Taylor's vegetating department of Alabama and Mississippi. Hood had been driven out of Atlanta and soon was to start his disastrous invasion of Tennessee. Johnson's Division was transferred to A. P. Hill's Corps in Lee's Army, responsible for the defense of Petersburg. When Grant sent the corps of Hancock and Gouverneur K. Warren to cut the Southside Railroad on October 27 by turning the south end of the Confederate lines, Johnson's Division from east and southeast of Petersburg was stretched out to man nearly five miles of trenches.[16]

James Longstreet, sufficiently recovered from the accidental wound inflicted by his own men five months previously in the Wilderness, came back to the helm of the First Corps on October 19. His return to duty left Lieutenant General Richard Heron Anderson without a command. He had taken Longstreet's place, made a famous march to Spotsylvania in May and then had not done as well with the Confederate advance on Cold Harbor on June 1.[17] To continue him in a command commensurate with his rank, a fourth corps was created in the Army of Northern Virginia. It was composed of Johnson's and Hoke's divisions, formerly the realm of Beauregard.

Anderson and Johnson were somewhat kindred spirits—unassertive, gentlemanly, lacking inspirational color or showmanship. Both were born on October 7, Johnson in 1817 and Anderson in 1821. They had known each other at West Point where the South Carolinian finished fortieth in the fifty-six members of the class of 1842. Scholastically they were on the same level, not quite up to median. Anderson had remained in the "Old Army" and was a captain when he resigned in March 1861. Short, thick, and stocky, he was given to meditatively smoking a meerschaum pipe while he let his staff run his corps. Like Johnson, he was personally brave, but not pushing or aggressive. Unimpressed Moxley Sorrell thought he was "of a rather inert, indolent manner for commanding troops in the field." He took especial pride in his ability with the needle, sitting on his bed after awakening in the morning to patch his clothing and mend his hats, boots, bridles and saddles with a well-stocked tailor's kit. Such tasks he regarded as "recreation."[18] There were also stories that he sometimes resorted to the bottle for relaxation.

Their temperaments being similar, it may have been inevitable that Anderson and Johnson should sink into the swamp of hopelessness together. After December, when Hoke's Division was detached and went back to North Carolina, Anderson's corps command consisted of little more than Johnson's deteriorating and hodge-podge division and so it remained until hours before the surrender. To each, the other communicated his increasing sense of the tragic futility of the dying cause and his want of enthusiasm for the desperate gambling efforts of Lee's Army to stave off the looming defeat.[19]

Meanwhile, Johnson engaged in another futile conflict with Lee's headquarters and the Richmond bureaucracy. He needed a new assistant adjutant general to replace Blakemore, who, fitted with an artificial leg, was serving on a general court-martial in the Department of Richmond. Johnson had tried to get Blakemore promoted to major, cavalry, after Bean's Station in December 1863. Buckner and Longstreet supported the request which Secretary Seddon denied. In September 1864, Johnson tried again on the grounds that Blakemore's gallantry at Drewry's Bluff merited the favor. Lee returned the papers with the information that no appointments were to be made under the new Staff Act until further orders. In February of 1865 Johnson revived the pleas, backed by Longstreet and Anderson. "His misfortune gives him additional claims to our sympathy," Longstreet said. Lee agreed on March 1 that Blakemore was deserving, but, as any vacancy was lacking, he disapproved again.[20]

For Blakemore's place, Johnson twice in June asked Adjutant Cooper to appoint Captain John E. Saunders, a former cadet at Western Military Institute in the mid-

1850s, who had been an aide to Johnson at The Crater. Saunders, a ward of Gideon Pillow's, had been on his guardian's staff at Stones River. Cooper's office delayed an answer to the request for seven weeks and then refused it on grounds that Saunders was originally an artilleryman and was not in the Adjutant General's Department. Johnson retained him as an aide. Johnson also asked that Captain Romley Erskine Foote, an Arkansan formerly adjutant in McNair's Brigade, who had been with Johnson in East Tennessee from December 21, 1863, be promoted to major.

In July Johnson also got Captain William H. Whitner, South Carolina-born resident of Florida, former adjutant to Brig. Gen. Roger A. Pryor. Whitner's left little finger had been shot off May 6 in the Wilderness, but he, Foote and Saunders all performed efficiently until Appomattox.[21] From the 23rd Alabama Sharpshooters, Foote picked young William Barfield as a courier, who also remained until the surrender.[22] For nine days in September Gracie replaced Johnson as division commander. Johnson was back on September 10, his absence unexplained in the records.[23]

As the days grew shorter in December and the scantily clad men in the slimy trenches looked ahead with dread to winter's tribulations, there were some flurries and alarms concerning Johnson's Division, whose strength stood at 553 officers and 6339 men present for duty as of October 31.[24] Union telegraph lines in Tennessee crackled with rumors that Johnson had arrived December 3 in Greeneville with two divisions and a force of cavalry.[25] Major General George Stoneman in Knoxville wired Thomas in Nashville December 6 with another story that Johnson was on the way to Bristol, Virginia.[26]

These were fruits of jumpy Federal imagination. More realistic was an urgent appeal from Beauregard in Savannah on December 18, for both Johnson's and Hoke's divisions to come at once to save the prized Georgia seaport whose surrender had been demanded by Sherman.[27] At the same time a powerful Federal fleet was moving on Wilmington, North Carolina, the last entry for blockade runners. Hoke, taken from Anderson's Corps, started December 20 not for Savannah but for Wilmington.[28] Governor A. G. McGrath of South Carolina wired President Davis that both divisions were necessary to hold the threatened lower portion of his state,[29] but Lee bluntly told the president that if he lost both divisions "it will necessitate the abandonment of Richmond with the present opposing force."[30] Davis was convinced. He wired Beauregard that since Sheridan's Army of the Shenandoah had joined Grant he could not give up both Johnson and Hoke.[31]

Certainly Lee could not have spared Johnson. In October, after Hoke had been withdrawn to the north of the James, Johnson had less than 7000 men to guard the trenches formerly occupied by his own division, Hoke's and part of Mahone's. In an emergency later in the month, with a small reinforcement Johnson defended nearly six miles of works,[32] which was spreading his troops vastly too thin for comfort.

Discontent walked with hunger and suffering as winter beset Johnson's men. Pitiful letters from homes menaced by the enemy, or no letters at all from areas already overrun by the Federals magnified the doubts and anxieties in the hearts of the discouraged soldiers stagnating in the filthy earthworks. Many decided that the game was up and they wanted no more of it. Some kept their arms, sneaked past rear area sentries and went home. Others, including lieutenants, within a few minutes of creeping distance across "no man's land," gave up to the enemy and curried favor by betraying locations and identifications of units.[33] Desperate efforts of the Richmond government promising amnesty for deserters who returned,[34] President Davis's pardons and reprieves and clemency generally did not dam the rising tide, accelerated by Federal offers to pay deserters $8 apiece for their weapons. The chief of ordnance of Meade's Army of the Potomac asked for $10,000 to be used in this way to entice Confederates across the lines.[35]

As conditions of existence grew more intolerable, the numbers who gave up mounted among Johnson's troops. Faith and hope were fading rapidly. Men left in groups instead of singly, increasing problems for pickets, provost guards and patrols. Johnson told Anderson he thought that more picket firing was necessary to prevent interviews between the lines,[36] but a few nights later he had to report to Anderson that twenty men of Faison's Fifty-sixth North Carolina had sneaked away.[37]

A plot for a mass desertion of fifty to sixty men was reported by Johnson to Anderson February 26, 1865. He said the plan, uncovered the night before, called for a group from the brigade of W. H. Wallace—those South Carolinians who had withstood the shock of the Union mine explosion so gallantly—to meet with others from three brigades of Cadmus Wilcox's Division at a rendezvous three miles from Petersburg where forage was usually unloaded from the Southside Railroad into wagons on a dirt road. Sergeants were about as unreliable as the men, Johnson added.[38]

Strangely some Federals deserted to Johnson's trenches. Many of these were recruits or conscripts in service only two weeks. They were useless as sources of information on Union dispositions. All came from the Seventh and Eighth New York and the Seventh and Eighth New Jersey and the Fifth New Hampshire—a total of 42 in October and 56 in November.[39] Thereafter there were scarcely any. The stories told by some of them raised Johnson's hopes. He reported that they said Hancock's lines were thinly held by inferior troops, all second rate and conscripts, and he had no doubt that "a good line of battle would sweep everything" opposite him and "capture and hold the whole of the enemy's works on my front."[40] On sober afterthought he must have realized soon how chimerical was this dream.

The pangs of hunger never ceased. The daily ration sometimes included an ounce or two of raw bacon, but usually was nothing more than a pint of corn meal. The available foraging area for miles around had been scoured clean. Supplies brought by the creaking railroads still operating were late and inadequate. Food boxes from home spoiled for failure to deliver or were stolen.[41] In December the story spread along Johnson's trenches that the women of Richmond were preparing a New Year's feast under the direction of Thompson Tyler, "king of the caterers." Contributions of beef, mutton, ham, venison, shoat, fowl and sausage were cooked and stored at the Ballard House. A bakery firm added hundreds of loaves of bread.[42] Scarcity of transportation delayed delivery to some units until January 2. Demand outstripped supply by a wide margin and there were many disappointed and still empty-bellied soldiers.[43]

Lack of forage and overwork took a terrific toll of Johnson's animals. He suggested to Anderson that thirty replacements be obtained and six weeks rest be given to fifteen teams of mules used in hauling timber, ammunition and supplies.[44] Whence would any replacements come? All horses, except those indispensable for moving guns and wagons, by high command order, were kept away from the front and out of range of Federal shells and bullets, aggravating the problem of mobility if some emergency demanded rapid movement.[45] Johnson proposed that front-line divisions be halved and those troops not in line be located in woods where they could get their own fuel without hauling.[46] Weakening the defense line while opposing Union numbers grew was not deemed advisable. It was a desperation measure at best.

The first days of spring brought a fictitious hope to the high command, certainly not shared by the dispirited rank and file. Optimistic John B. Gordon, 33-year old successor to the leadership of the decimated corps of Jubal Anderson Early, proposed an assault on Federal Fort Stedman, followed by a breakthrough to the Union rear and a sweep down the enemy works which would compel Grant to abandon the left of his line which was gradually creeping beyond Lee's capacity to contain it.[47] The vaporous dream visioned such a crippling of Grant's 125,000 soldiers that Richmond and Petersburg could be held with a reduced Confederate force and Lee could slip South, join Joseph E. Johnston and crush Sherman. Whereat, the fantasy continued, the united forces of Johnston and Lee would return and annihilate Grant.[48] Few were the realists among these wishful thinkers who saw that the effort was foredoomed to failure.

From Johnson's threadbare division, the brigades of Wallace and Ransom were loaned by Anderson to Gordon for the assault on Fort Stedman. Bushrod Johnson did not accompany them, nor did Anderson. Neither was asked to lead his own troops. It was to be wholly Gordon's show. At 4 A.M. on March 25, Gordon's force climbed out of the trenches, dashed across the open ground between the lines and clambered up and into the Union works. Surprise was complete. For a few minutes it looked like the Confederates might make it. But Union reaction was swifter and much deadlier than anticipated as soon as there was sufficient daylight. Gordon's men could not advance and were soon under heavy counterattack. The situation was the Battle of The Crater all over again with the roles reversed. At 8 A.M. Lee sent orders to withdraw. The Southern flight back across no man's land cost many lives. Some Confederates refused to run the gantlet and gave up as prisoners. When the bloody fiasco was finished, 3500 casualties were counted, 1200 of them from Johnson's brigades. The Union bag of prisoners totaled 1900.[49]

As the curtain raised on the final phase of the defense

of Petersburg and Richmond on March 27, Johnson's Division of 4800 ragged, emaciated and dispirited men occupied more than three miles of trenches on the extreme right of Lee's thread-thin defenses, near Burgess' Mill, where the Boydton Plank Road crossed Hatcher's Run, about six miles southwest of Petersburg.[50] Around this far end of Lee's Army, Grant chose to send the cavalry corps of Sheridan and the V Corps infantry of G. K. Warren on the morning of March 29.

Lee had only Pickett's division available for maneuvering to meet this threat, plus the cavalry divisions of his nephew Fitzhugh Lee and his son, W. H. F. ("Rooney") Lee in addition to Thomas Rosser's.[51] To strengthen Pickett, the brigades of Wallace and Ransom which had been riddled a few days previously at Fort Stedman again were taken from Johnson on March 30 and marched down the White Oak Road to Pickett at Five Forks. In a one-sided trade, the Virginia brigade of Eppa Hunton consisting of five skimpy regiments was detached from Pickett and given to Johnson.[52]

Friday morning, March 31, Lee rode in the rain to Johnson's position. Two lines of Union infantry were in front of the Confederate trenches with their left flank exposed. The South Carolina brigade of Samuel McGowan, near Burgess' Mill, was moved over and attached to Johnson, who was put in command under Anderson's supervision.

Johnson formed line of battle with McGowan on his right, Brig. Gen. Young M. Moody's Brigade led by Colonel M. L. Stansel in the center, and Hunton on the left, with Wise in reserve.[53] McGowan was directed to lead his and Stansel's men against the Union left flank and drive it across the front of Hunton and Wise, taken from the reserve on Lee's order and sent to Hunton's left.[54] The first attack succeeded in doubling back the Union left flank. Lee remained with McGowan and tried to get some artillery and cavalry support. But strong Federal counterattacks caused the left of the attacking force to waver. Reluctantly Lee had to consent to a withdrawal at 5 P.M. back to the main breastworks whence the morning start had been made. Johnson's brigades lost 800 killed, wounded and prisoners.[55] This was to be their last night in the mud and misery of the trenches.

Chance had given Johnson another opportunity to function under the eye of the army commander and thus modify in his memory the picture of torpid Johnson at The Crater. But Lee personally had dominated the action and issued the tactical orders without reference to Johnson or Anderson. Whatever impression Lee carried from the scene was erased by the news he received long after dark back at his headquarters in the Trumbull House at Edge Hill, that Pickett and Fitzhugh Lee had met and driven back Sheridan at Dinwiddie Courthouse.[56]

When the morning mists dissolved in front of Johnson's trenches on Saturday, April 1, the enemy was gone, too. Johnson's Division moved to the right across the Boydton Road, and waited. At 4 P.M. the sound of firing came from the vicinity of Five Forks, four miles to the West. The noise was the knell of Pickett's Division, wrecked by the cavalry of Sheridan and Ranald S. Mackenzie and Warren's infantry. During part of the time, Pickett and Fitzhugh Lee had been absent at Rosser's headquarters, enjoying a feast of broiled shad. The Federals captured 3244 men and four guns.[57] Survivors including Pickett were streaming north.

At 5:45 P.M. Johnson was ordered, through Anderson, to go at once to Church Crossing on the road to Amelia Courthouse to rescue and support whatever cavalry and infantry had escaped from Five Forks. In 45 minutes the brigades of Wise, Moody, and Hunton, around 3000 men, shouldered their meager equipment and were on their way. Behind them on their right as they tramped through the darkness up the Claiborne Road toward the Southside Railroad, came the threnody of heavy artillery fire from the direction of Petersburg. At 2 A.M., Sunday, April 2, Johnson halted his marchers at the road crossing and they went into bivouac[58] beside the road, in adjacent fields, farmyards or anywhere exhausted men could stretch out and sleep.

There was one last battle ahead of them to be fought. It would be a dark disaster!

ii. When the Generals Ran Away

Bushrod Johnson's men stretched their aching bodies awake at Church Crossing[59] as the dawn of Sunday, April 2, 1865, lighted a world greening with the promises of a Virginia spring. After a scanty breakfast the columns formed up. There was no word of Pickett's fugitives, no reports of the approach of Federal infantry. For several hours of welcome inaction, the men rested. At 11 A.M. came dreaded news. Petersburg's defenses had been broken and the enemy had cut the vital Southside Railroad. Orders from Lee told Anderson and Johnson to continue westward toward Bevill's Bridge over the Appomattox, to cross the river and wait for the main Confederate Army, fleeing westward north of the river. By noon, sloshing through ankle-deep mud, Johnson's men reached Namozine Creek,[60] swollen by recent rain, but passable over a narrow bridge.

There in late afternoon rode Fitz Lee and his survivors, fending off Sheridan's eager pursuers. Lee asked Johnson to deploy his infantry to check the Union horsemen, almost climbing up his back. Some of the footsore regiments formed line of battle and four times beat off enemy thrusts. After dark the pursuit broke off and the troops

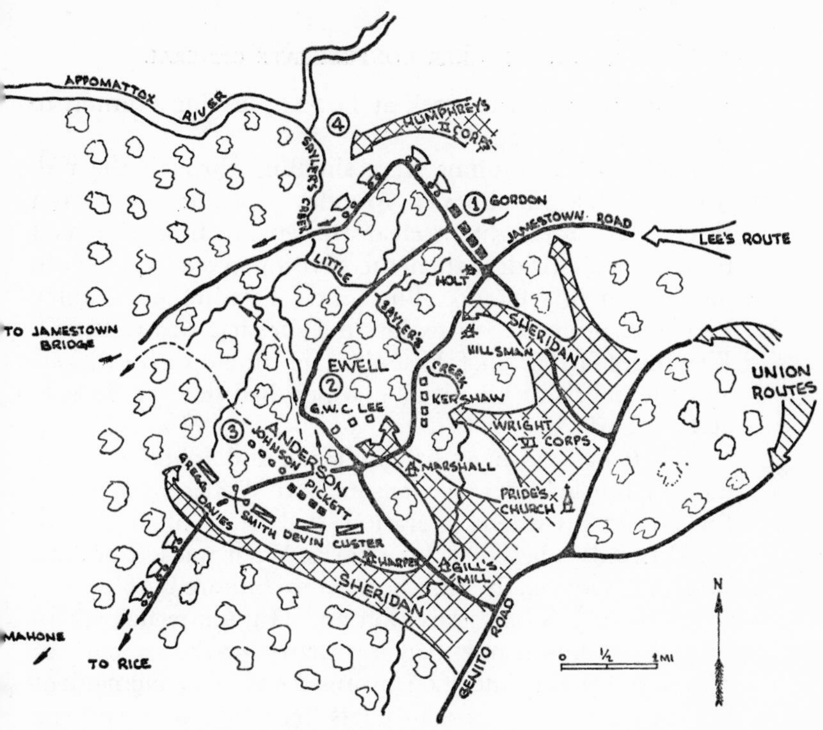

① GORDON (■■■■) FOLLOWS EWELL'S WAGONS

② EWELL'S (□□□) LAST STAND NEAR HILLSMAN'S

③ JOHNSON'S (oooo) AND PICKETT'S STANDS NEAR HARPER'S

④ FINAL ATTACK ON GORDON AT 5 P.M.

----• GENERALS' FLIGHTS (APPROX.)

UNION ATTACKS

UNION UNITS (CAVALRY)

DAVIES' ROADBLOCK

SAYLER'S CREEK

April 6, 1865

His frazzled troops overwhelmed by Sheridan's cavalry, Johnson leaves them to escape with Anderson and Pickett through the woods. He reports to Lee, who scorns and humiliates him before removing him from command. It is a tragic finale to his military career. (From description in SHSP, *XLII, pp. 136–151)* resumed crossing the creek at 11 P.M., leaving Hunton to protect their passage.[61]

The frazzled columns were shuffling through the red, sticky muck again at 6 A.M., Monday, April 3. There was a brief, sharp fire fight to clear the enemy from the road near Brown's Bridge, then the division passed over without further interference. But Johnson's adjutant, Romley E. Foote, promoted to major in February, was captured. Five miles farther on Johnson's men came up with Pickett and the debris of his division which had fled the debacle at Five Forks.[62]

Pickett had sad news for Anderson and Johnson. Many men of the brigades of Ransom and Wallace, loaned to Pickett for his recent operation, had been killed or captured two days before at Five Forks. What was left of both brigades, reduced in numbers from hundreds to scores, returned to Johnson's Division and Hunton went back to Pickett's. Johnson now had less than half the strength of a month before. Anderson assumed overall command of both divisions with probably less than 4000 men and the march was resumed toward Amelia Courthouse. Pickett was in the lead.[63]

Tuesday, April 4 was spent in a continual skirmish with Sheridan's horse soldiers in mounting numbers. Johnson moved slowly four miles behind Pickett, halting to deploy and fight, reform in column and move ahead, repeating the routine until darkness brought respite. The bone-tired and empty-stomached, unwashed and stinking men kept their spirits flickering by repeating the promise that food awaited them in Amelia Courthouse on the morrow.[64]

Ammunition there was in plenty in Amelia, but no food! There had been a failure in logistics and the special reserve of 350,000 rations in Richmond had never been shipped. While the hungry troops complained profanely, wagons were sent out in the countryside, already scoured to the bones. Pickings were slim indeed. Then men wandered off individually to hunt anything to eat and many never came back. Officers, equally exhausted and foodless, were losing both their will and their ability to maintain control.[65] The ammunition, ninety-five caissons of it, was destroyed.

In a chilly, nagging spring drizzle the painful trudge of the reunited army was resumed at 1 P.M. Wednesday, April 5. Now it pursued a mirage 104 miles southward at Danville, capital of the fugitive Confederate government, where a million and a half rations were stocked, the rumors said. Some of this precious food had been ordered shipped up the Richmond and Danville Railroad and the army would move to meet it.[66] Scarcely had marching resumed when Lee learned that the Federals were entrenching across his path southward toward Jetersville. He had no choice but to turn westward and plod all night in the hope of outdistancing the blue-clad pursuers before turning south again.[67]

As the straggling columns of Lee's army stumbled forward in the sooty darkness and disorder on the narrow mud road from Deatonsville to Rice, the limping hundreds of Pickett and Johnson moved in the center, behind Longstreet's abler units of Wilcox, Heth and Mahone with their string of wagons and ahead of Ewell's motley mixture of artillerymen without guns, a naval battalion, clerks and reservists in two divisions of Kershaw and G. W. C. Lee. Behind Ewell was another long train of lurching wagons and then came Gordon's valiants, trying to shield the army's rear from the endless nipping of Sheridan's troopers.[68]

Thursday's damp dawn bared a situation ripe for calamity. The gummy red clay road wound through thick woods, hiding the stabbing enemy. Sleepless and fatigue-wracked men mingled like zombies in disarray with wagons and guns. Many fell out, crept into the bushes and stayed there. Animals dropped from exhaustion. Broken wagons blocked the way until pushed aside into the brush. Ewell, Anderson, Johnson, and Pickett prodded and badgered equally tired juniors to drive shambling men and staggering animals ahead. Lee, whose magic presence might have energized the faltering, was three miles up ahead trying to stimulate Longstreet's Corps, trudging into Rice. He was virtually out of contact with more than half of his army.[69]

The rising sun catalyzed the Federals. Johnson's men were plugging along behind Pickett and ahead of Custis Lee's ex-office soldiers about midday when a strong enemy force dashed down upon them at the Pride's Church-Jamestown road crossing. From their main route on the Genito Road less than two miles southeast, the Blue horsemen in increasing strength and daring were jabbing, feinting, retiring and returning all along the Confederate lines, hunting weak spots through which to pour a devastating cataract. Between Johnson and Custis Lee seemed such a likely crevice and the Federals tried it. Captain Whitner of Johnson's staff quickly mobilized a few dozen stragglers. Their frantic rifle fire held the enemy in check until Johnson could deploy enough men with guns and waning energy to cover the road and Custis Lee could close up on Johnson's left. Sharp skirmishing continued for half an hour. The Confederates scraped up some temporary defenses while Pickett sent back some of his men to help. The enemy was momentarily repulsed and Anderson's force resumed its march across Little Sayler's Creek.

The wagons in the long column were especially vulnerable. Sheridan's horsemen shot the jaded beasts pulling them, wounded or killed the relatively unprotected drivers, broke wheels with a few quick axe blows and set fire to canvas covers. Something had to be done quickly to get rid of these creeping trains separating Gordon from Ewell and Ewell from Anderson. Whenever the firing died down, Pickett, Johnson, Custis Lee and Kershaw sent their men into the ditches and the brush beside the narrow road to let the vehicle move ahead behind Mahone, at the rear of Longstreet. Some of the wagons edged to the front of Pickett. Almost at once they became flaming roadblocks.

Then Anderson, weary and dispirited in mind as well as body, with marching orders requiring him to stay close behind Mahone, forgot to inform him that he had halted. Mahone kept going. As a result, the unprotected wagons rumbled into a widening void on high ground near the Harper plantation, a mile beyond the frail, pole bridge over Little Sayler's Creek.[70] Swift as hunting cheetahs the Union horsemen pounced on them. Teamsters were shot and sabered, horses and mules killed or crippled, vehicles overturned and set afire. By the time Pickett's men could rush up the hill to the rescue, the road was effectively blocked. The brigades of J. Irvin Gregg and Charles H. Smith and elements of the divisions of Thomas C. Devin and George A. Custer, dismounted, formed an arc from north to south across the road on which the troopers of Henry E. Davies's brigade sat their horses in a solid, massive barrier.

At the other end of the halted Confederate column, behind Ewell, another disaster had been distilled from confusion, fatigue and collapse of command. More of Sheridan's troopers were striking into the train still separating Ewell from Gordon. Ewell ordered the surviving vehicles to turn right on a road north from John Holt's house at his rear and proceed on the longer, but less exposed route to Jamestown Bridge.[71]

Here Ewell duplicated Anderson's mistake. He forgot to inform Gordon, whose men had been slogging behind the wagons for hours. Naturally they continued on behind the train as it turned to the northwest and marched farther and farther away from Ewell. Never suspecting he had lost any chance of help from Gordon, Ewell made a brief stand on the hilltop at Hillsman's and beat off his tormentors long enough to get across Little Sayler's Creek and to edge a half-mile up the hill toward Anderson.[72]

Bracing their men to move against the Federal roadblock ahead, Johnson brought up his lines north of the road and Pickett did the same on the south at Anderson's direction. Then Anderson noted that Custer's dismounted men, ready to attack, outflanked Pickett's left.[73] At the same time, two Union batteries were blasting at Ewell's rear and left from the hill at Hillsman's. He had no artillery to answer them. Infantry from Horatio G. Wright's VI Corps was swarming toward him behind Sheridan.[74] Dog-tired and perplexed, the two lieutenant generals, Ewell and Anderson, met between their troops near Swepp Marshall's to decide what to do. They could lean on no direction from Lee, who was far to the front, unaware of their peril. Ewell, the ranking officer, wanted to abandon the wagons to the enemy, quit the road and move the troops through the woods on the right to find the upper route to Farmville. Anderson favored uniting their forces for a smash through the roadblock ahead of Johnson and Pickett. While they sat debating irresolutely, the Federals resolved the issue by closing in on Ewell. He galloped down the hill toward the bridge to turn his men back to back with Anderson's and form a defense.[75] Springing from behind fence rails, brush and hastily dug earth, Ewell's Corps made a last, futile countercharge against Wright's surging infantry.

Anderson rode west up the hill to join beleaguered Johnson and Pickett. He had given little leadership and not much direction in the crisis. Meanwhile, without orders or informing anybody, impetuous Wise and his brigade which previously had been detached from Johnson's lines by Anderson, rashly attacked Gregg and Davies with two of his regiments, shook them momentarily but failed to push them back without support.[76] Then Wise drifted toward Pickett's feeble line which stretched across an open field with both flanks in the air. Johnson made a final effort at control by trying frantically to join his left flank with Pickett's right and link up with some of Custis Lee's men, being pushed back against him. Johnson had just put the scanty brigades of Wallace, Ransom and Moody in some puny semblance of a line of battle north of the road when the augmented Union guns on Hillsman's hill zeroed in on his rear and left flank.[77] Troopers of Gregg, Davies and Smith swarmed like angry hornets from three sides.

Vacillating Ewell left his own raging front and frisked back to see how Anderson fared. Far from succeeding, the breakthrough ahead of Anderson was being overwhelmed. As Ewell turned and scurried back toward his own lines, he was cut off and captured by Union troopers who had brushed past Pickett's left and were now between Anderson and Ewell. In the next few catastrophic moments, Ewell lost 2800 men by capture and his division chiefs, Kershaw and Custis Lee, were also made prisoners of war.[78]

Johnson was trying to adjust his wavering line of battle in a lane beyond a small open field and had ordered his men forward when Pickett galloped up and asked him to delay the attack for a minute while he finished trying to tie in his right flank with Johnson. Too late! An avalanche of Federals cascaded from the rear between and around the two little forces. Wallace's Brigade was overwhelmed first. The battle line formations disintegrated in wild disarray.[79] Wise's men stuck together and fought their way into the cover of the woods on the right. The instinct of self-preservation took command of the rest. Men broke ranks, flung away their weapons and stampeded for safety in any direction. A few officers tried desperately to hold them to their ground, then gave up and followed in disorganized flight, every man for himself. It was now after 4 P.M.

Abandoning efforts to quell the panic, Anderson, Johnson and a few staff officers plunged as frantically as the fleeing infantrymen into the sheltering trees to the north. Then, each goaded by his fear of capture, they separated. With Johnson went his courier William Barfield, Captain W. H. Whitner, his adjutant and Captain J. E. Saunders, his aide and former student. His other adjutant, Major R. E. Foote, had been captured at Namozine Creek three days previously.[80] Pickett and his medical director, Major M. M. Lewis, and his adjutant and apologist, Lieutenant Colonel Walter Harrison, yelled to a few men to fire in the faces of a squadron of Blue cavalry pounding down upon them. The volley slowed the pursuit long enough to let the three crash through the trees and get away.[81]

Five brigadiers also escaped in their separate ways: Matt Ransom, Moody and Wallace of Johnson; William R. Terry and George H. ("Maryland") Steuart of Pickett. Montgomery D. Corse and Eppa Hunton of Pickett were captured.[82] More than 1500 of the abandoned troops were made prisoners. Only Wallace and Wise retained much semblance of organization. Survivors of the other brigades wandered through the woods during the night and finally gravitated toward the rest of the army near Farmville the following day. Around 3300 of Anderson's Corps were paroled after the surrender.[83]

Of all the fugitive generals, only Johnson made the naïve mistake of facing Lee, who gave him ample cause to regret it. Pickett and Anderson roamed the area for the next two days looking for each other and for stragglers and thus avoided the army commander. It was well for them that they did.

After he gained the road to the rear of the woods which led to the leading elements of the army, Johnson, as he wrote later, "reported to General Lee who directed me with my assistant adjutant general to collect together all the scattered forces of Generals Anderson's and Ewell's commands."[84] Lee's biographer, Douglas S. Freeman, tells it less matter-of-factly. He quotes an eye-witness who described the scene in 1894 without using Johnson's name. There can be no doubt that Johnson was the general mentioned. Lee was watching the routed wreck of Anderson's Corps limping toward Longstreet's when "a general of exalted rank" arrived. A staff officer called Lee's attention to his presence. Lee would not even turn to look at him.

"All he did was move his right hand to the rear in a gesture of biting reproach," Freeman writes. Then Lee said slowly:

"General take those stragglers to the rear, out of the way of Mahone's troops. I wish to fight here."[85]

Darkness, Johnson wrote, "terminated the work before much progress had been made therein. Loss in my division was quite small." The latter statement was patently face-saving wishful thinking in the light of what had happened.

The next morning, Friday, April 7, near Farmville, Lee further abased Johnson. This story was repeated with gusto up to 1900 by three generations of the Wise family and the incident was witnessed and recorded by W. B. Freeman, father of Lee's biographer. Lee was still looking for survivors of the Sayler's Creek debacle north of the Appomattox when he encountered still unnerved Johnson who told him he believed his entire division had been destroyed and that Wise had been killed. This statement was contradicted shortly by the appearance of Wise, his brigade and what was left of Wallace's, 250 of Moody and 80 of Ransom.[87]

Wise loudly demanded food for his men. Lee told him where to find some in a nearby wagon train which had eluded Union raiders. Then, in Johnson's sight and hearing, Lee directed Wise to take command of all stragglers from Johnson's Division. Wise, noting hated Johnson within earshot, roared a condemnation of "officers who are deserting their men, who are disorganizing your army" and asked Lee if the order included "men of all ranks," an evident reference to Johnson.

Lee imposed no restraint. "Do your duty, sir!" he said and turned to suppress a smile. Wise moved off triumphantly past Johnson, sitting his horse in red-faced shame among Lee's staff officers and others who had heard and seen the show.[88]

Lee still had not washed his failing hands of the three high-ranking runaways. On the afternoon of Saturday, April 8, he had many things to monopolize his time and his thoughts. He had received and answered Grant's suggestions for surrender; he knew some of his paladins favored quitting, but he clung to a faint dream that he might attack early on Palm Sunday and cut his way out of the Blue encirclement. Actually in less than twenty-four hours he would give up. However, he found time in the midst of his anxieties to direct his adjutant, Walter H. Taylor, to issue orders to Anderson, Pickett and Johnson relieving them from command and sending them home. No censure was implied; no reasons were given. Many years later Taylor said that Lee told him why, but this was never divulged.[89] No similar action was taken against the five brigadiers who had joined the flight from Sayler's Creek, nor was anything ever done by Lee to his nephew Fitzhugh Lee or to Virginian Tom Rosser for being absent at the "shad bake" at the Five Forks annihilation.

Biographer Freeman is at pains to explain Lee's action, vulnerable to challenge as vindictive in the bitter hour of defeat. He argues that absorption of Pickett's and Johnson's survivors later by Gordon made the three generals "supernumerary" without commands befitting their ranks, that they could not be reassigned to replace others who had "done their full duty" and that to retain them in the army without any part in its future battles, if any, would be a "humiliation." Part of this thesis confronts the statistics that Wise and Wallace still had intact brigades, however small, and that 2277 officers and men of Johnson and 1031 of Pickett are listed as paroled after the surrender—

sufficient numbers to justify retention of the three for the few hours Lee must have well known were all that remained to his army. Some of the five fleeing brigadiers who escaped Lee's wrath led only company-sized units in these death throes as did others in the crumbling army.[90]

It is also difficult now to appreciate the reasons why Lee delayed forty-eight hours to penalize the trio for their conduct, until his gesture almost lacked significance. In the face of grim certainty of surrender was there a desire to blame, by inference, three scapegoats for tactical failures which might be laid to his own generalship? Was the penalty an expression of petulant impatience with failure on the part of one whose own leadership must so soon acknowledge for all time its lack of success? And finally, what impelled Lee to depart from his characteristically courtly behaviour to first snub and then publicly humiliate Johnson, a high ranking officer whose general performance of duty with fidelity and diligence deserved better treatment?

In sharp contrast was Lee's handling of Jubal A. Early two weeks before. Early left his army and ran away from a crushing defeat at Waynesboro, Virginia. Reluctantly responding to Richmond's pressure, Lee relieved Early and sent him home. But he softened the blow in a warm personal letter, assuring Early "my confidence in your ability, zeal and devotion to the cause is unimpaired."[91] Lee was under no popular or political pressure to fire Johnson, Pickett and Anderson. He acted on his own unforgiving volition and to them no salve was applied.

Anderson left for his South Carolina home at once. He never saw Lee again. In March 1866 in the midst of a bitter struggle against poverty he got a letter from Lee in Lexington, Virginia asking for details on his corps' part in the fatal finale. Lee was contemplating writing a history of the Army of Northern Virginia. Bearing no grudge, Anderson wrote a brief, self-exculpating story of Sayler's Creek, saying his troops "seemed wholly broken down and disheartened" and "gave way in confusion" after a "feeble effort to advance." He said nothing about his own flight and noted only that he had been relieved from duty on the afternoon of April 8.[92]

Johnson likewise never looked upon Lee's face again. He remained with the survivors of his division in Gordon's Corps until it camped about a mile from Appomattox Courthouse at 3 P.M. Saturday. Then, he said in his report, under instructions of Gordon to Brigadier General James A. Walker of Gordon's Corps, "my division moved out under the command of Brigadier General W. H. Wallace,"[93] chief of the South Carolina stalwarts who withstood the Federals at The Crater. Wallace led the division about 8 P.M. into the tiny town where it remained in line all night.[94]

Johnson wrote a fairly matter-of-fact report of the division's operations from March 28 to 8 P.M. Saturday, April 8 when apparently the order relieving him was delivered. He made no reference to Wise superseding him on Lee's verbal order, but said simply that about noon on Friday the seventh he was advised that the division had been assigned to Gordon. He glossed over the cataclysmic events of Thursday afternoon at Sayler's Creek thus:

> . . . my troops broke and moved rapidly to the west and gained the road to the rear which connected with the right or advanced portion of our army. I here reported to General Lee who directed me . . . to collect together all the scattered forces.[95]

Wallace's report was silent on taking over command on the last day. If Wise ever wrote any report, it has been lost. Wallace said his own brigade at Sayler's Creek "fell back" about a mile and was reassembled by him and marched toward the main body, arriving at High Bridge about 11 P.M. Thursday.[96] In the Union lists of members of Johnson's Division paroled after the surrender, Wallace's Brigade totaled 630 officers and men, ahead of Wise with 600, Moody, 578, and Ransom, 435. With Johnson and his staff of ten this totals 2277 for the division.[97]

Johnson's parole was dated Sunday, April 9 but was not signed until the tenth as were those of other generals and staff officers.[98] He wrote his report on Monday, the tenth and probably did not participate on Wednesday, April 12, when his men, still known as Johnson's Division, marched in the Confederate surrender parade behind Gordon's Corps.[99]

As he signs his report and his parole, Bushrod Rust Johnson writes "finis" to his service as a Confederate officer. Begun in the short-sightedness of approving the fatal site of Fort Henry, his career crumbles in the shame and disgrace of Sayler's Creek The troubled years between know few moments of glory, but hours of frustration and disappointment. There are some serious lapses from responsibility and some evidences of mediocrity of mind and spirit. But this is to be expected. Perfect military heroes exist only in the realms of romance.

Johnson faces a thorny dilemma at Fort Henry. If he concurs in the choice of the site recommended by the civilian engineers, Anderson and Foster, against the opinion of Donelson, he affronts the caste kindredship of West Pointers, often self-regarded as superior in training and judgement in matters military. The later overwhelming verdict of those doomed to survive or fall at this fort below flood level (Tilghman, Heiman, Taylor, and Gilmer), supports the expertise of the civilians and denounces the obvious inadequacies, hazards and vulnerability of the place. But not Johnson. His engineering background includes only what he has learned from Military Academy texts a score of years before and what civil engineering he himself has taught to his cadets. He never had any practical experience as a military engineer, nor had Donelson, whose army service thirty-six years before is limited to a single year. But

Donelson is a figure of political status in the Tennessee scene as well as being a brother alumnus. So Johnson takes his side against the better skilled, and rationalizes his option by stressing its excellent field of fire, which, as it develops, is a deciding advantage for the Federals. The episode is a definite debit against Johnson.

Fort Donelson is his first battle ordeal since Monterrey. In the confusion of command by Floyd and Pillow, Johnson exhibits more than average capacity. Although unaccustomed to his role, he proves himself a leader of proficiency and performance. Ignored and undercut by his two fumbling superiors, he shows a potential that flowers on later fields. More dash and decision when Forrest importunes for a general attack might have added luster. But his credits here are overshadowed by his questionable conduct when the firing ceases. He evades his military and moral obligations when he watches his comrades go to prison and then walks away to freedom. He presents an insincere and unattractive figure when he protests later that he had no part in the surrender although he personally had accompanied the flag of truce to Lew Wallace and escorted him back through the lines to Buckner.

His wound early in the disorder of Shiloh cheats him of a greater part in the glory of this first great battle of the West. Here Polk interferes and Bragg deprives, both neglecting their corps duties for lower echelon intervention, to the detriment of Johnson. Entirely courageous and disdainful of danger, Johnson directs and inspires his troops, rallies and encourages them in faltering moments. He measures up well to what the situation demands. This is to his credit.

The same Buckner he had deserted at Donelson demonstrates his confidence in Johnson at Perryville, assigning to him the task of spearheading the wedge into the Federals along Doctor's Creek and the Bottom House. Johnson justifies his chief's trust and acquits himself with professional competence in the face of fire that cuts down five of his mounts. But the persistent luck that is required to make a soldier good is denied to him when, out of ammunition, he is forced to give way to Cleburne. Nevertheless, Perryville may be scored on the bright side.

Stones River is another laurel. He persists in sustaining a drive that surpasses expectations and the capabilities of men. When it degenerates into unreasoning panic, he strives mightily to dam the flood of runaways and to rally and reform them beneath their colors. He is alert and resourceful—both attributes of leadership. He jealously fights for full credits for his men, another mark of the dedicated commander.

Johnson's shining apogee is the second day at Chickamauga. Favored with the trust of Longstreet after dubious Hood is removed by a Union bullet, Johnson functions at his optimum. He moves promptly and vigorously against the Brotherton House defenses. He is energetic and vigilant. His reaction to the chance gap in the Federal lines is immediate and imaginative; his troop dispositions are calculated to insure the maximum advantage. He perseveres in drawing out the utmost effort from his men when others yield to exhaustion. This day of glorious achievement is the brightest in his record.

There follows the frustrating, suffering period in East Tennessee, but none of this is to his discredit. Denied more than a secondary part at Knoxville, he does well at Dandridge and Bean's Station. He shows his continuing concern for the welfare of his men in his shoemaking enterprise at Cloud's Creek and his sensitivity and admiration for those who kept stout hearts in the season of appalling distress. He earns the plaudits of Longstreet and Buckner and their support for his promotion hopes.

Beauregard adds fulsome praise for his performances at Drewry's Bluff and Bermuda Hundred, the first appearances of Johnson and his Tennesseeans in the realm of

Lee's Army of Northern Virginia. The kudos are the last such entries to Johnson's account. He finds no warmth of welcome among the high-blooded Virginians who occupy two-thirds of the most responsible assignments under Lee and who are distrustful of men from the West. His long-sought promotion comes to him at last, not as a reward, but as a happenstance.

Thereafter Johnson's military balance sheet shows little but red. Deprived of his cherished brigade, his spirits seem to ebb. In the desperate hours at The Crater when his new and unfamiliar soldiers need intelligent direction he is strangely remiss and sluggish. Without protest he lets his responsibilities go to Mahone who reaps lasting glory. His disenchantment grows as he is assigned to a castoff corps commander equally disillusioned. In two weeks he loses two-thirds of his troops, taken from him and fragmented in bloody fiascos at Fort Stedman and Five Forks in which he has no part whatever. In his first standup fight after the decay of the trenches, at Burgess Mill, he is relegated almost to a spectator's role as the army commander himself personally directs the action.

Johnson reaches the depths of body and spirit at Sayler's Creek and its aftermath. Fatigue dilutes any energy or will among his used-up troops for driving the impeding Federals from their roadblock and only desperation spurs a mechanical effort to form up and fight. The end is swift and overwhelming. From the wild scramble to safety Johnson emerges safely and in his dazed agitation foolishly reports directly to Lee. He is curtly scorned. Next are added a public degradation and the crowning disgrace—relief from duty and command—all this far less than justice or understanding.

On balance, Johnson deserves a better farewell to arms. Among those under whom he serves, Lee's depreciative evaluation of him is shared only by Bragg, and even he grudgingly admits achievement "with some distinction."

Beauregard, Longstreet, Hardee, Polk, Buckner, Cleburne, Hindman, Pillow, and Floyd all have words of commendation, sometimes repeated, for his professional capacity. To say that he only functions best under their supervision is to forget that no one but the leader of an army or an independent command is totally free of high control and guidance in battle.

All this is behind Bushrod Johnson as he shakes the hand of his young courier William Barfield and tells him goodby[100] in the last of his farewells to his staff officers and rides away from Virginia. Ahead of him are fifteen more years in which to try to change the pattern of his life.

Notes

1. *Warner*, p. 11.
2. *OR*, XLII, pt. 1, p. 1284.
3. *Ibid.*
4. *Ibid.*, XLII, pt. 1, pp. 1263, 1266.
5. *Ibid.*, XLII, pt. 1, p. 1223; pt. 3, p. 1153.
6. *Ibid.*, XLII, pt. 1, pp. 1284, 1288.
7. *Ibid.*, XLII, pt. 1, p. 1235. Though united with Archer, the brigade was still listed on December 31, 1864 as part of Ewell's Department of Richmond.
8. Freeman, *Lieutenants*, III, p. 701; *SHSP*, XXV, pp. 17 ff.
9. *SHSP*, XVIII, p. 6.
10. *OR*, XL, pt. 3, pp. 770 f.
11. *Ibid.*, XLVI, pt. 2, p. 1239.
12. *Warner*, p. 114.
13. *Gracie*; see n. 71, chap. 8.
14. Freeman, *Lieutenants*, III, pp. 543 f.
15. *OR*, XLII, pt. 2, p. 31.
16. Map 141, *WP Atlas*.
17. Freeman, *Lieutenants*, III, p. 509.
18. G. Moxley Sorrel, *Recollections of a Confederate Staff Officer*, (New York: Neale Publishing Co., 1905), p. 254.
19. Freeman, *Lieutenants*, III, p., 631; *Dowdey*, p. 351.
20. *Blakemore file*, CSA Staff Papers; Original correspondence on Saunders in Confederate Collection, Tennessee Archives; Notes on Cadet Saunders in WMI Folder No. 1, *Owen Papers*; *Foote* and *Whitner Files*, CSA Staff Papers.
21. *OR*, XLII, pt. 3, p. 1200; *ibid.*, XLII, pt. 2, p. 1162.
22. *CV*, XIV, p. 109.

23. *OR*, XLII, pt. 2, pp. 1227, 1244.
24. *OR*, XLII, pt. 3, pp. 1186 f.
25. *Ibid.*, XLV, pt. 2, p. 69.
26. *Ibid.*, XLV, pt. 2, p. 80.
27. *Ibid.*, XLII, pt. 3, p. 1280.
28. *Ibid.*, XLII, pt. 3, p. 1283.
29. *Ibid.*, XLIV, pt. 1, p. 1000.
30. *Ibid.*, XLIV, pt. 1, p. 966.
31. *Ibid.*, XLIV, pt. 1, p. 969.
32. *Ibid.*, XLII, pt. 3, pp. 1140, 1142, 1180.
33. *Ibid.*, XLII, pt. 3, pp. 424, 893, 952, 1077, 1081.
34. *Ibid.*, XLVI, pt. 2, pp. 1228–1230.
35. *Ibid.*, XLVI, pt. 3, p. 75.
36. *Ibid.*, XLVI, pt. 2, p. 1195.
37. *Ibid.*, XLVI, pt. 2, p. 1239.
38. *Ibid.*, XLVI, pt. 2, p. 1261. Ella Lonn, *Desertion During the Civil War,* (New York: The Century Co., 1928) puts total Confederate desertions on all fronts at 1028 officers and 103,400 men.
39. *OR*, XLII, pt. 1, pp. 896, 897, 901, 906, 909, 914, 915, 916.
40. *Ibid.*, XLII, pt. 3, p. 1143.
41. Freeman, *Lieutenants*, III, p. 620.
42. *Richmond Examiner*, Dec. 31, 1864.
43. Freeman, *Lieutenants*, III, p. 621.
44. *OR*, LXVI, pt. 2, p. 1152.
45. Freeman, *Lieutenants*, III, p. 622.
46. *OR*, XLII, pt. 3, p. 1276.
47. Freeman, *Lieutenants*, III, p. 645.
48. Map 142, *WP Atlas.*
49. *OR*, XLVI, pp. 155 f., 196; *CV*, XIX, pp. 217 f.; *ibid.*, XXII, pp. 460–462.
50. Freeman, *Lee*, IV, pp. 25 f.
51. *Ibid.*, pp. 27 f.
52. Johnson's report, *OR*, XLVI, pt. 1, p. 1286.
53. *Ibid.*
54. Freeman, *Lee*, IV, p. 34; Johnson's report.
55. *OR*, XLVI, pt. 1, p. 1286.
56. Freeman, *Lee*, IV, p. 35.
57. *OR*, XLVI, pt. 1, pp. 1263 f.; *ibid.*, p. 836.
58. *Ibid.*, XLVI, pt. 1, p. 1288.
59. Now called Church Road on U.S. 460, ten miles from Petersburg.
60. *OR*, XLVI, pt. 1, p. 1288. Johnson's report gives detailed movements of his troops.
61. *Ibid.*
62. *Ibid.*; Foote File, CSA Staff Papers. Foote was taken to the Old Capitol Prison in Washington, thence to Fort Delaware on April 8. He was freed May 8 after taking the oath of allegiance.
63. Walter Harrison, *Pickett's Men,* (New York: D. Van Nostrand, 1870), pp. 148, 152; C. Irvine Walker, *Life of Lt. Gen. Richard Heron Anderson,* (Charleston: Art Publishing Co., 1917), p. 211. Clifford Dowdey, *Lee,* (Boston: Little, Brown & Co., 1965), p. 559, thinks Anderson's force could have totaled no more than 3500.
64. Freeman, *Lieutenants,* III, p. 689.
65. Freeman, *Lee,* IV, pp. 66 f.

66. *Ibid.*, 71; Map 144, *WP Atlas*; *OR Atlas*, Plate LXXVIII, No. 4.
67. Freeman, *Lee*, IV, p. 77.
68. Freeman, *Lieutenants*, III, p. 699.
69. Freeman, *Lee*, IV, p. 82.
70. *OR*, XLVI, pt. 1, pp. 1265, 1294, 1302; *Walker*, p. 211. See also Walter C. Watson's detailed description in *SHSP*, XLII, pp. 136–151.
71. *OR*, XLVI, pt. 1, pp. 1294 ff. Ewell wrote this report of the battle eight months later on December 20, 1865, from his home in Spring Hill, Tennessee to Lee in Lexington, Virginia.
72. Freeman, *Lieutenants*, III, p. 702.
73. *OR*, XLVI, pt. 1, p. 1107.
74. *Ibid.*, XLVI, pt. 1, p. 906.
75. *Ibid.*, XLVI, pt. 1, pp. 1294 ff.
76. *SHSP*, XXV, pp. 17 ff.; *OR*, XLVI, pt. 1, p. 1289.
77. *OR*, XLVI, pt. 1, p. 1290.
78. *Ibid.*, XLVI, pt. 1, p. 1295. The captor of Ewell and Custis Lee was Union Brigadier General Oliver Edwards who had received the surrender of Petersburg a few days before. For his feat at Sayler's Creek he was brevetted major general. Warner, *Generals in Blue*, p. 138.
79. *OR*, XLVI, pt. 1, p. 1290.
80. *CV*, XIV, p. 109. This account disagrees with the time and place of Foote's capture, given in *Foote File*, CSA Staff Papers.
81. *Harrison*, p. 157.
82. *OR*, XLVI, pt. 1, pp. 1277 f.
83. *Walker*, p. 211. Copy of Anderson's report in *Munford-Ellis Papers*, Duke University Library.
84. *OR*, XLVI, pt. 1, p. 1289.
85. Freeman, *Lee*, IV, pp. 84–86 and p. 86 n., quoting Colonel W. E. Cameron, who witnessed the event, in *Norfolk Landmark*, November 25, 1894.
86. *OR*, XLVI, pt. 1, p. 1289.
87. Figures in Johnson's report.
88. *SHSP*, XXV, pp. 13 ff. Contributed by Braxton Hall Wise, a grandson, this story of the shaming of Johnson by Lee purports to be an address by Henry A. Wise, probably around 1870, at a veterans' meeting near Cappahoosic, Glouster County, Virginia. Time and place are indefinite. A similar version appears in John Sergeant Wise, *The End of an Era*, pp. 433–435. This son of Wise, a New York lawyer, viciously attacks Johnson. See also Freeman, *Lee*, IV, pp. 96 f., and *Lieutenants*, III, pp. 714 f. Freeman says the scene was witnessed by his father, W. B. Freeman.
89. Letter of Walter H. Taylor, Lee's adjutant, to R. E. Cowart, Dallas, Texas, November 10, 1908. Copy in *Munford-Ellis Papers*. Cowart was colonel of the Seventh Georgia in Anderson's old brigade.
90. *OR*, XLVI, pt. 1, pp. 1277 f.
91. Text in Freeman, *Lee*, IV, Appendix IV–1, p. 508.
92. Copy of letter, Anderson to Lee, March 24, 1866 in *Munford-Ellis Papers*.
93. *OR*, XLVI, pt. 1, pp. 1290 f.
94. *Ibid.*, XLVI, pt. 1, p. 1291. Wallace biographers later asserted these troops fired the last shots by Lee's army shortly before the surrender.
95. *Ibid.*, XLVI, pt. 1, p. 1289.

96. *Ibid.*, XLVI, pt. 1, p. 1291. Henry A. Wise in *SHSP*, XXV, pp. 13 ff., says Wallace's troops "were ensconced" in the woods until Wise's men fired three volleys into the trees over their fellow Confederates to force them "to come out to us" and march "safely off the field."
97. *OR*, XLVI, pt. 1, p. 1278. The numbers of parolees included captives taken in all the actions in the final defense of Petersburg and on the retreat to Appomattox.
98. Original in *B. R. Johnson File*, CSA Staff Papers.
99. Freeman, *Lieutenants*, III, p. 748.
100. *CV*, XIV, p. 109.

11

SALVAGER IN THE WRECKAGE

i. Real Estate and Reconstruction

The stark reality that the cause he had embraced had been utterly destroyed was visible on every side to Bushrod Johnson as he rode away from Appomattox on the day after the formal surrender parade. War's ravaging hand showed its hideous marks across the scavenged landscape, in the still unburied bodies at Sayler's Creek, in the debris-strewn roads filled with dirty, weary, disheartened men on their way home to pick up the fragments of their lives and start all over. It was manifest, too, in his own soul.

Now forty-eight years old, worn with the fatigues and anxieties of nine months in the foul trenches of Petersburg climaxed by the calamity of his ejection from the army, Johnson weighed his doubtful future. His former means of civilian livelihood were gone. Dr. J. Berrien Lindsley had tried briefly in 1863 to revive the collegiate department of the University of Nashville during the Federal occupation and had failed.[1] In the disrupted economic state of most of the South's "finer families" upon whom the school must depend for its existence, there were scant prospects that Johnson could do any better in resurrecting the enterprise now that the war was over.

He could not seek a haven in any familiar spot in the North. In Wayne County, Indiana where his afflicted son, Charles, was still under the care of Dr. Nathan Johnson's family,[2] there would be scant toleration for an ex-rebel general, however much his kinsmen might have welcomed him with sympathy and understanding. His nephew Dr. Lemuel R. Johnson was prominent in Republican councils and in a few years would be rewarded with the Cambridge City postmastership by President Grant.[3] The second nephew, Judge Nimrod Hoge Johnson, common pleas judge in Centreville, soon to be elevated to the circuit bench, had survived politically the occasional references to his connection with Bushrod in the partisan opposition press, but these innuendos certainly would be revived and magnified by the presence of his ex-Confederate uncle.[4] Back in Belmont County, Ohio the atmosphere would be more hostile. Only his widowed sister Aletha was still there, with children and grandchildren to whom Uncle Bushrod may have been no more than a legend. They soon were to move away.[5]

Johnson probably did not travel alone on the long, sad return to Tennessee. His aide and former student, Captain J. E. Saunders and possibly his former adjutant and one-time cadet, Colonel R. Bogardus Snowden, both of whom lived in Nashville, may have been his companions. Their route from Appomattox would have taken them to Bristol and down the valley to Knoxville through sites of pain and trouble in the winter of 1863. Even though spring's magic was transforming the scenes, they could only have stirred unhappy recollections.

There was not much in Nashville to generate euphoria in the defeated when they arrived. The city was changed considerably from the place Johnson had left hastily in February 1862. Union troops under Bushrod's classmate George Thomas had turned the capitol hill into a fortress. A bloody two-day battle had been fought on the southern outskirts in December 1864 and ghastly relics of it were still much in evidence. Federal soldiers had taken over the buildings of the University of Nashville a few days after the fall of Fort Donelson. They turned Lindsley Hall into a hospital, where undaunted Dr. Lindsley continued to operate the university's medical school almost amid the cots of suffering or recuperating Yankees. After Appomattox, the tenants were in no hurry to leave. Not until September 11, 1865 was the last patient evacuated and the orderlies and pickets moved out, leaving the debris and trash of two-and-a-half years of untidy occupancy.[6] Buildings needed repairs and fences were gone.

As the chief city of a state wherein loyalties were sharply divided and bitter rancor remained, the community climate in Nashville was not favorable for any effort at financial recuperation. A Union occupation force was to remain for several years. The political situation compounded the state of chaos. The governor was William Gannaway ("Parson") Brownlow, seated under the shadow of Union bayonets on March 4, 1865 to succeed the military governor, Andrew Johnson, now president of the United States. An intense and single-minded East Tennessee Unionist, Brownlow was bitter and vengeful. He had suffered at the hands of secessionists and they now were the continuing targets of his wrath.[7] In June 1865 he had succeeded in obtaining from his like-minded legislature a law to limit the vote to unconditional Union men, including those resident in the state for six months, which let in carpetbaggers, and whites conscripted into the Confederate Army known to be true friends of the Union, which meant many East Tennesseeans. Rebels were disenfranchised for fifteen years.[8] In February 1867 an act was passed allowing Negroes to vote.

The Nashville city government was headed by Mayor A. E. Alden, a carpetbagger. He and his packed city council devoted themselves to a thorough system of public plunder through high taxes and manipulation of municipal funds.[9] Two serious cholera epidemics in 1866 halted all business activity while fearful residents fled the city, adding to its economic instability.

In spite of these insalubrious features of his environment, Bushrod Johnson was back among friends, former associates and wartime comrades when he returned to Nashville. Soon he joined in a real estate firm with two eminent Nashville residents. The senior partner was Samuel Read Anderson, Virginia-born 61-year old ex-postmaster in the Polk and Buchanan administrations, Mexican War lieutenant colonel and Confederate brigadier general in charge of conscription in Tennessee which he directed from exile in Selma, Alabama.[10] Anderson had been cashier of the Bank of Tennessee when the third member of Johnson's firm, Colonel Granville Physic Smith, had been president before the war. Smith, fifty years old, owed his odd middle name to a family friend. Also born in Virginia, he had been educated as a physician, but quit practice to become a banker. During the war he had served on Anderson's staff.[11]

The firm of Anderson, Johnson and Smith had an office at 30½ Public Square in 1866 and 1867. Johnson lodged in an adjoining room. He lived alone. His teenage son Charles either remained with the Nathan Johnsons in Indiana or with the Williams family for two years after they moved from Cambridge City, Indiana to Cincinnati at the close of the war. Charles's maternal stepgrandmother, Mrs. Mary R. Hatch, widow of Daniel G. Hatch, lived across the Ohio River in Covington, Ky., on East Fourth Street and may have sometimes shared in his care.[12]

Anderson and Smith owned considerable property in Edgefield, the flourishing suburb east of Nashville, across the Cumberland River. Johnson still had his remaining part of a tenth interest in the town of McGavock, bought nearly a decade previously with Richard Owen.

Somehow during the war, Johnson also had contrived to pay off the $6000 debt on the farmland in Illinois which he bought from the Williamses in 1861.[13] How he managed to do this out of his pay of $301 a month as a brigadier or what he received in depreciated Confederate paper money as a major general is a puzzle. He got some additional remuneration for forage for his personally owned horses and was compensated for the loss of some of them in battle,[14] but all of this was in currency worthless at the end of the war. The 1860 census indicated he owned personal property valued at $12,000 but no records disclose in what form this was, how it might have survived the Federal occupation, and how much was salvaged after the war.

During the war Johnson held the 320 acres in Osage County, Kansas he had deeded in 1861 to his son and also had a shaky title to six tracts of woodland in three Missouri Ozark counties of Madison, Shannon and Ripley, the whole totaling 1912 acres. How or when he acquired this is vague. He disposed of all of the Ozark property in 1867 to Mathias Martin and T. E. Delashmutt of Frederick, Maryland in payment for rights to the patent of Jackson & Clark's Improved Churn for the state of Tennessee. The agreement took into consideration the possibility that Johnson's title to the woodlands might be imperfect and provided for voiding the deal without court action in such an event. Anderson signed the agreement as a witness.[15] Records do not reveal the outcome, but apparently nothing came of the scheme.

Johnson also paid $1000 in cash to R. E. Mayer of Chester, South Carolina, for the rights to manufacture and sell an "Improved Soap" on which Mayer held a patent. Mayer also was to get one-third of the net profits of any factories established by Johnson for making the soap for seventeen years from April 10, 1866. His real estate partners, Anderson and Smith, signed the document as witnesses, indicating their assent if not participation in the enterprise.[16] Records again are silent on results, which apparently were nil. Both transactions evidence a combination of desperation and innocence in Johnson's efforts to find a steady source of income.

The firm's activity seems to have been no more than modest, probably insufficient to provide Johnson with a living. Real estate was stagnant and many ex-Confederate officers competed as brokers for the small amount of business. Notes, often unpaid and uncollectable, figured in transactions instead of cash. Because he needed money in November 1867, Johnson sold three of his McGavock lots to his partner Anderson for $1500, some of which was a transfer of interest in an 1866 judgement, in other words, only part in cash.[17] In one case productive of a few dollars in fees, Johnson in December 1867 was named a special commissioner by the chancery court of Maury County in a suit against Gideon Pillow, his fellow actor in the farce at Fort Donelson.[18]

Early in 1867 Johnson brought his son, called "Charley" in the family, back to Nashville. He enrolled him in E. I. Crocker's boarding school at White Springs Creek, about a dozen miles from downtown Nashville.[19] The boy was not robust and painfully slow to learn. The firm of Anderson, Johnson and Smith moved in 1867 to quarters at 54 North College Street over the Fourth National Bank and Johnson's adjoining living room was inadequate to house both father and son.[20] The lot sale to Anderson probably provided the boy's tuition expenses.

Meanwhile Johnson had submitted to the federal authorities his application for pardon and restoration to his civil rights. As a former U.S. Army officer who had "resigned and entered the rebel service" and as a graduate of West Point and a "rebel brigadier [*sic*] general" he was listed in Class 2 with such notables as Robert E. Lee.[21] There is no evidence that his plea was granted before the general amnesty proclamation of Tennesseean President

Andrew Johnson on Christmas Day 1868 restored Bushrod Johnson to status as a citizen.

During 1868 in Tennessee the political situation was nearing a critical showdown. Whites who were denied votes in Western and Middle Tennessee were restive. Some advocated downright rebellion. Others counseled legal organization against the Radicals, personified by Governor Brownlow, to reestablish a "white man's government." The Ku Klux Klan, organized with General Forrest as Imperial Wizard in April 1867, had carried on a campaign of intimidating Negroes, flogging Radicals, and "executing" men they judged guilty of murders in guerilla fighting in some areas.[22] There had been race riots in 1866 which had brought a militia law, used by Brownlow in 1867 and later repealed. In the election for the legislature in 1867 most of the winners were born in Tennessee or in the South; only nine were Northerners, but forty-three had served in the Union Army.

Brownlow called the legislature into a special session in July 1868 and asked reenactment of the militia law which gave him the power to use an extraordinary state guard force to restore order and put down insurrection. Firebrand newspaper editors, voicing the sentiments of the disenfranchised, warned and threatened the state government.

Around this powder keg, fortunately, a few cooler heads gathered, among them Bushrod Johnson. With his former comrades, B. F. Cheatham and George F. Maney, Confederate ex-generals, he took part in a conference with the militia committee of the legislature on July 31, 1868. Maney was president of the Tennessee and Pacific Railroad, and Cheatham was selling life insurance and nursing political ambitions. The next day, more former generals, including S. R. Anderson, John Calvin Brown, William B. Bate, George Gibbs Dibrell, W. B. Quarles, Forrest, and Pillow, met with Johnson, Maney and Cheatham and adopted a conciliatory memorial to the governor and legislature.[23]

They said Brownlow was mistaken in his statements that an effort was being made to overthrow the state government or that any revolutionary means were contemplated. They said that to their knowledge no secret nor public organization existed for the purpose of overthrowing the state government by unlawful means. This wording, of course, did not apply strictly to the Ku Klux Klan, whose aim was not to overthrow the government unlawfully, but to restrict or coerce voting through intimidation.

The statement argued that control of the state government did not require military means. It warned that to reorganize such a force as the extraordinary state guard would provoke, not prevent, a collision of the factions. Johnson and his fellow ex-generals pledged their influence to restrain the men formerly under their commands from resorting to violence and to persuade them to maintain order and peace. While they promised to support the laws, they said that they did so with the expectation that the lawmakers would "enact such measures to remove existing irritations," and they pointed out that there was bound to be dissatisfaction when a large mass of white men in the state were denied the right to vote and to hold office.[24]

Forrest gave dubious support to the position of his comrades. In a speech at Brownsville on August 10, he urged conservatives to rally to the generals' promises, but he denounced Brownlow and threatened personally to shoot Radical whites "if war comes."[25] Klan outrages continued.

President Andrew Johnson promised the use of Federal troops to protect the civil government. The legislators enacted the militia bill. For some time thereafter the state was quiet. A Democratic legislature in 1869 repealed the militia and anti-Klan laws. It ended disenfranchisement by the device of stating that every male citizen over 21 could vote on the question of electing delegates to a convention to draft a new state constitution. The convention was approved five to one. The new constitution was silent on denying the vote to rebels.[26]

Bushrod Johnson had no further active part in these events after his connection with the conciliation committee of July 1867. His was not the temperament to find pleasure or satisfaction in public controversy. His natural diffidence did not fit him for the raging arena of politics. In the past, a sense of outraged justice had propelled him into disputes over what he regarded as wrongs, such as credit for capture of the hospital at Stones River or the captured flags at Petersburg which earned him the hatred of Henry A. Wise. But generally, in quiet dignity, he went about his duties and occupations undramatically and without ostentation. For that reason there are fewer references to him in the chronicles of events in postwar Tennessee than can be found relating to more flamboyant characters.

He maintained his connection with some of his former cadets by correspondence. A few who lived for years after the war remembered his interest in those "who had been fine soldiers and who had done credit to their alma mater." Such a one was R. M. Tunno, Savannah, Georgia, who in 1906 quoted a letter received from Johnson in 1869.[27]

From Indiana in 1869 sad news came to Johnson of the tragic death of his nephew, Judge Nimrod Hoge Johnson, occupant of the Twenty-first Judicial Circuit bench since October 1868. The 48-year old jurist, returning from a visit to Indianapolis, halted in Cambridge City to visit his ailing mother, Sarah Hoge Johnson, 70. On her bedside table were several unlabeled bottles of medicine. One contained tincture of gentian, a mild stimulant tonic; another held aconite, a derivative of poisonous monk's hood or wolf bane, lethal in any quantity beyond a few diluted drops. The day was April 28, 1869.

Thinking to refresh himself after his trip with a swallow of gentian, the judge drank instead of the aconite. Within an hour he was dead in spite of frantic efforts of his father, Dr. Nathan, and his brother, Dr. Lemuel, to administer antidotes. He left a widow, Catherine Underwood Johnson, who never recovered from the shock before her death in 1904, and two sons, Henry Underwood Johnson, four times elected to Congress in the 1890s, and Robert Underwood Johnson, coeditor in the 1880s of *Battles and Leaders of the Civil War*.[28] A daughter, Clarissa, born of the judge's first marriage to Clarissa M. Ireland of New Paris, Ohio, also survived.[29] Nimrod and Bushrod had been teenage teachers together in the 1830s in Ohio.

How Johnson had adjusted to his straitened circumstances in postwar Nashville is revealed in a letter written to Richard Owen May 13, 1869.[30] Owen, professor of geology on the faculty of Indiana University since 1864, wrote Johnson in April asking for information on the status of his property in McGavock. Johnson made a careful study of the deed records and detailed the pertinent references in the Davidson County register's office. These involved some transfers, a suit for an unpaid note and an auction after a chancery court judgement. He described one transaction involving himself:

> I had to bid in one lot and pay lawyer's fee $50 and my share of cost to get any chance for my claim. I since sold the lot to a negroe [*sic*] and have not got even the first payment.

McGavock property values, he told Owen, were 33% or more lower than when the partners bought the tenth interest, but a proposed large cotton factory on Dr. McGavock's old home place, if built, might boost the prices. A new street railroad in McGavock had not helped the situation. He offered the services of Anderson, Johnson and Smith if Owen ever decided to sell.

Johnson expressed his pleasure at Owen's "comfortable position and of the satisfactory condition of your sons and of the evidences of general prosperity and happiness among all the members of your family. . . . I trust you will always have something bright for yourself and Mrs. Owen to look forward to."

Of himself he said "the most I have learned in the past is to place my enjoyment in action. I still look to the future for gratification in this and should not object to a modification in the form of foreign travel. I am first for making money, or trying to do so. It will give me action if it does not give me success: that is, the making of money."

He was trying several things, he said, among them a cement making plant due to begin operation in four weeks on the banks of the Tennessee River at Clifton in Wayne County where he also had an interest in a "bank of anhydrous oxide of iron" capable of being made into "an excellent paint of fine lustre and body" which he hoped to market.[31]

His son, Charley, he told Owen, had been in Crocker's school, "much better for him than the city," since his return from the North. He recalled to Owen that Crocker "used to send us some well-drilled scholars." "Charley is in excellent health and is a good boy without any bad habits as I thoroughly believe," he added. He told Owen of the tragic death of Judge Nimrod a fortnight earlier and said the rest of Dr. Nathan's family "are in their usual health."[32]

Owen apparently had asked Johnson if he intended changing his widower's status and to this Johnson replied:

> Your pleasant intelligence in regard to myself "is all but a dream at the best." I think of matrimony much as the old gentleman who was asked his advice on the subject. He replied "You will be sorry if you do and you will be sorry if you don't", and so I stand still by virtue of a sort of inertia. I have some very pleasant friends and love them with gravity and dignity becoming my years—and I find much happiness

in it—Why should I seek for more? Especially if I run the risks of killing the goose that lays the golden egg.[33] My kindest regards and best wishes to Mrs. Owen, yourself, your children and grandchcildren.

The nagging problem of the handicapped son to whom Johnson was devoted came up again in the spring of 1870. Owen was conscious of the harassed father's problem and he suggested Charley might come to live with his family and go to school in Indiana. The boy was restive and dissatisfied at Crocker's school. When Johnson wrote to Owen March 13, 1870 relative to a transfer of some of the McGavock property from him to Owen he asked Owen how much it would cost for boarding with the Owens and for tuition in school in Indiana.[34]

Johnson also revealed a soft-hearted attitude toward a couple owing notes to Owen on one of the lots. "I feel it is my duty to submit the whole matter to you," he wrote. "I know if the money is made out of them it will have to be done by law and greatly to their distress. . . . I confess I would dislike to attempt to make the collection by law and would rather return the notes and give you the property under any reasonable settlement."[35]

He recommended that Owen retain his lots "for some years yet" because he was convinced "Nashville will continue growing after a time" but if Owen wished to sell them and would indicate what prices he would accept, Johnson and his partners would try to market them. Deferential as always, Johnson wrote on the margin of the letter: "Please give me the usual titles by which you are addressed as I shall be pleased to observe them." He had been meticulously referring to Owen by his military rank of colonel.

Later in the year, on July 8, 1870, Johnson sold to Owen for $352.50 two small strips adjoining one of Owen's McGavock lots. Johnson had acquired these in a court action in May 1867. Johnson also bought and sold a few lots in what was called the Boyd Ament tract as guardian for his son.[36]

Although he did not take Owen into his confidence in the spring of 1870, Johnson was contemplating a return to the enterprise which had brought him the fullest success in his life—the military school—after five years of an uncertain livelihood in the real estate business. Conditions in the city and in Tennessee had become more stabilized. In May 1868 an exposé by the *Union and American* of the municipal financial skullduggery of the carpetbagger administration[37] had brought on litigation in courts uncontrolled by the regime and the Alden gang was ousted. The new state constitution restored the vote to former Confederates, many of whom now entered the lists for political office. The penalties of defeat were abating.

It seemed to be a time for trying to bring back something of the old days, to restore the well-loved ways of life and thought after a decade of nightmare. This improved ambience, Johnson felt, offered a chance to revive the school he had left in 1861, this time with a prestigious associate, one of the Confederacy's eight full generals, Edmund Kirby Smith.

ii. The Generals' School Surrenders

Edmund Kirby Smith floundered around without success trying to make a living for more than four years after he surrendered the last Confederate force, the Trans-Mississippi Department, to Union Major General Edward R. S. Canby at Galveston, Texas on May 26, 1865. Fearful of arrest he fled first to Mexico, then to Cuba. Back in the South in the fall, the forty-one-year old 1845 graduate of West Point cast about for something to do which would provide for his steadily increasing family and would be commensurate with the exalted dignity he had achieved in the rebel army.

Still unemployed in June 1866 in Lynchburg, Virginia, Smith decided to try his luck in either Kentucky or Tennessee. First he went to Washington, obtained Grant's signature on his parole, visited relatives in Baltimore and then traveled to Louisville, late in June. He was warmly welcomed there by the ex-Confederate element in the business world, who introduced him to those who might help him and then deluged him with advice. He pondered going into the commission business in Louisville or Cincinnati or trying something else in Memphis or New Orleans. The latter he ruled out as too unhealthy for his children.[38]

Finally he made up his mind and accepted the presidency of the Accident Insurance Co., of Louisville. His wife and two daughters joined him in August. A son, named for the father, was born soon afterward.

The insurance enterprise failed. Smith then tried the presidency of the Atlantic and Pacific Telegraph Co., which struggled for a year and died in 1868. His next venture was a military academy in New Castle, Kentucky,[39] in Henry County where to Drennon's Lick in 1851, Bushrod Johnson and Richard Owen had brought Western Military Institute. Before his school had a chance to taste any prosperity it was razed by a fire in 1869. Ex-General E. Kirby Smith must begin again.[40]

On the hunt anew for a means of livelihood, Smith came to Nashville and in the course of time he met and talked with Bushrod Johnson. They had not had much previous association. Johnson was gone from the U.S. Military Academy before Smith entered as a plebe in 1841 from Florida. Johnson was on commissary duty in Vera Cruz when Smith was winning brevets in battle at Cerro Gordo and Contreras in the Mexican War. In Bragg's invasion of Kentucky in 1862 their paths would have crossed only during the retreat and thereafter not at all because Smith went to the Trans-Mississippi Department.

As a neophyte in the school operating business, Smith sought the counsel of Johnson, more experienced, possessing contacts and cognizant of conditions in Tennessee. Fortune and circumstance were playing into their hands.

In 1855, the will of Montgomery Bell, the Tennessee iron master, left $20,000 to the trustees of the University of Nashville for the support of a school for boys. The money was invested but not used at the time, for two reasons. The university had Johnson's military academy as a going concern for its literary or collegiate department and the sum was deemed inadequate to operate another, separate school.[41] Presently the war brought a disastrous interlude.

Dr. J. Berrien Lindsley, chancellor of the University of Nashville before and during the war, failed to resuscitate the collegiate department of the university, which in 1867 was operating only a medical college. The university's board of trustees included both Unionists and ex-Confederates such as John Bell, 1860 candidate for president and later secessionist; John W. Bass, wealthy plantation owner and son-in-law of Felix Grundy; John M. Lea, friend of Andrew Johnson and prewar member; Edwin A. Ewing and Francis B. Fogg, Unionists.[42] Bushrod Johnson was favorably known to most of these, not as an ex-general so much as an educator of some success before the war.

By 1867 the Montgomery Bell bequest had grown to $46,000. With this money the university trustees set up Montgomery Bell Academy with a seven-year course of three years' elementary studies and four years' high school. Tuition was set at $60 and $80 respectively. Still chancellor of the university, Lindsley was named in June 1868 as the academy's professor of chemistry. W. S. Snow was chosen principal of the academy at an annual salary of $2500 and was given two assistants at $2000 each. The university owed Lindsley $12,000 in unpaid back salary, $837 for money advanced by him to start the academy and other claims for a grand total of $14,931. The trustees settled with him for $11,891 in October 1868.[43]

Lindsley's heart was set on reviving an undergraduate collegiate department of the university like the one he had set up in 1855. In July 1869 he proposed to the trustees that the academy, which seemed destined to grow, be enlarged into a college. The trustees vetoed the idea. He refused to drop the project, convinced that the university must be something more than a medical college if it were to continue to survive.

Lindsley thought he had the answer to his dream in Bushrod Johnson, friend and associate of long standing, and General Edmund Kirby Smith, whose name and rank carried distinction. The ex-generals proposed in a letter dated April 30, 1870 to reopen the literary or collegiate department of the university as a military school and operate Montgomery Bell Academy as a preparatory school. They asked tenure for fifteen years and the right to name their staff. When the trustees met on May 11, they were dubious at first and inclined to reject the proposal.[44]

Offering to give up his chancellorship, Lindsley put his support vigorously behind Smith and Johnson. He drafted a recommendation to the trustees and when they delayed their usual meeting, he got his views into print in the *Republican Banner* issue of May 25, 1870. He said the board faced a situation similar to that of 1855 when Western Military Institute was added to the university. Large and valuable college buildings, he said, were "situated within the limits of a wealthy, refined and growing city" but the income was "not sufficient to pay one-half the salary of the head of the institution" [the Chancellor] and "utterly inadequate even to the keeping in repair of its large and costly buildings and to the proper caring of its libraries, apparatus, etc. It has always depended and must for years continue to depend upon tuition fees for the payment of its corps of teachers."

All the risk in the generals' proposal, he said "is to be borne by the two distinguished gentlemen who propose to conduct a great school under your charter and with your cooperation." The only guarantee they demanded "is that they shall continue in their professorships for the short period of 15 years instead of being at the pleasure of the board and that they shall have the right to nominate their coadjutors and associate teachers in the school."

He made the prestige of Smith and the experience of Johnson his strongest selling points. His characterization of Johnson is an interesting appraisal:

> [Johnson] has so long been a resident of Nashville and is so well known as identified with collegiate instruction, that it is hardly necessary to detail his antecedents. In early life, he earned, by teaching, the means which enabled him to prepare for West Point where he received a thorough scientific training, which characterizes the U.S. Military Academy. For a period of 13 years previous to 1861 he was engaged in the work of an educator. He thus became personally acquainted with large classes of young men from the entire valley of the Mississippi. As a governor of boys and young men, the difficult work in all colleges, he made a high reputation.
>
> Retiring and perhaps diffident when appearing in public, slow and cautious in his utterances, he has doubtless been too lightly appreciated by the careless or prejudiced observer. Amid the excitement of the battlefield, his rare powers of command and discipline have been fully acknowledged. Calm, conscientious, unflinching and firm in the discharge of irksome and onerous duty, he has unfailingly won the confidence and respect, no less than the esteem, of many who have been associated with him, or have been under his care as pupils.[45]

After some compromising between the generals and the

trustees, Lindsley convinced enough of the board to accept their proposition by a vote of 11 to 7 on June 11.[46] The modifications provided that the trustees would select and pay the salaries of the faculty and would reserve the right to approve the course of study and methods of discipline. They would furnish, rent-free, buildings and necessary apparatus. The 15-year tenure of Johnson and Smith was agreed upon. Smith was elected Chancellor and Johnson was named principal of the collegiate department and professor of applied mathematics and engineering.[47]

Having accomplished what he set out to do, Lindsley dropped out of the picture. Chancellor since 1855, he had endured and survived the struggles and disappointments of the years of war and reconstruction and at the moment when it seemed he might begin to have things his way, he resigned June 6. He continued to teach in the medical school in which he was dean of the faculty and later he joined the Nashville city school system and engaged in public health work. He had a long career in both.[48]

Johnson and Smith worked feverishly through the summer of 1870 to get the school ready to open in September. A subscription campaign among Nashville residents raised $7000 as a starting fund for repairs and furniture.[49] The revenue of the Bell bequest was to pay the tuition of twenty-five academy pupils, the remainder to be pooled with other university revenues to maintain buildings and equipment. The literary or collegiate department, as in 1855–1861, resumed a military system but with less emphasis.[50]

Chancellor Smith was also named professor of natural history and geology on the faculty of the literary department. Later political economy and agriculture were added as his courses. Principal Johnson had additional tasks as treasurer of the university. A. D. Wharton was principal of the academy and professor of mathematics in the literary department. S. M. Clark was principal of the grammar school. There were also professors of Greek, Latin, physics and chemistry. W. A. Obenchain was commandant of cadets and professor of modern languages. Dr. Charles K. Winston, who had been surgeon of Western Military Institute in 1858–1861, again was named surgeon.[51]

As the first term got under way in September 1870, the academy with 239 students overshadowed the literary department with 32 cadets. Medicine and law totalled 211, making 482 overall for the 1870–1871 school year.[52] Among the students in the academy was Johnson's son, Charley, past seventeen years old. Smith moved his family, with a new baby girl, to the campus after classes began.[53] They lived in the President's House.

Tuition for college and academy boarders for twenty weeks ran from $150 to $175 with uniforms and books extra. Day students paid $12.50 for primary and $50 for college.[54] In the revived Order Book and Register of antebellum Western Military Institute now appeared familiar names of cadets such as Donelson, Robertson, McGavock, Cheatham, Pillow and Anderson. The disciplinary problems also had an accustomed ring: pranks, drinking and disobedience.[55]

Time and events had turned full circle for Johnson, now in his mid-fifties. Five years after the disrupting war he was again a schoolmaster, engaged in the habitual scenes of his hopeful progress of 1855–1861 and living in the same milieu he had occupied so briefly with his beloved Mary.

But this time there was a striking difference. Where he had formerly been the dominant force, even in his partnership with Owen, Johnson now was definitely in a subordinate role. The figure and personality of Edmund Kirby Smith held the spotlight from the very first. When the *Republican Banner* on September 29, 1870 hailed the opening of the revived university as "an ornament to the state" with "a new law department added to the collegiate and medical" schools, "with grounds and buildings renovated and the finest corps of instructors" all credit was given to "the conductorship of the able and experienced Chancellor." In subsequent news stories about school commencements, exercises and social events in the *Republican Banner* and the *Union and American* during the next three years, Johnson's name usually was missing while Smith's invariably appeared.

Neither general, however, was listed as participating in the community memorial meeting held in the Davidson County courthouse on October 15, 1870 to eulogize General Robert E. Lee, whose death on October 12, was marked by turned column rules on the *Republican Banner's* editorial page. But the next day, Sunday October 16, a gathering of ex-Confederates at the courthouse elected Smith vice president of the meeting and he, Cheatham, and Bate were among the speakers honoring Lee. Johnson was not noted as being present.[56]

Success was scanty for the two generals as the first term closed with Chancellor Smith awarding diplomas to two graduates.[57] The trustees voted $855 to Smith and Johnson on May 6, 1871,[58] which may have meant that each had only $427.50 for his year's labors in addition to free lodging in the President's House and free food at the cadet mess. Johnson did not get, as in prewar days, the profits of sales to the students from the shops and stores. Smith's family increased one child annually and he had the additional expense of sending them to Virginia during the malaria and cholera outbreaks which periodically menaced life in Nashville.[59]

The second term, starting September 1871, saw about the same total number of students, most in the academy, and less than three dozen cadets in the collegiate department—fewer than a fair-sized classroomful. Only 161 academy and collegiate department students signed the historical Register, among them, Charles C. Johnson, still a high school student at nineteen years old.[60] In November the trustees voted two payments of $860 and $875 to Smith and Johnson, which may have been the sum total of their remuneration for the school year 1871–1872. They were not voted any more money until July 1872.[61]

For a brief interval in January 1872 there was a moment of recollected glory for the two ex-generals. The occasion was the funeral of Lieutenant General Richard S. Ewell, 1840 classmate of Johnson, who died at his wife's home, Spring Hill, Tennessee on January 25. Johnson and Smith were among the pallbearers, who included ex-General John Calvin Brown, now Tennessee's governor, ex-Generals Anderson, Bate, Maney, Cheatham, W. H. Jackson, Beverly H. Robertson and Robert Doak Lilley of Virginia, once commander of Ewell's old brigade of the Second Corps. Bishop Charles Todd Quintard, Connecticut-born physician-chaplain to the corps of Leonidas Polk, conducted the service in Christ Episcopal Church and the body was escorted to the Old City Cemetery where fourteen years before Johnson stood beside the grave of his wife. Then the ex-Confederates assembled at the Maxwell House with Smith as chairman and Johnson as secretary to draft the customary resolutions of eulogy and condolence for the Ewell family.[62] It was a time for sad reminiscing about shared experiences and days of glory.

At the end of the term in June 1872, Chancellor Smith talked frankly to the trustees. He told them more than $8000 had been spent on building repairs and $6430 had been paid on back debts, but that little progress had been made in expanding enrollment. He urged doubling the student body in the academy which had been carrying the load for the rest of the university since 1870 because of its income from the Bell endowment. He advocated an effort for closer cooperation with the state, saying the University of Nashville was a "gift to all the people of Tennessee." The trustees listened politely, but did nothing.[63]

The commencement festivities were subordinated in the newspapers to the alumni meeting held at the same time, June 13. Judge John D. Phelan, a student in 1827, was the star of the event and the *Republican Banner* devoted four and a half columns to his reminiscences. Chancellor Smith came in for praise in the article, but Johnson was not mentioned.[64]

Two calamities struck the school in the 1872–1873 term. The nationwide depression of 1873 utterly disrupted land values in the South and put additional crimps on the resources of Southern families likely to send their sons to benefit from the tutelage of the former Confederate generals. Some students among the tiny cadet corps had to quit and return home. Then, at the end of the term, as at Johnson's school in 1849, a cholera epidemic scourged Nashville. The malady prevented any school commencement.[65] More than 1000 persons died on "Black Friday," June 20.[66]

There had been some futile tinkering with the collegiate department's curriculum in the 1872–1873 term. The military aspects were deemphasized. The class system was abolished and an elective organization substituted. A student could pick any of at least three two-year courses in Latin, Greek, French, German, English, mental philosophy and political economy, pure mathematics, chemical and natural philosophy, natural history, geology and engineering. Johnson's memory might have gone back to 1858 and his differences with Owen then over the military system versus the liberalized theories of his former partner. He was now, in fact, adopting some of Owen's ideas which he formerly had opposed to the point of no return and the severance of their prosperous association. The reformed curriculum produced only confusion and none of the new students it was designed to attract.[67]

In January 1873 the trustees voted their last payment

of record to Smith and Johnson, the sum of $907 to be divided and an extra $40 to Smith alone.[68] From September 1870 to June 1873, the generals had received a total of $4807, or $2400 apiece for three years' efforts. There was no prospect of any improvement. Smith made another "frank" statement to the trustees on May 30, 1873, suggesting the possibility of obtaining Federal land grant funds under the Morrill Act if the university were made into an agricultural and mechanical college such as were being established in many other states. The trustees again took no action and Smith's name disappears thereafter in the minutes of their meetings.[69]

The disastrous effects of the economic depression of 1873 and the summer cholera epidemic were reflected in the enrollment for the 1873–1874 term. The academy drew only 153, of whom 88 signed the Register, including Charles C. Johnson, now twenty years old and still in high school. Only thirty-one cadets entered the collegiate department.[70] It was brutally apparent that the school was doomed without outside financial help. Less than two miles away, in September, the foundation was laid for the first building of Vanderbilt University,[71] to which went the Medical Department of the University of Nashville in April 1874. With the loss of this long-enduring core of the University of Nashville, the deterioration of the generals' school was accelerated. Principal Johnson signed the last order in the old Western Military Institute Order Book on October 24, 1873, promoting Cadet R. Cheatham to corporal and adding a regulation that a permit from the principal was required by each cadet in the platoon-sized corps before absenting himself from any duty.[73] What was to be the last commencement was held in the Tennessee Hall of Representatives in the capitol June 11, 1874. Chancellor Smith conferred degrees on eight graduates: one Master of Arts, one Bachelor of Arts, three Bachelors of

Science and three civil engineers. If Johnson had any part in the program it was ignored by the *Republican Banner's* reporter.[74]

Outside financial help came to the university a few months later, but paradoxically when it arrived it ended the school as then operated. In January 1875, the trustees met with Dr. Barnas Sears, president of Brown University and general agent of the $2,000,000 fund set up by George Peabody, Massachusetts-born London banker, to advance education in the South. Sears suggested that money would be available for operation of a normal school for teachers rather than to shore up the tottering current operation of the University of Nashville.[75]

At the request of the trustees, the Tennessee legislature amended the charter of the University of Nashville to permit them to discontinue the strictly "literary or collegiate" functions and install a "scientific school" for instruction in botany, chemistry and metallurgy. The change also enabled them to arrange with the Peabody Fund for setting up a normal school for teachers. The end result was establishment of State Normal College with Eben S. Stearns of Massachusetts as president in the fall of 1875. It took over the buildings and grounds of the defunct university. This institution later was known as Peabody Normal School and today flourishes as the George Peabody College for Teachers in another location. Montgomery Bell Academy, continuing to enjoy the fruits of the iron master's bequest of 1855 proceeded on its separate and successful way. It perpetuates the University of Nashville in its legal status and carries the university's seal beside its own on its documents.[76]

These arrangements finished the University of Nashville. Bushrod Johnson and Kirby Smith sank with the wreckage. With his constantly increasing family, Smith left for the University of the South at Sewanee, where the former chief of ordnance of the Confederacy, Pennsylvanian Josiah Gorgas, West Point '41, was vice chancellor. For the eighteen years of life left to him, Smith remained at Sewanee teaching mathematics and looking after his family which eventually numbered eleven children.[77]

For Bushrod Johnson, 58 years old, the death blow to the university was calamitous. During its revival of four years he had derived at best a small and precarious income and had been forced to liquidate what was left of his real estate holdings in McGavock and Nashville. Any return to the real estate business which had scarcely sustained him between 1866 and 1870 was precluded by his own advancing age and the fact that his former associates, Anderson and Granville Smith, now 71 and 60 respectively, had separate new interests.[78]

In the summer of 1874 Johnson cleared up his affairs connected with the school and convinced himself that no further opportunity for recuperation remained. Reluctantly he made the decision to leave Nashville and fall back on his resources elsewhere. These included 320 acres of unimproved prairie land in Osage County, Kansas, south of Topeka, bought in 1859.[79] Johnson probably had never seen this property and it had little value or attraction as a place of refuge now. Then there was the farmland in Macoupin County, Illinois, purchased in 1860 from his niece, Ruth, and her husband, Alfred Williams, and paid off during the war. Johnson may never have visited this place either. It had been operated by a succession of tenants for fifteen years.

Johnson elected to go to neither of these places. Instead he opted to take Charles with him to St. Louis and enter the commission business in July 1874. It was a curious decision. He had no experience in this merchandising activity, he had no circle of acquaintances nor ex-associates in St. Louis and his reticent personality certainly did not fit him for salesmanship. He could hardly have believed his duties as a commissary in Mexico nearly thirty years previously gave him any qualifications. But he rented a residence in the 1000 block of Pine Street[80] and from it he conducted a precarious enterprise for six months which diminished further his slender resources. In November he was compelled to sell, at a loss, his last remaining property in Nashville.[81] The deal severed his last link to Nashville and to Tennessee.

To cut the ties which had grown for two decades must have been a difficult resolve. More than Ohio of his boyhood or Indiana of his mature years, Nashville had been his home. What fleeting financial success he had ever enjoyed had come to him there. The brief happiness and heartbreak of his marriage were identified with the city's familiar places. His failures and defeats, except for the final wreck of the university, had befallen him elsewhere in foreign scenes and amid people to whom he was a stranger. Acceptance, position and stature had been his portion in Tennessee. It must have wrung the heart of Bushrod Johnson to leave Nashville with the saddening realization that he might never return.

Notes

1. *Rule,* p. 37.
2. *Robert Johnson,* p. 13.
3. *Young,* p. 268.
4. See *supra,* Chapter Seven, references to newspaper stories after Johnson's walkaway at Fort Donelson.
5. *U.S. Census,* Belmont County, Ohio, 1860 and 1870.
6. *Minute Books,* I says Union occupancy began February 12, 1862. This is an error. The last Confederate forces did not leave Nashville until Sunday, February 23 and the Federals first appeared in Edgefield February 24. The departure date, September 11, 1865 is in *Minute Books,* I, p. 182.
7. John Trotwood Moore and Austin P. Foster, *Tennessee, The Volunteer State,* (Chicago: S. J. Clarke Publishing Co., 1923), p. 526.
8. *Ibid.,* p. 529.
9. *Tennessee Guide,* p. 185.
10. *Warner,* p. 10.

11. Data from genealogy of Smith family by Mrs. Jeff McCarn, furnished by reference library, Tennessee State Library.
12. *Berry Salter & Co., Business Directory for 1866–67,* (Louisville: n. p., 1866); *King's Nashville City Directory,* (Nashville: n. p., 1867); Information from Covington, Ky., city directories supplied by Mary Ann Morgan, librarian, Kenton County, Ky., Public Library.
13. Macoupin County, Ill., *Deed Record,* Vol. RR, pp. 358, 360.
14. Pay and forage vouchers and claims for slain horses in *B. R. Johnson File* in CSA Staff Papers.
15. Johnson's original copy, April 23, 1867 in Miscellaneous Collection, Tennessee Archives; information from Wyman Hoefer, circuit clerk, Doniphan, Missouri.
16. Johnson's original copy, July 16, 1867 in Miscellaneous Collection, Tennessee Archives.
17. Davidson County, Tennessee, *Deed Record,* Book 38, p. 509.
18. *Ibid.,* Book 38, p. 663.
19. Letter, Johnson to Richard Owen, May 13, 1869 in Business Papers, Folder No. 4, *Owen Papers.* Croker's school had elementary grades only.
20. *King's Nashville City Directory* 1868, p. 146.
21. U.S., Congress, *House Docs.,* 40 Cong., 1 Sess., pp. 570–572.
22. Philip A. Hamer, *Tennessee, A History* (New York: American History Society Inc., 1933) 4 vols. IV, pp. 636 ff.
23. *Moore and Foster,* p. 539, says ten ex-generals participated; *Hamer,* IV, p. 637, says thirteen, adding Joseph B. Palmer, George W. Gordon and Thomas B. Smith.
24. *Hamer,* IV, p. 638.
25. *Ibid.,* p. 639.
26. *Ibid.,* p. 650; *Moore and Foster,* p. 550.
27. *CV,* XIV, p. 109.
28. Richmond, Indiana *Palladium,* April 29, 1869; *Young,* p. 269.
29. *U.S. Census,* Cambridge City, Indiana, 1870.
30. Letter, Johnson to Owen, May 13, 1869 cited *supra,* n. 19.
31. These projects did not materialize. Johnson sold the properties for $1 to Narcissus P. Sanders on September 17, 1875, Wayne County, Tennessee *Deed Register,* Book M, p. 409.
32. Mrs. Nathan Johnson died in March 1871 and Dr. Nathan in January 1872. (Tombstones in Johnson lot, Old Capitol Hill Cemetery, Cambridge City, Indiana).
33. What Johnson was trying to convey by this cryptic phrase is not clear.
34. Letter, Johnson to Owen, May 13, 1870 cited *supra.*
35. *Ibid.*
36. Davidson County, Tennessee, *Deed Record,* Book 38, pp. 509, 663; Book 43, p. 526.
37. Nashville *Union and American,* issues of May and June, 1868.
38. Joseph H. Parks, *General Edmund Kirby Smith,* (Baton Rouge: Louisiana State University Press, 1954), pp. 495 f.
39. *Ibid.*
40. *Ibid.*
41. *Rule,* pp. 33 f. Bell owned or hired 400 slaves to work his foundries whose special product was a huge iron kettle used extensively in Louisiana's sugar refining industry.
42. *Hamer,* IV, pp. 659–673.

43. *Minute Books,* I, p. 223; *Howell,* pp. 44 f.; *Rule,* p. 38.
44. *Minute Books,* I, p. 254; *Parks,* p. 497; *Howell,* pp. 45 f.; *Rule,* pp. 38 f.
45. *Minute Books,* I, p. 258; Text also in John Berrien Lindsley "The Present Conditions and Prospects of the University", quoted in J. E. Windrow, *John Berrien Lindsley,* (Chapel Hill: University of North Carolina Press, 1938), p. 54.
46. *Minute Books,* I, p. 275.
47. *Ibid.,* p. 269; *Parks,* p. 498; *Rule,* p. 42.
48. *Minute Books,* I, p. 267; *Rule,* p. 42.
49. *Howell,* p. 51.
50. *Rule,* p. 43.
51. *Catalogue of the University of Nashville, 1870–1871,* (Nashville: Paul and Tarvel, 1871), p. 4.
52. *Ibid.,* p. 23; *Register,* September 14, 1870.
53. *Parks,* p. 498.
54. *Catalogue,* 1870–71, p. 27. Lucius Salisbury Merriam, *Higher Education in Tennessee,* (Washington: Government Printing Office, 1893), p. 51.
55. *Order Book,* entries for September and October 1870; *Register,* signers in September 1870.
56. *Republican Banner,* September 29; October 13, 15, 16, 1870; June 10, 16, 1871; February 23, June 3, 12, 14, 1872; *Union and American,* February 28, June 14, 1872.
57. *Republican Banner, Union and American,* June 16, 1871. Johnson was not mentioned in the news story of the commencement nor the alumni meeting afterward.
58. *Minute Books,* I, p. 296.
59. *Parks,* p. 498.
60. *Register,* September 1871. Some students who returned subsequently to signing the pledge of honor did not do so again. Among new signers were Edwin A. Tooke, 22, ward of General S. B. Buckner of Louisville, Ky., James Alleson Maney, son of General George E. Maney, and ex-Chancellor Lindsley's 13-year old son, John.
61. *Minute Books,* I, p. 296. There is an unexplained gap in this record from June 1870 to June 1872. Figures given here are from a report of A. Van Lindsley, M.D., treasurer of the trustees, made April 23, 1873. He was a brother of John Berrien Lindsley.
62. Nashville *Banner,* January 26, 1872; *Union and American,* January 25, 27, 1872.
63. *Minute Books,* I, p. 282.
64. *Republican Banner, Union and American,* June 14, 1872.
65. *Republican Banner,* June 12, 1873.
66. *Tennessee Guide,* p. 185.
67. *Merriam,* p. 51; *Union and American,* June 14, 1872.
68. *Minute Books,* I, p. 296.
69. *Ibid.,* pp. 300 ff.
70. *Register,* September 1873.
71. *Republican Banner,* September 16, 1873.
72. *Howell,* p. 56.
73. *Order Book,* October 24, 1873.
74. *Republican Banner,* June 12, 1874.

75. *Howell*, p. 56; *Rule*, p. 46.
76. *Parks*, p. 499; *Rule*, p. 46.
77. *Warner*, p. 112, pp. 279 f.
78. *Nashville City Directory 1874*, p. 349.
79. Osage County, Kansas *Deed Book* A, p. 127.
80. *St. Louis, Mo., Directory, 1875*. Data supplied by Reference Department, St. Louis Public Library, July 30, 1968.
81. Statement in letter, Johnson to Owen, June 25, 1875 in Business Papers, Folder No. 4, *Owen Papers*.

12

LAST DAYS AMONG STRANGERS

i. Cold Welcome for a Rebel General

Many of the 1875 residents of Macoupin County, Illinois, which lies midway between Springfield and St. Louis, had roots that went back to the upper South: Kentucky, Tennessee, Virginia and Maryland. But there had been no question of their loyalty to the Union in 1861. When President Lincoln called for volunteers, the young men of the area responded enthusiastically. So, too, did older leaders of the county's towns and hamlets, who left their families to learn the craft of arms and to take places at the heads of companies and regiments.

The 122nd Illinois Volunteer Infantry was recruited around Carlinville, the county seat, by an ex-Marylander, John Irving Rinaker, 31-year old lawyer. In the southwest corner of the county, Jonathan Rice Miles, native of Kentucky with a North Carolina father reared in Tennessee, had an active part in raising the Twenty-seventh Illinois, though he was 44 years old with three children and had business interests jeopardized by his departure.[1]

Many who left their homes never returned. They died in battles of the Army of the Tennessee at Chickamauga, Chattanooga or in fighting Hood around Atlanta. Others came home mutilated, broken or suffering ailments which, in time, killed them. Their families did not forget and were slow to forgive. Eleven years is not long enough for acceptance of sudden bereavement, nor reconciliation with aching grief, nor toleration of an abhorrent cause.

So there was some resentment and animosity when the story got around in January 1875 that a "rebel general" with a 22-year old son who was "odd" had come from St. Louis to live in the small house on the 191-acre farm next to John Andrews, three miles north of Brighton on the Jacksonville-Alton state road.[2] The general's place was in low repute in the neighborhood anyhow. The busy and thrifty farmers of the community looked askance at its tenants who were Henry A. Roundtree, 30; his wife, Elizabeth Haworth Roundtree, 32; her brother, William Haworth, 17; and her sister, Ida M. Haworth, 14. Folks around Brighton and Miles's Station, two miles away, regarded the family as shiftless, interested mostly in what they could take from the land and its owner, while letting buildings and equipment deteriorate, fields grow up in weeds, fences go unmended and animals badly attended.[3]

The opposite was the rule on the Andrews property. Joseph Andrews, son of a Revolutionary War soldier, who moved from Virginia to Todd County, Kentucky in 1817, came to Illinois in 1830 with his Virginia-born wife, Susan Ellis, and their seven sons. He took up 960 acres of land, some of it in adjoining Jersey County. His son, John, born in Sussex County, Virginia, south of Petersburg in 1815, was operating 400 prosperous acres in 1875 next to Bushrod Johnson's shabby and unkempt menage.[4]

John Andrews married Martha, sister of Jonathan Miles, born in Logan County, Kentucky, near the Tennessee border. Their eldest surviving son, among five children, was Hobart Miles Andrews, who enlisted in the 122nd Illinois. He survived its battles but contracted fever while on duty in Mobile, made no recovery in a New Orleans hospital and was mustered out in August 1865. He came home to die in December.[5]

His father never got over Hobart's death. He blamed it on the war and regarded Confederates and their cause as responsible for his loss. His surviving son, John Edward, had been too young to fight. John was the same age as Bushrod Johnson's afflicted Charles and had been attending Blackburn College in Carlinville[6] at the time the Johnsons came to the adjoining farm.

Some sufferance of Johnson's presence came eventually among his neighbors. It was born of pity for the son's condition and tolerance for the father's inept lack of initiative to improve the situation in his household. But they never could understand why a man who had the capacity to become a general could be so trusting of employees who were victimizing him. Johnson came to know Colonel Jonathan Miles, whose deceased wife, Eliza Stratton, had come from Robertson County, Tennessee, north of Nashville. Miles's Twenty-seventh Illinois had fought in some of the same battles as Johnson. He had been on furlough at Stones River, but at Chickamauga his regiment was in Sheridan's Division when Johnson's troops touched off the rout on the Union right. Miles also had marched to the relief of Knoxville in the same 1863 campaign fought by Johnson under Longstreet. The two ex-enemies, both born in 1817, had many notes to compare. Miles was regarded as well-to-do, owning a $28,000 flour mill at Miles' Station where he persuaded the Chicago and Alton Railroad to build a depot. In the 1870 census, his total worth was listed at $43,000.[7]

Johnson also became acquainted with Rinaker who had risen to brevet brigadier general, had been severely wounded at Parkers Crossroads and fought in the XVI Corps in the Army of the Tennessee.[8] It is ironical that Ohio Confederate Johnson's friends in his last days in a hostile environment were two Union ex-officers born in slave states.

With young John Andrews on the adjacent farm, Johnson formed a satisfying relationship. The young man's avid interest in widening his education appealed to the former schoolmaster. Johnson had managed to bring from Tennessee some of the library he had accumulated over the years and to young Andrews he loaned books on history, mathematics, science and engineering. When the books were returned, Johnson would quiz Andrews and discuss their contents with him. The friendly young neighbor provided the father of a stricken son with an agreeable substitute companion. The elder Andrews, however, never reconciled himself to the proximity of the "rebel general."[9]

Johnson allowed himself the illusion that his stay on the rundown farm was only temporary. He cherished the dream that sometime soon he would profit from some new enterprise and could move to a garden spot on the Pacific Coast "amid orange groves, vineyards and banana orchards" where he could "enjoy the sea breeze and look out on the good old ocean." Thus he confided to Owen in a letter in July 1875. Owen, unaware of the collapse of the school and Johnson's removal from Nashville, had written in June to Johnson in Nashville, asking about the McGavock property. The letter was forwarded to Brighton. Owen was then in Bloomington, Indiana teaching geology in Indiana University again after two controversial years (1872–1874) as the first president of Purdue University.

Johnson told his former partner of leaving Nashville and spending six months in St. Louis in the commission business with which, he said, he "became dissatisfied." He said the farm to which he had come six months previously "has been neglected, although valuable in a fine country" where he would "abide at least for a time" while he cleared up "other old interests before I make any more combinations or complications." He told of selling his McGavock lots, but purchasers "have failed to meet their obligation" to pay deferred payments, and he warned Owen that "hard times and scarcity of money" might adversely affect Owen's chances to sell his own Nashville lots.

Of his son, Charley, Johnson said he "does not look to be robust, but is rarely really sick. He has improved in strength since he has been on the farm. He and I set out this spring about one mile of hedge and have been attending to it since. It has been quite a tedious job. We propose to hold on to this place as a retreat from unfortunate adventures."

He hoped, he said, to sell all his property, "so that we can put everything else in our pockets and seek a desirable location in the West. . . . I may yet anchor on the shores of the Pacific. . . . You know that as long as there is any of the spice of life in us we must still have our pleasant anticipations and amount of happiness."[10]

Obviously, Johnson was putting his situation in the best possible light for the eyes of his former colleague. The farm hardly broke even with six persons dependent upon it. Past sixty years old in 1878, Johnson was feeling the effects of the tropical fevers he had survived at thirty and the privations and hardships of the trenches at forty-eight. With diminishing vigor he compelled himself to direct and assist in the farm work, with which he had little experience since the 1820 days in Ohio. Modern residents of the area recall stories of their grandsires about Johnson peddling fence posts, cut on his place, to his neighbors during the late 1870s. Straitened circumstances forced him to sell half of his Kansas property for $800 in 1878.[11] Three years previously he had received one dollar for his cement plant enterprise in Clifton, Tennessee.

He made at least one trip back to Tennessee. Probably in late 1879 he was the guest of his former student and one-time adjutant, ex-Colonel Robert Bogardus Snowden, who had settled in Memphis after a five-year residence in New York after the surrender. Snowden had been highly successful in land, railroads, insurance and industry and lived in a showplace plantation home "Annesdale" near Memphis.[12]

Snowden described the visit to the *Confederate Veteran* in 1906, when he commissioned an artist, Cornelius Hankins, to paint a portrait of Johnson which Snowden presented to the Tennessee Historical Society. It was unveiled with ceremony by Sumner Cunningham, editor of the southern veteran's magazine, and was hung initially in the library of the George Peabody College for Teachers. It is now displayed in the Confederate Room of the Tennessee State Museum. Snowden wrote in 1906:

> He was at my house "Annesdale" just before he died. I gave him a dining and many old Confederates were present. We kept up the affair until morning. Only myself is now living. He then spoke of going back to Mexico and investing in some enterprise in that country.

Mexico was no more than another of Johnson's "pleasant anticipations" like the Pacific Coast he mentioned to Owen in 1875. He was back in Illinois in the spring of 1880. His health was bad. Then on April 10, 1880 (if credence can be placed in the date given in the 1906 *Confederate Veteran*), mentally incompetent Charles, 27, and Ida Haworth, 18, were married.[13] There is no record of any license issued in Macoupin County. When the 1880 U.S. Census tabulation was made three months later in July, the couple was listed as having a month-old son, Alonzo Haworth Johnson. The conclusion is inescapable that the tenant family, noting the progressive decline of Bushrod Johnson and counting on his habitual unassertiveness, made sure the property would not pass from their hands at his death by contriving a "shotgun wedding" situation. The daughter of John Edward Andrews, who operated her father's farm until 1958, told this writer that her father felt Charles's incapacity had been taken advantage of by deliberately compromising him with the girl at a time when Bushrod either was absent or too ill or too indecisive to frustrate the sordid plot. A year later, at Charles's death, a further incident occurred which testified to the mercenary motives involved in the relationship.

Sometime in the summer of 1880, Johnson was stricken by a cerebral hemorrhage and left paralyzed. Scarcely aware or totally unaware of passing events, and probably casually cared for, he lingered for several weeks. Dr. F. A. Clement of Brighton attended him. Death came September 12, 1880. He was twenty-five days less than sixty-three years old.

Unaccountably, Dr. Clement dated the death certificate September 10, 1881, incorrect both as to day and year.[14] Courthouse attachés in Carlinville explain that physicians in 1880, because of the distance over dirt roads from the county seat, often waited for months before filing death certificates and Clement may have misdated the paper accidentally.

In Nashville, the passing of a once-familiar figure went almost unnoticed, although only five years had gone by since his departure. Only the *Nashville Banner,* on September 15, printed three sentences in the fifth column of an inside page:

DEATH OF BUSHROD JOHNSON

> A telegraphic dispatch received last night chronicles the death of Maj. Gen. Bushrod Johnson, formerly a well known citizen of this place. For several years past he has been a resident of Brighton, Ill., at which place he died. General Johnson was a distinguished officer in the Confederate Army and had a host of friends throughout the entire South.[15]

No former comrades or associates among this "host of

friends" gathered in his erstwhile home to pass resolutions of respect or condolence characteristic of the era. The Nashville *Daily American* ignored the obituary entirely. Swiftly, Bushrod Johnson had passed from the memories of his former townsmen.

Johnson was buried in the churchyard cemetery of the Miles Station Methodist Church. The grave then, and still is, by itself at the western edge of the small burial ground. A marble, urn-surmounted shaft was erected in the style of the times with this inscription:

Gen. Bushrod R. Johnson
Died
Sept. 12 1880
Aged
62 years 11 Mos 5 days[16]

At the base this verse was carved:

A valiant leader, true hearted and sincere
An honored soldier, who held his honor dear
A cultured scholar with mind both broad and deep
An honest man, the noblest work of God.[17]

The ironic epilogue to Johnson's career, perpetuated in the engraved marble, is the absence of any reference to the Confederate Army. This lends credence to the local folklore, related by Miss Andrews, that the monument was supplied by Colonel Miles, whose more imposing memorial is a few yards away, because Charles Johnson was mentally incapable of providing the stone for his father and the tenant family coterie unlikely to have done so.

There is a modern sequel to this. Years after Johnson's death the church was disbanded and torn down. The cemetery became unkempt and fenceless. Any care of graves was left to descendants of those buried there. Sometime in 1960 vandals pushed the time-defaced headstone down across Johnson's mound. In 1963 the trustees were prodded into repairing and reerecting the stone by the threat of an effort, sponsored by a Tennessee historical group, to get court approval for the removal of Johnson's body to Nashville for reburial beside his wife.[18]

Johnson left no will and there was no administration of any estate. The farm and the Kansas prairie land had long been in the name of the son. Charles was taken ill in December 1881, only fifteen months after his father's death. As he lay dying, on December 13, 1881, Dr. Clement, who had attended Bushrod in his last illness, wrote a will naming himself as executor without bond for Charles's estate. He tried to arouse Charles to sign it. An illegible scrawl resulted.[19] William Haworth, brother of Charles's wife, Ida, and Henry Roundtree, her brother-in-law, signed as witnesses to the "signature."

Charles died about December 15, 1881. The exact date is not known because Dr. Clement never filed a death certificate. Where he was buried is not disclosed in any records.

The 19-year-old widow, Ida, objected in court on December 22 to probate of "the purported will," contending that Charles was "not of sound mind," did not know what he was doing and did not sign the paper voluntarily. Haworth and Roundtree testified they were present when Clement wrote the paper, but they admitted they had not seen the actual "signing" and they added their names as witnesses some time later when Clement brought the paper to them. Confronted with their stories, Dr. Clement withdrew his application to probate the will and Ida Haworth Johnson was named administratrix.[20]

The estate subsequently was appraised at $8800. Ida sold thirty-six detached acres and some personal property of Charles's and his father's to clear up current debts in 1883. One item was Bushrod's Colt Brevette revolver, engraved with his name and carried through the war. A British sailor eventually bought it in New Orleans in

1890 for $3. He kept it for sixty-five years and sold it to an English collector who in 1957 resold it to a gun fancier in Dallas, Texas.[21]

About 1885 Ida Haworth Johnson was married to Addison Reese and moved with him and Bushrod's grandson, Alonzo, to Carterville, Williamson County, Illinois, 150 miles distant in southeastern Illinois. In 1897 she sold the 191-acre farm[22] where Bushrod Johnson had spent the last five years of his frustrated life.

Alonzo Haworth Johnson, last of the blood of Bushrod, lived with his mother and stepfather in Carterville. Like his father, Alonzo was mentally handicapped. When he was fifteen years old, his mother, Ida Johnson Reese, applied to the Williamson County Circuit Court for the appointment of S. H. Bundy as his guardian. The request was granted November 18, 1895.[23] Eight years later, on September 7, 1903, Bundy, as Alonzo's guardian, sold the 160 acres remaining in Osage County, Kansas acquired by Bushrod Johnson in 1859. The land brought $3005; Johnson had paid $150 for it 44 years earlier. It was a last legacy from the Quaker Confederate to a grandson seen only through eyes dulled by paralysis in the summer of 1880.[24]

Alonzo died March 4, 1904 from "consumption," never having married. His stepfather had preceded him in death in 1903, as had a half-brother Edward, who died in infancy in 1893. The three are buried beside each other in the Reese family lot in Carterville.[25] What happened to Ida Haworth Johnson Reese after the deaths of her husband and sons is undisclosed.

At the time of Bushrod's death in 1880, two of the Indiana members of the family, his great-nephews Henry and Robert, had begun their distinguished careers, and his Iowa first cousin, once removed, William Windom of the Spencer family, was rounding out more than twenty years in Congress, as Representative and Senator. In a few months, President Garfield named him Secretary of the

Treasury,[26] to which post he also was chosen by President Benjamin Harrison.

Henry Underwood Johnson, in 1880 prosecuting attorney of Wayne County, Indiana, became a state senator in 1887 and served four terms in Congress, 1891–1899. His active life ended at the age of eighty-nine in 1939.[27] His son, Nimrod Hoge Johnson II, was once city treasurer of Richmond, Indiana and a utility firm executive. Robert Underwood Johnson, three years younger than Henry, in 1880 had been for seven years with *Century* magazine from which he resigned as editor in 1913. In 1883 with Clarence Clough Buel, he persuaded Union and Confederate officers to write their stories of the Civil War's battles and controversial tactics; these became the highly successful *Battles and Leaders of the Civil War.* In World War I his efforts to provide ambulances and relief for Italy won him appointment by President Woodrow Wilson as ambassador to Italy in January 1920. He served to July 1921. He was director of the New York University Hall of Fame, 1919–1937, and secretary of the American Academy of Arts and Letters.[28] He died in 1937, aged eighty-four.

Robert's son was Owen McMahon Johnson, (1878–1952), prolific writer for fifty years of novels and short stories dealing sometimes satirically with American customs and behavior. One popular series of his works had as its theme life in preparatory school and college as experienced by his hero, Dink Stover.[29]

France awarded the Legion of Honor to Robert, to Owen in 1919 for work in France during World War I, and to Owen's son, Owen Denis de la Garde Johnson after World War II for his efforts in the Resistance. This is probably the only instance of such an honor being bestowed upon three generations of the same family.

Two generations of descendants of Ruth Johnson Williams (her daughter Alice Williams Brotherton [1848–1930][30] and her grandson, John Williams Brotherton) acquired notable literary reputations in Ohio.

Fame which snubbed Bushrod Johnson was more generous to his deserving kindred.

ii. The Final Reckoning

The ancient Greeks believed that to every man is allotted a mixture of good and evil which he cannot avoid. He may struggle, as Oedipus did, against his apportionment, but it will be futile. Inevitably, the measure assigned to him will overtake him. Indeed, by his own folly, he may even increase his share of ill fortune.[31] Perhaps it is in this context that the qualities of mind and heart of Bushrod Johnson may best be assayed, for almost as surely as the Greeks' predestination, his character and temperament condemned him to no more than a pittance of success and a full meed of adversity, some of which he deserved.

He emerges from the shadows as neither hero nor antihero, but something of both—a figure often bland and undramatic, a man of multiple contradictions. There are fleeting moments that generate admiration for his unquestioned courage, respect for his demonstrated professional competence, sympathy for his misfortunes and understanding for his failures. He ranks among the best in his battle performances at Shiloh, Perryville, Stones River, Chickamauga, Bean's Station, and Drewry's Bluff. All of his superiors in these tests of military skill have naught but praise for his capacity and diligence. Their commendatory endorsements on his perennial pleas for promotion reflect their abiding respect for his ability. His behaviour at The Crater and Sayler's Creek is the baleful exception.

In civilian life as an educator he earns equally high repute. He is accepted and respected in an environment alien to his background. The Nashville community manifests its confidence and esteem in him by its willingness to draw on its own meager resources to give him money to revive his school in 1870. Tennessee today still counts him as one of hers. His constant provisions for the welfare and future of his handicapped son are evidences of his enduring dedication and conscientiousness. These are his passive virtues.

But there is an obverse to this admirable image. The quiescent Quakerism of his birth and upbringing seem to be in periodic conflict with his acquired martial qualities of will and action. What results is a tragic psychological malaise of recurrent childish artlessness coupled with lapses from duty having vastly disproportionate consequences. There is an intermittent compulsion, as of a Quaker conscience, to purge a troubled heart, to ask remission, to seek a source of reassurance in situations where a more mature character could sustain itself. Naiveté colors the obscure "proffit" letter far more than moral turpitude. Johnson appears utterly guileless in letting himself be persuaded to propose a shadowy scheme without "injustice to U.S." to a scarcely known superior quite certain to take steps to keep his own probity unsullied. He forgets or ignores his own moral obligation. The immature turning to a father image shows in his desperate explanation to President Polk that his offer to Seawell was really a "request for advice." He exhibits this insecurity again after the walkaway at Fort Donelson when he goes to Pillow with his uneasy conscience and with callow sophistry similar to that of 1847 justifies his desertion of the soldierly Buckner by arguing that he wanted to share the fate of his troops, but not, as it turns out, their imprisonment in the North. He feels no compulsion to support and sustain his chief. At The Crater the father figure is Beauregard whose easy rationalization to give Mahone the whole responsibility for recovering the captured trenches is accepted gratefully by Johnson without demur.

It is characteristic of his essential nature that Johnson's reactions are similar in his grandest and most tragic hours. As nightfall halts the bloody work at Chickamauga, weary but triumphant, he spends three solid hours riding around in the darkness, hunting not for Longstreet, his immediate superior, but for Bragg, the army commander, "to report his position" and hopefully to hear his commendation. From the dire disorder of Sayler's Creek, after the collapse of his control, Johnson does not search for Anderson, his corps commander, but speeds directly to agitated Lee to report that he personally is safe though his division is wrecked. Even after being rebuffed by the army commander, Johnson still lacks the sagacity to avoid Lee's petulant presence and so he is the target in the humiliating scene the next morning. In both instances there is the spectacle of a 46-year old soldier of training and experience conducting himself typically as the youngest of nine children might act when trouble, pain or pride sends him seeking comfort or praise from some accustomed source. Equally puerile is the lack of frankness, candor or sincerity in his tendency to rationalize his deficiencies.

Johnson's endemic reluctance, hesitancy and self-effacement, his cautious manner which Lindsley says "prejudiced observers" all seem part of the same pattern. He has no thought of making an issue of the choice of the fatal site of Fort Henry, but rather tries to justify the disadvantages acutely apparent to less taciturn observers. He is unwilling to assume direction in Pillow's absence during the drive on Grant's right at Fort Donelson where resolute response to Forrest's plea for a general charge might have ensured a breakout. At Chickamauga with Hood wounded and Longstreet absent, the question of his or Kershaw's right to area command wastes time and aggressive impetus while Johnson ponders and defers. Irresolution stands in the way of tidying the shambles in his Illinois household, obvious to all his neighbors. Reticence allows connivers to compromise his incompetent son while neglect and ruin take over the only valuable property he has left.

This is the dark side of Bushrod Johnson, the folly the Greeks saw as adding to man's share of evil. It costs him his future in the "Old Army." It denies him from having more than passing recognition of his meritorious service in the Confederate Army and brings him disgrace at the end. Except for the published aspersions of the Wise clan for two decades after his death, it buries him in historical oblivion thereafter.

Chance, as much as inheritance, shapes his personality. The baby in a family bereaved by the death of four children in a brief period, he is the object of extraordinary, rather than normal attention. He is overloved and overprotected. As a Quaker lad in a community which "bears testimony against war" and who wants to be a professional soldier he is a curiosity. His brother's unsympathetic attitude echoes the neighborhood's. A simple rural youth in the midst of strangers for the first time at West Point, he is defensively withdrawn and the "loud talking" and "profane swearing" for which he is penalized are symptomatic of his inferiority complex. His classmates never recall him.

In manhood, the murky secret of his sudden separation from the army is a burden to be borne in silence and its disclosure always to be feared. Until his own death the company and care of his afflicted son are a continual reminder that his brief married life ended in heartbreak and sorrow. All these are cumulative ingredients to produce the introvert, continually denied happiness and good fortune, yet eagerly cherishing the "pleasant anticipations" that somehow the morrow can supply the deficiencies of the present day. It is his portion that his lot is never improved.

In fitting recompense, the best of Bushrod Johnson lived longest in the memories of the valiant Tennessee Brigade which shared his brightest hours. For half a century these veterans spoke of him with respect and admiration at their reunions, regretting that he had been "underrated" and that "justice to this true patriot and fine soldier has been very tardy." Their final judgement in 1911 declared that he deserved "the homage of every man who reveres Dixie" and that "he was gallant, faithful and capable as any general."[32]

Until they died, the men of Johnson's Brigade were proud that he had led them. They gave him their trust in battle; their abiding loyalty was a measure of his leadership. To a commander, no grander accolade can come.

Notes

1. Charles A. Walker, supervising editor, *History of Macoupin County, Ill.,* (Chicago: S. J. Clarke Publishing Co., 1911), 2 vols., I, p. 58; *History of Macoupin County, Ill.,* (Philadelphia: Brink, McDonough & Co., 1879), p. 169. *Macoupin History,* hereafter.
2. This is now (1969) U.S.67. Sentiment of the community described by Miss Phoebe Andrews, La Jolla, California, quoting her father, John Edward Andrews.
3. Miss Andrews' statement.
4. *Walker,* I, pp. 407 f.
5. *Macoupin History,* p. 178.
6. Data from Miss Andrews.
7. *Macoupin History,* p. 170; *U.S. Census,* Macoupin County, Ill., 1870.
8. *Walker,* I, p. 58.
9. Miss Andrews' statement.
10. Letter, Johnson to Owen, June 25, 1875. Business Papers, Folder No. 4, *Owen Papers.* This may have been the last contact between them.
11. Osage County, Kansas, *Deed Book* 7, p. 205; Wayne County, Tennessee, *Deed Register,* Book M, p. 409.
12. *National Cyclopedia of American Biography,* XXXII, p. 46.
13. *CV,* XIV, p. 13.
14. Macoupin County, Ill., *Death Record,* 1–91, p. 1177. Charles Dudley Rhodes in *DAB,* X, p. 91 gives September 12, 1880; Clement A. Evans in *Confederate Military History* has December 7, 1880.
15. *Nashville Banner,* September 15, 1880.
16. This date also disagrees with Clement's certificate.

17. *CV*, XV, 551 prints a letter from R. D. Fletcher, Thayer, Illinois who visited the grave in 1907 and describes it.
18. Correspondence on this project in possession of Stanley F. Horn, Nashville, and this author.
19. Miss Andrews quotes her father's opinion that Charles lacked the capacity to sign his name under any circumstances.
20. Original "will" and subsequent papers in Macoupin County, Ill., *Index to Wills*, B; *Order Book*, M.
21. Harry C. Knode, "Bushrod's Pistol" in *The American Arms Collector*, July, 1958, pp. 74 f.
22. Macoupin County, Ill., *Deed Records*, Book FT, p. 106.
23. Data in letter to author from Williamson County, Ill., Circuit Court Clerk.
24. Osage County, Kansas, *Deed Book* 119, p. 306.
25. Inscriptions on tombstone on Reese family grave lot in Carterville, Ill., Cemetery. Alonzo's death certificate in Williamson County, Ill., *Death Records*, 1904.
26. *Congress Directory*, p. 1836.
27. *Ibid.*, p. 1125.
28. *DAB*, XXII, Supplement Two, pp. 348 f.; *Robert Johnson*, p. 189.
29. *National Cyclopedia of American Biography*, XLI, pp. 33 f.
30. *Robert Johnson*, p. 28. William Coyle, Ed. *Ohio Authors and Their Books*, (Cleveland: World Publishing Co., 1962) p. 80.
31. H. J. Rose, *Gods and Heroes of the Greeks*, (Cleveland: World Publishing Co., 1958), p. 63.
32. *CV*, VI, p. 248; XIV, p. 13, 545; XV, p. 551; XIX, p. 272.

BIBLIOGRAPHY

Manuscript Sources

Chicago Historical Society, Chicago, Ill.: one Johnson military letter, June 6, 1864.

Duke University Library, Durham, N.C.: Letters and references to Bushrod Johnson and Richard Heron Anderson in *Munford-Ellis Family Papers.*

George Peabody College for Teachers Library, Nashville, Tenn.: *Order Book,* Western Military Institute, 1847–1873.

Maryland Hall of Records, Annapolis, Md.: Microfilmed copies of records of Goose Creek Quaker Meeting.

Mississippi Dept. of Archives and History, Jackson, Miss.: *Charles Clark Papers.*

Montgomery Bell Academy, Nashville, Tenn.: *Register of Cadets,* Western Military Institute, 1847 to present.

National Archives, Washington, D.C.:

1. Record Groups No. 94, 153, *et al.*; The Adjutant General's Department, U.S. Army: Index of letters sent and received; copies of letters sent and originals of letters received, 1840–1847, pertaining to Bushrod Johnson.
2. Confederate Army Staff and General Officer Papers: Files of B. R. Johnson, W. T. Blakemore, R. E. Foote, W. H. Whitner, R. H. Anderson.
3. Regimental Returns: Third U.S. Infantry, 1840–1847.
4. U.S. Military Academy Admittance Papers: Correspondence with and pertaining to Bushrod Johnson.

New Harmony, Indiana: Private collection of papers of Richard Owen, including Johnson's letters to Owen, 1851–1875 and much material relating to their partnership. Researched by special permission of Kenneth D. Owen, Houston, Texas; *Elliott Family Papers.*

Tennessee State Library and Archives, Nashville, Tenn.: University of Nashville Records: *Trustees Minute Books,* 1852–1906; Colonel Johnson's Cash Receipts and Expenditures, 1858–1862; Microfilm records of Western Military Institute, 1847–1872.

Isham G. Harris Papers: telegrams to Harris from Johnson, January 1862.

Two business agreements by Johnson in 1867.

U.S. Military Academy Archives, West Point, N.Y.: Class and promotion records of B. R. Johnson, 1836–1840; Official Registers of officers and cadets; Post Order Books.

Virginia Historical Society, Richmond, Va.: *The Diary or Prison Journal of John H. Guy*; *John Kirkwood Mitchell Papers*: two military letters by Johnson, May 1864.

Public Documents

Pennsylvania: Pennsylvania Archives, Series 2, III.

U.S. Bureau of the Census:

1. Indiana: Wayne County, 1850, 1860, 1870.
2. Illinois: Macoupin County, 1870, 1880.
3. Kentucky: Georgetown, Scott County, 1840, 1850, 1860; 1850, 1860 slave schedules; Nicholas County, 1850.
4. Ohio: Belmont County, 1820, 1830, 1840, 1850, 1860, 1870; Muskingum County, 1830.
5. Tennessee: Nashville, Davidson County, 1860, 1870; 1860 slave schedules.

County Records: Deeds, Taxes, Marriage, Death, Probate, Burial

1. Illinois: Macoupin County, Deed, Death, Probate Records
   Williamson County, Death Record.
2. Indiana: Wayne County, Deed, Will Record.

3. Kansas: Osage County, Deed Record.
4. Kentucky: Henry County, Marriage Record.
Scott County, Deed, Estate Records.
5. Missouri: Ripley County, Deed Record.
6. Ohio: Belmont County, 1810 Tax List, Deed, Marriage, Probate Records.
Muskingum County, Deed, Marriage Records.
7. Tennessee: Davidson County: Deed Register.
Wayne County, Deed Register.
8. Virginia: Loudoun County: Bargain and Sale Record.
9. Miscellaneous: Record of Interments, Old City Cemetery, Nashville, Tenn.

Collected Source Material, General Reference Works, and Serial Publications Other than Newspapers

Battles and Leaders of the Civil War, 4 vols. New York: Thomas Yoseloff, Inc., 1958.

Confederate Veteran, 40 vols. Nashville, Tenn., 1893–1932.

Hamersly, Thomas H. S., *Complete Army and Navy Register of the U.S., 1776–1887.* New York: T. H. S. Hamersly Publishing Co., 1888.

Heitman, Francis B., *Historical Register and Dictionary of the United States Army.* 2 vols. Washington: Government Printing Office, 1903.

Military Review. The U.S. Army Command and General Staff College, Fort Leavenworth, Kansas.

Southern Historical Society Papers, 49 vols., Richmond, Va., 1876–1944.

U.S. War Department, *The War of the Rebellion: A Compilation of the Official Records of the Union and Confederate Armies.* 70 volumes in 128 plus 3 vol. Atlas. Washington: Government Printing Office, 1880–1927.

Biographies and Personal Narratives

Albjerg, Victor Lincoln. "Richard Owen" in *Archives of Purdue,* No. 2 (March 1946). Purdue University, Lafayette, Indiana.

Alexander, E. Porter. *Military Memoirs of a Confederate.* New York: Charles Scribner's Sons, 1907.

Barbour, Philip Narbourne, *Journals of the Late Brevet Major Philip Narbourne Barbour and his Wife.* New York: G. P. Putnam's Sons, 1936.

Bernard, George S. *War Talks of Confederate Veterans.* Petersburg, Va.: n. p., 1892.

Biographical Directory of the American Congress, 1774–1961. Washington, D.C.: Government Printing Office, 1961.

Boyd, James F. *Life and Public Services of Hon. James G. Blaine.* Philadelphia: Publishers Union, 1893.

Bridges, Hal. *Lee's Maverick General.* New York: McGraw-Hill Co., Inc., 1961.

Buck, Capt. Irving A. *Cleburne and His Command.* Jackson, Tenn.: McCowat, Mercer Press, Inc., 1959.

Campbell, William Bowen. "Mexican War Letters of Col. William Bowen Campbell of Tennessee, written to Gov. David Campbell of Virginia, 1846–47." *Tennessee Historical Quarterly,* I.

Cullum, George W. *Biographical Register of the Officers and Graduates of the U.S. Military Academy.* 2 vols. New York: D. VanNostrand, 1868.

Deas, Major George. "Reminiscences of the Campaign in the Rio Grande." *Historical Magazine,* II.

De Peyster, J. Watts. "A Military Memoir of William Mahone, Major General of the Confederate Army." *Historical Magazine,* VII.

Ewell, Richard S. *The Making of a Soldier.* Richmond, Va.: Whittet and Sheperson, 1935.

Freeman, Douglas Southall. *R. E. Lee.* 4 vols. New York: Charles Scribner's Sons, 1935.

———, *Lee's Lieutenants.* 3 vols. New York: Charles Scribner's Sons, 1944.

Furber, George C., *The Twelve Months Volunteer.* Cincinnati: U. P. James, 1857.

Grant, U. S., *Personal Memoirs of U. S. Grant.* 2 vols. New York: Chas. L. Webster & Co., 1885–86.

Harrison, Walter, *Pickett's Men.* New York: D. Van Nostrand, 1870.

Hitchcock, Ethan Allen, *Fifty Years in Camp and Field.* New York: G. P. Putnam's Sons, 1909.

Howells, William Cooper, *Recollections of Life in Ohio, 1813–1840.* Cincinnati: The Robert Clarke Co., 1895.

Johnson, Allen and Malone, Dumas, *Dictionary of American Biography.* 20 volumes, plus index and supplements. New York: Charles Scribner's Sons, 1928.

Johnson, Robert Underwood, *Remembered Yesterdays.* Boston: Little, Brown & Co., 1923.

Johnston, William Preston, "Student Life at Western Military Institute" in *Filson Club History Quarterly,* XVIII.

———, *Life of Albert Sidney Johnson.* New York: Appleton & Co., 1878.

Kegley, Tracy M., "Bushrod Rust Johnson—Soldier and Teacher" in *Tennessee Historical Quarterly,* VII.

Leland, Winfield Meyer, *Life and Times of Col. Richard Mentor Johnson of Ky.,* published Ph.D. dissertation, Political Science, Columbia University, New York, 1932.

Lewis, Lloyd, *Captain Sam Grant.* Boston: Little, Brown & Co., 1950.

———, *Sherman, Fighting Prophet.* New York: Harcourt Brace & Co., 1932.

Longstreet, James, *From Manassas to Appomattox.* Dallas, Texas: Dallas Publishing Co., 1896.

Lytle, Andrew Nelson, *Bedford Forrest.* New York: Minton Balch & Co., 1931.

Meade, George G., *Life and Letters of General Meade.* 2 vols. New York: Scribner and Son, 1913.

McCall, George Archibald, *Letters from the Frontiers.* New York: Lippincott, 1868.

McSherry, Richard, *El Puchero.* Philadelphia: Lippincott, Grambo & Co., 1850.

National Cyclopedia of American Biography. 44 vols. New York: J. T. White Co., 1893–1962.

Oswandel, J. Jacob, *Notes of the Mexican War.* Philadelphia: n.p., 1885.

Park, Joseph H., *General Edmund Kirby Smith.* Baton Rouge: Louisiana State University Press, 1954.

Ridley, Bromfield, *Battles and Sketches, Army of Tennessee, 1861–1865*. Mexico, Mo: Missouri Printing and Publishing Co., 1906.

Ripley, R. S., *War With Mexico*. 2 vols. New York: Harper & Bros., 1849.

Russell, Charles Edward, *Blaine of Maine*. New York: Cosmopolitan Book Corp., 1931.

Sherman, W. T., *Memoirs*. New York: D. Appleton & Co., 1875.

Stanwood, Edward, *James Gillespie Blaine*. Boston: Houghton Mifflin, 1905.

Tucker, Glenn, *Hancock the Superb*. Indianapolis, Ind: Bobbs Merrill, 1960.

Walker, C. Irvine, *Life of Lt. Gen. Richard Heron Anderson*. Charleston, S. C.: Art Publishing Co., 1917.

Wallace, Lew, *An Autobiography*. New York: Harper & Bros., 1906.

Warner, Ezra J., *Generals in Gray*. Baton Rouge, La.: Louisiana State University Press, 1959.

———, *Generals in Blue*. Baton Rouge, La.: Louisiana State University Press, 1964.

Wilcox, Cadmus M., *History of the Mexican War*. Washington, D.C.: Church News Publishing Co., 1892.

Windrow, J. E., *John Berrien Lindsley*. Chapel Hill, N. C.: University of North Carolina Press, 1938.

Wise, John S., *The End of an Era*. Boston: Houghton Mifflin Co., 1900.

Wyeth, John Allan, *That Devil Forrest*. New York: Harper & Bros., 1959.

State, County and Specialized Histories

Altstetter, Mabel and Watson, Gladys, "Western Military Institute" in *Filson Club History Quarterly*, X.

Caldwell, J. A., *History of Belmont and Jefferson Counties*. Wheeling, W. Va.: Historical Publishing Co., 1880.

Collins, Lewis, *Historical Sketches of Kentucky*. Cincinnati: J. A. & U. P. James, 1850.

Everhart, J. F., *History of Muskingum County*. Columbus: Ohio State Journal, 1882.

Fertig, James Walter, *The Secession and Reconstruction of Tennessee.* Chicago: University of Chicago Press, 1898.

Folmsbee, Stanley J., Corley, Robert E., and Mitchell, Enoch L., *History of Tennessee.* Nashville: Lewis Historical Publishing Co., Inc., 1960.

Gaines, B. O., *History of Scott County.* 2 vols. Printed by author, Georgetown, Ky., *ca.* 1900.

Hamer, Philip A., *Tennessee, A History.* 4 vols. New York: American History Society, Inc., 1933.

History of Macoupin County, Ill., Philadelphia: Brink, McDonough & Co., 1879.

Howell, Isabel, "Montgomery Bell Academy," unpublished MS thesis, History Department, Graduate School of Education, George Peabody College for Teachers, Nashville, Tenn., 1940.

Jordan, Philip D., *The National Road.* Indianapolis, Ind.: Bobbs Merrill Co., 1948.

McKelvey, A. T., *Centennial History of Belmont County, 1801–1901.* Chicago: Biographical Publishing Co., 1903.

McGregor, Lt. Col. Edward W., "The Leavenworth Story" in *Military Review,* XXXVI.

Moore, John Trotwood and Foster, Austin P., *Tennessee, The Volunteer State.* Chicago and Nashville: S. J. Clarke Publishing Co., 1923.

Perrin, William Henry, *History of Bourbon, Scott, Harrison and Nicholas Counties* [Kentucky]. Chicago: O. L. Baskin & Co., 1882.

Rule, James C., *History of Montgomery Bell Academy.* Nashville: n. p., 1954.

U.S. Federal Works Agency, Works Progress Administration: *Dinwiddle County, Va.*, Dinwiddie County School Board, 1942. *Kentucky, A Guide to the Bluegrass State,* Hastings House, New York, revised edition, 1954.

Walker, Charles A., supervising editor, *History of Macoupin County, Ill.* 2 vols. Chicago: The S. J. Clarke Publishing Co., 1911.

Young, Andrew W., *History of Wayne County, Indiana.* Chicago: Robert Clarke & Co., 1872.

Genealogical Works

Hinshaw, William Wade, *Encyclopedia of American Quaker Genealogy*. 6 vols. Ann Arbor, Mich.: Edwards Bros., Inc., 1950.

Jenkins, Howard M., *Genealogical Sketch of Descendants of Samuel Spencer of Pennsylvania*. Philadelphia: Ferris and Leach, 1904.

Rust, Ellsworth Marshall, *Rust of Virginia*. Privately printed, Washington, 1940.

Newspapers

Indiana: Richmond, *Palladium*
Jeffersonian

Ohio: St. Clairsville, *Belmont Chronicle*
Gazette
National Historian

Tennessee: Nashville. *Nashville Banner*
Republican Banner and Nashville Whig
Union and American

City Directories

Covington, Ky.: Data supplied by Reference Dept., Kenton County Public Library.

Nashville, Tenn.: *Nashville City and Business Directory*, Vol. III, 1857, Smith, Camp & Co.; Vol. IV, 1859, E. G. Eastman & Co.; Vol. V, 1860-61, L. P. Williams & Co.; *King's Nashville City Directory*, issues for 1867, 1868, 1869, 1870, 1871, 1872, 1874, printed for the proprietor, Nashville.

Richmond, Ind.: *Sutherland and McEvoy's Richmond and Cambridge City Directories for 1860 and 1861*, published by compilers, no location given.

St. Louis, Mo.: Data from 1860 and 1875 issues supplied by Reference Department, St. Louis Public Library.

Accounts of Battles and Campaigns

Bearss, Edwin C., "Unconditional Surrender" in *Tennessee Historical Quarterly,* XXI (March–June 1962)

Connelly, Thomas Lawrence, *Army of the Heartland.* Baton Rouge: Louisiana State University Press, 1967.

Fort Henry and Fort Donelson Campaigns. Fort Leavenworth, Kansas: The General Service Schools, 1923.

Dowdey, Clifford, *Lee's Last Campaign.* Boston: Little, Brown & Co., 1960.

Downey, Fairfax, *Storming of the Gateway.* New York: David McKay Co., Inc., 1960.

Esposito, Col. Vincent T., *The West Point Atlas of American Wars.* 2 vols. New York: Frederick A. Praeger, 1959.

Gracie, Archibald, *The Truth About Chickamauga.* Boston: Houghton Mifflin Co., 1911.

Seymour, Digby Govan, *Divided Loyalties.* Knoxville: University of Tennessee Press, 1963.

Steele, Matthew F., *American Campaigns.* Washington: U.S. Infantry Association, 1935.

Tucker, Glenn, *Chickamauga, Bloody Battle of the West.* Indianapolis, Ind: Bobbs Merrill Co., 1961.

Turchin, John B., *Chickamauga.* Chicago: Fergus Printing Co., 1888.

Watson, Walter C., "Sayler's Creek" in *Southern Historical Society Papers,* XLII.

Wise, Barton Haxall, "Address by Henry A. Wise," in *Southern Historical Society Papers,* XXV.

Background Material

Boatner, Mark, *The Civil War Dictionary.* New York: David McKay Co., Inc., 1959.

Clark, Thomas, *Frontier America.* New York: Charles Scribner's Sons, 1959.

Hesseltine, William B., and Smiley, David L., *The South in American History.* Englewood Cliffs, N. J.: Prentice-Hall, 1960.

McRea, J. H., "The Third Regiment of Infantry" reproduced

in Rodenbaugh, T. F., and Haskin, W. L., *The Army of the United States.* New York: Maynard Merrill & Co., 1896.

Merriam, Lucius Salisbury, *Higher Education in Tennessee.* Washington, D.C.: Government Printing Office, 1893.

Millis, Walter, *Arms and Men.* New York: G. P. Putnam's Sons, 1956.

Lonn, Ella, *Desertion During the Civil War.* New York: The Century Co., 1928.

Thomas, Allan C., and Richard H., *A History of the Friends in America.* Philadelphia: John C. Winston Co., fourth edition, 1905.

Wooster, Ralph A. *The Secession Conventions of the South.* Princeton, N. J.: Princeton University Press, 1962.

Miscellaneous

Dickoré, Marie, Collection of Kentucky funeral invitations, Ohio Historical Society Library, Columbus.

Pillow, Gideon J., *Address Delivered Before the Agatheridan and Erosophian Societies of the University of Nashville,* Nashville: Cameron and Fall, 1856.

School Catalogues:

Catalogue and Regulations of Western Military Institute for 1847, Cincinnati: Herald of Truth Print, 1848.

Catalogue of College Department, Western Military Institute, University of Nashville, School Year, 1854–55, Nashville: Cameron and Fall, 1855.

University of Nashville Collegiate Department, Western Military Institute, Announcement for 1857–58. Photostat in Tennessee State Library, publisher's name missing.

Catalogue of the Literary and Medical Departments of the University of Nashville, 1858–59, Nashville: John T. S. Fall, 1857.

Catalogue of the University of Nashville, 1870–71, Nashville: Paul and Tarvel, 1871.

Regulations of the Military College, the Literary Department of the University of Nashville, Nashville: L. P. Williams Co., 1859.

INDEX